The natural rate of unemployment

The natural rate of unemployment

Reflections on 25 years of the hypothesis

Edited by

Rod Cross
University of Strathclyde

CAMBRIDGE
UNIVERSITY PRESS

Published by the Press Syndicate of the University of Cambridge
The Pitt Building, Trumpington Street, Cambridge CB2 1RP
40 West 20th Street, New York, NY 10011-4211, USA
10 Stamford Road, Oakleigh, Melbourne 3166, Australia

First published 1995

Printed in Great Britain at the University Press, Cambridge

A catalogue record for this book is available from the British Library

Library of Congress cataloguing in publication data
The Natural rate of unemployment: reflections on 25 years of the
  hypothesis/[edited by] Rod Cross.
      p.   cm.
  ISBN 0 521 47298 9 hbk; ISBN 0 521 48330 1 pbk
  1. Unemployment. 2. Unemployment – Effect of inflation on.
I Cross, Rod.
HD5707.5.N383 1995
331.13'72 – dc20   94-20097   CIP

ISBN 0 521 47298 9 hardback
ISBN 0 521 48330 1 paperback

VN

For Irena

Contents

Contributors

Bruno Amable, INRA and CEPREMAP, Paris
Albert Ando, Pennsylvania and NBER
G.C. Archibald, University of British Columbia
Olivier Blanchard, Massachusetts Institute of Technology and NBER
Flint Brayton, Board of Governors of the Federal Reserve System
Andrew Caplin, Columbia
Bernard Corry, Queen Mary and Westfield College
Rod Cross, ICMM, Strathclyde
Maria Demertzis, Strathclyde
Meghnad Desai, The Lord Desai of St Clement Danes, London School of
    Economics and Political Science
Huw Dixon, York and CEPR
Frank Hahn, Cambridge
Jérôme Henry, Banque de France
Andrew Hughes Hallett, Princeton, CEPR and ICMM, Strathclyde
John Leahy, Harvard
Frédéric Lordon, CEPREMAP, Paris
Ian McDonald, Melbourne
David Peel, Aberystwyth
Hashem Pesaran, Cambridge and UCLA
Edmund Phelps, Columbia
Ron Smith, Birkbeck
Alan Speight, Aberystwyth
James Tobin, Yale
Richard Topol, CNRS and OFCE, Paris
Simon Wren-Lewis, ICMM, Strathclyde and CEPR

Preface

Olivier Blanchard

Twenty-five years ago, Edmund Phelps and Milton Friedman developed the 'natural rate' hypothesis. The essence of their argument was that there was such a thing as a 'natural rate of unemployment', that it was quite stable, and that, in the words of Phelps in his essay for this volume, it was a strong attractor of the actual rate of unemployment.

There is no denying that the natural rate hypothesis took the analysis of labour markets from the ad hocery of the Phillips curve to more solid methodological ground. But, 25 years later, one can hardly be impressed by its empirical success.

We have learned, or perhaps relearned, that:

The natural rate is at best a weak attractor. Even in the best of worlds, which in this case must mean the United States over the post-war period, the natural forces which return unemployment to normal are weak at best. Natural forces are not what have gotten us out of the recessions in the post-war US. Expansionary fiscal and monetary policies have.

The natural rate is often as much an attractee as it is an attractor. Robert Solow used to joke that the natural rate was whatever the average unemployment rate had been over the previous three years. The joke has been on Europe in the 1980s. The natural rate appears to have rejoined the actual rate all the way up. High unemployment coexists with stable inflation, a standard indicator, under the natural rate hypothesis, that Europe is now roughly at the natural rate.

These facts were, I am sure, the trigger for this volume. Some of the chapters document and reflect on the facts. Some of the chapters reflect on the underlying theory, then and now. Together, they provide a rich overview of the issues. But the reader must be warned. The time is not one of synthesis, and no clear, fully worked out, alternative hypothesis is in sight. The macro facts are fairly clear. But the specific channels are much less so. What we have are questions. Through which channels does the actual rate attract the natural rate? Is it through changes in the composition of unemployment, in the behaviour of the unemployed, through changes in labour market institutions and arrangements? Indeed, how do labour market institutions influence how the actual rate affects the natural rate? And what can be the role of both supply and demand policies? Fortunately for researchers, unfortunately for Europe, we still have few of the answers. The work has just begun.

1 Introduction

Rod Cross

As Keynes remarked, 'the ideas of economists and political philosophers, both when they are right and when they are wrong, are more powerful than is commonly understood' (Keynes, 1936, p. 383). The natural rate of unemployment hypothesis formulated by Edmund Phelps (1967) and Milton Friedman (1968) provides testimony, having wielded a powerful influence on thought about what determines, and what can be done about, unemployment from the 1970s onwards.

The distinguishing feature of the hypothesis is not so much what it says about the determinants of unemployment, as what it says about the factors that *do not* influence the natural or equilibrium rate of unemployment. The standard definition of the natural rate is as depending on 'the actual structural characteristics of the labour and commodity markets, including market imperfections, stochastic variability in demands and supplies, the cost of gathering information about job vacancies and labour availabilities, the costs of mobility, and so on' (Friedman, 1968, p. 8). This in itself does not rule out an influence for the aggregate demand for goods stressed in the preceding Keynesian wisdom regarding unemployment: aggregate demand could influence the 'actual structural characteristics of the labour and commodity markets', and hence the equilibrium rate of unemployment. The innovation comes instead in the preclusion of nominal magnitudes, which of course affect aggregate demand, from the list of factors affecting the natural rate: '[the] crucial element is that nominal magnitudes must be sharply distinguished from real magnitudes, and that nominal magnitudes in and of themselves cannot determine real magnitudes' (Friedman, letter to the author, 2 November 1990). Thus the natural rate hypothesis postulates autonomy in the 'structural characteristics of labour and commodity markets', and applies the doctrine of monetary neutrality to unemployment. This was evident in Friedman's introduction of the natural rate hypothesis by way of analogy to Wicksell's concept of a natural rate of interest (Friedman, 1968), the formal equilibrium characteristics of which had been elucidated by Frisch (1936). Phelps, in his essay in this volume (chapter 2), points out that his own formulation of the natural rate

1

hypothesis followed the real–nominal dichotomy to be found in Lerner in the 1940s, and in the teachings of Fellner in the 1950s.

Paraphrasing Alan Coddington's (1982, p. 101) comments on Keynesian economics, the natural rate hypothesis cantered briskly into the 1970s, faltered in the 1980s, and stumbled somewhat uncertainly into the 1990s. The main cause of loss of confidence was not so much reservations regarding the hypothesis itself, which had been expressed since the hypothesis was launched, but more the weight of evidence. It was by no means clear that the hypothesis was consistent with the upward shift in unemployment, particularly evident in European countries, during the 1980s (see Solow, 1987 and Blanchard, 1990 for assessments). As Keynes also remarked, the ideas from which those in authority 'distil their frenzy' are not necessarily the most recent (Keynes, 1936, pp. 383–4). Thus in the 1990s policies towards unemployment continued, by and large, to be distilled from the natural rate spring: supply-side measures to 'improve' the 'structural characteristics of labour and commodity markets' are still seen as the key to achieving lasting reductions in unemployment; and the perception remains that anti-inflation policies can be pursued without lasting costs in terms of higher unemployment.

Given this tension between the conventional wisdom provided by the natural rate hypothesis and the weight of evidence, a volume of essays which reflects upon, and assesses, the natural rate hypothesis is of more than what the sports commentators infelicitously refer to as academic interest. The aim of this volume was to gather together a set of assessments of the status of the hypothesis 25 years on, a period of time sufficient to have thrown up severe evidential challenges to the hypothesis and various re-formulations of how the 'structural characteristics of labour and commodity markets' affect equilibrium unemployment. The distinguishing feature of the natural rate hypothesis is its application of the classical dichotomy between real and nominal variables to equilibrium unemployment, so the theme underlying the assessments is inevitably one of whether this neutrality proposition is theoretically and evidentially plausible. The chapters fall under four broad headings.

The theoretical framework

Appropriately enough, the first essay in Part I, 'The origins and further development of the natural rate of unemployment' (chapter 2), is by Edmund Phelps, the co-originator of the hypothesis. Phelps describes how his formulation of the hypothesis grew from an attempt to understand the theoretical background to the Phillips curve, this work, ironically enough, being initiated during a visit to Cambridge, UK. Two aspects of the natural rate hypothesis are distinguished: the application of the real–nominal dichotomy to equilibrium unemployment time paths; and the idea that the natural rate is a strong attractor for actual unemployment. Phelps points out that, contrary to what is often supposed, his original work on the natural rate did contain a substantive model of the determinants of equilibrium unemployment, and that in his own framework involuntary unemployment occurs in natural rate equilibria in the sense that the workers affected would prefer not to be at the sharp end of the rationing. After outlining the rich set of theoretical models bred by the hypothesis, Phelps records reservations concerning: whether the hypothesis draws too sharp a distinction between nominal and real variables, and so cannot capture phenomena such as debt deflation; whether convergence of the actual to the natural rate will occur; whether, in view of insider–outsider effects, the natural rate is a zone rather than a point; and whether the coexistence of wage bargaining and incentive wage effects on wages is captured.

James Tobin, a vigorous critic of the natural rate framework for understanding unemployment (see his 1971 American Economic Association Presidential Address, for example), writes in chapter 3 on 'The natural rate as new classical macroeconomics'. Tobin focuses on the Friedman (1968) version of the hypothesis as a precursor of the Lucas (1972) restatement of it as a rational expectations equilibrium, which in turn gave rise to the Lucas–Sargent–Wallace policy ineffectiveness proposition. The serious defect in the framework is seen as the failure to take account of the fact that wages and prices are denominated in the monetary unit of account, and that economy-wide adjustments in heterogeneous markets will see real wages and prices deviate from equilibrium values for reasons endemic to the processes of adjustment. This is taken to be the key insight of Keynes, implying that downward adjustments in money wages may not reduce real wages and unemployment, the result being involuntary unemployment in the real sense captured by survey-based measures of unemployment. Tobin reiterates his own alternative view of unemployment—inflation interaction, which arises from random intersectoral shocks which keep individual labour markets in diverse states of disequilibrium. The outcome is a set of S-shaped Phillips curves for individual markets and for the economy at large. At high and low unemployment rates the inflation–unemployment locus is close to vertical, as in the natural rate hypothesis, but at intermediate rates of unemployment the locus is fairly flat, indicating a range of unemployment rates consistent with a particular rate of inflation. The assessment is that, although the natural rate hypothesis conveyed a sensible warning against excessively expansionary demand policies, the hypothesis has been both wrong and harmful in its message that expansionary demand policies cannot, in any circumstances, yield lasting reductions in unemployment.

Frank Hahn's essay (chapter 4), 'Theoretical reflections on the natural rate of unemployment', puts the natural rate in the class of 'shaky and vastly incomplete theories'. Hahn assesses the coherence of the equilibrium constructs used in natural rate models in which it is taken as axiomatic that labour is on its supply curve. In the case of perfect competition the problem is the lack of an axiomatic foundation for behaviour out of equilibrium. Hahn points out that in such circumstances non-competitive behaviour, in which workers do not compete for jobs by accepting lower wages, can yield a perfect equilibrium for a range of unemployment rates bounded from above (see Hahn and Solow, 1995). For the 'realistic' case of imperfect competition the problem is the absence of any rigorous general theory which would yield a natural rate concept. In special cases, such as concave profit functions and no strategic interactions, underemployment can arise, and there is nothing in the limited theoretical constructs available to rule out multiple equilibria. Hahn points out that the natural rate is an aspect of a neoclassical steady state growth path, and outlines reasons why such steady states might not exist, may involve non-linear relationships and multiple equilibria, and be path dependent. Hahn concludes that natural rate models reflect 'pseudo-theorising', and that the way forward involves taking account of features such as non-linearities and heterogeneity in agents and sectors of economic systems.

The classical dichotomy between monetary and real variables underlying the natural rate hypothesis provides the theme for Huw Dixon's 'Of coconuts, decomposition, and a jackass: the genealogy of the natural rate' (chapter 5). The 'jackass' is Paul Samuelson's description of his youthful belief in the classical dichotomy. Dixon traces the dichotomy back to Hume, and argues that the natural rate hypothesis version of the dichotomy was largely derivative of the concept of full employment laid down in Patinkin's *Money, Interest and Prices* (1965). The role played by 'decomposition' arises from Patinkin's suppression of the wealth effect on labour supply, which gives rise to a vertical aggregate supply curve, which in turn allowed Patinkin to decompose his system of equilibrium equations, the labour market equilibrium equation being solved in isolation from the rest of the system of equilibrium equations. The new slant given to the classical dichotomy by Friedman is discussed, along with the subsequent re-formulations of the micro foundations in terms of perfectly competitive markets with informational deficiency by Robert Lucas, and in terms of dynamic equilibria in real business cycle models. The 'coconuts' refer to Peter Diamond's search model (1982) in which trade frictions in a perfectly competitive framework yield multiple natural rates of unemployment.

Dixon argues that multiple (discrete) natural rate equilibria, or a natural range (continuous) of equilibria, are likely to be more relevant to economies with imperfectly competitive markets than the unique equilibrium postulated by the natural rate hypothesis.

Adjustment, ranges of equilibria and hysteresis

A theme recurring in various guises in the above assessments of the natural rate theoretical framework was the idea that there may be multiple natural rate equilibria, or a range of natural rates of unemployment, consistent with a particular rate of steady or anticipated inflation. This theme is taken up in more specific detail in a grouping of studies in Part II which discuss adjustment processes, models yielding ranges of equilibria, and hysteresis in economic systems.

Andrew Caplin and John Leahy's essay 'The economics of adjustment' (chapter 6) focuses on the role of information in adjustment processes triggered by the evolution of consumer tastes and production techniques. The two standard approaches to adjustment problems are search theory, which emphasises the difficulties involved in locating appropriate uses for resources, and the adjustment cost approach, which highlights the costs inherent in transferring resources to different uses. The basic models ignore externalities to adjustment processes, so resources unused during adjustment processes, such as unemployed people, do not reflect a misallocation of resources. Extensions of the basic models to take account of externalities in search processes and adjustment costs have been made but, Caplin and Leahy argue, have taken a narrow view of the learning processes involved. They argue, along lines somewhat similar to the newspaper beauty contest described in Keynes' *General Theory* (1936, p. 156), that the way agents learn from observing the behaviour of other agents is a key aspect of the externalities involved in adjustment processes. Caplin and Leahy illustrate their argument by discussing how agents learn from the behaviour of other agents in three cases where resources are known to be in sub-optimal uses: vacant office buildings; arms manufacturers in Central and Eastern Europe; and redundant steel workers. Allowing unemployed workers to learn about the distribution of wage offers by observing the behaviour of other unemployed workers creates externality and free rider problems which prevent the unemployed from searching with sufficient intensity for social optimality. Information about adjustment is underprovided, providing a plausible role for government policy to improve the allocation of resources.

Chris Archibald's essay 'Hysteresis and memory in the labour market' (chapter 7) addresss the adjustment problem on the demand side of the labour market, and asks what determines the division between firms who hire and fire labour on a spot market, and those who treat labour as a fixed or quasi-fixed factor which is not adjusted in response to spot market conditions. Workers have utility functions which imply trade-offs between wages and job security, job security and unemployment benefits, and wages and unemployment benefits. Given that firms are less risk averse than workers, profit maximisation implies that lay offs and new hires of workers will occur in discrete doses. At low output prices firms will abandon quasi-fixed employment commitments, closing down shifts or plants. At high output prices it also pays firms to abandon fixed employment commitments and compete for more labour on the spot market. In between there is range of prices in which employment levels remain fixed, it being optimal for firms to offer *Zaibatsu-style* employment security. This implies that the history of past shocks to output prices will determine the division between spot and fixed employment firms. Hence any equilibrium rate of unemployment will not, *contra* the natural rate hypothesis, be independent of shocks experienced in the past.

Ian McDonald argues in chapter 8 that the behaviour of inflation at high rates of unemployment is inconsistent with the natural rate hypothesis, and suggests instead a range of equilibrium rates of unemployment. His essay, 'Models of the range of equilibria', begins by reporting the evidence on the relationship between inflation and high unemployment for a variety of countries and periods. The pattern evident in the 1920s, 1930s and 1980s is that high unemployment has a temporary effect in reducing the rate of inflation, and not the continuing effect claimed by the natural rate hypothesis. McDonald then surveys analytical models which yield ranges of equilibrium outcomes, beginning with customer market models in which the frequency of search is low relative to frequency of purchase. Such models have a discontinuity in the marginal revenue curve, implying that a particular price is consistent with a range of values of marginal cost. On their own, customer market models involve only voluntary unemployment, and suggest procyclical movements in real wages rather than the acyclic movements observed. After reviewing bargaining and insider–outsider models, McDonald argues that concern for relative wages is a key aspect of the wage determination process. This implies a kink in the utility functions for workers or unions which, when combined with the customer market kink in marginal revenue functions, yields a range of equilibrium rates of unemployment consistent with the observed acyclic patterns of real wages.

The term 'hysteresis' was first coined by James Alfred Ewing in 1881 to refer to effects which remain after the initial causes are removed, the context being the behaviour of electromagnetic fields in ferric metals. In the 1980s it became fashionable to invoke such hysteresis effects to explain why unemployment remained high after the temporary shocks experienced at the beginning of the 1980s. Bruno Amable, Jérôme Henry, Frédéric Lordon and Richard Topol's essay 'Hysteresis revisited: a methodological approach' (chapter 9) contrasts the interpretation given to 'hysteresis' in the economics literature with hysteresis as a general systems property. They argue that the economics literature used the term incorrectly to refer to the properties of *linear* systems of equations with unit roots in the case of difference equations, and zero roots in the case of differential equations. Such special cases do not capture the key features of systems with hysteresis in the proper sense of the word. The general properties of systems with hysteresis have been articulated in the work of the Russian mathematician Mark Krasnosel'skii and associates (Krasnosel'skii and Pokrovskii, 1989). The authors point out that hysteresis is a property of *non-linear* systems with *heterogeneous* micro elements. Such systems display *remanence*, that is they do not revert to the *status quo ante* after a temporary shock is removed; and they have a selective memory of the *non-dominated extremum values* of the input shocks experienced. They argue that such properties are relevant to equilibrium rates of unemployment.

Rod Cross in chapter 10 poses the question, 'Is the natural rate hypothesis consistent with hysteresis?'. He outlines how hysteresis was introduced into NAIRU (non-accelerating inflation rate of unemployment) models of the equilibrium rate of unemployment in an attempt to reconcile the models with the fact that unemployment remained anomalously high in the 1980s. The 'hysteresis' in such models, however, was nothing more than persistence in deviations of actual unemployment from the natural rate. Cross uses the Krasnosel'skii techniques to show how *non-linearities* and *heterogenieties* in economic agents gererate unemployment equilibria which depend on the *non-dominated extremum values* of temporary demand shocks experienced. Hence hysteresis equilibria for unemployment depend on past shocks to nominal variables, and so violate the neutrality proposition underlying the natural rate hypothesis (NRH). The natural rate hypothesis is thus not consistent with hysteresis.

Empirical tests and macro models

In the first study in Part III, Hashem Pesaran and Ron Smith assess the empirical tests of the natural rate hypothesis in their essay 'The natural rate hypothesis and its testable implications' (chapter 11). After reviewing the Lucas–Sargent–Wallace version of the hypothesis, they ask whether the equations used by Robert Barro and others to test the natural rate hypothesis are valid. If output is trend stationary, as natural rate proponents have often assumed, the Barro-type regressions are not a valid representation of the natural rate hypothesis. If, as seems more likely, output is difference stationary, the regressions are spurious. Pesaran and Smith point out that a Keynesian model, in which a government controls optimally a set of policy instruments, produces a reduced form which is difficult to distinguish from that of a new classical model, the proxies for the government output targets being difficult to distinguish from the proxies for the natural rate. The conclusion is that, in the absence of a precise formulation of the determinants of the natural rate of output or employment, it may be impossible to test the hypothesis.

David Peel and Alan Speight's essay, 'Non-linear dependence in unemployment, output and inflation: empirical evidence for the UK' (chapter 12), contrasts the natural rate and hysteresis accounts of equilibrium unemployment, and tests for the presence of non-linearities as suggested by the hysteresis approach. The data set used covers monthly unemployment, inflation and industrial production in the UK 1972–93. They begin with linear representations of the data generation process for the three time series. Although they cannot reject the null of a unit root form of 'hysteresis' in unemployment, they point out that such tests have low power, and proceed to test for non-linear representations. They find that the growth rate of industrial production and the differenced inflation rate can be well represented as AR–GARCH (autoregressive, generalised autoregressive conditional heteroscedasticity) processes, and strong evidence of non-linearity in unemployment in both bilinear and SETAR (self-exciting threshold autoregressive) forms. Evidence of non-linear interaction between unemployment and past thresholds in both unemployment and industrial production is also found. While these tests do not deal with the precise forms of selective memory implied by hysteresis systems analysis, they are consistent with past shocks having remaining effects by way of thresholds.

Natural rate models have experienced less severe difficulties in explaining unemployment in the US, where steady inflation unemployment equilibria have varied less than in Europe. Albert Ando and Flint Brayton's essay, 'Prices, wages and employment in the US economy: a traditional model and tests of some alternatives' (chapter 13), assesses the ability of the price–wage sector of the MPS model maintained at the Board of Governors of the Federal Reserve System to explain the behaviour of unemployment and inflation in the 1980s and early 1990s. They compare and contrast the MPS model with the early NAIRU model of Richard Layard and Stephen Nickell, and ask whether the 1970s' version of the MPS model can track the subsequent behaviour of inflation and unemployment in the US. Ando and Brayton conclude that the traditional MPS model tracks satisfactorily the behaviour of US unemployment and inflation in the 1980s and early 1990s.

In this model the natural rate is determined by demographics, 'permanent' productivity growth and the unemployment insurance replacement ratio, and modified by the wedge between producer and consumer prices. In contrast with the new classical models, they find no evidence of direct effects of money on inflation.

The influence of the natural rate hypothesis on macroeconometric models, and the light such models can throw on the limitations of the hypothesis, are discussed in Simon Wren-Lewis' essay, 'The natural rate in empirical macroeconomic models' (chapter 14). Wren-Lewis discusses the influence of the natural rate hypothesis on macroeconometric models in the UK, describing the evolution from expectations-augmented Phillips curve representations to the imperfect competition foundations, to which consistent (rational) expectations solutions are applied, which are used at present. This is in contrast to the large US models, which tend not to apply rational expectations (RE) solutions. The importance of the natural rate hypothesis in providing a consistency check on macro models is illustrated with regard to the effects of the wedge between producer and consumer prices on natural rate solutions. Wren-Lewis then outlines three examples where macroeconometric models yield departures from the natural rate hypothesis. The first is the response of the natural rate to a demand shock: even removing nominal inertia from the wage and price equations yields protracted real effects arising from a combination of price dynamics, exchange rate movements and real exchange rate effects. The second example is where demand elasticities differ between sectors: if the government's demand elasticity differs from the private sector's, for example, a change in government spending has a permanent effect on the natural rate. The third example arises in a vintage specification of capital: if the goods market mark-up depends on marginal productivity, and the labour market mark-up on average productivity, then in a vintage, rather than Cobb–Douglas, specification of production, changes in the marginal–average productivity relationship will lead to changes in the natural rate.

Political economy

The studies in Part IV touch more specifically on political economy, broadly defined as the art of managing a state's economic affairs. The essay by Maria Demertzis and Andrew Hughes Hallett (chapter 15) poses the question, 'Is the natural rate of unemployment a useful concept for Europe?'. Despite the problems with the ERM, monetary union remains the official target of the European Union. Demertzis and Hughes Hallett ask what the implications of union, in the form of a single currency or integrated product markets, would be in a Europe characterised by the present segmentation of labour markets and substantial differences in unemployment rates. They ask whether such a union would lead to an increase in the union-wide natural rate of unemployment, and a deterioration in the unemployment–inflation 'sacrifice ratio'. Three cases are considered: a convex downward sloping Phillips curve in each region/member state; vertical Phillips curves; and linear, region-specific Phillips curves. They demonstrate that in all three cases aggregating the inflation–unemployment relationships over the member regions/states leads to a displacement effect which raises the natural rate of unemployment and leads to a deterioration in the sacrifice ratio. Using quarterly data for Germany, France, Italy and the UK, 1975–90, they estimate the quantitative significance of the displacement effect. For 1990, the estimate is that the natural rate of unemployment would have been $\frac{1}{2}\%$ point higher if the four countries' product markets had been fully integrated.

The essay by Meghnad Desai (the Lord Desai of St Clement Danes) (chapter 16) offers a 'Fundamentalist Keynesian view' of the natural rate of unemployment. Desai distances himself from both the new classical and new Keynesian views on equilibrium unemployment, returning instead to the original Phillips curve and Keynes' *General Theory* in order to construct an account of equilibrium unemployment. Regarding the original Phillips paper of 1958, Desai argues that there is a missing equation: Phillips had equations for wages (explicit) and prices (implicit), but a third endogenous variable, unemployment. Dissatisfied with the natural rate procedures of closing this system by invoking 'some non-existent dynamic Walrasian model' for the natural rate, or by involving a quantity theory equation for prices, Desai returns to the 'Keynes effect' of chapters 19 and 20 of the *General Theory*. In this effect an increase in the ratio of nominal money to the wage and import bill reduces the rate of interest and this stimulates investment and employment. A small macroeconometric model is estimated for the UK, providing at least weak support for the existence of a long-run effect of the money stock on unemployment. The second part of Desai's essay deals with the problem of the non-homogeneity of labour, neglected in the natural rate literature, but the focus of special attention in Keynes' discussion of wage units in chapter 4 of the *General Theory*. Desai constructs an index of employment weighted in terms of wage units or earnings, and compares the evolution of this index with the conventional measure of employment in terms of bodies. This provides a new perspective on UK employment levels 1948–91, indicating, for example, the disproportionate impact of unemployment on lower paid workers during 1980–91.

Bernard Corry's essay 'Politics and the natural rate hypothesis: a historical perspective' (chapter 17) addresses the question of how the natural rate hypothesis acquired conventional wisdom status. He argues that economists find it difficult to settle theoretical disputes by appealing to empirical evidence, and that instead theoretical disputation tends to prevail. The theoretical disputes in turn are often a 'facade for different political agendas' involving the relative merits of free markets and state intervention. Corry traces the background to the emergence of the natural rate hypothesis back to Keynes, pointing out that, contrary to popular myth, in the *General Theory* prices and wages rise during the process of recovery from a depression. This formed the background to A.W. Phillips' Ph.D. thesis *Dynamic Models in Economics* (1953) and Phillips' famous curve, in which causality ran from aggregate demand to output and unemployment, and hence from unemployment to inflation. Given the prevailing mood of interventionism, the Phillips curve was used to buttress the need for incomes policies designed to ameliorate the inflationary consequences of the pursuit of fiscal and monetary policies to keep unemployment low. The restatement of the case for free markets at the micro level was well under way in the 1960s, but lacked 'overpinning' at the macro level. Corry argues that it was not a empirical breakdown of the Phillips curve, which did not happen in the UK, but rather the ability of the natural rate hypothesis to complement the micro case for free market provision that explained the adoption of the natural rate hypothesis. By including the technical novelty of rational expectations, the way was paved for the free market revolution enshrined in the policy ineffectiveness proposition. According to Corry's thesis the political tide of the 1990s has turned in favour of intervention, which in turn has turned opinion away from the natural rate hypothesis account of equilibrium unemployment.

References

Blanchard, O.J., 1990. 'Unemployment: Getting the Questions Right and Some of the Answers', in J.H. Drèze and C.R. Bean (eds.), *Europe's Unemployment Problem*, Cambridge, MA: MIT Press

Coddington, A., 1982. *Keynesian Economics, the Search for First Principles*, London: Allen & Unwin

Diamond, P., 1982. 'Aggregate Demand Management in Search Equilibrium', *Journal of Political Economy*, 90, 881–94

Ewing, J.A., 1881. 'On the Production of Transient Electric Currents in Iron and Steel Conductors by Twisting Them When Magnetised or by Magnetising Them When Twisted', *Proceedings of the Royal Society of London*, 33, 21–3

Friedman, M., 1968. 'The Role of Monetary Policy', *American Economic Review*, 58(1) (March), 1–17

Frisch, R., 1936. 'On the Notion of Equilibrium and Disequilibrium', *Review of Economic Studies*, 5, 100–5

Hahn, F.H. and Solow, R.M., 1995. *Critical Essay on Modern Macroeconomic Theory*, Cambridge, MA: MIT Press and Oxford: Blackwell

Keynes, J.M., 1936. *The General Theory of Employment, Interest and Money*, New York: Harcourt Brace and London: Macmillan

Krasnosel'skii, M.A. and Pokrovskii, A.V., 1989. *Systems with Hysteresis*, Berlin: Springer-Verlag

Lucas, R.E., Jr., 1972. 'Expectations and the Neutrality of Money', *Journal of Economic Theory*, 4(2), 103–24

Patinkin, D., 1965. *Money, Interest and Prices*, New York: Harper & Row, 2nd edn

Phelps, E.S., 1967. 'Phillips Curves, Expectations of Inflation and Optimal Unemployment over Time', *Economica*, 34(3) (August), 254–81

Solow, R.M., 1987. 'Unemployment: Getting the Questions Right', *Economica*, 53, S23–34

Tobin, J., 1972. 'Inflation and Unemployment', *American Economic Review*, 62(1) (March), 1–18

I

The theoretical framework

2 The origins and further development of the natural rate of unemployment

Edmund Phelps

The idea of the natural rate of unemployment, more generally the equilibrium path of the unemployment rate, challenged the main tenets of Keynesian thought: that doctrine held that the unemployment rate was a function of effective demand, and demand management could aim for the unemployment rate deemed best. In the new Keynesian version, fiscal policy was to be governed by neoclassical considerations while monetary policy was to engineer a point on the unemployment–inflation trade-off – on the Phillips curve.

Modelling of the natural rate idea led to two propositions. One of these was a conclusion from the model sketched in my 1968 paper (Phelps, 1968, part 2). Management of monetary demand cannot engineer an arbitrary unemployment rate other than the natural level without sooner or later generating a continuing disequilibrium manifested by rising inflation or mounting deflation – then collapse.[1] Maintaining the unemployment rate below the natural level, for example, would ultimately or immediately pull the actual inflation rate above the expected rate, which would drive up the expected rate; but each such rise would push the actual rate up by as much, leaving the disequilibrium undiminished.

The other proposition was implied by my 1967 paper (Phelps, 1967) and rather a similiar thesis was forcefully argued by Milton Friedman in his 1968 paper (Friedman, 1968). Monetary policy can make a permanent difference only to nominal variables: a policy to generate a finite increase or decrease in the inflation rate will generate only a transient dip of the actual unemployment rate relative to the path it would otherwise have taken. In particular, the actual unemployment rate, though occasionally hit by such shocks, is constantly homing in on the natural rate. This last part – equilibration – makes this the stronger proposition of the two, as we could believe the former without having much faith in the homing in.

Some of these terms need defining, since some authors use them in other senses. 'Equilibrium' here means, as theorists from Marshall to Hayek meant, that expectations of wages, etc. are borne out, absent a new and

15

unforeseen shock; 'disequilibrium' means a gap between expectations and outcomes. Under the maintained assumptions, each equilibrium path of the unemployment rate (indexed by its starting point) converges to the path of the natural rate – conceived as a path independent of monetary policy, at least approximately. The current natural rate may be defined as the current stationary rate: the level of the unemployment rate such that it would be unchanging for the moment as least.[2] For analytical convenience the natural rate was taken to be a constant, hence equal to the equilibrium stationary state level.[3] The first proposition assumes that in the stated circumstances there is a tendency for expectations to narrow the disequilibrium unless policymakers keep people off balance. The second proposition assumes that the tendency to equilibrium is general. Then the actual unemployment rate converges to one of the equilibrium 'glide paths', all of which converge to the natural rate path.

Strikingly, this message that economists took away from the natural rate discussions of the late 1960s – the neutrality of money and inflation and the homing in – was less a theory of employment determination than a set of *axioms* that we might require of such a model independently of what substantive building blocks the model is made from.[4] Indeed, the concept of the natural rate, as I have on occasion acknowledged, had existed for decades prior to the arrival on the scene of Milton Friedman and myself. The postulate that inflation was neutral for the equilibrium path of output, employment and some other 'real' variables was introduced by Abba Lerner in the 1940s and by William Fellner (a great teacher of mine) in the 1950s.[5] Perhaps my 1967 paper and Friedman's were more emphatic and explicit about homing in to the natural rate (on which I was more cautious in my 1968 paper).

There was a tendency among quite a few scholars, myself included, to forget that my 1968 paper on equilibrium unemployment sketched a *substantive model* of the determination of the *size* of the natural unemployment rate and the course of the equilibrium unemployment rate path which leads to it. The 1968 paper by Friedman also had a substantive side, though it sketched departures of the labour force (to which employment was equal) from its equilibrium path: unemployment does not appear.

The present commentary on the natural rate begins by looking back: to what my model of equilibrium unemployment was, and how that model arose. The second section argues that the full implications of this model and kindred sequels – all featuring what I prefer to call 'incentive wages' – have not, until very recently at any rate, been grasped. The discussions of 1968 hit upon one implication of central consequence for Keynesian thought, the scope of monetary policy. But, I will maintain, there are other ramifications of this kind of model of equilibrium unemployment – implications for fiscal policy and other non-monetary impulses – that are, if judged empirically plausible, no less devastating for Keynesian doctrine.

Background to the original model

It might be thought that the late 1960s modelling of the Phillips curve and, as a byproduct, the natural rate grew out of great agitation and yearning for light. In fact, the Keynes–Phillips orthodoxy was sailing on smooth waters, the object of much congratulation, rather like the liner *Titanic* prior to its collision with the fateful iceberg. In the present case the iceberg was the neutrality axiom of Lerner and Fellner. What made a collision of the Phillips curve with neutrality inevitable was that sooner or later someone – or some *two* – would provide one or more micro–macro models of the Phillips curve, and with that development the difficulty of maintaining that inflation was non-neutral, which the Keynes–Phillips position implies, would be exposed.

My efforts at a theoretical understanding of the Phillips curve began in earnest over the summer of 1966 in the Sidgwick Avenue building at Cambridge, and my first few months at the University of Pennsylvania in the autumn. In the preceding winter I had written a paper on optimal inflation/unemployment control, published in 1967, in which an expectations-augmented quasi-Phillips curve was written down:

$$p - p_{-1} = \phi(u) + p^e - p_{-1}, \tag{1}$$

equivalently

$$p = \phi(u) + p^e, \tag{1'}$$

where p is the money price level being set, p^e is what it is expected to be, and u is the unemployment rate. But there was nothing about the microeconomics of the function ϕ. Furthermore, the money wage level was implicitly the passive partner of the price level rather than the other way around, as Phillips and most practitioners supposed. A microeconomic understanding of the relation between inflation and unemployment did not yet exist.

With the benefit of hindsight the puzzles I was struggling with can be reduced to a few basic problems: How can there be involuntary unemployment, particularly in conditions of equilibrium in the expectational sense? How could the unemployment rate remain, however briefly, below its natural level? In such a infra-natural state, what is the process by which nominal wages go on spiralling upward? How might one introduce into this model the Lerner–Fellner acceleration hypothesis that as long as monetary policy, say, kept the unemployment rate below its natural level, the rate of increase of the average wage would steadily increase? I had only a foggy notion at best of the answers to any of these questions. However, I did have the sense that the way to the answers was somehow to lay out a model – not a complete system of differential equations but nonetheless a serviceable description of a highly stylised hypothetical economy.

There were bits of labour economics that I started from with each new attempt at a model. I had read a little of Dunlop and Slichter, the Harvard labour economists, Paish, the LSE economist, and Wallich, my colleague over several years at Yale. From them I took away the impression that when the economy is pressured, at least for a time, into operation at a level in excess of its equilibrium steady state level, the low unemployment rate poses various inconveniences for firms, which try in turn to cope by setting higher wage rates. I also had a more recent memory of the dynamics of employment arising from employee turnover behaviour as it was modelled by Richard Lipsey in an otherwise econometric paper of his on wage inflation and employment (1960). Yet these insights, however necessary, were missing something fundamental, it seemed to me. They did not put us into the mind of the firm, or its personnel manager. Man is a thinking, expectant being! What was needed was a model of a sequence: the firm's expectations, its subsequent actions and those of the others, the discovery of the others' actions, the formation of new expectations, and so forth.

I had also read the (1964) paper on wages and employment, replete with econometric estimates, by Sargan of LSE. This paper postulated a required nominal wage level that is an increasing function of the employment rate (hence decreasing in the unemployment rate), given expectations of the price level. I took from this paper the rather important point that the rate of increase of nominal wages is a function not just of the *level* of unemployment but also the *change* of employment. It also encouraged my impression that when firms plan to increase employment they offer an increased wage simultaneously; the wage is not completely described as a feedback response to discovery of changes in the market wage and the total unemployment rate. On the other hand, at the embryonic stage of my thinking then, this paper was a distraction and an unnecessary complication. For weeks, I focused exclusively upon expectations of the price level by the personnel manager and his employees rather than their expectations of what the general money wage level was going to be.

By the time I was settled into the University of Pennsylvania I had a 'story' about labour market equilibrium and wage dynamics – to use the phrase I finally used as a title. The unemployment rate might move to so low a level that, to moderate the associated quit rate, every firm wants to offer its employees a better *real* wage as an inducement not to quit with such readiness; but as all firms pass along the implied money wage increase, the price level increases in proportion (beyond what it was going to do anyway), an increase that is unexpected; to keep the unemployment rate down, there must be a succession of such wage increases and hence continually unexpected inflation – greater than whatever rate was expected. In such a scenario, the unemployment rate was below equilibrium; the steady state equilibrium must be one with a larger rate.

One day, though, it struck me that something was terribly wrong with that story. Suppose that each wage increase is accompanied by a proportional incease of productivity, so that the price level remains unchanged and the real wage is increased. Then it would be implied by the original story that the reduced unemployment rate was consistent with equilibrium. With each advance of the real wage and productivity, the equilibrium volume of unemployment would be reduced again, with unemployment vanishing in the limit. Furthermore, as I went on to see, it is presumably the effect of its increased wage scale on the expected *relative* wage that the firm counts on to induce a reduction of the quit rate. Employees might not respond as assumed to a higher money wage if they could observe the same increase in money wage rates at all the other firms.

The model was then reconstructed: the quit rate is a decreasing function of the firm's relative wage. For simplicity, only the relative wage and the unemployment rate determine the quit rate, not the real wage. In the revised version, if the unemployment rate is driven to a sufficiently low level, every firm raises its wage in the expectation of achieving an increase in its relative wage in order to induce a moderation of its quit rate; but as all firms try to outpay one another the result can only be disappointment – a disequilibrium in which expectations of the money wage at other firms are found to be too low. Equilibrium in the labour market thus requires a large unemployment rate – large enough to dissuade the representative firms from attempting an unrepresentative outcome. The resulting Phillips curve was

$$w - w_{-1} = \phi(u) + w^e - w_{-1}, \tag{2}$$

where w denotes the money wage level. The equilibrium steady state unemployment rate, which makes $\phi(.)$ equal to zero, is a positive number. If monetary policy keeps on yanking up firms' nominal demand prices in order to induce firms to go on employing beyond the steady state rate, firms will pass along each round of wage increase in proportionally higher prices; money wages will continue to go up, round after round, always in excess of what firms expect them to go up by.

A number of features of this model stood out. As already noted, the invariance of labour market equilibrium to whatever inflation rate was expected was a sensational aspect. This was not because there was intense substantive interest on the part of economists in whether a steady inflation of, say, 6% per year, might make for tighter labour markets than 5%. As I suggested at the start of this chapter, the fascination lay in the implication that Keynesian aggregate demand management – through monetary policy, at least – could not achieve an arbitrarily chosen unemployment rate within some admissible and reasonable range. Keynesian forces could only make transient departures from the gravitational pull of the natural rate.

A second feature was that the unemployment existing at the natural rate, and indeed virtually everywhere on any equilibrium path, was involuntary – not just in Keynes' sense of the term but in the everyday sense that the unemployed could not get a job by offering their labour for less than the going wage. As far as I can recall, this point was not well understood by me at the time of writing, nor for some time after.[6] But eventually it became clear to me why the model implied that an unemployed worker could not obtain a job that way: if the firm were to accept such a worker at a lower wage though that worker did not apparently differ from employed workers with regard to the likelihood of quitting, the firm would have to assume that the worker's quit rate would be higher as a result; but that trade-off would be sub-inoptimal for the firm to accept since it had already calculated the optimum on the wage-quitting opportunity locus.

Another feature – an 'optional extra' – of the model was the property that, starting from unemployment in excess of the natural level, the equilibrium path would approach the natural rate only gradually. The argument was simply that firms will not jump their employment rolls to the natural level since they face rising marginal cost of imparting firm-specific training, or induction programmes, to new recruits. Whether a specified unemployment rate today will generate unexpected inflation thus depends on the rate yesterday. The augmented Phillips curve became

$$w - w_{-1} = \phi(u, u_{-1}) + w^e - w_{-1}. \tag{2'}$$

Hence there was an equilibrium path of the unemployment – a path along which the expected wage is always matched by the actual wage, hence a path given by $\phi(u, u_{-1}) = 0$ – that approaches the natural rate only asymptotically. This was the notion of 'persistence'. In contrast, the idea of 'hysteresis', as used in my 1972 book, at any rate, referred to the effect of unemployment history on the natural rate, either a permanent effect or a long-lasting one.

In another respect, however, the spirit of the model was uncomfortably remote from the behaviour of aggregate data: the setting evoked by the paper suggested that firms would raise their wages – up or down – immediately in response to a shock, then learn what the general wage was doing once the data for that week or month were finally collected, processed and released. But in reality, though the preponderance of firms may change their wages by discrete amounts, instantaneously or when it suits them, the weekly time series of the average wage rate appears to be virtually continuous – without large increases no matter how large and widely perceived the shock. This modelling problem was met in a formal way by the apparently artificial device of imposing on the individual firm a gradual response of its wage; implicitly there was some lag in the reporting of the daily or weekly wage. In the last section of the text, however, there was a verbal discussion of the importance of moving to a more complex version of the model that would allow for overlapping wage rates that are revised in a non-synchronous and regular manner, as from a uniform distribution. In an altered version of that paper prepared for a January 1969 conference on which the (1970) conference volume was based, a version that suffered from effects to make it closer to the companion paper by Dale Mortensen, I sketched the algebra of the wage rate leap frogging by such firms for the special case in which unemployment is held at the natural rate. But the major work remained for the 1970s in New Keynesian papers by John Taylor, Guillermo Calvo and myself.[7]

As a result of synchronous wage-setting and either fixed mark-up pricing or an auction market for goods, the model implied that if expectations were rational, instead of adaptive as I had supposed, a jump in demand would generate what could be regarded as a disequilibrium disturbance, resting on forecast errors by the firms about the upcoming wage level, only for as long as it took for the wage data (or other proxy date) to come in. Once the data were in, wage rates would jump the remaining distance needed to put the economy again on an equilibrium track. This was the thrust of Robert Lucas' (1972) model, based on my parable of imperfectly communicating 'islands'. Fortunately, by the early 1970s, Friedman's wonderful example of the peso problem arrived to give one sort of reply: if, in an economy that was at the fixed natural rate, the central bank went on a money-creating spree having always the same probability of ending with the present 'period', then employment will be above natural as long as the spree continues, as wage-setters will not have treated its continuation as a certainty; employment will drop below its natural level in the first period after the rampage is over, regaining the natural level gradually. So there *can* be booms and slumps, not just weekly vibrations. The other reply, which was developed both independently and collaboratively by Roman Frydman and myself in the 1980s was the argument that expectations cannot be presumed to be rational in a world in which the correct model (or theory, as I tend to say) is a souce of continuing disagreement. Then your rational forecast is not my rational forecast, unless we are fellow travellers down the same model's road. Then the economy can take a non-equilibrium path for a long time, even indefinitely. (Even in the 1968 paper, I might add, a certain ambiguity arises over whether the economy assuredly approaches the natural rate path – hence the distinction between the concept of the natural rate and the natural rate hypothesis.[8])

There was another missing feature – trade unions. In the economics of those days, the fashion had been to suppose that the necessity for so high an unemployment rate in order to contain inflation was ultimately a consequence of the presence of labour unions, which grew aggressive whenever the labour market became tight. I took a different view, and in a paper where so little had been eliminated in the interest of simplicity and tractability, I felt it was necessary to draw the line somewhere. Labour unions were banished. Since then, there has been a considerable amount of modelling of unions. It has become clear what unions can add to the story. But a rough idea of the quantitative importance of that addition is not yet in hand.

One last comment. The above account glosses over the confusions and ambiguities that were present in my mind over the months of writing the paper and for months afterwards. The worst of these was the unfortunate remark early in the exposition that it would be necessary to think of the labour force as heterogeneous in order to make sense of positive unemployment as an equilibrium phenomenon. In fact, though, heterogeneity of workers plays no role in the defensive upward push of the product wage in response to the turnover problem that is the driving force behind the creation of unemployment in the model; it is the heterogeneity of firms in the minds of workers that underlies labour turnover. Worker heterogeneity merely plays a supporting role as one of the contributors to the marginal cost of hiring; it is needed to underpin firms' concern about the quit rate only if marginal hiring costs do not include any firm-specific on-the-job training costs, which ultimately I came to depend on more. The next-worst confusion was created by the property of rising marginal hiring costs on which the existence of continuous equilibrium paths depended; it led to a variable vacancy rate, which played a role alongside the unemployment rate as a determinant of the rate of wage inflation. Some readers mistook the resulting model as generalisation of an excess demand model of wage dynamics (in which excess demand was measured by the excess of vacancies over unemployment).

If I have gone on rather lengthily about this now rather old piece of work, it is because it will be useful to have a good idea of what that model of the natural rate was for grasping the simple propositions of the next section on the determinants of the natural rate and hence the possible causes of its long-term swings and shifts.

Further developments

Natural rate models, to repeat, are so constructed that, if they contain nominal variables at all, the equilibrium path from every initial condition is invariant to 'money' and to the purely monetary effects of disturbances generally. The presence of non-synchronous wage- (or price) -setting introduces nominal variables into equilibrium near-term behaviour, but it does not alter the two main propositions: that keeping the unemployment rate bounded away from the natural rate path must ultimately result in inflation or deflation rising to a problematic level, and that a small change in monetary policy will make only a transient difference for the path of the unemployment rate. The riskiness of this doctrine warrants comment. There is another large aspect of the subject, however, with at least as urgent a claim on our attention.

The question arises: what *are* the key determinants of the size of the natural rate – money not being one, by construction – and in what direction do they pull? My 1968 paper observed that faster growth of the labour force would produce a higher natural rate through the rising marginal cost of training. There was also the suggestion that faster steady growth, if it entailed a higher average rate of layoff in the economy, would also produce a higher natural rate. But there was little more than that. It is striking that this paper and all the succeeding papers in the next months and years did not explore the 'comparative statics' of the natural rate. In time this omission in the theory was elevated to the status of a normal property – that the natural rate was a constant, as if a force of nature, a magical thing that is not itself caused.

This constancy, which served only to cover up the yawning gap in our understanding of the natural rate, may lie behind the suspicion with which natural rate doctrine has come to be regarded in some quarters in the past dozen or so years. Natural rate models can hardly be satisfactory if the natural rate, in any suitably general view, has been pulled to and fro by real shocks of the evolution of real conditions while our *models* of the natural rate continue to treat it as a parameter rather than a variable.

There has been a crying need, then, for a *general equilibrium view* of the natural rate – defined now in the general sense of the *current* equilibrium stationary rate, given the *current* capital stock and any other state variables. (It is the unemployment rate that, if it were the actual rate at the moment, would make the current rate of change of the associated equilibrium unemployment rate path equal to zero.) In such a framework, the equilibrium unemployment path from a given initial point is still driven by a natural rate, but the latter is a *variable* of the system – an endogenously moving target that the equilibrium path constantly pursues.

If we view the natural rate path as endogenous, pushed like other economic variables by non-monetary forces, and take on board the rest of natural rate doctrine – actual unemployment tending soon to equilibrium, and all equilibrium paths approaching the natural path – we arrive at a new paradigm: *a non-monetary equilibrium theory of unemployment movements* – an endogenously moving-natural rate theory of movements in the *actual* rate of unemployment.

Over the past several years I have managed to develop to a rudimentary, working stage a general equilibrium theory of this kind in the form of a family of intertemporal micro–macro models. Each one revolves around a distinct kind of asset acquired by the firm that is of importance for its hiring decisions: the trained employee, the customer and fixed capital equipment. Collectively these models provide a 'structuralist story' of how the equilibrium unemployment path is determined and thus disturbed by changing parameters and conditions. The evidence so far encourages me to believe that this theory does rather well at explaining the *shifts* and *long swings* of the unemployment rate in the postwar experience of the Western industrial countries. A detailed exposition of this approach, with a statistical and historical investigation of its explanatory power, is presented in my recent monograph (Phelps, 1994). It is possible, though, to give a glimpse of what the approach has to offer by taking up two themes regarding the closed economy.

One of these themes concerns the effect of shocks to the technology. Consider a one-time shock to the level of labour augmentation appearing in all production functions. In the admirable rendering of the natural rate by Steven Salop (1979), the implication in this regard went unnoticed. Such a productivity shock had no effect on the natural rate path and, accordingly, on the equilibrium path from the initially given unemployment rate; the shock was followed instantly by a neutralising increase of the real wage at each firm, hence no change in the quit rate, and no reason for firms to speed or slow their hiring of labour, the wage having offset the increased productivity of employees. This was a comforting result from one point of view since it meant that secular progress did not have the counterfactual implication of an ever-decreasing unemployment rate; but it likewise implied that there was no near-term disturbance to the employment rate either. This result was a consequence of the wage–wage view of labour turnover behaviour of my 1968 paper on which Salop built. In the later, utility-theoretic formulation by Carl Shapiro and Joseph Stiglitz (1984), the contrast was complete. Such a labour-augmenting shock, in driving up the economy-wide real wage, decreased the propensity to quit, causing the supply wage to shift up less than the demand wage in the employment–wage plane, with the result that the employment rate is increased and the wage rises proportionately less than productivity. This finding was a consequence of the utility function chosen and the background setting.

The models I have developed take an additional step in introducing the income from wealth in the quitting or shirking function contained by the model. Nevertheless, a one-time productivity shock has no effect on the natural rate, nor on the equilibrium path from the given initial condition, in the two models where there is no slow-moving state variable (other than, as in one model, the stock of employed workers, hence the employment rate itself). In the model where there *is* such a state variable in the form of the stock of fixed capital, however, there is an effect on the natural rate: if the capital stock could increase in proportion to productivity, to which level it will tend gradually as saving and investment jump up, there would be no effect; the wage rate at the firm, in the economy as a whole, and the employees' non-wage income would all increase in proportion to productivity; as a result, the demand wage and the supply wage (or incentive wage) would increase equally, putting the unemployment rate at its preshock level. But since the capital stock cannot increase, there is a near-term effect. It tends to be contractionary through an important channel since the implied drop in capital relative to the new-found level of labour augmentation operates to raise the real rate of interest and lower the real price of the capital good; the latter effect in turn operates to move the capital goods sector down its (new) supply curve and, since that is the labour-intensive sector, thus to reduce the demand wage relative to the new level of labour augmentation.[9]

The effect of an unanticipated positive increase in the *rate* of labour-augmenting progress expected to prevail over the indefinite future is another story. It might be thought that the effect would be exhilarating for the economy, precipitating new doses of investment. But in fact the prospect of new levels of real income in the future propel an expansion of consumption, while not providing the technical means for increased supply of output in the present, with the result that the real price of assets has to seek a lower level, with real interest rates accordingly pushed up. In one model the effect is a drop in the capital goods output supplied; in both cases employment is contracted. Thus it may happen that the growth rate of an economy is the enemy of its employment rate.

The emerging general equilibrium theory makes demand shocks as much as supply shocks the great movers and shakers of the economy's equilibrium path. In the version constructed here, the theory sees shifts in profitability and thrift as prime sources of disturbances. Adjustments of domestic assets and of wealth operate to amplify or ultimately to tend to correct the early effect on unemployment.

Here the theory is an echo of pre-Keynesian doctrine in sounding the theme of slump through 'undersaving': public debt and other fiscal stimulus to consumer spending are seen as contractionary. Yet the results have in common with Keynesian doctrine the theme of slump through 'under-investment': in particular, government armaments purchases (and in all but special cases manpower buildups too), as occur in wartime, and more generally any government spending on goods produced by the capital goods sector of the economy are implied to be expansionary – without any reference to the liquidity of a money economy, which is crucial to the Keynesian analysis.

The pre-Keynesian part follows from a very simple mechanism. An increase of consumer demand, whether the response to a spontaneous increase of the rate of pure time preference or the artefact of a recent increase of public debt, creates an excess of consumption demand over consumption supply, with the result that real asset prices have to drop and real interest rates rise in order to eliminate that excess demand. The repercussion of these changes in financial prices is an induced decrease in the amount of investment of the various types that firms are willing to undertake. The effect in turn is a decline in the equilibrium path of the employment rate.

The Keynesian part arises from the property that an increased demand by the government for the capital good serves to pull up the relative price of the good whose production is the more labour-intensive and thus to pull up the demand wage in the aggregate employment–wage plane. As an empirical matter, however, it is not clear that this effect is generally strong; it may be confined to a small sub-set of capital goods.

Introducing the interactions of open economies adds further twists to the story. It is found to be theoretically possible that a consumption-demand stimulus in an open economy, if it small enough, will have an expansionary effect at home – a result more Keynesian than that obtained by some Keynesian models – while having a contractionary effect abroad (in proportion to its size). This is the same 'locomotive' in reverse, or 'crowding out' at a distance, previously found in the part-monetary models of Fitoussi and Phelps (1988). The argument is that the fiscal largesse of the country on its own citizenry drives up the domestic real interest rate and thus the world real interest rate, which entails a real exchange rate depreciation abroad, the effect of which is to push up the natural unemployment rate abroad.

The empirical sections of the monograph suggest that this theory of equilibruim unemployment succeeds to an important degree in shedding light on the contrasts between the long period of extraordinarily high economic activity from the early postwar years to the end of the 1960s and the two nearly global slumps in the 1970s and 1980s. (The view of the 1990s it offers is not far from the mark either.) Of course, other non-classical representatives of the equilibrium approach to unemployment also exist: the insider–outsider models (especially their non-monetary versions), and the still embryonic models based on modern finance notions of credit rationing to firms and households. So it is not suggested that the particular models of the natural rate that I have developed are the only vehicles for a structuralist approach to slumps and booms.

Some reservations

The thrust of these reflections is clear. The natural rate idea remains a powerful concept for macroeconomic analysis. The endogenisation of the natural rate in the work of Salop, Stiglitz and myself – and the parallel work of a less micro founded sort by Kouri, Bruno and Sachs, Fitoussi and Phelps, and Newell and Symonds, to mention only a few – has freed the natural rate to do a great deal more work than it was called upon to do earlier.

Yet it would be remiss of me not to draw back for a critical look at the edifice that has been going up. How much of the macroeconomic world can be captured by a theory that emphasises the natural rate, downplaying monetary factors and channels and downplaying expectational disequilibrium, and that bases the natural rate on incentive wage considerations – quitting, shirking, and adverse selection?

The claim that money and inflation are neutral deserves more qualification than it usually receives. The monetary aspects of the economy do not possess the sort of linearity that we imply in our usual models. In the neighbourhood of the normal range of the economy, money may be neutral 'in the small'. A 1% increase or decrease of the money supply will make little difference. A change of 15 or 25 per cent, however, may make a large difference. And in the neighbourhood of such a disturbed range, even a small change of the money supply may make a large difference. It is remarkable how firmly and how early Irving Fisher got a hold of this point, and how little attention was paid to it by Keynes and most Keynesians.

Fisher's point may be important for understanding the various forces behind the high unemployment of recent years. It is plausible that the slump of the 1990s is not altogether a holdover of the lengthy 1980s' slump in the economies but is, rather, *in part* to be explained by the huge drop in inflation over the 1980s, which has left households and corporations saddled with larger levels of real indebtedness than they anticipated when they took on much of this debt in previous years. By the same logic, it must be that some of the 1980s' slump – particularly the high unemployment rates still lingering toward the end of the decade – is also to be explained by this phenomenon of 'debt deflation', in Fisher's term. Very likely the bulging levels of real debt overhang had a sobering effect on households and firms contemplating their customary accumulations of real assets and financing them by the customary mix of debt and equity. If this hypothesis is true and quantitatively important, it means, as I see it, that the natural rate hypothesis is not as good an approximation of reality as it first seemed to us in the 1960s. However, no purpose would be served by conceding this small but valuable piece of territory to the resurgent monetary forces until the econometric scouts have confirmed that the insurgents have solid control of it. At the time of writing, the relevant econometric tests have not yet been performed. Scraps of circumstantial evidence and supporting observations are useful but not conclusive.

The reliability of convergence to the natural rate path is, in my view, no less serious an issue. It is one thing to suggest a broad tendency toward equilibration (not in any exact way, of course) over a range of circumstances and histories, and quite another to close the door to the intuition, ventured by Keynes and a few others, that there are apt to be episodes in which the economy lingers away from equilibrium or moves back and forth past the correct expectations to have. Research by Roman Frydman and myself, some of it collabourative, has sought to identify some conditions that may block convergence to equilibrium. On the other hand, if my recent econometric work implementing the variable natural rate theory (mentioned on p. 26 above) is basically right, there is – on average, at any rate – a tendency for the unemployment rate to approach the natural rate path. A question very much left open, however, is whether, following a shock, there is a systematic tendency for a stampede, culminating in overshooting – a phenomenon perhaps traceable to expectational errors or perhaps to a desire of each enterprise manager not to be seen having taken fewer precautions than other managers even if the situation of the enterprise does not call for them.

Finally, is the labour market really a matter of incentive pay and nothing else? Of course not. Students should understand that seeing N papers in a row without a mention of the word 'union', say, or 'insiders' and 'outsiders', should not be taken to indicate that the author doubts the importance of those considerations. The more convenient model is always preferred, and as between equally convenient models, the one in which the writer has a vested interest is selected.

The insider–outsider theory greatly enriches the dynamics of employment, and it has interesting implications for the real wage response to shocks. Some models by Andrew Oswald and by Assar Lindbeck and

Dennis Snower (1989, for example) are among those that have had an impact in the 1980s. It does not seem that these models are contrary by their very nature to the natural rate concept. There are insider–outsider models in which the unemployment rate gravitates back to the level that could be regarded as the natural rate. Indeed, there are elements of the 1960s' models, such as the marginal costs of hiring, that have fed directly into insider–outsider models. A careful recognition of such costs tends to generate a natural rate *zone* instead of a point, since the employment level to which a firm will downsize its workforce when starting with an excess of employees is possibly greater than the level to which it will increase its workforce when starting with a deficiency.[10] One could go further with the contention of similarity, arguing that these models offer another dimension – the extortion dimension – of incentive pay: wages are set high enough that the workforce will not sabotage production, refuse to work with new recruits, and so forth.

Lastly, trade unions. To Europeans it must seem a sort of wilfulness to have left them out. As I commented earlier, unions had been overemphasised in the preceding years and, as a reaction, I took the position that unions were inessential for explaining why equilibrium unemployment was substantial. Since then, of course, a number of models of unemployment centred on trade unions have appeared. Models of the insider–outsider type in which unions figure have already been mentioned. With the (1991) monograph by Richard Layard and his colleagues has come another model of wage-setting and unemployment based on bargaining between unions and imperfectly competitive firms – a sort of Nash–Zeuthen model focusing on unemployment. Yet these union models do not incorporate considerations of incentive pay, just as incentive models do not have unions.

We are stuck with the fact that every tractable model can offer only a slice of reality. I feel fortunate to have seized on a slice that, despite so many years, has gone on yielding rich insights into the determination of unemployment.

Notes

1 The process of rising inflation would cause the rate finally to hit a barrier such that sellers of money would find no takers, money having ceased to play any useful role. The process of rising deflation would cause the rate finally to reach a level such that sellers of real wealth claims would be unable to find any takers, money having come to dominate all non-monetary assets such as equities and consumer durables.

2 This definition of the natural rate seems to be very convenient in econometric work. In a purely theoretical paper it might be more natural (no pun intended)

to define the natural rate as the equilibrium steady state path.
3 Clearly the thrust of the doctrine would survive if the natural rate became a *path* instead of a constant, even an endogenous path provided it is invariant to monetary policy.
4 Dahrendorf would say that the proposition belongs to critical rather than to theoretical economics; see Dahrendorf (1993).
5 These papers were widely known. Lerner's, in the *Review of Economics and Statistics* (1949), was the stimulus to Friedman's famous complaint that, contrary to what Lerner had implied, inflation had *some* real allocative maleffects, namely the time-consuming efforts of people to economise on cash balances.
6 Among those who zeroed in on this aspect of the model were Dale Mortenson and some of his colleagues at Northwestern, Donald Gordon, then at UBC, and Arthur Okun at Brookings.
7 The first wave of new Keynesian models, developed at Columbia in the latter half of the 1970s, is discussed in Phelps (1991).
8 I could not be certain that the distrinction was really there were it not that I remember some readers having called attention to it, William Nordhaus for one.
9 Another effect works the other way, as the deficiency of capital relative to the long run means that non-wage income is decreased relative to the wage, which tends to decrease the propensity to shirk in the model and thus to reduce the supply wage (or incentive wage). As a consequence of this contrary tendency, there is no theoretically unambiguous result regarding the unemployment effect of a permanent shock to the level of labour augmentation and of a change in the initial capital stock.
10 Appendix A to the 1970 version of my paper has some equations bearing on the dynamics of employment under the explicit presence of rising marginal hiring cost. Without doubt that discussion is somewhat confused, having been written in late 1966, well before the significance and real meaning of the model I was working on had become more or less fully clear to me.

References

Dahrendorf, R., 1993. *Essays in the Theory of Society*, Stanford, CA: Stanford University Press
Fellner, W. J., 1959. 'Demand Inflation, Cost Inflation, and Collective Bargaining', in P.D. Bradley (ed.), *The Public Stake in Union Power*, Charlottesville: University of Virginia Press
Fitoussi, J.-P. and Phelps, E.S., 1988. *The Slump in Europe*, Oxford: Basil Blackwell
Friedman, M., 1968. 'The Role of Monetary Policy', *American Economic Review*, 58(1) (March), 1–17
Layard, R., Nickell, S.J. and Jackman, R., 1991. *Unemployment: Macroeconomic Performance and the Labour Market*, Oxford: Oxford University Press
Lerner, A. P., 1948, 'The Inflationary Process – Some Theoretical Aspects', *Review of Economics and Statistics*, 31 (August).

Lindbeck, A. and Snower, D.J., 1989. *The Insider–Outsider Theory of Employment and Unemployment*, Cambridge, MA: MIT Press

Lipsey, R.G., 1960. 'The Relation Between Unemployment and the Rate of Change of Money Wage Rates in the United Kingdom, 1862–1957: a Further Analysis', *Economica*, 27 (February), 1–31, reprinted in AEA Series (1966), *Readings in Business Cycles*, 456–87

Lucas, R.E., 1972. 'Expectations and the neutrality of money', *Journal of Economic Theory*, 4 (April), 103–24

Phelps, E.S., 1967. 'Phillips Curves, Expectations of Inflation and Optimal Unemployment Over Time', *Economica*, 34(3) (August), 254–81

1968. 'Money Wage Dynamics and Labor Market Equilibrium', *Journal of Political Economy*, 76 (August), part 2, 678–711

1970. 'Money Wage Dynamics and Labor Market Equilibrium', in E.S. Phelps *et al.*, *Microeconomic Foundations of Employment and Inflation Theory*, New York: Norton and London: Macmillan (1971)

1972. *Inflation Policy and Unemployment Theory*, London: Macmillan

1991. *Seven Schools of Macroeconomic Thought*, Oxford: Oxford University Press

1994. *Structural Slumps: the Modern Equilibrium Theory of Unemployment, Interest and Assets*, Cambridge, MA: Harvard University Press

Salop, S.C., 1979. 'A Model of the Natural Rate of Unemployment', *American Economic Review*, 69 (May), 117–25

Sargan, D., 1964. 'Wages and Prices in the UK: a Study in Econometric Methodology', in P.E. Hart, G. Mills and J.K. Whitaker (eds), *Econometric Analysis for National Economic Planning*, London: Butterworth

Shapiro, C. and Stiglitz, J.E., 1984. 'Equilibrium Unemployment as a Worker Discipline Device', *American Economic Review*, 74 (June), 433–44

3 The natural rate as new classical macroeconomics

James Tobin

Friedman, Lucas, and market clearing

In retrospect, Friedman's 1967 Presidential Address to the American Economic Association (Friedman, 1968) was the opening shot of the new classical macroeconomics, the precursor of Lucas's 'misperceptions' explanation of Phillips curve observations and of the 'policy ineffectiveness proposition'. Like Lucas (1973) and other new classicals, Friedman deploys ancient classical money-is-a-veil doctrine to argue that only real prices and real wages can determine real quantities of production and employment. Apparent relations between money prices and real quantities, like the Phillips curve, are bound to be ephemeral, especially if policymakers try to exploit them. The Friedman–Lucas doctrine is that the economy behaves as if markets were determining real prices all the time. Those prices are the arguments in supply and demand functions, and equalities of demand and supply shape the path of the economy.

The natural rate, according to Friedman, is 'the level that would be ground out by the Walrasian system of general equilibrium equations' (1968, p. 8). The sentence continues with the proviso that 'imbedded' in these equations are 'market imperfections, stochastic variability in demands and supplies, the cost of gathering information about job vacancies and labour availabilities, the cost of mobility, and so on, phenomena that no one knows how to imbed in them'. After this gesture Friedman forgets about these awkward non-Walrasian phenomena and applies classical doctrine unconditionally.

How do deviations from the natural rate occur? There are two possible answers, not necessarily exclusive, new classical and Keynesian. In new classical theory, departures from the natural rate result from distortions of demand and supply schedules because of misperception, misinformation, or incorrect expectations regarding the real wages and prices relevant to those schedules. Markets still clear, supply still equals demand, just as in natural rate equilibrium, but the prices, wages, and quantities determined in those markets differ from natural rate outcomes. Friedman describes graphically the dynamics of the expectational adjustments that lead to accelerations of prices up or down when employment and output are higher or lower than their natural rate values. Lucas introduces here the powerful tools of rational expectations, but that does not make his story essentially different from Friedman's. Both of them say that unanticipated monetary policy and inflation can raise employment temporarily, but only temporarily and only by fooling workers and employers.

Keynes and uncleared markets

Keynesian 'full employment' is the counterpart of the natural rate. It too is a real classical equilibrium, in which equality of the marginal productivity of labour and the marginal disutility of work determines real wages and the volumes of employment and output. But the Keynesian explanation of departures from full employment is quite different from the Fried-man–Lucas description. It is that markets are not clearing. Lapses from full employment occur when there is excess supply of labour, involuntary unemployment. Some workers are unemployed even though they are willing to work at prevailing real wages, or less, and are no less efficient and productive than employed workers. This involuntary unemployment arises not because of the usual classical culprits, interferences with competition by trade unions and government regulations, but because market prices adjust slowly, certainly not instantaneously, to aggregate demand shocks (Keynes, 1936, Book I).

The idea that adjustments to shifts of supply and demand curves are not immediate would not have troubled the classical economists of Keynes' generation. It is only their latter-day successors, Friedman,[1] Lucas, and other new classicals who assume that observed prices and quantities are continuously the outcomes of price-cleared markets. 'Real business cycle' theorists represent the ultimate in this intellectual tradition; they do not even recognise the distortions of supply and demand schedules that explain departures from the natural rate in Friedman and Lucas. For them, the natural rate is just the actual rate, whatever it is today.

Frictional and involuntary unemployment

A simplistic aggregate interpretation of either Keynes' full employment or Friedman's natural rate would imply that in those equilibria unemployment would be zero – involuntary unemployment, that is. Voluntary choice to be out of the labour force is not at issue. The US Census Current Population Survey measure of unemployment is a close empirical approximation to the relevant concept of involuntary unemployment; it counts as unemployed persons who were not employed any time during the survey week but report that they have been looking for work during the past four weeks.

Keynes is almost as cavalier as Friedman on this point. He allows 'frictional' unemployment to coexist with full employment, and he gives several reasons that 'there will always exist 0in a non-static society a proportion of resources unemployed "between jobs" ' (Keynes, 1936, p. 6). However, a better theory of the relation of unemployment and inflation would provide a more complete account of frictional unemployment, and of Friedman's various addenda to Walrasian equations.

A more crucial question for each of the two theories is whether they ever imply involuntary unemployment. The Keynesian model obviously does. In natural rate theory, however, labour markets are always clearing. Although workers may misperceive and underestimate the real wages they face, they are getting as much employment as they desire in present circumstances as they understand them. The Census would not count them as unemployed. Of course, new classical macroeconomists have never regarded involuntary unemployment as reported in surveys as meaning anything they need to explain. Critics may regard that omission as a serious defect.

Keynes' monetary economy

Both Keynes' full employment and Friedman's natural rate relate nominal wage or nominal price change to discrepancies from those equilibria. In Friedman and Lucas, these movements are the market-clearing results of adjustments of demand and supply to revised estimates of current and future real wages and prices. In Keynes, they are the natural competitive responses to excess supply or excess demand. While classicals, new or old, viewed markets as generating real prices and wages, Keynes stressed that we live in a monetary economy, in which the wages and prices determined in markets, both in equilibrium and during disequilibrium adjustments, are wages and prices expressed in the monetary unit of account. Because these adjustments take real time, real wages and prices will deviate from their equilibrium values for finite periods of time, perhaps even for extended periods of time. But this does not reflect money illusion in agents' behaviour, nor irrational expectations, nor imperfect or asymmetrical information.

The Phillips curve is the natural extension to economy-wide labour markets of the conventional dynamics of supply and demand both in Marshallian sectoral markets and in Walrasian general equilibrium. Until the last 20 or 30 years economists of all persuasions recognised that supply and demand do not clear continuously, that it takes real time for prices and quantities to adjust to shifts in the curves. The common scenario, long used by teachers and texts of introductory economics, was and is that prices move down when there is excess supply, roughly proportionately to the amount, and likewise move up in response to excess demand. This informal but intuitive dynamics convinces students that supply/demand analysis makes sense. For a single market, small relative to the whole economy, it is reasonable to interpret these movements as adjustments in both real and nominal prices at the same time.

Keynes' important insight was that this story does not carry over to economy-wide adjustments of money wages to excess demands or supplies. Clearly the economy-wide nominal prices of commodities, which translate money wages into real wages, are not independent of nominal labour costs. The dynamics are much more complex and chancy than uncritical analogy to the textbook story for single small markets suggests. Indeed, as Keynes pointed out, downward adjustments of money wages may not reduce the real wage at all, and may not eliminate or reduce the unemployment that triggered them. Yet new classicals ignore Keynes (1936) chapter 2 (see also chapter 16 in this volume). They finesse all the anomalies raised by the fact that their models make behaviour depend only on real prices while actual markets generate nominal prices.[2]

In labour markets unemployment and vacancies are consequences and indicators of failures of markets to clear at prevailing prices. To describe the failure another way, prices are not flexible enough, instantaneously flexible enough, to equate demand and supply at every moment of time. As older generations of economists took for granted, excess supplies and demands – unemployment and vacancies respectively in particular labour markets – commonly occur and trigger movements of prices and quantities – specifically money wages and employment.

Keynes argued, of course, that nominal wages are sticky. His argument exploited the truth that money wages are determined in a host of disaggregated markets, not in a single economy-wide market or national negotiation. In every particular market workers and employers might well believe that a money wage cut would be a cut in their wages relative to those of workers elsewhere, and resist it on those grounds. Although Keynes purported to be adopting the classical assumption that both product and labour markets are purely competitive in the absence of monopolistic combinations or government regulations, his discussion of the realities of labour markets seems to recognise monopolistic competition and bilateral bargaining as normal features of wage determination.

The Phillips curve

Phillips (1958) was well within Marshallian and Keynesian traditions when he plotted nominal, not real, wage changes against unemployment rates.

Friedman missed the point when he called this choice a 'basic defect'. This is not to deny that changes in money wages in labour markets will reflect expected nominal wage and price movements throughout the economy, as well as pressures from excess supply, unemployment, and excess demand, job vacancies. If the real economy and monetary quantities are growing at different rates, equilibrium nominal prices will be moving too. In a full and continuing equilibrium, expectations will be confirmed by future events. If equilibrium prices are moving, consumers, workers, and business managers will anticipate those trends.[3]

The Phillips curve came to prominence on the American macroeconomic scene in the 1950s, when money wages and prices appeared to accelerate while employment was less than what was regarded as 'full'. A new category of inflation had been discovered and a new term invented, 'cost-push' as distinguished from 'demand-pull'. But a name is not an explanation, and there was no theory of the sources of cost-push. A different approach, consistent with Phillips curve observations, was to regard 'full employment' as a zone rather than a point, and inflation not as an either–or discontinuity but as a matter of degree, depending on the prevalence of excess demand markets in the economy.

Essential to this rationale is recognition of three characteristics of the sources of Phillips curve observations. Two of them I have already discussed: that, as Keynes stressed, the wages and prices determined in markets are expressed in the monetary unit of account, and that *disequilibrium* in a market – excess supply or demand at prevailing prices – is a crucial source of changes in wages or prices. The third is the multiplicity of labour and product markets and the diversity of the demand/supply circumstances of the several markets.

The Beveridge curve

We know from common obervation that excess supplies and excess demands exist simultaneously in the economy. Specifically, in some labour markets unemployed workers outnumber job vacancies, while in others at the same time vacancies exceed unemployment. One might, as I suggested (Tobin, 1972), define a single labour market narrowly enough so that vacancies and unemployment do not coexist within it.

At any moment there are both vacancies markets, those with excess demand, and unemployment markets, those with excess supply. Of course, the identities of markets within the two classes are always changing, as supply/demand balances shift. Yet over the economy as a whole there is considerable stability in the relation between aggregate vacancy and unemployment rates, as they vary in business fluctuations. This is a negative relationship: high vacancies go with low unemployment, and vice versa. Moreover, the marginal decrease in vacancies per unit increase in unemployment declines with the unemployment rate. This relation is often called the Beveridge curve. William Beveridge (1945) defined employment as full if unemployment is no more numerous than vacancies. In this context it is easy to define frictional unemployment, namely the maximum amount of unemployment consistent with Beveridge's criterion of full employment.

In practice it is difficult to implement this conceptual framework literally, because vacancies and idle workers cannot be measured so that one vacancy is really comparable to one unemployed worker. But the framework is useful. For example, consider the frequently recurring controversy whether observed increases in unemployment are frictional or structural, on the one hand, or cyclical and 'Keynesian', on the other. In the former case, there would be in effect an increase in the natural rate or, to use a more appropriately neutral term, the non-accelerating inflation rate of unemployment (NAIRU), and demand stimulus would not be the appropriate remedy. In the latter case, there would be an increased shortfall from full employment, and Keynesian demand policy would be called for. In the former case, the Beveridge curve would have shifted outward, in a way that increased both vacancies and unemployment. In the latter case, there would have been movement along an unchanged Beveridge curve, not an outward shift.

'Stochastic macroequilibrium' and the NAIRU

In my own Presidential Address in 1971 (Tobin, 1972), I described a Phillips curve theory based on what I called stochastic macroequilibrium: 'stochastic because random intersectoral shocks keep individual labor markets in diverse states of disequilibrium; macroequilibrium, because the perpetual flux of particular markets produces fairly definite aggregate outcomes of unemployment and wages.' In this model I was following contributions by Lipsey (1960), and by Archibald and Holt (in Phelps, *et al.* 1970). Here it is again.

The microeconomics of the Phillips curve is that money wages rise in excess demand labour markets and fall in excess supply markets, in approximate proportions to the amounts of excess demand or supply. These are movements relative to market-clearing wages, which may themselves be moving. Economy-wide average wage change depends on both vacancies and unemployment. The macro Phillips and Beveridge curves arise as joint outcomes of the events in individual markets and of the distribution of excess demands and supplies among them. As the aggregate number of jobs increases relative to the labour force, more markets will experience vacancies and fewer will exhibit excess supplies of workers. The rate of wage inflation will be greater, and as the norms of wage settlements rise in response, Friedman's unbounded acceleration may occur.

Individual markets are subject to stochastic shocks in supply and demand. If these shocks were to cease, adjustments of prices and of quantities – e.g. movements of workers towards markets with higher wages and greater excess demands – could bring equilibrium with markets cleared. The only aggregate quantity of jobs compatible with such an equilibrium is a quantity equal to the labour force. This equilibrium would carry with it a 'natural rate' of unemployment, namely zero, at stable wages and prices.

Suppose, however, the macroeconomic environment is stable, as measured by the aggregate number of jobs, while the distribution of these jobs among individual markets is constantly changing. Even if the distribution of excess demand and supply across markets remains constant, the positions of individual markets in the distribution are in continuous flux.

What is happening to money wages depends on the dynamics of adjustment to excess demands and supplies. Since these adjustments take time, there are bound to be some vacancies and some unemployment. The balance between them will vary with the macro environment, the aggregate of jobs. Beveridge full employment will not necessarily result in average wage change of zero (relative to the equilibrium trend). The NAIRU can well involve unemployment in excess of vacancies, jobs fewer in aggregate than the labour force. This would happen if downward adjustments of wages in excess supply markets are slower than upward adjustments in excess demand markets. Non-linearity of response of this kind introduces an inflationary bias to the system. The same non-linearity of response would imply that the NAIRU is higher the greater the dispersion of excess demands and supplies across markets.

The model also allows for mobility of workers towards markets with higher wages and more vacancies. Within limits, the greater is such endogenous mobility the fewer will be the mismatches reflected in frictional unemployment and the lower will be the NAIRU.

My 1971 model assumed – with one exception – that, for any given aggregate quantity of jobs relative to labour force, increases in average money wages over time would ultimately feed fully into wage determination in every sector. This is a recipe for a vertical long-run Phillips curve *à la* Friedman. But I did point out a possible exception, a way in which a long-run trade-off might be preserved. Suppose that in any market money wages will not actually decline unless and until a high rate of unemployment has persisted for several periods. This barrier might temporarily prevent the wage change in the sector from falling as far below the general norm as would be appropriate to prevailing excess supply in the sector. If the wage change norm were high, that rate of unemployment would without delay generate a wage increase appropriately below the norm but still non-negative. But if the wage increase norm were so low that it would take a money wage decline to bring about that same differential, the decline would be postponed and for a while there would be no change. Eventually, however, this barrier would give way.

This phenomenon is realistic, whether or not it is irrational. Even if it could be said to show money illusion, it is not a permanent non-homogeneity in any market. However, the positions of markets are always shifting. So there may always be some markets at the nominal barrier, their identities always changing. If so, increasing the aggregate number of jobs will at the same time reduce the unemployment rate and increase the average rate of wage inflation. The effects of actual wage change on the wage norm are diluted by the fact that money wages remain unchanged in those sectors at the money wage floor. There is a permanent trade-off in aggregate, though not in any one market. But the long-run Phillips curve will still become vertical when the average wage increase and the general wage increase norm are high enough so that no adjustments in any market would require nominal wage cuts. I am afraid that critics did not understand this subtle and ingenious argument; they just thought I was committing a vulgar error.

In conclusion

The symmetry between accelerating inflation and accelerating deflation in Friedman's model has always been hard to believe. Unemployment lower than the natural rate spells exploding inflation, he says, and unemployment higher spells galloping disinflation and deflation. In contrast, in Keynes open-end inflation results from an 'inflationary gap' in aggregate demand, while a 'deflationary gap' leads to comparative stability of prices or price trends. The asymmetry stems from Keynes' observation of the downward stickiness of money wages.

I am inclined to believe in an S-shaped short-run Phillips curve for both individual markets and the economy at large (as I suggested in Tobin, 1955). At low unemployment rates and high vacancy rates, the curve would become quite steep. At high unemployment rates and low vacancy rates, as for example in 1982 in the US, the marginal response of wage inflation to additional unemployment would be increasing. For intermediate unemployment and vacancy rates the curve would be fairly flat, making it hard to locate any precise NAIRU. In this central flat range, transient microeconomic ups and downs in prices and wages would be more important than macro events and policies. After all, it is difficult to believe in a knife-edge natural rate or full employment, implying that small changes in the tightness of labour markets have immense qualitative and quantitative consequences. *Natura non facit saltum*, so it says on Marshall's title page.

The NAIRU is not a Walrasian solution. It has no particular claim to be called 'natural' or 'optimal'. Its dynamic and distributional determinants come from institutional features of markets and from stochastic intermarket flux rather than from rational utility maximising determinants of real supply and demand relations. We economists do not, not yet anyway, have a general theory of optimisation applicable to dynamic adjustment mechanisms, because neither the objectives of such behaviour nor the constraints upon it can be, except in simple specific cases, formulated in terms of the utility and production functions which make us feel comfortable and on which we base ordinary supply and demand functions. Our models should of course be consistent with rational behaviour, including the absence of money illusion, in equilibrium. But in a monetary economy, in which markets, imperfect or perfect, grind out money wages and prices along with real quantities, we have no right to rule out *a priori* money effects on real variables during disequilibrium adjustments. This was Keynes' message, and both friends and foes in the profession were quite obtuse and wrong in attributing to him gratuitous assumptions of irrational money illusion.

In the end, the most destructive feature of natural rate theory is not its sensible warning against overdoing policies to expand aggregate demand in order to reduce unemployment below an inflation-safe rate. It is its inhibition against expansionary demand policies in any circumstances. This comes from new classical macroeconomics and real business cycle theory, and they are next-of-kin heirs of Milton Friedman's 1967 Presidential Address, very likely the most influential article ever published in an economics journal. Its influence reached way beyond the profession – for example, to European and Japanese governments and central banks and to *The Economist* and other opinion leaders. Europe has never really recovered from the recessions of 1974–5 and 1979–82, and now the entire advanced democratic capitalist world is stagnating.

Notes

1 Until I re-read Friedman's Presidential Address in order to write this chapter, I had the impression that Friedman accepted a Keynesian non-market-clearing explanation of unemployment in excess of the natural rate. Now, however, I think

the wage and price adjustments in his paper are better interpreted as corrections of expectations than as responses to excess demand or supply. The spirit of Lucas is also evident in Friedman's stress that the monetary authority 'cannot use its control over nominal quantities to peg a real quantity'. The word 'peg' does leave some ambiguity, about the length of time for which a particular value of a target variable is the policy objective. But the spirit of his paper, reinforced by the critical dismissal of 'fine tuning', suggests that the monetary authority should eschew any real target at any time.

The Presidential Address is not the only evidence of Friedman's drift towards a new classical or 'real business cycle' position. In his ultimate defence of his position that fiscal policy has no macroeconomic consequence he embraced the classical view that price flexibility keeps the economy at full employment (natural rate) anyway. He said, 'It is important that we try to determine as accurately as possible the characteristics of the demand function for money, including the elasticity of demand with respect to interest rates. But in my opinion no "fundamental issues" in either monetary theory or monetary policy hinge on whether the estimated elasticity can for most purposes be approximated by zero or is better approximated by -0.1 or -0.5 or -2.0, provided it is seldom capable of being approximated by $-\infty$' (Friedman, 1966, p. 85). This cannot be true unless real aggregate output is independent of interest rates and that cannot be true unless perfect or near-perfect price flexibility keeps the economy at full employment independent of fiscal and monetary policies and events.

2 Dillard (1988) called this contradiction the 'Barter illusion in classical and neoclassical economics'. I have discussed these issues at length elsewhere (Tobin, 1993).

3 That norms for wage increases would reflect actual experience and expectation of economy-wide wage and price inflation was widely appreciated before 1967 by economists who found the Phillips curve a useful macroeconomic tool. The famous or infamous Samuelson–Solow article (1960) recognises this explicitly. Consider also the following part of a paper presented in October 1966:

[We do not] know the answer to the . . . basic question whether continuation of 4 percent unemployment would, so long as it generates any inflation, generate an accelerating inflation. This would be the orthodox prediction: Wages and other incomes rise because people want real gains, and the bargaining power of the individuals and groups depends on the real situation. If they find that they are cheated by price increases they will simply escalate their money claims accordingly. On this view the Phillips curve would blow up if growth at a steady utilization rate were maintained . . . On this interpretation, the only true equilibrium full employment is the degree of unemployment that corresponds to zero inflation – any higher rate if utilization can be called excess demand. This is a dismal conclusion if true, because it appears to take a socially explosive rate of unemployment – more than 6 percent in the USA – to keep the price level stable (Tobin, 1967).

I would add that when President Kennedy's Council of Economic Advisers in 1961 set 4% unemployment as the goal of macro policy, we were not proposing to take a ride up a Phillips curve to purchase lower unemployment than the 7% then prevailing at the expense of more inflation. We believed, maybe wrongly but not obviously so then or now, that 4% was at that time consistent with stable low inflation. We proposed also to take out insurance by incomes policy, 'wage-price guideposts'. Inflation accelerated in the late 1960s when Vietnam war fiscal and monetary policy carried unemployment down to 3%.

References

Beveridge, W.H., 1945. *Full Employment in a Free Society*, New York: W.W. Norton

Dillard, D., 1988. 'The Barter Illusion in Classical and Neoclassical Economics', *Eastern Economic Journal*, 14 (October–December), 299–318

Friedman, M., 1966. 'Interest Rates and the Demand for Money', *Journal of Law and Economics*, 9 October, 71–85

1968. 'The Role of Monetary Policy', *American Economic Review*, 58(1) (March), 1–17

Keynes, J.M., 1936. *The General Theory of Employment, Interest and Money*, New York: Harcourt Brace and London: Macmillan

Lipsey, R.G., 1960. 'The Relation between Unemployment and the Rate of Change of Money Wage Rates in the United Kingdom, 1862–1957: A Further Analysis', *Economica*, 27 February, 1–31; reprinted in AEA Series (1966), *Reading in Business Cycles*, 456–87

Lucas, R.E., Jr., 1973. 'Some International Evidence on Output–Inflation Tradeoffs', *American Economic Review*, 63(3) (June), 326–34

Phelps, E.S. *et al.*, 1970. *Microeconomic Foundations of Employment and Inflation Theory*, New York: W.W. Norton and London: Macmillan

Phillips, A.W., 1958. 'The Relation between Unemployment and the Rate of Change of Money Wage Rates in the United Kingdom, 1861–1957', *Economica*, 25 November, 283–99

Samuelson, P.A. and Solow, R.M., 1960. 'Analytical Aspects of Anti-Inflation Policy', *American Economic Review*, 50 (May), 177–94.

Tobin, J., 1955. 'A Dynamic Aggregative Model', *Journal of Political Economy*, 63(1) (April), 103–15

1967. 'Unemployment and Inflation: The Cruel Dilemma', in A. Phillips (ed.), *Price Issues in Theory, Practice and Policy*, Philadelphia: University of Pennsylvania Press

1972. 'Inflation and Unemployment', *American Economic Review*, 62(1) (March), 1–18

1993. 'Price Flexibility and Output Stability: An Old Keynesian View', *Journal of Economic Perspectives*, 7 (Winter), 45–65

4 Theoretical reflections on the 'natural rate of unemployment'

Frank Hahn

Introduction

Phillips (1958) started it with what he claimed was an inverse relation, derived from historical data, between unemployment and the rate of change in money wages. This suggested that the price of lower unemployment was inflation – the famous 'trade-off'. The paper gave rise to some rudimentary theorising. It soon dawned on those interested that workers were concerned with wages in terms of wage goods and employers in wages in terms of product prices. Since the theory quickly became a branch of macro-economics and since as a first step it was easier to deal with a closed economy and to neglect taxes, the distinction between the two wage deflators was ignored and one simply considered 'real' wages. Thus the real Phillips curve was born, that is, a relation between unemployment and real wage was the object of enquiry.

All of this coincided with the counter-revolution in macroeconomics. For present purposes this entailed the hypothesis that labour is at all times on its supply curve – 'involuntary' unemployment was impossible. This was treated as an axiom. A distinction, however, was made between the long run and short run. In both 'runs', again axiomatically, markets clear but in the short run expectations may be falsified while in the long run they are correct. (This must be understood in the sense of expectations being 'rational' or not.) The natural rate of unemployment and its twin the 'non-accelerating inflation rate of unemployment (NAIRU)' refer to the long run. In fact, they refer to the steady state (with some allowance for white noise). Unemployment is 'search unemployment'. The steady state equilibrium is taken as unique and 'super-neutral', that is, values of real variables are independent of the inflation rate. The long-run supply curve of labour is vertical.

The short run is a story of mistakes. Unemployment below its steady state level (below the natural rate) is possible if rising nominal wages wrongly signal rising real wages, and rising prices wrongly signal (to firms) lower real wages. Workers in these circumstances supply more labour because they substitute future for present leisure. The mistakes gradually become apparent and the economy returns to the natural rate. To stay permanently at unemployment below this, mistakes must continue, and the only way to ensure that is to have accelerating inflation.

The policy lessons were clear. While governments might possibly affect the natural rate of unemployment by improving the efficiency of search (e.g. by housing policies) or by making search more costly by reducing unemployment benefits, there was nothing else – certainly not macro policy – which could reduce it. Thus Keynes was buried.

Steven Nickell in a wide-ranging survey (1990) writes that if the world looks as just described, unemployment would not be of great interest. He continues: 'Indeed, for many, it is transparently obvious, and has been so since the 1930's that unemployment reflects a waste of resources and severely penalises those who are subjected to it, mainly unskilled and semi-skilled workers.' He therefore favours an approach via theories of non-competitive wage determination such as union bargaining, efficiency wages, 'insider–outsider' theories and contract theories. He goes through these very well but incorporates them into a model which, while far less extreme than the classic American variety, is still essentially of that form. At the end he concludes that it is clear that 'any real explanation of long run shifts in unemployment must come from the supply side'.

Equilibrium

Friedman (1969), who had a theorist's instincts, defined the natural rate of unemployment as that rate which 'would be ground out by a system of general equilibrium equations taking account of market imperfections, stochastic variability of demand and supply, cost of mobility, etc.' (p. 102). Clearly not an Arrow–Debreu setting. He did not say whether he had a sequence of short runs or the long run in mind and, of course, the task of implementing his definition in either case is formidable. As far as I know it has not been done even on a macro level where, for instance, 'optimum search' is explicitly incorporated in a model.

But I start further back and ask: why equilibrium? There is an uninteresting view of equilibrium which I believe is, or was, held in mid-west America to mean that at any time an agent does what that agent believes to be best. This is not on its own helpful in thinking about the equilibrium of a market or of an economy. Here we are thinking of interactions of agents and of coordination.

Consider the usual real wage–employment diagram with a traditional monotonically upward sloping supply curve and a monotonically declining demand curve. The two curves intersect, say, at (w^*, l^*) and that is what we call an equilibrium. Why? Because at the point neither workers nor firm have an incentive to deviate from their supplies and demands. In order to establish that we need to say what the outcome of a deviation would be. In a perfectly competitive economy this is simple, since for the workers and firm, $w*$ is given. When competition is not perfect matters are more difficult and I return to that below. But at the moment what interests me is the analysis of points like (w, l) with $w > w*$ and $l < l*$.

Notice first of all that points on the labour supply curve represent the sum of the derived labour supply of workers. We have as yet no information on what workers would regard as best actions when some of them find that they cannot sell as much labour as they want. In particular recall the maintained competitive hypothesis that w is a parameter as far as the individual worker is concerned. The same applies to the firm. Moreover in specifying the economic environment of the firm – price, nominal wage, production function – we have not included any observation of labour supply. I am repeating a commonplace: we have no axiomatic foundations for behaviour out of perfectly competitive equilibrium.

Let me give an example based on theory proposed by myself and Solow (1994) and anticipated by Weibul.

Suppose our diagram is a macro diagram. Let the market be periodically repeated. If at $w > w*$ the unemployment rate is u, interpret that as the probability – the same for all workers – of not finding a job on any occasion when the market operates. Now, forgetting all about 'money wages being given', let us calculate the expected gain in utility for any worker of accepting a wage less than w' on the assumption that if he does, all others will do so also. That is, in this situation the norm is 'compete for jobs'. Compare this expected utility with that under a regime 'do not compete for jobs', i.e. stick to w. It can be shown that the 'non-competing' norm is a perfect equilibrium for a range of values of u bounded above by some critical $\bar{u}$. (For details see Hahn and Solow, 1995; Hahn, 1987.)

On this theory, then, there is $w > w*$ and $l < l*$ where no agent 'deviates' and that is also an equilibrium. Note that each worker acts in his own best interest. Each unemployed worker would prefer to work at w but that emphatically does not mean that he would prefer to accept a lower wage. On Keynes' definition his unemployment is *involuntary* – if the demand for labour increases at w the worker is willing to supply labour at w. But the market is in equilibrium on the non-deviation definition. Involuntary unemployment in equilibrium is simply an indication that the equilibrium is inefficient; there is a misallocation between work and leisure. Such inefficient equilibria are the daily diet of game theorists.

While I like the Hahn–Solow theory here the reader need not buy it to see the point which is being made. For instance s/he may be taken by theories of efficiency wages. At the efficiency wage $\hat{w}$ (when the elasticity with respect to the wage of the efficiency multiplier is one), firms demand a certain amount of labour $\hat{l}$. If at $\hat{w}$ more than that is supplied, a willingness on the part of the unemployed to lower their wage would do them no good. Once again as far as deviations go $(\hat{w}, \hat{l})$ is an equilibrium.

Once we leave the realm of perfect competition we do not even have a rigorous general equilibrium theory to help us with Friedman's definition. At least we have one only for special cases: concave profit functions (e.g. constant mark-up on constant costs) and no explicit strategic interactions. Walter Heller (1986) has demonstrated the pathologies which can arise in even a miniature model of strategic interaction, in particular the possibility of underemployment. Clearly one would also like to include the possibility of increasing returns, etc. So the first point to be made is that what most of us regard as the more realistic economic setting is at present without serious theoretical analysis and so all claims to know answers should be treated with considerable reserve.

But we can make a number of fairly straightforward points. First let me enthusiastically quote Blanchard and Summers (1988): 'Abusing the language somewhat . . . labour demand may refer to the equilibrium locus of price and employment decisions taken by monopolistically competitive firms given the nominal wage' (p. 194) (see also Dow, 1990). Blanchard and Summers are the first in the literature I have come across who understand and emphasise that this locus is *not* a demand curve for labour (in the real wage–employment space) in the usual sense. Estimates of 'the demand curve for labour' in which we are to think of the real wage as the independent variable do not, for the case of imperfect competition, inspire confidence. (If there is a constant mark-up or constant average cost the curve should be horizontal.) In any case abusing not only language but theoretical sensibilities, if we interpret the curves as applying to the macro economy then analysis of the case $w > w^*$ becomes harder than it already is.

It becomes harder because workers do not 'call' a product wage but usually a money wage. Just as governments do not control the real money stock, workers (in general) do not control the real wage. Nothing wrong with Keynes here. Every undergraduate knows the way we could argue that as a matter of comparative statics a lower money wage could lead to a lower real wage via cash balance effects. In other words one can argue that there exists a money wage which will be consistent with our conventional equilibrium notion. But that is to ignore the process of falling money wages. I do not propose to attempt a full-scale dynamic analysis now – except in the simplest case I do not know how to go about it. But I can report that in a simple model of overlapping generations, (a) convergence is not guaranteed and (b) one can show that monetary policy can achieve more efficiently what falling money wages can achieve (Hahn and Solow, 1994).

There are, however, a number of simpler points to make. Under imperfect competition there is no compelling reason to suppose that the 'demand' for labour is negatively sloped nor is there any reason to suppose that it has only one intersection with the 'supply' curve. Increasing returns are quite sufficient to give us what we want here. Blanchard and Summers (1988) argue that apart from the usual increasing returns there are also legal reasons connected with layoffs and quits which may lead to an upward sloping curve. They also show how 'insider–outsider' phenomena and union power can lead to downward sloping supply curves of labour. Of course if there are mulitiple equilibria then even if we can be sure of convergent dynamic processes, initial conditions ('history') will play an important role in which equilibrium is eventually established.

But even such splendid economists as Blanchard and Summers carry on the discussion in what is essentially a pseudo-partial equilibrium framework. They also neglect a point which seems to me of some importance. They are not alone in this.

In the simplest, non-strategic theory of imperfect competition, firms' demand for labour will depend on the position of the demand curve they believe themselves to be facing as well as on its elasticity. Almost all the discussions which I have seen suppose that firms know their 'true' demand curves. It does not require a great deal to see the externality problem – the 'true' demand curve facing any one firm will depend on the incomes earned, and so the outputs of all other firms which in turn depend . . . It is very easy to construct cases where no firm is mistaken in the demand curve it faces and yet there exists an equilibrium of the economy when all 'true' demand curves are displaced to the right. In other words, if all firms believed their demand curve displaced to the right they would produce and sell more (see, e.g. Heller, 1986). Of course this argument relies on labour not being on its supply curve in the first equilibrium of the firm, and one needs to look whether this is consistent with equilibrium in the sense in which I have already argued.

An important point emerges here which seems to be rarely made. Suppose that wherever the demand curves, they have the same (constant) elasticity and that production is everywhere under constant returns. Ignore all arguments to the contrary and suppose that an excess supply of labour induces falling money wages. We must now follow a path, not just of wages but of prices and of the rest of the economy. I shall return to this below. Here I note that there is no guarantee of convergence, leave alone monotone convergence to some steady state. So, if nothing else, the process will generate extra uncertainty. By the prevailing theory it cannnot change the equilibrium real wage. Keynes' central point here is that government can short-circuit this process since after all it is a complicated and unsafe way of increasing real cash balances. In fact Keynes maintained that it was desirable not to have money wages fall in the way we supposed. Certainly one could say that involuntary unemployment was not due to money wages not falling (if they do not fall) but to the monetary authorities not acting. But whatever one says, one should not maintain the tautology that if all prices were 'perfectly flexible' then indeed all markets would clear. Nor should one say that unemployment is due to real wages being 'too high' unless one thinks that the world is perfectly competitive (see Dow, 1990).

Returning to the theme of this section, I have argued that not only is there nothing either in theory or in the data to exclude multiple equilibria, but our conventional theory may mis-specify equilibrium. That is because these theories do not describe states which are not equilibrium states – they do not describe allocations outside conventional equilibrium. But if there is one lesson which game theory has taught us it is that equilibrium cannot be described unless we know the consequences of deviations – that is, payoffs for all strategy profiles. When we neglect to do this we neglect a possibly large class of equilibria – that is, here, wage–employment pairs such that neither employers nor workers wish to deviate from them. I have given some examples of these non-conventional cases.

The long run

It is an amusing paradox that the outstanding proponents of an important strand of Marxism are the neoclassical growth theorists. The strand in question is historical determinism and the implied impotence and irrelevance of human intervention in the historical process. The natural rate theory is a prime example of this. It is interpreted as the unemployment which would persist in steady state neoclassical equilibrium. It is unique and no long-run deviations from this rate are possible. It must now be added that this extreme view is being abandoned not only by neoclassical macroeconomists (see, e.g., Lucas, 1988) but by most sensible economists. Macroeconometricians have found it harder to do so mainly because they seem to be able to deal only with linear (or log-linear) equations.

But before we follow this particular hare it is worthwhile considering the 'orthodox' position a little more closely.

One could start with the celebrated Solow model (1956) except that it falls foul of modern standards of neoclassical analysis by *assuming* a fixed saving rate and an inelastic supply of labour. It also neglected money. So more recent theory, while continuing at Solow's level of aggregation and with nice concave production functions exhibiting constant returns to capital and labour, insists on the 'proper micro foundations'. When these are provided one quickly finds oneself happier with Solow's use of ad-hoc propensities. For these foundations are provided by a representative 'Ramsey agent'. That is, an infinitely-lived all-knowing agent. At the very best this can be interpreted under extremely restrictive circumstances as mimicking the outcomes of an Arrow–Debreu economy over the infinite future. This may be an interesting exercise and indeed it may also yield some insights. But its descriptive merits must be very much in doubt. ('Calibrating' such a model and claiming that it is not contradicted by time series does not add to its persuasiveness.)

But let us look a little more closely. The representative agent is endowed with an instantaneous utility function $u(c, m, l)$ where c is consumption, $m = $ real cash balances and l is labour supply. Including m is explained by the 'convenience yield' of money. But there are ways of avoiding this – for instance by 'cash in advance' constraints. The agent is interested to maximise V subject to constraints of feasibility, where

$$V = \int_0^\infty e^{-\rho t} u(c_t, m_t, l_t)\, dt.$$

If there are stochastic factors to take into account, then V is replaced by its expectations. Stochastic processes are almost always taken to be iid, but I shall not go into detail here.

Matters are straightforward if there is no technical progress (for simplicity consider a stationary population). One easily finds the conditions for the steady state:

$$-\frac{u_l}{u_c} = y(k) - ky'(k) \tag{1}$$

where $y(k)$ is output per man as a function of capital per man.

$$y'(k) = \rho. \tag{2}$$

$$\frac{u_m}{u_c} - \Pi = 0 \tag{3}$$

where Π is the inflation rate.

Now equations (1) and (2) define the real steady state variables provided $\frac{u_l}{u_c}$ is independent of m. This assumption was made, for instance, by Sidrauski (1967). This is the basis of the claim of super-neutrality of the steady state (the vertical Phillips curve) – Π cannot affect the real variables k, l and c. This is a special case not only because of the utility assumptions but because it does not carry over to other models of accumulation, e.g. models based on overlapping generations.

But the absence of technical progress will not do – it is a very uninteresting 'long run'. So let k stand for capital per efficiency unit of labour employed where it is assumed that there is exogenous technical progress at the rate α which is 'labour-augmenting'. Suppose we look for a steady state in the Ramsey model which now also means $\dot{l} = 0$.

Equation (1) on this assumption becomes

$$-\frac{u_l}{u_c} = e^{\alpha t}[y(k) - ky'(k)]$$

where k is now the ratio of capital to efficiency unit of capital employed. Plainly one now needs more 'separability' assumptions. Consumption will be rising at the rate α. k is constant at $k*$ so for $\dot{l} = 0$ we want the marginal utility of consumption to be falling at the rate α *and* the marginal disutility of leisure constant when l is.

These seem to me to be rather odd assumptions. Looking back over the past 150 years, an increase in the consumption of leisure is plain. Leisure is not an inferior good. The cost of leisure in terms of consumption is rising, and one needs to suppose that this exactly offsets the income effect on leisure. As I say, this is pretty odd over the long run.

It is therefore by no means clear that a steady state as usually defined exists. Of course it is possible that employment will be changing over time while the fraction of those engaged remains constant. At this stage no judgement can be made since it will have been noticed that search, etc. has not been formally modelled. Indeed search may provide problems for the representative agent since at any time there is a distinction between searchers and those who are employed. I return to this in the next section.

But now we note that apart from the difficulties with labour supply we have an extremely primitive growth model. Technical progress is exogenous (and of a particular kind and at a constant rate) and we have no means of analysing one of the striking features of economic history, which is innovation-induced changes in the composition of output and the structure of industry. Indeed it is such changes which will explain the need for the reallocation of labour and so the search associated with that. There are now a considerable number of 'endogenous growth' theories which of course must not be taken too literally. Common features are: increasing returns (to research, for instance), externalities and, as a consequence, multiple steady states (when they exist). Of course these models are constructed with an eye to the kind of answers one is looking for, so that rather special functional forms and other assumptions are employed. But this is an instance where the special and unrealistic detail does not prevent us learning lessons which are likely to be of much wider applicability.

Assuming that the economy we are studying is in some steady state while there is a number of these of course makes the history of the economy relevant. It also opens the possibility that policy might be able to bring about a transition from one steady state to another. This is then relevant to the policy-impotence doctrine. But even neglecting this, these theories of endogenous growth – or most of them – make it clear how mis-specified a linear or log-linear model may be. This is especially true of the pricing equation of these models.

This leads to another question which is rarely addressed. In much of the literature there is an identification of trend with steady state, for instance the trend rate of productivity growth. There is no theoretical warrant for this identification. But there is even less to be said for the conclusions which seem to have been drawn. For instance, in real trade cycle models the economy is indeed in continuous rational expectations equilibrium but there is no such thing as *the* natural rate. Employment, and so one presumes search unemployment, is varying all the time. There is no particular interest to the 'average' unemployment rate over the cycle.

This is not a quibble. The labour market is, in many of these models, taken to clear instantly (although it is not clear how search is grafted on to this assumption). But in the world we need to have signals to agents: for instance the requirement of a higher real wage must be signalled by higher money wages or lower prices or both. The real Phillips curve is in perpetual motion and we need to see how we get from a point on one to a point on the other. It may well be that the only way is by 'overshooting', that is, by a (temporary) inflationary phase. Our judgement here however is sharply different from the conventional one: the inflationary phase is needed to allow the economy to accommodate to new realities arising from technical progress.

Indeed one is tempted to enunciate a doctrine of a 'natural rate of inflation'. The reallocation of labour is probably more readily accomplished when those desiring more raise money wages. For reasons explored in contract and other theories, those requiring less may dismiss workers rather than lower money wages. One feels pretty confident that such a theory could, at the prevailing level of rigour of macroeconomics, be constructed.

But let us return again to the question of endogenous steady states. Let us consider only one example where there is learning by doing.

Suppose there is a steady state from which there has been a deviation to lower unemployment due to 'mistakes'. Agree that the mistaken price expectations will be corrected in due course. Will the economy return to the same steady state real wage, etc.? No, because the phase of higher than steady state investment and employment will have led to the accumulation of new knowledge (I am using Arrow's 1962 formulation). Indeed these errors may be a way of correcting the intrinsic externalities of Arrow's economy. Considerations like these should make us pause before we aver that unemployment below 'the natural rate' *just* causes inflation.

One can only be amazed at the neglect of investment and of the capital stock in theories of the natural rate. The reason is of course that in steady state of the old-fashioned sort there is a unique capital/labour ratio. Nonetheless even here, short-run analysis requires special attention to be given to investment. The habit is to write total demand as proportional to the real money stock and not to include the interest rate. In old-fashioned steady state this does not matter, everywhere else it does. Even though these writers happily use the marginal product of labour equals real wage condition, they seem unaware of what it is this marginal product depends on. Including a trend term will do for the model with exogenous labour augmenting technical progress for an economy in steady state. Otherwise it will not. It is surprising that policy advice is supported by such a slender reed and totally unsurprising that the estimated curves keep shifting. These shifts may have something to do with labour supply conditions (e.g. higher real wages reduces the number seeking full-time employment), but it may also have something to do with investment and the nature of technological change. None of these are usually modelled.

To sum up. The 'natural rate' has been employed as an element in a wage and price adjustment model. The only interpretation which I think can be consistently given to it is that it is a steady state unemployment rate and that in the absence of accelerating inflationary policies, the actual path of the economy seeks this steady state. I have given reasons for (a) the possible non-existence of a steady stae, (b) the possibility of multiple steady states and hence the inappropriateness of linear models, (c) the possible dependence of the steady state on the path taken. There also loom the problems discussed on p. 45 of the appropriate definition of equilibrium. For instance the Hahn–Solow theory gives a whole interval of NAIRUs. These are all negative points and I discuss this feature in the final section below. Here I conclude that no-one should be surprised that empirical work based on poor theory has by and large performed so badly.

Search and involuntary unemployment

I have repeatedly stressed that traditional search theory finds no *formal* representation in macro theories of the natural rate. It is referred to, or better appealed to, but it is not connected with the theory proposed.

One of the first problems is that from the utility side of these stories one has, in natural rate theories, to think of the supply of hours. (Strictly speaking, of the first noticeable time difference.) On the other hand unemployment statistics refer to people. There is some fine empirical work on aspects of the labour supply decision, but macro theorising has made it hard to incorporate. It must however strike one that many workers cannot choose their hours of work (I know that some can). It is an interesting question why that should be the case; an answer probably turns on externalities and on production functions where the cooperative nature of work is properly modelled. In any case we can think of two kinds of unemployment: being without a job and supplying less labour than one would like.

The last of these – the case where the hours constraint has a positive shadow price – is a form of involuntary unemployment: the real wage exceeds the shadow wage. I have not seen it discussed.

The first kind of unemployment is explained as resulting from turning down a job offer in the hope of finding a better one. A proper search theory in the spirit of an ignorance of particulars of particular firms would be a theory in which search is for the highest utility. It does not take much to convince most people that the wage is only one element here. Location, prospects of being retained once hired and all sorts of other aspects enter the picture. One can construct much more elaborate models – at least including the most obvious elements – but the assumption that workers know the distribution of offers of utility becomes pretty strained.

But in any case it seems to me that the theory is fundamentally at variance with the facts. One must suppose that workers searching in the first instance search in their geographical neighbourhood and that they know wages and conditions in most of the firms; there are employment exchanges and advertisements. In any event, traditional search theory leaves a very profitable niche for suppliers of this information since workers will plainly be willing to pay for it.

The true picture therefore seems to be quite different: workers know the wages and conditions of work at various firms but they do not know whether they will be hired if they apply. That is not only due to lack of information on whether a particular firm will judge the particular applicant to be of the right quality. But also because there may be more applicants than the jobs offered by the firm. One can of course allow for some fuzziness in the information of offers by particular firms and so for the possibility that when this is resolved the job will be refused. But that seems to be a minor element.

The search for the highest 'wage' will be conducted in newspaper advertisements and in employment exchanges. The search for a job is the costly part. When a job is not offered then since the worker was willing to take it he is involuntarily unemployed. The probability of getting any job will depend on the number of job seekers who are likely to be applicants for it. I have set out this approach partially elsewhere (1987), and I am encouraged by some natural rate theorists who seem as dissatisfied with the current search approach as I am.

This way of looking at search certainly reinstates involuntary unemployment as 'labour off its supply curve'. At least this is true as long as workers *are* applying for jobs or have ceased to do so because they correctly estimate the probability of getting a job to be very low. This leaves the question of unemployment benefits. These will certainly be relevant in determining the range of jobs a worker applies for and will therefore tend to lower the success rate of applications. On traditional reasoning the gap between the wage and the unemployment benefit must at least cover the disutility of working although the traditional theory is at fault in not noting (in the utility function) the disutility of having no job. However it should be remembered that as long as a worker is willing to take a job which covers this gap and is judged to be of appropriate quality, he is involuntarily unemployed.

I have, in the past, been taken to task for bringing up the notion of 'involuntary unemployment'. But it is an important category. It is so because it is a misallocation between leisure and work and also between types of work. The Ph.D. in mathematics driving a taxi is probably misallocated in a straightforward way. The policy implications are also quite different, as is the theory required. The latter must turn on a mechanism by which the involuntarily unemployed cause wage and price changes. There is no decent theory here.

Some conclusions

Theories of the natural rate are amongst the class of shaky and vastly incomplete theories. This has been recognised by some of the practitioners (see Nickell, 1990 and some of the references cited there). Unfortunately, even if understandably, he and others are nonetheless keen to get down to econometrics long before an integrated and reasonable theory has been assembled. One of the consequences is an array of log-linear equations. These have proxy variables from many of the important phenomena which they discuss but do not formulate in a way in which the theory can have some bite. None of these authors (perhaps because they are engaged in macroeconomics) consider the possible role of inflation in the allocation of labour or of the innovations which make reallocations desirable. Imperfect competition appears in its most primitive 'mark-up' guise and no attention is paid to the many theories of slow price adjustments. The capital stock is ignored as is investment, which is one of the more peculiar aspects of these theories. One could go on. It would be interesting to know how much these economists would be prepared to bet on their results coming about.

The practical consequences have nearly all been bad, as one would expect when prognostication and advice outrun what can seriously be prognosticated or advised. Keynes' project of preventing a discrediting of the market economy has been much harmed. Not because it has been found that Keynesian theories are flawed but because it has been concluded that governments are powerless in the face of malfunctioning markets. Paradoxically the conclusion emerges from models in which markets never malfunction. For instance, fluctuations occur under Ramsey optimisation and workers are always on their supply curve. It is hard to think of a flaw in Keynesian theory which is as gross.

But while obviously I consider these very damning faults, it would be wrong to ignore the merits which there are. Prime amongst these is very interesting work, both theoretical and empirical, on micro labour markets. Contract theories, bargaining theories, search theories as well as careful studies of the characteristics of the unemployed are all serious contributions. But they are not well used, and perhaps cannot be well used in a macro model. If only they tried some models with just a few sectors! Of course one expects there to be some relations between unemployment and wage changes. But my strong guess is that these are only properly modelled when involuntary unemployment is allowed for. What is sad is all the pseudo-theorising about 'the' natural rate and the ever-increasing estimates of that rate. If there is any truth in that, the fate of capitalism must be in grave doubt.

References

Arrow, K.J., 1962. 'The Economic Implications of Learning by Doing', *Review of Economic Studies*, 29, 155–73

Blanchard, O.J. and Summers, L.H., 1988. 'Beyond the Natural Rate Hypothesis', *American Economic Review, Papers and Proceedings*, 78(2) (May), 182–7

Dow, J.C.R., 1990. 'The High-wage Theory of Unemployment: Theory and British Experience 1920–1989', *Proceedings of the British Academy*, 76

Friedman, M., 1969. *The Optimum Quantity of Money*, London: Macmillan

Hahn, F.H., 1987. 'On Involuntary Unemployment', Supplement to the *Economic Journal*, 97, pp. 1–17

Hahn, F.H. and Solow, R.M., 1995. *A Critical Essay on Modern Macroeconomic Theory*, Cambridge, MA: MIT Press and Oxford: Blackwell

Heller, W.P., 1986. 'Co-ordination Failure under Complete Markets with Application to Effective Demand', in W.P. Heller, R.M. Starr and D.A. Starrett (eds.),

Equilibrium Analysis, Essays in Honour of Kenneth J. Arrow, vol. II, Cambridge: Cambridge University Press

Lucas, R.E., 1988. 'On the Mechanics of Economic Development', *Journal of Monetary Economics*, 22, pp. 3–42

Nickell, S., 1990. 'Unemployment: A Survey', *Economic Journal*, 100(401), 391–439

Phillips, A.W., 1958. 'The Relation Between Unemployment and the Rate of Change of Money Wage Rates in the United Kingdom, 1861–1957', *Economica*, 25 (November), 283–99

Sidrauski, M., 1967. 'Rational Choice and Patterns of Growth in a Monetary Economy', *American Economic Review, Papers and Proceedings*, 57, 534–55

Solow, R.M., 1956. 'A Contribution to the Theory of Economic Growth', *Quarterly Journal of Economics*, 70, 65–94

5　Of coconuts, decomposition, and a jackass: the genealogy of the natural rate

Huw Dixon

Introduction

The concept of the natural rate of unemployment was formulated in 1968, by Friedman and Phelps. In Friedman, it plays the central role in his theory of the relationship between short-run and long-run Phillips curve. However, in this chapter, I will focus not on its role within the theory of inflation *per se*, but rather on the fundamental notion of equilibrium, the natural rate itself. The natural rate stands in a tradition of ideas that may be loosely called *classical* or *monetarist*. We may well ask, therefore, two questions: first, how does the idea of the natural rate (NR) differ from its predecessors; secondly, how have more recent ideas developed or diverged from it? A full and proper answer to both of these questions would require a degree of scholarship and comprehensive grasp of the broad sweep of the history of economic thought which, alas, eludes me. However, I intend to approach both questions in terms of a series of snapshots and observations which will be drawn together towards the end of the chapter. Without spoiling the story, I conclude that the natural rate as an *equilibrium* concept was largely derivative of Patinkin's concept of full employment, as laid out in his *Money, Interest and Prices* (first published in 1956). However Friedman nowhere ever lays down a specific theory of the natural rate itself, and as such the concept has proven sufficiently loose and vague to fit a variety of subsequent models of equilibrium.

The classical dichotomy

The origin of the notion of the natural rate lies in the view that (at least in the long run or some 'stationary state') real variables in the economy are determined by 'real things' such as preferences, technology, population and so on. To use Pigou's phrase, money acts as a 'veil', behind which the real economy operates (Pigou, 1941). The notion of the classical dichotomy itself was not formalised much by the classical economists. Perhaps its first

57

formal statement was by Patinkin (1965), whose ideas I will discuss later. However, in a very revealing essay written by Paul Samuelson in 1968, he defined the notion as a one-time believer. To quote at some length:

> Mine is the great advantage of having been a jackass. From 2 January 1932 until some indeterminate date in 1937, I was a classical monetary theorist. I do not have to look for tracks of the jackass embalmed in old journals and monographs. I merely have to lie down on the couch and recall in tranquility . . . what it was that I believed between the ages of 17 and 22 . . . We thought that *real* outputs and inputs and price ratios depended essentially in the longest run on real factors such as tastes, technology and endowments. An increase in the stock of money . . . would cause a proportional increase in *all* prices and values (1968, pp. 1–2).

As Samuelson stated, the idea or concept was not formalised. The essential idea was one of *homogeneity* of equilibrium equations in money and prices:

> A. Write down a system of real equations involving *real* outputs and inputs, and *ratios* of prices (values), and depending essentially on real tastes, technologies, market structures and endowments. Its properties are invariant to changes in the stock of money.
> B. Then append a fixed supply of money equation that pins down (or up) the absolute price level, determining the scale factor that was essentially indeterminate in set A . . . (1968, pp. 2–3).

In statement A we have the real equilibrium of the economy in which real factors determine *relative* prices, and in B the monetary side of the economy acts as a scaling factor to determine *absolute* prices. This is stated most simply in the quantity equation: real output Q is fixed, and the money stock merely acts to determine $P(MV = PQ)$, with a direct proportionality if the velocity is constant.

However, the earliest notion of the dichotomy to my knowledge is in David Hume (1750):

> Money is nothing but the representation of labour and commodities, and serves only as a method of rating or estimating them. Where coin is in greater plenty – as a greater quantity of it is required to represent the same quantity of goods – it can have no effect, either good or bad, taking a nation within itself; any more than it would make an alteration in a merchant's books, if instead of the Arabian method of notation, which requires few characters, he should make use of the Roman, which requires a great many.

Similar statements can be found in a variety of subsequent writers including (apart from Walras, Fisher and Cassel) Davenport, James Mill, Hawtrey (see Patinkin, 1965, Note I, pp. 454–62 for a brief history of the idea of the dichotomy).

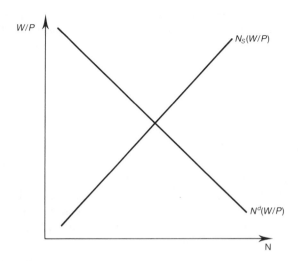

Figure 5.1 Patinkin's model of full employment

Patinkin and full employment

Money, Interest and Prices is perhaps as great in its vision as Keynes' *General Theory*. Whilst the latter has a greater abundance of originality, the former has a greater clarity of insight and formal expression. Don Patinkin states his theory of the labour market and corresponding notion of the full employment equilibrium in just three pages of *Money, Interest and Prices* (in the 1965 edn, pp. 127–30). These pages deserve great attention: they state the labour market model that became the standard foundation for the aggregate supply curve in the aggregate demand/aggregate supply (AD/AS) model. Although Patinkin himself did not formulate the AD/AS representation, it is implicit in his *Money, Interest and Prices*.

Patinkin presents his model of full employment diagrammatically (in his figure 10 on p. 129) as has become standard in macroeconomics textbooks. Labour demand depends on the real wage (and capital which is fixed), as does labour supply. Amending Patinkin's notation to reflect subsequent usage we have the familiar figure 5.1.

Two points need to be made about this model. First, Patinkin equates the notion of full employment with the competitive equilibrium in the labour market. Secondly, Patinkin suppresses the wealth effect on the labour supply. It is worth quoting at some detail from Patinkin on the suppression of the wealth effect:

To the extent that an individual operates on the principle of utility maximisation, the amount of labour supplied will depend on the real wage rate . . . Thus we write

$N^S = N^S(W/P)$ . . . It will be immediately recognised that we have greatly oversimplified the analysis. Both the demand and supply equations should actually be dependent on the real value of bond and money holdings as well as the real wage rate . . . Finally, full analysis of individual behaviour would show the supply of labour to depend on the rate of interest. If we have arbitrarily ignored these additional influences, it is because the labour market as such does not interest us in the following analysis; its sole function is to provide the bench mark of full employment (1965, pp. 128–9).

The suppression of the wealth effect from the labour supply is crucial, and has proven to be most durable, giving rise as it does to the vertical aggregate supply curve. It has the important feature that although the labour market functions in a system of general equilibrium equations, it can be treated as a partial equilibrium equation. Output, employment and the real wage are all determined in the labour market without reference to the rest of the economy (usually the money and goods markets).

Whereas the classical dichotomy rested on the *homogeneity* of equilibrium equations, Patinkin's model of full employment went further. Patinkin made the system of equilibrium equations *decomposable*, in that the labour market equation could be solved in isolation to the rest of the system of equilibrium equations. Since the level of output, employment and the real wage are determined by the labour market equilibrium alone, changes on the 'demand side' of the economy (the goods and money markets in the IS/LM framework) can have no effect on them. To see that this goes a lot further than the classical dichotomy, it implies not only that money is neutral, but also that changes in *real* demand-side factors will have no effect on output and employment. For example, an increase in real government expenditure will have no effect on the level of output and employment (although it will of course reduce the other components of demand such as consumption and investment – the 'crowding out effect'). If there is a non-zero wealth effect on the labour supply, matters are rather different. Real balances (and real bond holdings if Ricardian equivalence fails to hold) enter into wealth, and these depend on the *nominal* price level. Hence the position of the labour supply curve depends on the demand-side factors which determine the nominal price level. The labour market equilibrium condition is now given by (1), where for simplicity we assume that real balances are the only form of wealth, and there is no taxation or non-labour income:

$$N^d(W/P) = N^s(W/P, M/P). \tag{1}$$

Note that (1) is still homogeneous to degree zero in (W, P, M), so that the homogeneity underlying the classical dichotomy will not be affected.

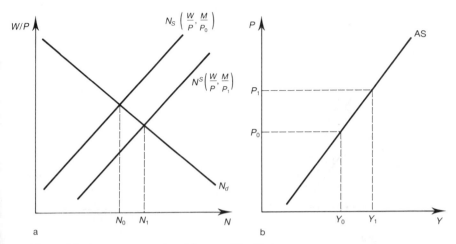

Figure 5.2 Aggregate supply with a wealth effect

However, the labour supply function will shift with P and M. Treating M as constant, if leisure is a normal good, a rise in P will reduce real balances, and hence increase the labour supply at any given real wage level, shifting the labour supply curve to the right, as in figure 5.2a, thus tracing out the upward sloping AS curve in figure 5.2b.

With the wealth effect on labour supply unsuppressed, the equilibrium system of equations does not decompose, and in fact it is easy to show that an increase in real government expenditure will not have a zero multiplier: the expenditure multiplier will be strictly positive but less than unity. In figures 5.3a and 5.3b we contrast the effect of an increase in the money supply and an increase in government expenditure. In figure 5.3a we can see that the increase in real government expenditure Δg shifts and the AD curve to the right, the distance of the shift being Δg if output markets clear.[1] From (1) above, the increase in g has no direct effect on the AS curve. The equilibrium moves from A to B, with some crowding out of the initial stimulus provided by Δg as nominal prices (and wages) rise from P_A to P_B. Clearly the increase in government expenditure has a real effect on the level of aggregate output and employment. This stands in contrast to the effect of a proportional increase of the money stock: as depicted in figure 5.3b, a proportionate increase in M to λM shifts both the AD and AS curves upwards equally, so that nominal prices rise proportionately to λP; the real side of the economy is unaffected.

Patinkin's notion of full employment added two things to the classical dichotomy. First, it identified the long-run equilibrium output with the now textbook competitive labour market, depicted in figure 5.1. Second, it

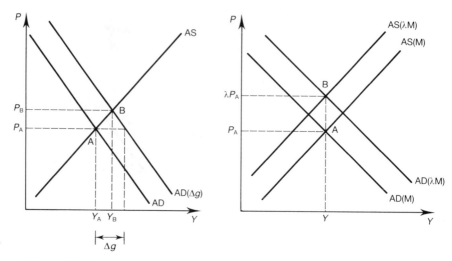

Figure 5.3 Macroeconomic policy without decomposition. a Fiscal policy;
b Monetary neutrality

added the property of decomposability, so that in addition to montary
neutrality total output, employment and the real wage were all independent
of *any* change in the demand side of the economy, whether real or nominal.
The vertical aggregate supply curve was born. The notion of decomposability has perhaps been the most crucial and pervasive. The notion that the
labour market equilibrium might be non-competitive had always been
recognised. However the first *formal* inclusion of imperfect competition in
the output market in a Patinkinesque framework was done by Ball and
Bodkin (1963). Following Joan Robinson's *Accumulation of Capital*, they
introduced the 'degree of monopoly' into the labour demand equation:

We add a profit maximizing condition: $(1 - \mu).f'(N) = W/P$, where W is the
money wage, P is the price level, and μ represents the degree of monopoly power
existing in the economy. μ is equal to $1/\varepsilon$ where ε is the elasticity of demand, on an
economy wide basis (Ball and Bodkin, 1963, p. 61).

In this case, the familiar figure 5.1 becomes as in figure 5.4. Imperfect
competition in the output market shifts the 'labour demand curve' to the
left (since with imperfectly elastic demand in the output market, the firm's
marginal revenue product is less than $P.f'(N)$).

Output, employment and the real wage are less than under perfect
competition. However, there is still a unique equilibrium level of employment. Furthermore, the equilibrium satisfies the classical homogeneity

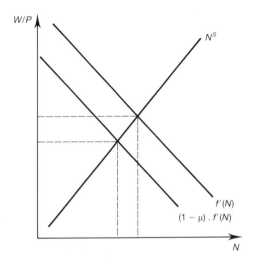

Figure 5.4 Ball and Bodkin's (1963) model of full employment with price-setting firms

property, and also Patinkin's own property of decomposability if the wealth effect on the labour supply is suppressed. Thus Patinkin's notion of full employment was perfectly compatible with imperfect competition.

Friedman and the natural rate hypothesis

Twelve years after Patinkin's *Money, Interest and Prices* had been published, and the same year that Samuelson had called his younger classical self a 'jackass', Friedman's Presidential Address (1968) was published. This paper is one of the great classics: it turned out to be both prophetic and seminal. However from the perspective of the study of the natural rate, it is elusive and frustrating. The other papers which Friedman wrote about the natural rate are his IEA lecture *Inflation vs Unemployment: an evaluation of the Phillips curve* (1975), and his Nobel lecture *Inflation and unemployment* (1977). Turning first to the 1968 definition of the natural rate, which has become ingrained in many generations of students, its meaning is more enigmatic than it seems:

At any moment of time, there is some level of unemployment which has the property that it is consistent with equilibrium in the structure of *real* wages . . . The 'natural rate of unemployment' . . . is the level that would be ground out by the Walrasian system of general equilibrium equations, provided there is imbedded in them the actual structural characteristics of the labor and commodity markets, including market imperfections, stochastic variability in demands and supplies, the costs of gathering information about job vacancies, and labor availabilities, the costs of mobility, and so on (1968, p. 8).

This 'definition' is remarkable for its vagueness. It is not a definition at all, but rather a research programme! Certainly, Friedman himself never attempted to present a formal theory of the natural rate which includes the various 'market imperfections' he lists. It is rather an assertion of the belief that the real side of the economy possesses a unique (long-run) equilibrium. The belief in the uniqueness of equilibrium is so deep that it is rarely stated as such by Friedman (although its implicit assumption permeates Friedman's work).

In Friedman's IEA lecture we find only a few comments:

The term 'the natural rate' has been much misunderstood . . . It refers to that rate of employment which is consistent with the *existing real conditions* in the labour market – The purpose of the concept separates the monetary from the non-monetary aspects of the employment situation – precisely the same purpose that Wicksell had in using the word 'natural' in connection with the interest rate (1975, p. 25).

The nearest we come to an explicit formulation of the microeconomic theory or the natural rate is also in Friedman's IEA lecture: turn to p. 16 figure 3, and what do we find? We find Patinkin's model of full employment, the competitive labour market with the labour supply depending only on real wages! Friedman's discussion of it is prefaced by the qualifier 'for example', but his discussion of it demonstrates the continuity with Patinkin in stressing both the homogeneity property of equilibrium and the decomposability of the labour market from the rest of the economy. The homogeneity comes across most clearly from Friedman's statement that what matters is the actual or anticipated real wage: 'the real wage can remain constant with W and P separately constant, or with W and P each rising at the rate of 10% a year, or falling at the rate of 10% a year, or doing anything else, provided both change at the *same* rate' (1975, p. 16). The notion of decomposability is implicit in his use of Patinkin's model, and the use of the phrase 'real conditions in the labour market' in the earlier quote from 1975.

Thus far, Friedman's natural rate seems to be nothing new: it is solidly in the classical tradition, and more specifically in the footsteps of his erstwhile Chicago colleague Don Patinkin. So what, if anything, was new about the concept of the natural rate as found in Friedman?

1 Friedman's main contribution was to restate the classical notion of a unique long-run equilibrium in terms of the then contemporary theories of the labour market: namely search models. Although he did not

actually formulate any of these himself, he did describe the process of deviations from the natural rate in terms of 'reservation wages' and so on. In fact, although partial equilibrium models of search and imperfect information abounded, it was not until 1979 that Salop's model of the natural rate was published. The real question is whether the notion of a unique long-run equilibrium unaffected by macroeconomic policy can survive if put in these terms.

2 Furthermore, Friedman became explicit about the role of imperfect competition in the natural rate. This is clearest in his argument that whilst trade unions cannot cause inflation, they can influence the natural rate. The direct statement of this view is in an answer to a question after the IEA lecture:

> Trade unions play a very important part in determining the position of the natural level of unemployment. They play an important role in denying opportunities to some classes of the community that are open to others. They play a very important role in the structure of the labour force and the structure of *relative* wages. But, despite appearances to the contrary, a *given* amount of trade union power does not play any role in exacerbating inflation. Industrial monopolies do not produce inflation; they produce high relative prices for the products they are monopolising, and low outputs for these products (1975, pp. 30–1).

Friedman argued that the only way to have a long-run influence on the level of unemployment was to reform the labour market (in the lecture text he talks of removing 'obstacles' and 'frictions').

3 Friedman *integrated* the classical theory with the Phillips curve, to formulate the vertical 'long-run Phillips curve'. Essentially, this synthesis rested on restating classical notions of homogeneity in terms of inflationary expectations. Whereas Patinkin had formulated his theory in terms of the *levels* for wages and prices, Friedman formulated it in terms of rates of *change*. Thus the natural rate becomes the level of employment which is consistent with fully anticipated inflation and constant real wages.

4 He also formulated a theory of *deviations* from the natural rate in terms of unanticipated inflation. Employment deviates from the natural rate because of forecast errors.

5 On the level of economic *policy* Friedman's formulation of the natural rate in terms of labour market equilibrium was very influential. In the UK it gave rise to the focus on labour market reform that characterised the Thatcher years (1979–91).

These are all important points, each one deserving an essay to itself. However, we must hurry on to subsequent developments.

Lucas–Rapping and the Lucas archipelago

Still staying at Chicago we turn to R.E. Lucas, who developed and formalised the natural rate in terms of a competitive market-clearing framework. There are two versions of this enterprise. The first was the Lucas–Rapping paper published in 1969 (written more or less contemporaneously to Friedman's address). This took the basic demand–supply model of the labour market and added to it an *intertemporal*, dynamic model of household labour supply (even if it had only two periods). This introduced the notion of intertemporal substitution in the labour supply: high wages today elicit a higher labour supply in part because it may mean that today's wages are high relative to future wages: the short-run responsiveness of wages is enhanced if the increase is seen as transitory as opposed to permanent.

The second paper was published a decade later (Lucas, 1979), and introduced the 'island' story of the natural rate in terms of a signal extraction problem. Each market is an island, and the aggregate economy is the archipelago. Agents in this economy have good information about their own 'island' market, but not the economy in general (the 'archipelago'). As rational agents, they have to distinguish between increases of nominal prices on their island that represent *real* increases in the price on their island relative to the general price level, and general inflation. Using optimal statistical forecasts based on the relative variances of aggregate economy-wide shocks and island-specific shocks, the agents apportion a certain proportion of any deviation of actual from expected prices to market-specific factors, and hence increase output, giving rise to a short-run Phillips curve.

Both of Lucas' models follow in the spirit of Friedman's definition of the natural rate, in that they put informational problems at the centre of the analysis; uncertainty about the future in the Lucas–Rapping model, and imperfect information about aggregates such as the price level and money stock in the 1979 one. In this sense, Lucas provided the micro foundations, the theory that was lacking in Friedman's notion of the natural rate. However, there was a different agenda as well. This agenda consisted in seeing all markets as competitive: unlike Friedman, Lucas gives little weight to the notion of non-competitive markets. The Lucas world view puts individual rational choice at the centre of a world of competitive markets. Institutional arrangements and customs are seen as irrelevant to the task of explanation: they are themselves endogenous, being designed 'precisely in order to aid in matching preferences and opportunities' (Lucas, 1981, p. 4). Fluctuations in economic activity are explained in terms of rational households varying labour supply in response to current and future wages and prices. For Lucas, this is the 'only account', there being 'no serious alternative' (1981, p. 4).

Real business cycles

Lucas had formalised the notion of the natural rate in a way that rested, at least partly, on imperfect information or forecast errors. However, implicit in his conception of the importance of intertemporal substitution was the notion that even with full information and perfect foresight, fluctuations in economic activity would occur in response to changes in the underlying characteristics of the economy: changes in technology and tastes. The natural rate had been an essentially *static* concept. This is clear in the discussion of the real equilibrium in classical writers such as Pigou and even Patinkin where the adjectives 'stationary state' and 'comparative statics' are used. This carries over to Friedman's discussion of the natural rate which is in entirely static terms. In this framework, *dynamics* becomes the discussion of short-run deviations around the long-run static equilibrium.

Real business cycle theory took the notion of competitive equilibrium, and extended it to a fully *dynamic* equilibrium. In this view there is an intertemporal equilibrium that extends through time. Variations in output and employment represent the fluctuations in equilibrium as rational households and firms maximise over a relevant time horizon (usually infinite!). Real wages respond to productivity shocks: the labour supply responds to the profile of real wages over time, hence leading to the business cycle. Thus, if real wages in time t are relatively high, this may cause households to exploit this fact by supplying more labour in t. This development makes the concept of the natural rate irrelevant. In this dynamic setting there may exist no real distinction between the actual and the equilibrium level of employment: the equilibrium level of employment is itself fluctuating. In real business cycle theory, then, the concept of the natural rate itself has become largely redundant, although (as the adjective 'real' indicates) the spirit of the classical dichotomy is very much present.

The NAIRU: unions and imperfect competition

Outside Chicago matters were developing rather differently. At the LSE there emerged a framework for modelling the labour market which I shall call the CLE view (CLE being the Centre for Labour Economics, a research centre operating at the LSE in the 1980s). Friedman had put the labour market at the centre of his notion of the natural rate. Richard Layard and Steven Nickell developed an empirical model of the UK labour market which put imperfect competition at the centre of the natural rate, in distinct

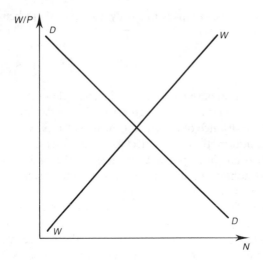

Figure 5.5 The NAIRU

contrast to the Lucas developments. Two papers provided the basis for this approach (Layard and Nickell, 1985, 1986). One of the key features of the natural rate stressed by Friedman was that it is the only level of unemployment that is consistent with non-accelerating inflation. Layard and Nickell therefore renamed the natural rate the 'non-accelerating inflation rate of unemployment', or NAIRU. The approach reflected an increased interest in imperfectly competitive markets in the early 1980s. The notion of equilibrium in the CLE approach can be represented by a diagram which looks deceptively familiar (figure 5.5).

The downward sloping curve DD is a familiar 'labour demand curve', reflecting the fact that imperfectly competitive firms equate marginal revenue with marginal cost, which is the same thing as saying that the firm employs labour up to the point where the real wage equals the marginal product of labour scaled down by $(1 - \mu)$ as in Ball and Bodkin (1963). The upward sloping curve WW is, however, rather more innovative. Layard and Nickell modelled the wage determination process as a bargain between the representative firm and union. The bargaining solution adopted was the Nash bargaining solution. The details of this need not concern us here; suffice it to say that the wage depends on the *outside options* (often called 'fallback positions') of the firm and the union. The nature of the bargaining solution is that the better the outside option of an agent, the better that agent does. Layard and Nickell modelled the outside option of unions as the expected income of union members if they become unemployed. If unemployed, the worker obtains a job at the going wage W/P with probability $(1 - u)$, where u is the unemployment rate, and stays unemployed with probability u. Hence the higher is employment in figure 5.5, the better is the outside option facing the union's members, and the higher the wage which results from the bargain. Thus the upward sloping curve WW represents the fact that unions are able to obtain higher wages when employment is high (unemployment low), rather than labour supply conditions.

The great merit of the NAIRU approach is that it enables the natural rate to be modelled empirically. Nickell and Layard were able to classify factors into those which affected the WW curve (union power, labour mismatch, unemployment benefits, etc.), and those which affected the DD curve (world energy and commodity prices, capital stock, etc.), to track the changes in the NAIRU over time. This is an enterprise that Friedman himself never undertook, since he always emphasised the ineffable and unknowable quality of the NR: 'One problem is that it [the monetary authority] cannot know what the natural rate is. Unfortunately, we have as yet no method to estimate accurately ... the natural rate of unemployment' (1968, p. 10).

An evaluation of the natural rate hypothesis

I have given a brief sketch of some of the ideas giving rise to, and arising from, the natural rate. The history is by no means comprehensive, but I have given what I believe to be the main salient points (although I must apologise to search theorists for omitting them).

The concept of the natural rate is very solidly rooted in the classical tradition. In its simplest form it consists of two hypotheses:

(a) There exists a unique equilibrium for the economy determined by real factors in the economy (classical dichotomy).
(b) Equilibrium output, employment and the real wage are determined in the labour market (decomposability).

Part (b) is perhaps a little injudicious. Friedman himself only ever talked about *monetary* policy in the context of the natural rate: he clearly believed in the neutrality of money, and conceived of it in terms of the homogeneity of the system of equilibrium equations. However, in practice, both Friedman and others have followed Patinkin's approach in locating the real macroeconomic equilibrium primarily in the labour market: output, employment and the real wage are all tied down within the labour market. This notion of decomposability is common to all of the approaches we have explored from Patinkin's notion of full employment to new classical theories and the NAIRU.

The phrase 'natural rate' is itself a masterpiece of marketing, akin to the phrase 'rational expectations (RE)'. In terms of hypotheses (a) and (b) it is a blank space, an invitation for economists to insert their own ideas and fashions in order to define their own notion of the 'real equilibrium'. By not specifying any particular theory of the natural rate, Friedman avoided the problem of obsolescence. I commented that the definition of the natural rate given by Friedman was a research programme rather than a definition: after 25 years no one has yet managed to combine all of the elements identified by Friedman into one coherent model, and probably never will.

The only real difference between the concept of the natural rate and Patinkin's notion of full employment is that the latter is specific (a model of the competitive labour market), and furthermore the only concrete version of the natural rate offered by Friedman himself was the same as Patinkin. However, the phrase 'full employment' has lots of connotations, such as that there should not be much unemployment, and that workers are on their supply curve. One of the reasons that Friedman opted to stress search theory in his Presidential Address was that it focused on the *voluntary* decision of workers to accept or reject job offers. The terminology 'natural rate' served to divert attention from the word 'full', and hence to accept that in equilibrium there might be unemployment, and indeed that since this unemployment was 'natural' it was not necessarily a bad thing. In that sense the change of language Friedman introduced prepared the intellectual ground for the shift of political objectives away from full employment to reducing inflation, and the acceptance of ever-higher levels of unemployment in the ensuing 25 years. Another shift in policy emphasis resulting from this change of language was that unemployment was seen as a primarily *microeconomic* concern. The way to reduce unemployment was not through macroeconomic policy, but through policy towards the functioning of markets – the labour market in particular – in order to remove 'frictions' and 'imperfections'.

Thus far I have tried to clarify the concept of the natural rate, rather than criticise. However, I will now offer a series of critical observations on the natural rate from a theoretical and practical point of view. First and foremost, the notion that there is a unique equilibrium level of output and employment is an extremely strong assumption. Most macroeconomic models are highly stylised in their aggregative structure, using representative markets and agents. These assumptions tend to bias models towards having a unique equilibrium. However, the possibility of multiple equilibria should not be dismissed as merely a curiosity. Friedman cast his 1968 discussion of the natural rate in terms of search theory. However,

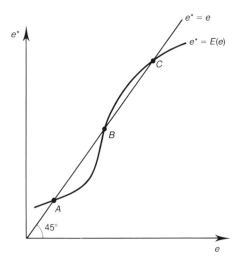

Figure 5.6 Multiple equilibria in Diamond's (1982) coconut model

subsequent research has shown that the possibility of multiple equilibria in
search models is endemic. The most notable model here is Peter Diamond's
'coconut' model (1982). Consider an island with coconut trees. Islanders
eat coconuts, but there is a taboo against eating coconuts that you have
picked yourself. In order to enjoy the succulence of a coconut and sample
the delights of coconut milk you need to pick a coconut and then search for
someone to swap coconuts with. The cost to you of getting a coconut
(finding and climbing a tree) is a fixed production cost: however, the
(expected) cost of finding a partner varies with the number of people
searching for a partner. If there are many individuals wandering around the
island with coconuts, the expected search cost of finding one of them is low:
if there are only a few of you, the search cost will be high. This is a basic
search externality, in that the incentive to 'produce' a coconut depends
positively on the proportion of the population similarly engaged. One
obtains something like figure 5.6, which follows Diamond more in spirit
than detail.

    Let us define the proportion of the islanders engaged in picking coconuts
and searching for partners as e. As an individual, the marginal expected
returns to picking a coconut are increasing in the proportion of people
likewise engaged. Thus the more people are engaged in producing
coconuts, the more individuals will find it in their interest to pick coconuts:
this is captured by the function $e^* = E(e)$, where e^* is the proportion of
people who want to pick coconuts given that a proportion e are so doing.

An equilibrium lies on the 45° line: the actual number of coconut pickers equals the number of would-be coconut pickers. Since E is upward sloping, there may be multiple equilibria, as at points ABC in figure 5.6. Furthermore, these equilibria may be welfare ranked: more people eat coconuts the bigger is e. As Diamond stated:

To see the importance of this finding, consider Friedman's (1968) definition of the natural rate of unemployment as the level occurring once frictions are introduced into the Walrasian economy. This paper argues that the result of actually modeling a competitive economy with trade frictions is to find multiple natural rates of employment. This implies that one of the goals of macroeconomic policy should be to direct the economy towards the best natural rate (1982, p. 881).

This sort of finding has become known as a *coordination failure* problem (Cooper and John, 1988): the economy may have multiple equilibria which are Pareto ranked, and the free market may fail to ensure that the economy ends up at the best one.

The second issue is that even if there is a natural rate, if it is not perfectly competitive it will not be Pareto optimal (indeed the coconut model shows that even competitive models with externalities might not be so). In this case the *decomposability* property of the natural rate model becomes rather suspect. It rather artificially imposes a unique equilibrium on the labour market irrespective of the demand side of the economy. Properly modelled, strong assumptions are needed to rule out fiscal policy (or any other real demand 'shock') from having an effect on the equilibrium. If we start from an initial position where there is too little output and employment, then there is the possibility that if fiscal policy can raise output, it will have a welfare improving effect. Indeed, if you drop the decomposability assumption, you will not obtain a natural rate model, but rather a *natural range* model: although there may be a unique equilibrium for a given macroeconomic policy (mix of monetary and fiscal policy), there is a *range* of equilibrium levels of output and employment available as policy is varied. If these are welfare ranked, then the government can choose from a range of equilibrium options (see, for example, Dixon, 1988, 1991). Both of the possibilities discussed here: multiple (discrete) natural rates and a continuum (natural range) are both more likely to be of interest in imperfectly competitive economies, since non-competitive equilibria start off being Pareto inefficient.

Thirdly, one has to consider the empirical evidence for the natural rate hypothesis. This is discussed in some detail in other chapters in this volume, so I shall not dwell on it. It is almost impossible to refute any hypothesis in economics on the basis of econometric evidence. However, the casual empiricist would be able to see huge fluctuations in employment over the past 25 years: these surely point strongly to the presence of strong hysteresis effects, and possibly multiple equilibria (for empirical evidence on the latter, see Manning, 1992).

Conclusion

The natural rate has clearly been a powerful idea. It is a phrase that captured and continues to capture a point of view, a perspective: it views unemployment outcomes as 'natural' and unavoidable from the macro-economic level. Indeed, the phrase 'full employment' had much the same ideological force in the preceding quarter of a century: it embodied the notion of abundance and stability as being attainable through sound macroeconomic management. It is interesting to note that the actual theory used to model both full employment and the natural rate may be the same: we find the same demand and supply model of the labour market in Patinkin's 1956 model of full employment and Friedman's natural rate in his Nobel lecture. As economics moves on and develops, economists will no doubt continue to use the label 'natural rate' to apply to equilibrium states. The continuity in the label may belie a difference in substance. At some stage in the fullness of time someone will grasp the spirit of the age and think up a new name, a new attitude. I only hope that they do not simply relabel and recycle yet another version of Patinkin's diagram of the labour market.

Note

1 For a formal derivation of the effects of fiscal and monetary policy with wealth effects see classic graduate texts of the 1970s (Ott, Ott and Yoo, 1975, ch. 12; Barro and Grossman, 1976, ch. 1).

References

Ball, R. and Bodkin, R., 1963. 'Income, the Price Level, and Generalised Multipliers in a Keynesian Economy', *Metroeconomica*, 15, 59–81
Barro, R. and Grossman, H., 1976. *Money, Employment, and Inflation*, Cambridge: Cambridge University Press
Cooper, R. and John, A., 1988. 'Coordinating Coordination Failures in Keynesian Models', *Quarterly Journal of Economics*, 103, 441–63
Diamond, P., 1982. 'Aggregate Demand Management in Search Equilibrium', *Journal of Political Economy*, 90, 881–94
Dixon, H., 1988. 'Unions, Oligopoly, and the Natural Range of Unemployment', *Economic Journal*, 98, 1127–47
   1991. 'Macroeconomic Policy in a Large Unionised Economy', *European Economic Review*, 35, 1427–48

Friedman, M., 1968. 'The Role of Monetary Policy', *American Economic Review*, 58(1) (March), 1–17

1975. *Inflation vs Unemployment: an Evaluation of the Phillips Curve*, Institute of Economic Affairs Occasional Paper, 44, London: IEA

1977. 'Inflation and Unemployment', *Journal of Political Economy*, 85, 451–72

Hume, D., 1750. Of Money, *Essays*, Oxford: Oxford University Press

Layard, R. and Nickell, S.J., 1985. 'The Causes of British Unemployment, *National Institute Economic Review*, 111 (March), 62–85

1986. 'Unemployment in Britain', *Economica*, 53, 121–69

Lucas, R.E.J., 1979. 'An Equilibrium Model of the Business Cycle', *Journal of Political Economy*, 83, 1113–44

1981. *Studies in Business-Cycle Theory*, Cambridge, MA: MIT Press

Lucas, R.E.J. and Rapping, L., 1969. 'Real Wages, Employment, and Inflation', *Journal of Political Economy*, 77 (September/October), 721–54

Manning, A., 1990. 'Imperfect Competition Multiple Equilibria and Unemployment Policy', *Economic Journal*, 100, Supplement, 151–62

1992. 'Multiple Equilibria in the British Labour Market: some Empirical Evidence', *European Economic Review*, 36, 1333–65

Ott, D.J., Ott, A.F. and Yoo, J.H., 1975. *Macroeconomic Theory*, New York: McGraw-Hill

Patinkin, D., 1965. *Money, Interest and Prices*, New York: Harper & Row, 2nd edn

Pigou, A., 1941. *The Veil of Money*, London: Macmillan

Robinson, J., 1960. *Accumulation of Capital*, London: Macmillan

Salop, S., 1979. A Model of the Natural Rate of Unemployment, *American Economic Review*, 69 (March), 117–25

Samuelson, P., 1968. 'Classical and Neoclassical Monetary Theory', *Canadian Journal of Economics*, 1, 1–15

II

Adjustment, ranges of equilibria and hysteresis

6 The economics of adjustment

Andrew Caplin and John Leahy

Introduction

As consumer tastes and production techniques evolve over time, the economy must adjust to the changing circumstances. It must reallocate its resources away from less desirable goods and less productive technologies towards newly desirable and more productive ones. The economics of adjustment takes as its subject matter the analysis of the manner in which these changes occur. It studies how individual economic agents decide to reallocate resources in response to economic disturbances and how markets aggregate these individual adjustment decisions. The importance of the subject arises from the fact that matching resources to their appropriate uses is a very difficult, costly and time-consuming process. As a result it is possible that resources may remain misallocated for some time as the process of adjustment works itself out.

In this chapter we focus on the role of information in the adjustment process. In most situations agents make their adjustment decisions under great uncertainty. They need to know the best use for their resources, the best location to adjust to, and the best means of adjustment. They face difficulties, however, in deciding exactly which uses, locations, and means are the best. At each stage of this decisionmaking process they need to gather information in order to make their decisions effectively. Faced with such uncertainty, it is natural that agents will make use of all sources of information at their disposal, including the observed behaviour of others who are in similar situations and contemplating similar adjustment decisions. We argue that a careful consideration of the role that information plays, especially the process of learning from others, is crucial to understanding the nature of the adjustment process. A consideration of this role quickly leads to a class of information externalities that have not been incorporated into the adjustment literature.

The economics of adjustment is a broad area that covers a wide variety of different problems. Milton Friedman's original definition of the natural rate places unemployment in this class of economic problems:

The 'natural rate of unemployment' [he wrote in his Presidential Address] . . . is the level that would be ground out by the Walrasian system of general equilibrium equations, provided there is imbedded in them the actual structural characteristics of the labor and commodity markets, including market imperfections, stochastic variability in demands and supplies, the cost of gathering information about job vacancies and labor availabilities, the costs of mobility, and so on (1968, p. 8).

Friedman's definition stresses the frictions inherent in labour markets and the difficulty of reallocating labour in response to shocks. The natural rate of unemployment is positive because stochastic supplies and demands make it necessary for labour to adjust, because it is costly to transfer resources from one use to another, and because it takes time to gather information concerning how labour should best be employed.

Labour is not the only factor which faces adjustment problems. Many of the same problems plague markets for other factors such as land and capital. Office buildings frequently remain vacant as owners look for desirable tenants (see below). Home owners often spend months searching for buyers for their homes. Producers must decide when to open and close factories and where to locate new production. In each of these cases the need to adjust to changing economic circumstances causes resources to be temporarily misallocated due to the cost and effort inherent in finding better uses.

At a broader level, there are times when the entire economy faces an adjustment problem. A prime example of this is the situation faced by the nations of Eastern Europe where resources must adapt to an entirely new political, economic, social and legal system. Here the uncertainty surrounding the adjustment process is particularly acute; no one has a very clear picture of what the ultimate deployment of resources in these economies will look like. Similarly, one may view a developing economy as facing an adjustment problem. Developing nations must cope with many levels of uncertainty in deciding how to concentrate their resources in their development effort. In this sense, the economics of transition, growth and development share much in common with the economics of adjustment.

Returning to the theme of unemployment, much of the Keynesian tradition in macroeconomics builds upon the idea that adjustment problems, including problems of coordination and price stickiness, can cause unemployment to remain sub-optimally high for a long period of time. When and how such high levels of unemployment might arise and whether or not government action might ease the adjustment process are all issues that can be included under the general heading of the 'economics of adjustment'.

As the above examples indicate, there is a vast range of economic issues that are all aspects of the economics of adjustment. We begin our discussion of these issues by describing existing approaches that economists use to study adjustment problems. Much of this effort has focused on the question of why it might be optimal for resources to be temporarily unemployed and on whether or not markets achieve the optimal rate of reallocation. After outlining existing approaches, we argue that this literature has paid inadequate attention to the informational problems that are involved in the adjustment process.

Current approaches to the economics of adjustment

The literature on economic adjustment has taken two general approaches towards examining the problems involved in reallocating resources. The search-theoretic approach emphasises the difficulties involved in locating appropriate uses for resources, whereas the adjustment cost approach highlights the costs inherent in transferring resources from one use to another. In their simplest form, both approaches explain why it is optimal for a cerain fraction of the economy's resources to remain in what otherwise might appear to be sub-optimal uses.

A benchmark model of labour misallocation due to adjustment costs would begin with a worker who after a shock to the economy is located in state A when the worker's optimal state of employment is state B. Depending on the focus of the model, these states may represent unemployment and employment, different industries or geographical regions, or some other aspect of the economic environment that might be relevant to the worker's productivity. The model would then posit: (1) an adjustment cost function that specified how costly it would be for the worker to move from A to B or, if relevant, to some intermediate position; and (2) a loss function that specified how costly it would be for the worker to remain in state A or move only part of the way towards state B. Given the description of the state space, the adjustment cost function, and the loss function, it is then straightforward to determine the worker's optimal adjustment policy; this policy will simply weigh appropriately the costs and benefits of adjustment.

If the costs of moving all of the way to state A exceed the benefits, the worker will optimally remain sub-optimally employed. Yet because there is no inherent reason that the privately perceived gains and losses should differ from the social ones, the misallocation that arises out of this benchmark adjustment cost model, however regrettable, is optimal from a social perspective. This basic model has been extended to situations in which the states A and B change over time, and to situations in which these changes are stochastic. These extensions affect the optimal adjustment policy but not the fact that this policy is socially optimal.

The questions addressed in adjustment cost models are when to adjust and by how much to adjust, not where to adjust. While many extensions of the benchmark model introduce uncertainty about the future state of the economy, adjustment cost models rarely consider uncertainty about the economy's current state. Agents in these models know exactly where resources would move if adjustment were costless. The adjustment costs merely impede this desired reallocation.

Search models introduce a degree of realism by allowing for situations in which workers do not know exactly where the best jobs are located. In the benchmark search model, a worker knows the distribution of wages in the economy, but not the location of any particular wage offer. Meeting a potential employer is equivalent to drawing a wage from this distribution. The question facing the searcher is whether to accept a given wage offer or to continue to search for a better one. The optimal policy involves calculating the wage that makes the searcher indifferent between the two alternatives and accepting all offers in excess of the reservation wage.

Like adjustment cost models, search models explain why workers might choose to remain unemployed. If the gain to finding better employment in the future exceeds the cost of remaining unemployed today, then search is optimal. Also like adjustment cost models, there is no intrinsic reason why search should lead to inefficiency. To the extent that private agents correctly judge the nature of the trade-offs involved, their decisions should be optimal from both an individual and social perspective.

In reaction to the optimality of the benchmark models described above, several authors have introduced externalities into the adjustment process. Mussa (1986) catalogues the possible distortions that might affect adjustment cost models. He discusses taxes, credit constraints, minimum wage laws, and monopoly power. The exercise, however, does not present a clear picture of the optimality of market-based adjustment. Depending on how the distortions affect the relative costs and benefits of adjustment, they may either excessively promote or hinder the process of reallocation. Mussa concludes, 'There is no presumption that the pace of adjustment . . . is too rapid or too slow.'

Others have considered the role of externalities in search models. Here two externalities have been emphasised in the literature. First, Mortenson (1982) observes that any match will result in a situation of bilateral monopoly in which the worker and the firm bargain over the surplus of the match. To the extent that this surplus is divided among the two parties, a party that rejects a match in favour of continued search does not take into account that part of the surplus that would accrue to the other party. In this sense, search is inefficient as too few matches are accepted. The second class of externalities concerns the technology by which workers and firms find matches. Tobin (1972) argues that congestion effects will cause the equilibrium rate of search unemployment to be inefficiently high. Gavin (1993) uses similar logic to argue that the unemployment resulting from adjustment in Eastern Europe is inefficient. Diamond (1981), however, argues that thick market externalities may lead to the opposite conclusion: an inefficiently low level of search unemployment. In the Diamond model, higher unemployment thickens the market and improves the quality of matches. Again, as in adjustment cost models, there is no presumption that the pace of adjustment is too slow, rather than too fast.

In broad terms, the existing approaches to the economics of adjustment surveyed above place emphasis on the nature of the costs of adjustment, and the time it takes for individual agents to sample enough information to determine where to move. While both of these issues are undoubtedly important, we feel that current approaches have neglected an important source of external effects on the search process: externalities that arise in the process of gathering and processing information.

We believe that learning is one of the central issues in adjustment. Agents face a tremendous amount of uncertainty in making their adjustment decisions. Their first task is to gather information in order to make informed decisions. The existing literature takes a very narrow view of this learning process. In as much as learning has been studied, it has been viewed as a private affair. An individual searches against a fixed distribution of offers in a manner that does not interact directly with the learning of other market participants. Yet others' actions and behaviour may prove to be an important source of knowledge and experience. We believe that the extent to which one agent may learn from observing the behaviour of other agents has important implications for the adjustment process.

In the next section we argue by example that there are important lessons that agents learn from watching the behaviour of other agents. After presenting these examples we describe, in the following section, how these externalities alter the qualitative nature of the adjustment process.

Three stories and a general approach

The informational issues involved in adjustment can best be appreciated by considering actual situations. We therefore begin with three cases in which resources are currently known to be in sub-optimal uses, and discuss how the owner of the resource can go about learning the appropriate use of the resource.

The case of the vacant office buildings

As our first case, consider a world in which there are a large number of currently unoccupied buildings in a given area, each with a separate owner.

Owners show potential tenants their vacant office space and entertain offers to take occupancy. Because it is costly to commit the building to any one of its potential uses, owners will not make a commitment easily. They will weigh the current offer against the possibility of receiving a better offer in the future. The situation is similar to the benchmark search model except that we have a group of offices instead of only one.

In the standard search-theoretic view, there is a fixed distribution of valuations among the potential tenants, and this makes it a straightforward matter for the owner to decide on the cutoff for accepting an offer. There are many situations, however, in which it is far from straightforward for either the landlord or the potential tenants to work out how they are to value the office space. The reason for this is that uncertainty has many dimensions. For example, owners need to ensure that rent is paid. For this they need to know if this particular tenant is creditworthy, and they need to form expectations regarding the potential success of the tenant's business. Will this tenant be successful in the future and therefore able to pay higher rents, or will the tenant file for bankruptcy leaving the owner in need of a new occupant for the office? Other issues arise from the fact that signing on a particular tenant commits the property to a particular use. This raises questions concerning the appropriate use for the property. What lines of business are likely to thrive in the coming years? What sort of business will occupy neighouring buildings? What sorts of synergies will these businesses create, and what sorts of tenants would be willing to pay higher rents to take advantage of these external economies?

The important point here is not that information is complex or multifaceted. Such complications can be handled within the context of the benchmark search model by allowing agents to search against a more general class of distributions. The important point is that with potentially so much uncertainty from so many different sources, agents can be expected to use all of the information at their disposal to inform their choices. In particular, when there are several property owners in a similar situation searching for tenants, there is the possibility that each may learn from the others.

The uncertainty surrounding many of the questions raised above can be greatly reduced by such observation. An owner can obtain a guess as to the creditworthiness or reliability of a prospective tenant by observing the behaviour of other tenants with similar characteristics. An owner can gain some information on the relative merits of various uses for the property by observing the choices that others make. Similarly, an owner can gain information as to the future character of a neighbourhood by watching what other owners do with their property.

What emerges is the picture of a market in which everyone is watching everyone else, deciphering each other's every move, attempting to learn what they can about the market. If one owner mothballs a building waiting for business conditions to improve, then all will become slightly more pessimistic about the current situation. If one building is rented for an unexpectedly large amount then all infer that the value of their real estate has risen. If one owner decides to rent to a firm in a particular industry, then all take a close look at the advantages of letting to a similar firm.

These sorts of information spillovers occur all the time. An example, although not from real estate, concerns the sale of the Baltimore Orioles baseball club. Upon hearing that the rival club had sold for $170 million, an owner of the Boston Red Sox was quoted as saying that the sale would 'have a significant impact on what this teams [sic] sells for and increase the value of all baseball franchises.' 'Frankly,' he continued, 'I'm surprised the price was that high. I figured it would be somewhere in the area of $140 [million].'[1] From this reaction, it is clear that the Orioles' sale conveyed positive information that affected the valuation of other clubs.

In another example, Bed, Bath and Beyond, a retailer specialising in linens and bathroom accessories, opened a superstore in a vacant building on lower Sixth Avenue in New York and was successful in drawing shoppers to the area. As a result many other buildings were quickly rented to retailers. Rents in the area rose from the low $20 a square foot that Bed, Bath and Beyond was paying to nearly $40 per square foot in negotiations a year later. Following Bed, Bath and Beyond's success, 'the owners of a parking lot on 23rd Street, whose original plans to build an apartment building on the site were quashed by a combination of the depressed market and city red tape, are now wondering whether the space might serve a lucrative commercial use.'[2] Again the experience of one searcher appears to have provided valuable information to others trying to make similar decisions.

The case of the East European arms manufacturer

It is clear that there is currently a tremendous mismatch between the actual employment of labour and capital in Eastern Europe and its optimal employment. This has led to a large discussion of the nature of the adjustment mechanism, much of it focusing on the relative costs and benefits of gradual versus accelerated adjustment. The picture that is typically painted in these discussions is that of an economy that is off target, where the main issue is how to adjust to that ultimate target. Again, we feel that this misses the crucial issue of just how agents actually go about assessing the optimal use for resources that are currently poorly employed.

There are many unanswered questions concerning adjustment in East Europe. Just how much heavy industry will survive the transition to a market economy? What will happen to the science establishment, the arms industry, and the nuclear power industry? To be concrete, consider a plant with a trained workforce that is currently manufacturing arms, but knows that it is about to lose its key contract with the state. What should it do? Should the factory close, should it produce arms for export, or should it convert to another use? Once these broad decisions are made a whole set of subsidiary issues must be addressed. If the factory is to be closed, can anything be salvaged for scrap? If new orders are to be sought, which countries are likely to be interested, and how does one tailor products and market them in the country? If the factory is to be converted, what is the best product to produce?

Again with such pervasive uncertainty the factory managers will look anywhere for information. One important source will be the experience of other factories in the local region, and of other arms manufacturers in general. By studying the decisions that others in similar situations have made and are making the managers may indirectly benefit from the information gathered by others prior to their decisions. They will be able to avoid decisions that turned out to be mistaken and to emulate those that succeeded.

The case of the redundant steel workers

One may regard an unemployed worker as facing many of the same issues. Just as a landlord must find the appropriate tenant and a plant manager must decide on the appropriate product, unemployed workers must find appropriate employment. In general, a worker's performance and pay will depend on the quality of the worker's match with a given firm, and this quality will depend in turn on how well a worker's skills fit with the needs of the firm, how well these skills mesh with those of other workers, how well the worker's personality fits with those of other workers and so on. Because their pay depends on the quality of the match, unemployed workers are likely to spend some time searching for a good match. The search literature has considered this problem to be a private one, one of a worker searching against a fixed distribution of matches or wage offers and optimally deciding which ones to accept. The literature on external effects has merely added the effect of one worker's search to the arrival rate of matches for others.

The questions facing unemployed workers are of course much broader than whether a given wage is greater than the reservation wage. Workers must decide where even to begin looking for a firm to match with. They must decide whether to remain in their current line of work or to search for employment in another field. If switching fields appears to be the best policy, workers must decide which ones offer the best prospects for employment for a worker of their type, and which firms within those particular fields present the best prospects for long and prosperous matches.

It is clear that if any of the characteristics that add to the success of a match between a particular type of firm and a particular type of worker are publicly observable then workers and firms should use this knowledge to improve their chances of making successful matches. By observing the behaviour of workers with similar skills and characteristics a worker can learn which types of firms value workers with characteristics similar to his/her own.

Because firms tend to hire workers that match well with the firm, and because workers with the same firm tend to acquire similar skills and knowledge, workers will not have to look far to find other workers with similar characteristics whose behaviour they might find informative. An unemployed steel worker will tend to observe the behaviour of other unemployed steel workers, since these people are likely to share many of the same skills, educational achievements, and social attitudes. Are these other workers remaining in town waiting to be called back to their jobs? Are they taking other jobs? What type of jobs? Are they happy? Are they moving away? Where are they moving? Are they finding work in their new locations? The answers to these questions will influence where, and with what intensity, the steel worker searches for new employment.

In all three examples, there is a tremendous amount of missing information. As in the standard search model, individuals will take time to gather and process the information that is relevant to this decision. But unlike the standard search model, information is an incredibly complex multifaceted object, and there are multiple sources of information relevant to the optimal use of the resource. In particular, in all three cases much that is relevant to one individual's decision can be clarified by watching the decisionmaking processes of other actors. In the case of the vacant offices, one of the relevant sources of information is the rental history of neighbouring offices. In the case of Eastern European arms manufacturers, one of the sources of information is the decision of similar arms manufacturers, on how to convert their factories. In the case of the redundant steel workers, there are the search histories of other workers laid off in steel and allied heavy industries.

Information spillovers and optimal search

The possibility that agents gain information from the search behaviour of other agents raises questions concerning what exactly it is that agents learn, and how it is that they learn it. In order to understand how informational spillovers influence the adjustment process, one needs to know what aspects of individual behaviour are observable, what the relevance of these observations is to other market participants, and how these observations affect the others' search behaviour. At a broader level, one needs to know how these influences on individual behaviour affect the operation of the market as a whole. In general, the answers to these questions will depend both on the source of the uncertainty and the way in which information is shared among workers. To get a flavour for the types of interactions that are possible, we discuss several possible cases in detail. To fix ideas we stay with the example of unemployed workers searching for new employment.

We begin with a simple case. Suppose that each worker is unsure about some aspect of the distribution of wage offers, possibly its mean or variance, and that all workers draw their wages from the same distribution. In this case, it is easy to see why the offers received by other workers would prove useful; they provide additional information regarding the unknown aspect of the wage distribution. Suppose further that there are no problems with information sharing. At the end of the day, all workers meet and provide complete accounts of their search activity. In this way, there is a common pool of information that all workers use in determining their reservation wages.

Even in this simple setting a number of informational externalities are present. First, as workers weigh the costs and benefits of increasing their search effort, they will only consider the value to themselves of receiving an additional offer and fail to take into account the value of this offer to others. For this reason, it is very likely that there will be too little search from a social standpoint. Information, as a public good, will be underprovided by the market. Second, the public good aspect of information leads to a free rider problem. If search is costly and requires effort, then each worker has an incentive to conserve energy and allow others to gather information for them. This too will lead to too little search in equilibrium. Finally, if and when workers do accept job offers they may not take account of the fact that by accepting an offer they stop searching and this stops the flow of information to others. Note that this third channel implies that unemployment spells are sub-optimally short because workers accept too many offers, whereas the first two imply that spells are sub-optimally long due to insufficient search effort. All three, however, imply that there is too little information from a social perspective. Ideally, agents should search more and search harder, but a combination of externalities and free rider problems prevents them from doing so.

One unrealistic aspect of this simple story of information sharing is that the flow of information between workers stops once a worker has accepted a job. In many cases the situation is exactly the opposite. Certain aspects of the match between a worker and a firm are observable only after a worker accepts a job offer and begins to work. We therefore consider what would happen if instead of learning about the distribution of wages, workers were learning about the quality of a match between their skills and those required by the various types of employment open to them. To be specific, assume that there are many types of employment and that *ex ante* each job has a known and identical distribution of initial wage offers against which all workers search. Workers differ in that each possesses a certain combination of skills and attributes. The source of uncertainty is that workers do not know which jobs match well with their particular set of skills, and the quality of this match will determine future wage growth on the job. For simplicity, we assume that the quality of the match between a particular worker and a firm is captured by a single parameter that is observable to the match participants and the public at large only after a job has been taken.

Since the distribution of initial wage offers is known there is nothing that workers can learn from the search experience of other workers. Workers can, however, learn from others' matches. When a worker with a certain set of skills discovers a particularly good match, all workers with similar skills will learn something about their match with that profession.

In this case, the information externality manifests itself in too few matches. Workers fail to take account of the value to others of the information that accepting a job offer reveals. For this reason unemployment spells will tend to be too long from a social perspective. As before there is also a free rider problem since agents have an incentive to wait for others to take jobs and reveal the quality of their matches. This free rider problem reinforces the effect of the information externality. It causes searchers to be even more selective in the matches that they accept. Unemployment spells become even longer, and the shortage of information even more acute.

In each of these examples, we have assumed that information sharing was a simple task. In the first case, it was possible to observe the entire search history of other workers. In the second case, it was possible perfectly to observe the quality of other workers' matches. In many situations, such information is neither simple to observe nor easy to convey. Nor is it the case that all information is equally easy to share. It is quite possible that a worker learns more from the fact that a co-worker has taken a job than from the observation that this co-worker is still unemployed. A worker may remain unemployed for a number of reasons. The worker may have received no offers from employers or the worker may have received only poor offers or the worker may not even have searched at all. Unless the channels of communication are very good much of this experience may remain unobservable. An accepted job is potentially far more informative. One could learn the industry, location, and possibly even the wage of the job that was accepted, all of which may be valuable informatiion to a searcher.

The fact that there is imperfect information sharing among the unemployed workers has further important ramifications for the search process. Consider a case in which the distribution of wage offers is uncertain, as in the first case above, but rather than sharing information on wage offers, workers only learn about the wages that are accepted. In this setting, successful matches between workers and firms create information that is useful to other workers attempting to decide how to use their unemployed labour, whereas continued unemployment is an ambiguous signal for the reasons described above.

The limited sharing of information in this example make the information externality and the free rider problem even more clear. To see this it is useful to compare the incentive to accept a match in this market setting to the benchmark search model in which each agent searches in isolation. Because matches in the market setting create information that is valuable to other searchers, social optimality dictates that agents should accept jobs more readily than they would if they were searching in isolation. This is the information externality at work. Due to the free rider problem, however, the result is precisely the opposite; workers become more selective in the market setting in order to learn from others' matches. As a result the market produces individual spells of unemployment that are unambiguously longer than would be socially optimal because each individual delays acceptance in order to learn what others have done.

These examples illustrate possible ways in which the consideration of information spillovers may enrich our understanding of economic adjustment, and therefore of the natural rate of unemployment. One general feature in all of the above cases is a tendency toward the underprovision of information by the private market. This shortage of information affects the efficiency of the search process and provides a possible role for government policy to improve the allocation of resources. Whether this shortage of information leads to a natural rate of unemployment that is above or below its optimal level, however, remains an open question that can be resolved only by analysing formal models of informational spillovers.

In this chapter we have argued that many topics in economics, including the theory of the natural rate of unemployment, can be viewed as part of the broader theory of the economics of adjustment. We have argued that existing approaches to the economics of adjustment take a very narrow view of the role of information. We have outlined an approach to this topic that stresses the role of learning and information externalities, and discussed through examples how these concerns alter the qualitative nature of the adjustment process. In particular, there appears to be a general bias towards the underprovision of information. The economic significance of this underprovision of information will likely vary from market to market.

Notes

We thank the National Science Foundation for financial support.
1 Figures and quotes are from McDonough (1993, p. 65).
2 Quotes and figures are from Deutsch (1993).

References

Deutsch, C., 1993. 'From the Carriage Trade to the Category Killers', *New York Times* (27 July 1993)

Diamond, P., 1981. 'Mobility Costs, Frictional Unemployment, and Efficiency', *Journal of Political Economy*, 89, 798–812

Friedman, M., 1968. 'The Role of Monetary Policy', *American Economic Review*, 56(1) (March), 1–17

Gavin, M., 1993. 'Unemployment and the Economics of Gradualist Policy Reform', Columbia University, mimeo

McDonough, W., 1993. 'In the Long Run, Oriole Sale Could Pay Off for Red Sox', *Boston Globe* (7 August 1993), 65–6

Mortenson, D., 1982. 'The Matching Process as a Non-Cooperative Bargaining Game', in J. McCall (ed.), *The Economics of Information and Uncertainty*, Chicago: University of Chicago Press

Mussa, M., 1986. 'The Adjustment Process and the Timing of Trade Liberalization', in A. Choksi and D. Papageorgiou (eds.), *Economic Liberalization in Developing Countries*, Oxford: Basil Blackwell

Tobin, J., 1972. 'Inflation and Unemployment', *American Economic Review*, 62 (March), 1–18

7 Hysteresis and memory in the labour market

G.C. Archibald

Introduction

In a most lucid paper on hysteresis in economic systems, Cross (1993, references here are to the draft of June 1992; see also Cross, 1988) has reminded us of the difficulties of 'forces acting at a distance', whether spatial or temporal. If the distance is temporal, the difficulty may be resolved if the objects of study have memories. Whether physicists following Ewing have succeeded in endowing molecules with 'memories' I do not pretend to know. In dealing with the labour market, we are dealing with human agents who certainly have memories, and institutions created by these agents whose design may well be altered in response to shocks, or at least sufficiently severe shocks.

In this chapter I shall consider first, and briefly, the way memory may affect the supply side of the labour market, and then at greater length the demand side. The discussion here will necessarily be somewhat lengthy, since I wish to draw on earlier work (Archibald and Chinloy, 1987) which is not well known, and I wish to make this chapter reasonably autonomous. The advantage is that we shall find an economic interpretation of Cross' 'hysteresis operators' which accounts for their heterogeneity across the market, the peculiar importance of certain (non-dominated) shocks, and the asymmetry of behaviour in upswing and downswing. My hope is that the Archibald–Chinloy model will provide some basis, albeit informally, in optimisation theory for hysteresis in economic behaviour. Some testable implications will emerge as the analysis proceeds. I offer some brief conclusions in the final section.

The stock of human capital

The supply side of the market can be dealt with in summary, indeed cursory, fashion since so much that I rely on to provide memory has been established in recent years, and may now be said to be common knowledge.

It is now well established that human capital can depreciate and grow

90

obsolete just like non-human capital, and is likely to depreciate faster ('rust') if it is unused. Serious and prolonged unemployment entails a running down of the capital stock. If, in addition, many school-leavers cannot find jobs, or are only fitfully and casually employed, less capital is formed than 'normally' would be or will subsequently be wanted. This is enough for 'memory' in an immediate and effective sense. There is, however, more. It is not uncommon for workers to be made redundant after repeated assurances that they would not be. Their 'trust' or confidence is damaged, and they may not wish to participate further in the labour force if they can avoid it. It is now well understood that the long-run costs of severe and prolonged unemployment may be substantially greater than the immediate costs. How much greater we shall perhaps yet discover. There is at least no mysterious question of 'forces at a distance' on the supply side of the labour market.

The model

My purpose in this section is the more ambitious one of providing an explanation of memory and hysteresis operators on the demand side of the labour market. The difficulty is obvious: at first sight, a profit maximising firm, whether it maximises short-run profit or present value, has no business to have a memory! It turns out that the work that Peter Chinloy and I did (1987, hereafter AC) for quite another purpose provides the desired explanation. Our purpose was to argue against the view, increasingly common in North America in the 1980s, that unemployment insurance benefits merely encourage workers to take 'paid holidays' or, if unemployed, to unduly extend the search period. We argued that workers are naturally interested in the security of their income flow, as well as its immediate amount. That security can be provided by 'on-the-job' security, or public provision for income security, and we argued that the better the latter, the less of the former would be demanded. A small international cross-section of countries provided supporting evidence: the better was public provision for income security, the less we found on-the-job security in such matters as average length of tenure or severance or redundancy pay. We argued that the less it cost a firm to dismiss a worker, the more willing it would be to hire one: 'easy fire, easy hire.' Again, we found ample supporting evidence in our (small) cross-section sample. Thus Japan, with the worst public provision, had the least flexible labour market: its inability to absorb the 'baby boom' generation into the labour market appeared mainly in the form of diminished participation rates. Canada and the US, with the 'best' public provision, had far the best record for 'absorption', and the least on-the-job security. West Germany and the UK, with relatively mean public provision and serious constraints on the behaviour of individual firms, had only intermediate 'absorption' records.

We are not here concerned with these matters, but I thought that I should explain the original reasons for a model which I wish to exploit, and must now at least sketch here. We simply endow each worker with a state-independent von Neumann–Morgenstern utility function and assume that he seeks to maximise expected utility. Thus

$$E(U) = qU(W) + (1 - q)U(X) \tag{1}$$

where q is the probability of remaining in the present job, W is the wage rate, and X the unemployment benefit. (If this appears unduly static or one-period, we may maximise the expected value of the integral over the appropriate horizon: it makes no difference to the qualitative results.) Totally differentiating (1) and rearranging, one obtains the marginal rate of substitution between wages and job security:

$$\partial W/\partial q_{(U = \bar{U})} = - [U(W) - U(X)]/qU'(W) \equiv r(W, q \,|\, X) < 0. \tag{2}$$

Similarly,

$$\partial q/\partial X < 0 \tag{3}$$

and

$$\partial W/\partial X < 0. \tag{4}$$

(2) tells us that the worker will trade wages for job security, (3) that he will trade job security for unemployment benefit (income security), and (4) that he will trade wages for unemployment benefit. Differentiating again, it is easily found that all three level surfaces have the expected curvature properties.

From the point of view of social policy, the most important of these inequalities is probably (3): the worker will accept a lower level of job security in exchange for greater income security. From the point of view of the firm, with which we are here concerned, the most important is (2): the worker will accept a lower wage in exchange for increased job security. Thus the firm can save current wages by offering more job security than it would in the completely flexible or 'spot' case. I assume now and throughout that the firm is less risk averse than its workers. It thus has a complex intertemporal maximisation problem. If demand for its product (or its price) is stochastic, the problem is a stochastic control problem which appears to be analytically intractable. We can bypass this by ignoring internal solutions ('some' additional security) and considering only the two extreme cases, which we may call S (spot) and F (fixed). In the S case, the firm behaves in textbook fashion, hiring and firing labour as a truly variable input. (We must bear in mind throughout that firms can be no more spot than current legislation governing redundancy payments and the like allows. It is doubtful if any firms in the UK can be as truly spot as some in Canada, although there is, of course, a substantial F-sector in that economy too. I shall not repeat this qualification.) In the F (fixed)-case it offers a package of wages $\bar{W}$ and employment $\bar{L}$ within some defined range of price realisations. Now labour is at least a 'quasi-fixed' factor, as in Oi (1962).

This concentration on the extreme cases is indeed a simplification, but it does not seem that it need cost us much. We may look on an economy as a convex combination of F-firms and S-firms, and we shall see how, in a downswing or recession, F-firms may be forced to become S-firms. We shall also be able to ask if a recovery is likely to be symmetrical. Indeed, the simplification may save us something, for this is *not* implicit contract theory in another wrapping. In the literature on that theory, it is common to assume just two states, good and bad. The implicit contract is not to lay off as many workers in the bad state as the firm would in the spot case. It is implicitly assumed that this will not alter its hiring in the good state, which is, in general, inadmissible: restrictions on layoff imply restrictions on hiring. In the bad state, the implicit contract is not incentive-compatible to the firm and, given asymmetric information, it is unenforceable. Thus there is a distinct advantage to ignoring internal solutions to the control problem, and considering the economy as a convex combination of S-firms and F-firms. Analysis in the S-case is familiar, so I concentrate on the F-case. First, I note, what is obvious, that just as this model does not offer implicit contract theory in another guise, it may not be identified with the 'insider–outsider' approach unless, at least, 'insiders' are to be identified as employees of what I here call F-firms and 'outsiders' as employees of S-firms (and perhaps the unemployed), which seems a little strained.

For this purpose, we exploit the variable profit function, the maximum of revenue *less* variable cost, given the production function $Y(K, L)$ and fixed capital $\bar{K}$. The firm is assumed to be a price taker in the output market, with price P independent of its output. (No qualitative results are altered if we introduce an imperfectly competitive inverse demand function $P(Y)$.) The S-firm will choose labour input, L, to maximise variable profit

$$\pi(W, P \mid \bar{K}) = \max_L \{ P Y(\bar{K}, L) - WL \} \tag{5}$$

which yields the labour demand function

$$L = - \partial \pi(W, P \mid \bar{K}, L)/\partial W. \tag{6}$$

Since this is, by assumption, the spot case, there are no (or only trivial) costs to altering the level of employment. Both (5) and (6) have the usual properties.

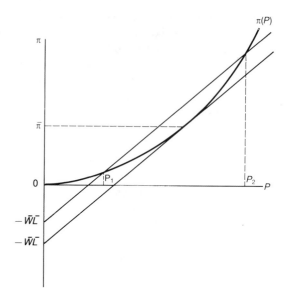

Figure 7.1   Possible contracts: spot and fixed cases
Source: Archibald and Chinloy (1987)

Now in the F-case the firm offers a guarantee of employment level $\bar{L}$ over some range of realisations of P. Its variable profit becomes

$$\bar{\pi} = PY(\bar{K}, \bar{L}) - W\bar{L}, \tag{7}$$

where $\bar{L}$ is the number guaranteed employment. This relation is linear in $\pi - P$ space with intercept $-W\bar{L}$. If F-firms and S-firms paid the same wage W prior to the realisation of the price P the profits from both strategies would be equal at only one point, where $L = \bar{L}$ and $\pi = \bar{\pi}$. It appears that the spot strategy dominates and that no firm would commit itself to $\bar{L}$. This is illustrated in figure 7.1 (taken from AC with corrections not made there).

From (2) above we know, however, that workers will accept a lower current wage in exchange for greater job security. Let the wage accepted in return for the firm's commitment to $\bar{L}$ be $\bar{W} < W$, the spot wage. The variable profit function for varying prices with fixed employment $\bar{L}$ and wage $\bar{W}$ now shifts upwards, as shown in figure 7.1. The amount of the shift depends, of course, on the firm's perception of the distribution of prices and its attitude to risk, the workers' risk aversion, and the outcome of any bargaining process, formal or informal, between the two sides. Since we cannot model the firm's stochastic control problem, we cannot assert that $\bar{L}$

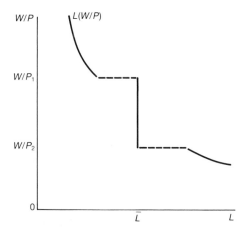

Figure 7.2   Discontinuities in labour demand in the fixed case
Source: Archibald and Chinloy (1987)

will be chosen such that the spot wage W and $\bar{L}$ will generate $\pi = \bar{\pi}$ as shown: figure 7.1 is merely illustrative. Given the shape of $\pi(P)$, however, it is clear that the upward shift in the linear variable profit function associated with $\bar{L}$ due to a wage of $\bar{W}$ gives two intersections, as illustrated, at points such as P_1 and P_2. Outside these limits, the firm 'goes spot', at one extreme because the high level of demand induces it to compete for labour in the spot market, at the other because the low level of demand forces it to abandon fixed commitments. Any interior solution, with fixed L and W, not necessarily the $\bar{L}$ and $\bar{W}$ somewhat arbitrarily illustrated here, is adopted because it *pays*. We might say that the firm extracts rent from the risk aversion of the worker. Its ability to do this is lower the higher is public provision for income security, as the alternative to private provision for employment security.

It is easily seen that the demand for labour of the F-firm is discontinuous. Assume that P has support on an interval $[\underline{P}, \bar{P}]$ where $0 \le Pg091 \le P_1 \le P_2 \le \bar{P} \le + \infty$. The three sub-intervals, with their implications for variable profit, are

$$\begin{array}{ll} \underline{P} < P < P_1 & \bar{\pi} < \pi \\ P_1 \le P < P_2 & \bar{\pi} \ge \pi \\ P_2 \le P < \bar{P} & \bar{\pi} < \pi. \end{array} \tag{8}$$

Demand for labour depends on which sub-interval is realised. We measure W/P on the vertical axis of figure 7.2 (taken again from AC) and the level of employment that maximises variable profit on the horizontal. Suppose that the level of nominal wages is fixed at W, while prices are free to vary. Then we have

$$W/P > W/P_1 \qquad L = \partial\pi/\partial P$$
$$W/P_1 \geq W/P \geq W/P_2 \qquad L = \bar{L} \qquad\qquad (9)$$
$$W/P_2 > W/P \qquad L = \partial\pi/\partial P.$$

This only formalises the proposition that, between P_1 and P_2, the firm adopts the fixed strategy because it pays and, outside those limits, goes spot.

One testable implication emerges at once. At the individual firm level, we expect layoffs and new hires to occur in discrete doses, not with the continuous adjustment of a spot market. When realisations of P are 'bad enough' (at P_1) the firm has to abandon its commitments and make layoffs which may certainly be substantial as the night shift is abandoned or a whole plant closed. When demand is high, it pays to abandon commitments and to compete for more labour in the spot market, possibly in a large enough dose to reopen a plant or man another shift. That hirings and firings by the individual firm are made in discrete doses seems to be consistent with common observation, and is supported more formally (by Hamermesh, 1989, for example). A neat and persuasive explanation in terms of catastrophe theory may be found in Johnes (1988). That demand for labour at some aggregate level may nonetheless appear continuous is familiar (see, for example, Johansen, 1961).

Implications: memory and hysteresis

It is now almost trivial to identify P_2 and P_1 with the a and b of Fab, the hysteresis operator of Cross (1993). There is no difficulty in identifying the 'dominant shocks' of that paper as realisations of price outside the limits of P_1 and P_2: realisations within are shocks not large enough to induce any change in behaviour, actual *or* desired. The values of P_1 and P_2 (or a and b) are, of course, peculiar to the individual firm. They depend on its perception of the distribution of demand for its product, its attitude to risk, and its 'solution' to the stochastic control problem, as well as the risk aversion of its workers and the bargain it actually makes with them. Diversity, or heterogeneity, seem assured. There is, however, a small difficulty. I have assumed for expositional simplicity that the firm is a price taker, rather than endowing it with the inverse demand function of imperfect competition. This implies that, within an industry or trade, there can be no interfirm differences in the realisations of price, although there may be differences in expectations, cost, and the degree of risk aversion. We might drop the price taking assumption at the cost of minor algebraic complexity, whence I do not think this difficulty important. Heterogeneity, from whatever causes, implies that aggregation is required.

Appropriate and ingenious aggregation techniques have been suggested by Caballero and Engel (1992), and will not be explored here. They, however, rely on the idea of an instantaneous *desired* level of employment, which would be achieved in a 'frictionless' world, and a discrepancy, due to 'friction', between that and an adjustment actually made. Friction is to be attributed to adjustment cost, in some broad sense, but is not rigorously defined. The difference between that approach and the model discussed here is obvious. *Between a* and *b*, or P_2 and P_1, the firm does not *wish* to adjust (though others, with different parameter values, may). When it goes spot, it presumably does encounter adjustment costs, perhaps particularly heavy ones at P_1, and indeed might well hesitate on the brink! Once in the spot market, it of course encounters the normal adjustment costs on a regular basis. We may notice informally that, at 'bad' realisations, close to P_1, the firm may not be anxious to attain the boundary production $Y(\bar{L}, \bar{K})$. Thus there may be an appearance of 'overmanning', and, when the firm is forced to go spot, it may be thought to be 'shaking out the slack'. I do not believe that existing optimising theory offers much explanation of this sort of behaviour, and certainly not theories from which a natural rate hypothesis may be derived.

With the model developed, let us now consider behaviour in the cycle. In a serious downswing, firms that have been in the F-sector will be forced to abandon commitments and go spot. This alters the weights between the F-sector and the S-sector, and in a way which obviously raises doubts about the meaning of base-weighted indices of wage rates. (As the actual weight shifts from *F* to *S*, measured wage rates may well appear more sluggish than are market rates.) Further predictions require assumptions about relative wage rates which were not incorporated in the model developed in the last section. It seems at least a plausible conjecture that F-firms are mainly employers of skilled labour (particularly if the skills are highly firm-specific). This skilled labour has bargained with the firm for additional job security at the cost of a wage lower than it might have had in the spot market. Some skilled workers made redundant when a firm goes spot *may* (if their skills are not too firm-specific) obtain work in the spot market at higher wage rates (in, for example, the oil industry). The majority will obviously try to avoid the spot market and hope for re-employment by F-sector firms. Those who remain in the surviving F-sector firms may even receive higher wages as productivity increases. What happens to the measured 'skilled/unskilled differential' obviously depends on how it is measured.

The major question now is whether recovery can be symmetrical. If the answer were 'yes', then hysteresis would be unimportant. I think that the answer must be 'no', but, again, the argument must be somewhat informal, since the AC model, sketched above, explains the behaviour of firms in the F-sector in 'good' or normal times, but has no direct implications for their behaviour after they have been forced to go spot. Let us consider this. At the bottom, the weights have changed: the ratio of F-firms to S-firms has fallen, and may indeed continue to fall as financial reserves fall, old customers fail, and so on. For surviving F-firms, recovery means little change in behaviour, apart from a probable desire to increase output. Spot firms are, and remain, spot, and doubtless react fairly quickly. The firms of interest are those that were F and have been forced to go spot. Will they automatically return to the F-sector as realisations of price start to exceed P_1? There are several reasons for thinking that they will not. They will find the labour market in some ways 'easier' than when they were last in the $P_1 - P_2$ range. There will not be so many established competitors with established labour forces in the F-sector. Spot wages are unlikely to appear so high that avoiding them is a major interest. And labour that has been unemployed or driven into the spot market is unlikely to be bargaining aggressively.

There is also the matter of learning. The management team of the individual firm has individual and 'collective' memory. Any university department has both, too. We all know how fragile the collective memory is. It is nominally recorded in minutes of meetings which no one ever reads. That apart, ordinary turnover ensures the feebleness of the collective memory. Much will depend on what individuals may have learned from recent experience. We are much too ready, I suggest, to think of learning as a convergent process, perhaps bumpy, but none the less convergent, towards 'truth' (truth in this case being action conducive to the profitability of the firm). I suggest that it is much more likely to display sinusoidal waves, doubtless damped but continually restarted by shocks. In this case a dominant shock will produce a strong overreaction. Part of the 'learning' will doubtless be embodied in changes in Standard Operating Procedures, the 'routines' of Nelson and Winter (1982), for at least some years to come. The 'cliché of the quarter' or 'platitude of the year' in the management of the firms that were in the F-sector and have gone through the traumatic experience of being forced to go spot is likely to be 'let's not get burned like that again'.

They might indeed have difficulty in doing so. Given what will have been happening to the stock of human capital (see p. 91 above) it will take time and experiment to rebuild the sort of labour force with which any sensible management would wish to make an F-agreement. I obviously assume here that we are dealing with disturbances too severe to be dealt with by 'layoff with recall'. I am considering F-firms that have been driven spot, and a labour force components of which have been given plenty of time to deteriorate, together with new entrants of whom a substantial proportion have had little or no opportunity for any serious on-the-job learning.

There is another reason for expecting asymmetry, not at all implied by the model developed above, but which does follow from earlier economic investigations. Consider the view of the firm developed by Coase (1937). Coase suggested that the firm is a sub-set of the economy in which allocation proceeds by command rather than market because some coordination can be done more cheaply that way. Thus the firm is an extra-market coordinating unit, operating with the 'routines' of Nelson and Winter. A familiar feature of prolonged recession is the closure of firms, whether by bankruptcy or voluntary liquidation. Closure entails, of course, the loss of the 'routines' and dispersal of the people who know how to operate them, as well as the rundown of physical equipment. Given the risks and costs of establishing a firm and its routines, as well as its plant, I cannot see how recovery can be symmetrical: it is more likely to be slow, expensive, and littered with error.

We may finally ask what may happen to the firm's perception of the distribution of demand. It is unlikely to be unchanged. Indeed, the more Bayesian its revision, the more, in prolonged recession, it will be revised downwards. (Business confidence?) This suggests one obvious generalisation: the more the expectations of economic agents are revised in a Bayesian manner, the more the whole system will be path dependent.

Conclusion

There is no need to summarise this brief chapter. Certain conclusions seem obvious.

Anyone may define any 'natural' rate of unemployment he pleases. The difficulty is that such a rate is almost certain to be path dependent, a shifting target and, in the present state of knowledge, an elusive one. About all that we can say with confidence is that, the longer a recession lasts, the higher it is likely to be. It does not seem to be a very useful concept. What we urgently need to know is what *rate* of recovery can be managed without encountering the supply-side constraint in an inflationary manner.

Note

I owe this chapter to the stimulus provided by Rod Cross, both on paper and in discussion. I am indebted to him, to Peter Chinloy, and to Geraint Johnes for comments on an earlier version. I am of course responsible for both errors and opinions.

100   G. C. Archibald

References

Archibald, G.C. and Chinloy, P.T., 1987. 'Job Security Versus Income Security', in *Labour Market Adjustments in the Pacific Basin*, P.T. Chinloy and E.W. Stromsdorfer (eds.), Boston, MA: Kluwer Nijhoff

Caballero, R.J. and Engel, E.M.R.A., 1992. 'Microeconomic Adjustment Hazards and Aggregate Dynamics', *NBER Working Paper*, 4900, Cambridge, MA: NBER

Coase, R.H., 1937. 'The Nature of the Firm', *Economica*, NS 4, 386–405

Cross, R. (ed.), 1988. *Unemployment, Hysteresis and the Natural Rate Hypothesis*, Oxford: Basil Blackwell

1993. 'On the Foundations of Hysteresis in Economic Systems', *Economics and Philosophy*, 9(1) (Spring), 53–74

Hamermesh, D.S., 1989. 'Labour Demand and the Structure of Adjustment Costs', *American Economic Review*, 79(4), 674–89

Johansen, L., 1961. *Production Economics*, Amsterdam: North-Holland

Johnes, G., 1988. 'Shake-outs and Shake-ins of Labour: an Example of the Riemann–Hugouiot Catastrophe?', *Indian Economic Journal*, 36, 24–9

Nelson, R.R. and Winter, S.G., 1982. *An Evolutionary Theory of Economic Change*, Cambridge, MA and London: Harvard University Press

Oi, W., 1962. 'Labour as a Quasi-Fixed Factor', *Journal of Political Economy*, 70, 538–55

8 Models of the range of equilibria

Ian McDonald

Introduction

An important contribution of the theory of the natural rate of unemployment is to show that a major influence on the actual rate of inflation is the expected rate of inflation. The high rates of inflation experienced in the 1970s and the 1980s in many industrialised capitalist economies would be hard, maybe impossible, to explain without the idea that the expected rate of inflation influences the actual rate. In the 1970s and the 1980s people expected the price level to increase and this expectation influenced their actions in setting wages and prices, thus ensuring that the price level did increase.

The weakness of the theory of the natural rate of unemployment is its postulate of a unique equilibrium rate of unemployment. The behaviour of inflation at high rates of unemployment is inconsistent with a unique equilibrium rate of unemployment and thus with the theory of the natural rate of unemployment. Instead there appears to be a range of equilibrium rates of unemployment. This chapter records some empirical evidence which suggests the existence of a range of equilibrium rates of unemployment and then discusses how customer market analysis and theories of involuntary unemployment can yield a reasonable model of the range of equilibria. A crucial requirement of a reasonable model is an acyclic pattern of real wages.

The remainder of this chapter is organised into five sections. In the second section empirical evidence which suggests the existence of a range of equilibrium unemployment rates is presented for a number of countries. In the third section customer market analysis, one of the two theoretical mechanisms from which a range of equilibria can be derived, is explained. However in a satisfactory theory of the range of equilibria there must be involuntary unemployment and there must not be a strong procyclic or countercyclic pattern of real wages. The remainder of the chapter discusses models of the range of equilibrium unemployment rates in the light of these two requirements. In the fourth section theories of trade union behaviour are

101

discussed and in the fifth section theories of unvoluntary unemployment which do not rely on the existence of trade unions are discussed. In these two sections a second theoretical mechanism from which a range of equilibrium unemployment rates can be derived, the Bhaskar theory of wage relativities, is discussed. A sixth and final section concludes the chapter.

Some empirical evidence on the range of equilibria

According to the theory of the natural rate of unemployment, a rate of unemployment greater than the natural rate should exert downward pressure on the rate of inflation. High unemployment, according to the natural rate theory, should reduce the rate of inflation below the expected rate of inflation. Assuming that the expected rate of inflation declines with the actual rate of inflation, either because the expected rate of inflation follows an error-learning mechanism or because the lower actual rate of inflation is foreseen, high unemployment should cause a decreasing rate of inflation. In practice the proposition that high unemployment causes decreasing inflation is contradicted by a large number of counter-examples. It is true that episodes have occurred where high unemployment reduces inflation. The empirical problem for the natural rate theory is that in many cases the rate of inflation has stopped decreasing even when the rate of unemployment has remained high. The tendency for high unemployment to cause decreasing inflation is, in practice, temporary. It disappears. The temporary nature of this tendency is inconsistent with the theory of the natural rate of unemployment.

Figures 8.1–8.4 show the inflation and unemployment experience of the last 30 years for four OECD economies (US, UK, Germany and Australia). In each of these countries a fall in the rate of inflation in the early 1980s was associated with a rise in the rate of unemployment. But as the rate of unemployment stopped increasing, the rate of inflation stopped decreasing. In each of these countries there was a year when inflation had stopped decreasing even although the rate of unemployment was high. These years were 1983 for the US, 1984 for the UK, 1985 for Germany and 1984–5 for Australia.

The temporary effect of high unemployment in causing decreasing inflation is evident in data on inflation and unemployment for many different times in many countries. Consider, for example, the data used by Phillips in his paper on the Phillips curve (Phillips, 1958). This data was for wage inflation and unemployment in the UK from 1860 to 1957. As shown by that data, in the UK from 1860 to 1957 there were periods in which unemployment rose to high rates. In each case the rate of inflation stopped decreasing while the rate of unemployment was high. These years were 1867, 1878, 1885, 1893, 1901, 1907 and 1921.

% change in GNP deflator

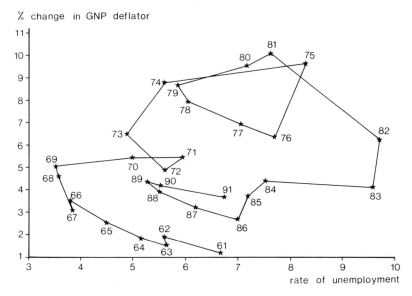

Figure 8.1 Inflation and unemployment, US, 1961–91
Source: *OECD, Economic Outlook*, extracted from *Data Express*

% change in GNP deflator

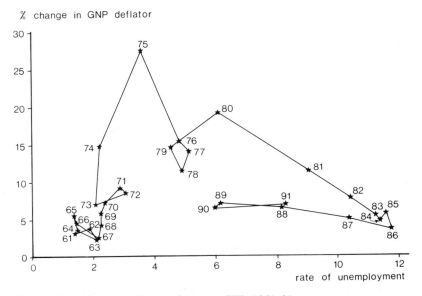

Figure 8.2 Inflation and unemployment, UK, 1961–91
Source: OECD, *Economic Outlook*, extracted from *Data Express*

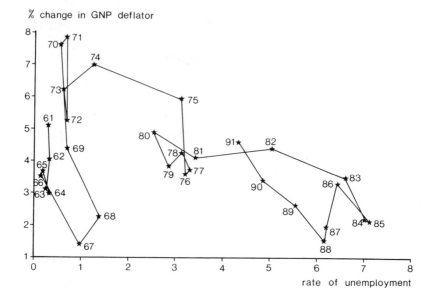

Figure 8.3   Inflation and unemployment, Germany, 1961–91
Source: OECD, *Economic Outlook*, extracted from *Data Express*

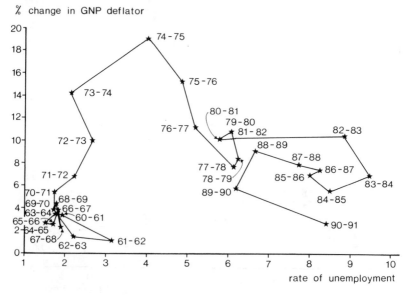

Figure 8.4   Inflation and unemployment, Australia, 1960/1–1990/1
Source: Australian Bureau of Statistics, *Australian National Accounts, National Income and Expenditure* (June 1992), cat. no. 5206.0

rate of unemployment

Figure 8.5   Unemployment, UK, 1860–1991
Sources: 1860–1965: Feinstein (1972)
1966–91: OECD, *Economic Outlook*, extracted from *Data Express*

The highest rates of unemployment experienced by most industrialised capitalist economies occurred in the interwar period, 1918–39. Furthermore, in this period extremely high rates of unemployment persisted for long periods of time. The UK suffered from high unemployment throughout the 1920s and the 1930s. Norway suffered from high unemployment in the latter half of the 1920s and throughout the 1930s. Other economies did better in the 1920s but suffered very high rates of unemployment throughout the 1930s. Data on inflation for the interwar period for the 13 industrialised capitalist economies reported in Maddison (1991) provides strong evidence supporting the proposition that the effect of high unemployment in causing decreasing inflation is temporary. Given the severity and the persistence of high rates of unemployment in the interwar period, if the proposition of a temporary effect of unemployment in causing decreasing inflation was not true then it is most likely to be contradicted by the evidence from the interwar period. In fact the evidence from the interwar period does not contradict the proposition of a temporary effect.

Figure 8.5 shows that, for the UK, the interwar period was characterised by the highest rates of unemployment over the period 1860–1991. Furthermore the period of high unemployment between the wars was much longer than the other periods of high unemployment. Before the First World War, the business cycles were characterised by periods of high

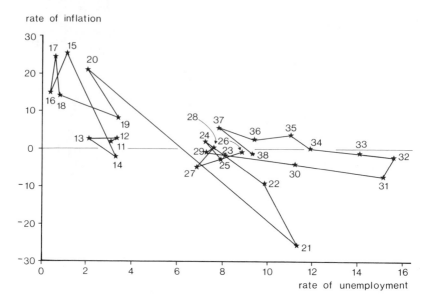

Figure 8.6   Inflation and unemployment, UK, 1911–38
Source: Consumer price index: Phelps Brown and Hopkins (1950)
        Unemployment: Feinstein (1972)

unemployment of three or four years. By contrast, the interwar period was characterised by 20 years of high unemployment, from 1921 to 1940. In this interwar period there was plenty of time for high rates of unemployment to cause decreasing inflation. However they did not. As figure 8.6 shows the rate of inflation in the 1920s and the 1930s in the UK shows no tendency to be decreasing. The high negative rate of inflation in 1921 is followed for the rest of the 1920s and the 1930s by rates of inflation close to zero. It is not the case in this period that the rate of inflation was decreasing whenever the rate of unemployment was high. Instead there are many years when the rate of unemployment was high and the rate of inflation was not decreasing. No persistent effect of high unemployment to cause decreasing inflation can be detected.

Of other industrialised countries, Norway is closest to the UK in experiencing high rates of unemployment in the 1920s and the 1930s. As figure 8.7 shows for Norway, this experience of 13 years of high unemployment (1926–38) did not cause decreasing inflation.

Figures 8.8–8.18 show the interwar experience of inflation and unemployment for the 11 other economies reported in Maddison (1991). These economies did not share the experience of the UK and Norway of high rates of unemployment for most of the 1920s. They all did experience high rates

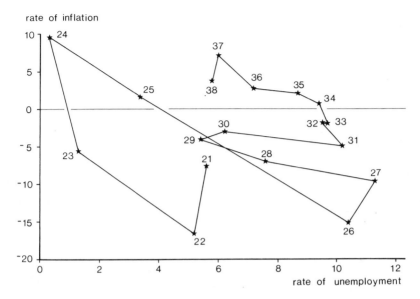

Figure 8.7   Inflation and unemployment, Norway, 1921–38
Source: Maddison (1991)

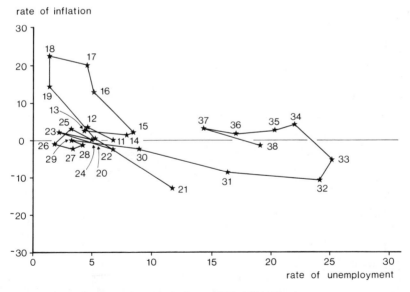

Figure 8.8   Inflation and unemployment, US, 1911–38
Sources: Consumer prices: Maddison (1991)
            Unemployment: Lebergott (1964)

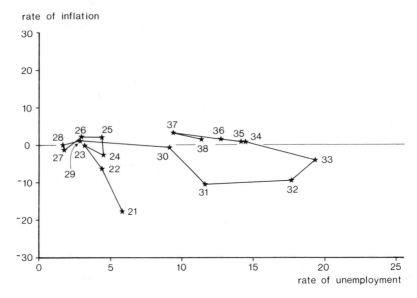

Figure 8.9   Inflation and unemployment, Canada, 1921–38
Source: Maddison (1991)

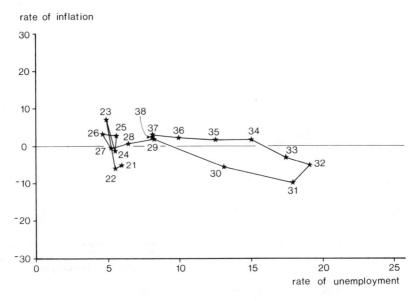

Figure 8.10   Inflation and unemployment, Australia, 1921–38
Source: Maddison (1991)

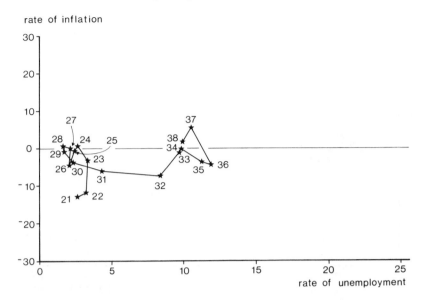

Figure 8.11   Inflation and unemployment, Netherlands, 1921–38
Source: Maddison (1991)

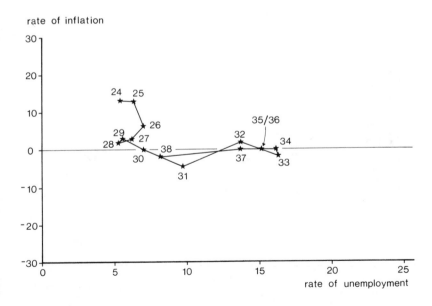

Figure 8.12   Inflation and unemployment, Austria, 1924–38
Source: Maddison (1991)

rate of inflation

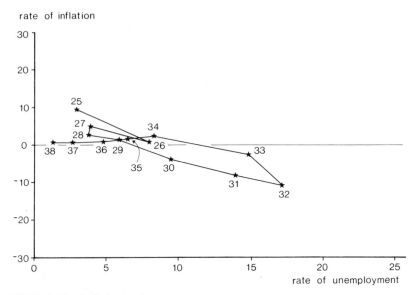

Figure 8.13   Inflation and unemployment, Germany, 1925–38
Source: Maddison (1991)

rate of inflation

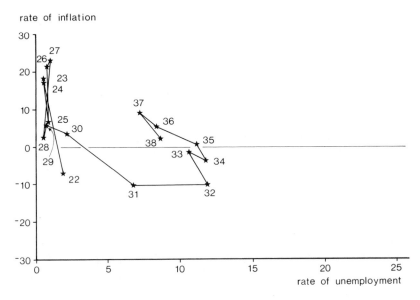

Figure 8.14   Inflation and unemployment, Belgium, 1922–38
Source: Maddison (1991)

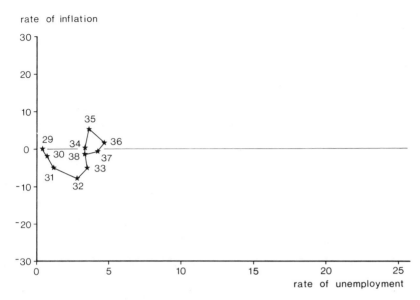

Figure 8.15   Inflation and unemployment, Switzerland, 1929–38
Source: Maddison (1991)

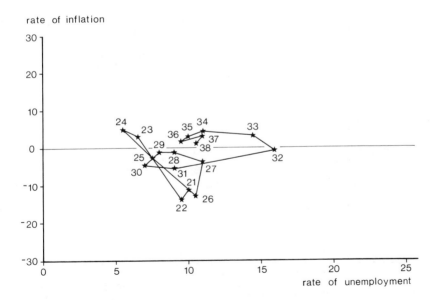

Figure 8.16   Inflation and unemployment, Denmark, 1921–38
Source: Maddison (1991)

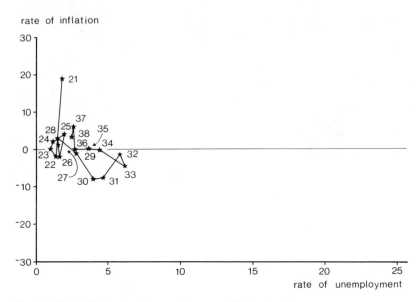

Figure 8.17   Inflation and unemployment, Finland, 1921–38
Source: Maddison (1991)

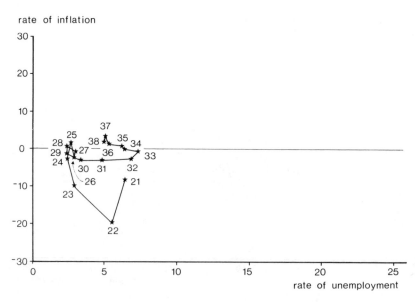

Figure 8.18   Inflation and unemployment, Sweden, 1921–38
Source: Maddison (1991)

of unemployment in the 1930s for, with the exception of Germany, periods of at least 8 years. In none of these countries was the rate of inflation decreasing throughout the 1930s.

The inconsistency of the experience of inflation and unemployment in the 1930s with the theory of the natural rate of unemployment has been commented on before. Rees (1970) took Lucas and Rapping (1969) to task for applying their natural rate model to the 1930s depression in the US. Further empirical investigation of their model (in Lucas and Rapping, 1972) revealed that '[B]y 1934 . . . actual wages and prices had returned to their normal levels', implying that 'in 1934 the unemployment rate should have been at its 1929 or 1930 level, as opposed to the observed 22 percent level . . . [the] theory continues to "miss" for the remainder of the depression years' (Lucas and Rapping, 1972, p. 190). Gordon (1988, p. 272) in describing the pattern of the price level in the US in the 1930s concluded 'A low level of output did not exert continuing downward pressure on the inflation rate'. Gordon argues that the European experience in the 1980s is similar.

It might be argued that the effect of high unemployment in causing decreasing inflation occurs with a lag. For example, Sachs and Larrain (1993, p. 72) say 'In the short run, the wage adjustment is too slow to ensure full employment, but in the long run, wages eventually adjust by enough to re-establish full employment and the classical equilibrium'. However the evidence cited here does not support this view. The evidence cited here suggests that the rate of adjustment of wages and prices slows down during a period of persistent unemployment, indeed the adjustment stops, rather than speeds up. Lucas and Rapping (1972) found their model of the natural rate was in closer conformity with the facts in the early years of the interwar depression than in the latter years.

Models of the natural rate of unemployment have the property that product and labour markets can be in equilibrium at any rate of inflation. This proposition uses the concept of the expected rate of inflation. In equilibrium the expected rate of inflation supports the actual rate of inflation. Thus the natural rate theory implies that the size of the rate of inflation cannot be used as an indicator of whether the economy is in equilibrium. Instead the change in the rate of inflation is suggested by the theory of the natural rate of unemployment as an indicator of equilibrium. A constant rate of inflation is a sign of equilibrium. Applying this idea to the inflation–unemployment experiences described above suggests that economies have been in product and labour market equilibrium at a variety of rates of unemployment. This variety of rates has included rates of unemployment as high as 20%. The deficiency of the theory of the natural rate of unemployment is its property of a unique equilibrium rate of

consumption real wage

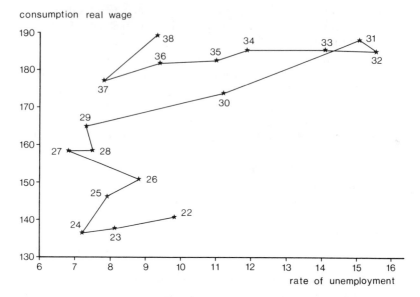

Figure 8.19   The consumption real wage and unemployment, UK, 1922–38
Sources: Consumption real wage: Phelps Brown and Hopkins (1950)
               Unemployment: Feinstein (1972)

unemployment A more realistic theory would replace the unique equilibrium rate of unemployment with a range of equilibrium rates of unemployment.[1]

There is a large empirical literature investigating the cyclic behaviour of real wages. The conclusion of this literature is that real wages are acyclic. This literature fails to find a strong and consistent procyclic or countercyclic pattern to real wages. Some studies find a mild procyclic pattern, some studies an acyclic pattern and other studies a mild countercyclic pattern. A reasonable description of these results is that real wages are roughly acyclic. A dramatic example of this acyclic behaviour of real wages is in figure 8.19, which shows data on real wages for the UK for the period 1922–38. The worsening of the depression in 1929 to 1931 did increase real wages. The following six years of very high rates of unemployment were associated with little change in real wages, even although the rate of unemployment fell by about 10 percentage points. It was argued above that the unchanging rate of inflation in these years suggest that they were years of equilibrium in the product and labour markets. A feature of these equilibria, shown by figure 8.19, is an acyclic real wage.

A reasonable macroeconomic model must be able to explain a wide range of rates of unemployment which are consistent with an unchanging rate of inflation and an unchanging real wage. This criterion will be used below to assess various models of the range of equilibria.

Customer market analysis

The microeconomic foundations

A range of equilibrium rates of unemployment can be derived from customer market analysis. This derivation depends on customer market analysis implying price stickiness, specifically that, for a profit maximising firm, a particular selling price is consistent with a range of values of marginal cost. In this section the microeconomics of customer market analysis are explained.

The crucial characteristic of a customer market is that the frequency of search by purchasers is low relative to the frequency of purchase. For a market in which the frequency of search is relatively low, the term 'customer market' is a most appropriate description. The defining characteristic of a customer is a predisposition to return to a supplier for his or her next purchase. Someone who searches before each purchase would not be aptly described as a customer.

In the literature the phrase 'customer market' appears to be associated most often with the work of Okun, especially Okun (1981), and with Phelps, especially Phelps and Winter (1970) and Phelps (1985). In Okun (1981) the term 'customer market' is applied where a continuing relation between a buyer and a seller exists. While it is not clear exactly what mechanism of price determination Okun had in mind, he emphasised the idea that sellers would tread carefully to avoid upsetting customers and in particular would refrain from those price increases which customers would regard as 'price gouging'.

Phelps and Winter (1970) developed a formal model in which the size of a firm's clientele responds gradually to the price set by the firm. However in the model of Phelps and Winter there is no price stickiness. The Phelps and Winter model is symmetric, in that the function connecting the rate of change of the clientele to price has a continuous first derivative. There is no break in the first derivative at the point of a constant size of clientele and from this property it follows that there is no price stickiness. Sibly (1992c, ch. 2) has pointed out that the symmetric nature of the Phelps and Winter model rests on a flawed description of the behaviour of customers. In the Phelps and Winter model the behaviour of a customer does not allow a reasonable role for the customer's memory. Consider the behaviour of a customer following an increase in price by the firm patronised by that customer. Before switching to a new supplier the customer, in the Phelps and Winter model, has to wait until he or she happens to hear of a firm offering a better price. This requirement that all customers have to wait to hear of a beter price does not sit well with the description in the Phelps and Winter model of how people receive information about prices. In the model information is received continuously at a rate determined exogenously. 'Customers learn of prices . . . only through "word of mouth" . . . [they] meet at random and compare notes on prices when they do meet' (Sibly, 1992c, p. 20). It would be more in keeping with the assumption of the model that customers receive information about prices continuously to assume that, when a firm raises its price its customers will remember information received earlier about prices of other firms and that at least some of these customers will switch to another firm immediately. By contrast, if a firm lowers its price, the lower price, being new information, will not generate an immediate increase in the firm's clientele. All potential customers will have to 'wait' until they hear, through the random, word of mouth mechanism, of the price decrease. By making the unreasonable assumption of memory-less customers, the Phelps and Winter model is symmetric with respect to price increases and price decreases and does not predict price stickiness. Sibly (1992a) shows how the word of mouth process of information acquisition can cause price stickiness when the memory of a customer is allowed for.

The idea that search is infrequent relative to purchase has been developed in a number of publications. The earliest systematic analysis appears to have been by Scitovsky (1952, pp. 272–81), who also pointed out the implication of sticky prices. In McDonald (1991a) the seller, described as a shop, sells many products and chooses prices to maximise profits over an infinite time horizon. Pricing strategies by shops in which prices can vary over the infinite time horizon are not allowed. Sibly (1992a) shows that variable price strategies are not profit maximising and thereby gives an underpinning for the assumption of a fixed price strategy. In the McDonald (1991a) model purchasers are assumed to search at potential suppliers at an exogenously determined frequency. Sibly (1992b) develops a model in which the frequency of search is determined by the speed at which uncertainty about the price charged by an alternative supplier increases. An additional explanation of the timing of search arises when search costs vary over time. For example travellers enrolled in a frequent-flyer programme may plan to search other airlines immediately after using up their accumulated points.[2]

A firm selling in a customer market will be selling a large part of its output to people who have bought from it previously. Furthermore the firm will not receive a large number of enquiries about its price from people who are purchasing from other firms. An increase in price by this firm will be noticed

price

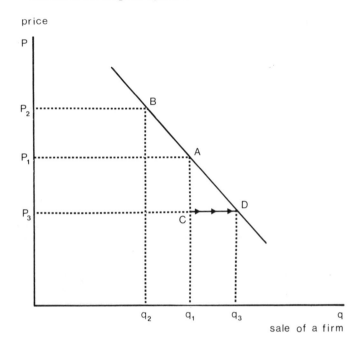

Figure 8.20   The behaviour of demand for a firm selling in a customer market

immediately by its customers. Some of these customers, having noticed the higher price, will be induced to look around at other firms. The price rise will jolt them into searching. The firm will quickly experience a decline in its sales. On the other hand, a reduction in price by this firm will cause a much slower response of sales. Buyers at other firms, because they do not visit this firm, will hear about the lower price only gradually, as the word gets around. The initial response to the reduction in price will be limited to any increase in purchases by existing customers, which will be very small, and to the purchases from people who happen to be searching that firm at the time of the price reduction, which will also be very small.

The response of customers to price changes by a firm selling in a customer market is illustrated in figures 8.20 and 8.21. Up to time t_1 the firm is charging a price of P_1 and selling q_1 units of output. At time t_1 if the firm raises its prices to P_2 sales adjust immediately to the level q_2 shown at point B in figure 8.20. The path of sales following this increase in price is shown in figure 8.21 as ABF with the vertical drop of AB at time t_1. On the other hand, if at time t_1 the firm lowers its price from P_1 to P_3 sales will increase only gradually as the news of a lower price gets around. In figure 8.20 price and quantity will follow the path ACD, with the drop from A to C being

sales of a firm

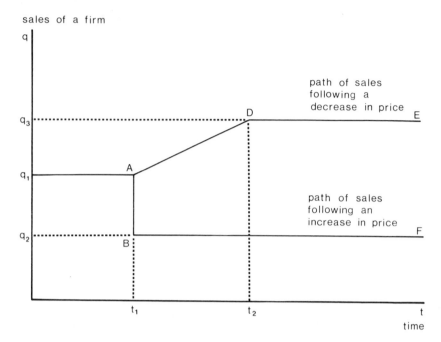

Figure 8.21   The time path of sales following a change in price for a firm selling in a customer market

instantaneous. In figure 8.21 the upward sloping segment AD shows the gradual increase in sales. At time t_2 all potential customers who were purchasing from other firms will have found out about the lower price and will have switched to this firm. This firm's sales has reached the higher level of q_3, at which level the sales remain.

The different response rates of customers to price increases and price decreases leads to a discontinuous marginal revenue curve, as shown in figure 8.22. The discontinuity in the marginal revenue curve is at the initial level of sales. The extra revenue earned from an increase in sales to one unit greater than the initial level, labelled mr^+ in figure 8.22, is less by a discrete amount than the revenue lost by a decrease in sales to one unit less than the initial level, labelled mr^- in figure 8.22.

Why a differential response rate in sales causes the marginal revenue curve to be discontinuous, that is to have a vertical section, can be seen with the aid of figure 8.23. From an initial combination of P_1 and q_1 imagine price is reduced to P_3. In a non-customer market sales would increase immediately to the level q_3. Imagine for simplicity that there are just two periods, this week and next week. The extra revenue, if the increase in sales

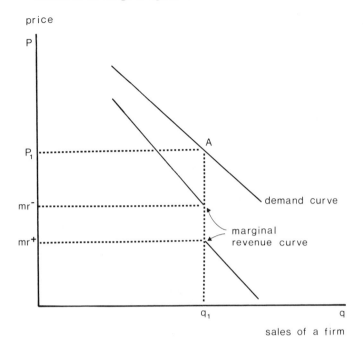

price

Figure 8.22   The discontinuous marginal revenue curve

is immediate, is $(P_3 q_3 - P_1 q_1)$ in each of the two periods, adding up to an increase in total revenue of $2(P_3 q_3 - P_1 q_1)$. Now, to allow for a customer market effect, imagine the increase in sales is slow. In the first period sales increase to q_4 as shown in figure 8.23 and in the second period sales increase further to q_3. Extra revenue in the first period is $(P_3 q_4 - P_1 q_1)$ and in the second period extra revenue is $(P_3 q_3 - P_1 p_1)$. Thus the increase in total revenue is $P_3(q_3 + q_4) - 2P_1 q_1$. Marginal revenue, being expressed as a flow per period, is the increase in total revenue divided by 2. With an immediate increase in sales to q_3, the non-customer market case, marginal revenue is

$$mr^+ \text{(non-customer market)} = P_3 q_3 - P_1 q_1 \qquad (1)$$

and with the slow increase in sales, the customer market case, marginal revenue is

$$mr^+ \text{(customer market)} = \frac{P_3 q_3 + P_3 q_4}{2} - P_1 q_1. \qquad (2)$$

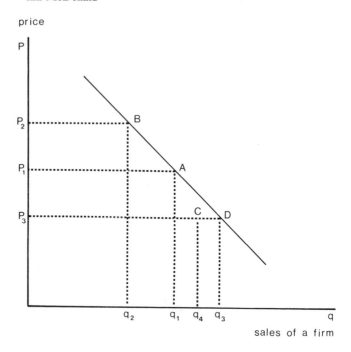

Figure 8.23   Why the marginal revenue curve for a firm selling in a customer market is discontinuous

Subtracting (2) from (1), gives

$$mr^+ \text{(non-customer market)} - mr^+ \text{(customer market)} = \frac{P_3(q_3 - q_4)}{2} \quad (3)$$

which is positive because q_4 is less than q_3. Therefore, given that the marginal revenue curve in a non-customer market is continuous, in a customer market the marginal revenue curve is discontinuous.

A discontinuous marginal revenue curve will create price stickiness, in that a change in marginal cost or demand may cause no change in profit maximising price. This stickiness of price is illustrated in figures 8.24 and 8.25. In figure 8.24 the impact of changes in marginal cost is illustrated. The initial position of the marginal cost curve is mc_1. This curve, mc_1, intersects the marginal revenue curve at the level of output of q_1, implying that the output q_1 sold at a price P_1 is the profit maximising combination of quantity and price. Now imagine there is a downward shift in the marginal cost curve from mc_1 to mc_2. If we think of the firm under consideration as a retailer then a reduction in the wholesale price, the price the retailer pays for

price

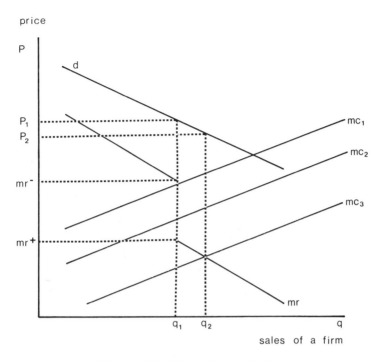

Figure 8.24   Price stickiness with shifts in the marginal cost curve

supplies of the product to be sold, will cause a significant downward shift of
the marginal cost curve. In practice the amounts paid by retailers to
wholesalers account for about 80% of the marginal cost of retailers. With
the marginal cost curve of mc_2 the profit maximising level of output and
price remains at q_1 and P_1 because the marginal cost curve, mc_2, intersects
the marginal revenue curve within the discontinuity. In this case the retail
price is sticky. A larger fall in the marginal cost curve to mc_3 will lead to a
lower price. The marginal cost curve mc_3 intersects the marginal revenue
curve at the level of output q_2 which is greater than q_1. If wholesale price fell
by an amount sufficient to generate the marginal cost curve of mc_3 then the
retailer would be induced to cut price and await the gradual increase in
sales.

As shown by figure 8.24 changes in marginal cost can occur which have
no effect on the profit maximising price of output. For any marginal cost
curve that lies in the range of mr^+ to mr^- at the level of output of q_1, the
profit maximising price is P_1. This price stickiness does not arise in the
conventional theory of the firm in which the marginal revenue curve is
continuous.

price

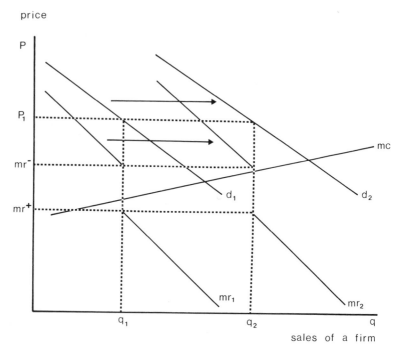

Figure 8.25   Price stickiness with shifts in the demand curve

It can also be shown that, with a discontinuous marginal revenue curve, a change in demand can leave the profit maximising price of output unaffected. Consider figure 8.25. The initial demand curve is d_1 with a discontinuous marginal revenue curve of mr_1. At this initial level of demand the profit maximising level of output is q_1 and the profit maximising price is P_1. An increase in demand caused by, for example, an expansionary aggregate demand policy which raises people's disposable incomes, will shift the demand curve to d_2 and the marginal revenue curve to mr_2. The discontinuity now occurs at the level of output of q_2. The marginal cost curve intersects the marginal revenue curve within the discontinuity at the level of output q_2, implying that the increase in demand has led to an increase in output with no change in profit maximising price.

In deriving the discontinuous marginal revenue curve, the possibility that the retailer will advertise a decrease in price has been ignored. By advertising a decrease in price a firm will speed up the increase in sales and reduce, maybe eliminate, the discontinuity in the marginal revenue curve. However advertising will introduce a discontinuity on the cost side. While it may be profitable to advertise a decrease in price, it does not pay to advertise a price increase. Because of this asymmetry the property of sticky prices would not be overturned by including advertising in the analysis. Sibly (1992c, ch. 6) analyses the effects of advertising on the degree of price stickiness in a customer market.

Empirical evidence which supports the price stickiness predicted by customer markets has been found by a number of investigators. Some of the literature is reviewed briefly in McDonald (1990, ch. 4). It is a general characteristic of prices that retail prices fluctuate less than wholesale or producer prices. The relatively smaller fluctuations in retail prices are consistent with customer market analysis, as suggested by the analysis using figure 8.24.

A model of the size of the discontinuity in the marginal revenue curve

An expression which determines the size of the discontinuity in the marginal revenue curve can be derived in the following way.

Consider a retailer selling one good (the more complicated case of a retailer selling many types of goods is shown to yield a similar equation determining the size of the discontinuity in the marginal revenue curve in McDonald, 1991a). Let $\{n_0, P_0\}$ denote the size of the initial clientele and the initial price. Assume n_0 is the equilibrium number of customers given the initial price, i.e. $n_0 = n(P_0)$ where the function $n(P)$ determines the number of customers in equilibrium. It is assumed that $n'(P_0) < 0$. For $P < P_0$, a price reduction, the gradual increase in the size of the clientele is assumed to be described by

$$n_t = n_0 + (n(P) - n_0)t/T \qquad \text{for } 0 \le t \le T \qquad (4a)$$

and,

$$n_t = n(P) \qquad \text{for } t \ge T \qquad (4b)$$

where t stands for time and T is the length of time taken for the size of the clientele to reach its new equilibrium size following a decline in retail price. For a price increase, $P \ge P_0$, the reduction in the size of the clientele to the new equilibrium size is assumed to occur instantly and so

$$n = n(P) \qquad (5)$$

Assume that the price paid by the shopkeeper for the good, called the wholesale price or the producer price and denoted P^w, is the only component of the retailer's marginal cost. Furthermore assume that the retailer's actions are determined by maximising profits over an infinite time horizon. Then it can be shown (using equations (5) and (7) in McDonald and Spindler, 1987) that the size of the discontinuity in the marginal revenue curve is, using the mr^+ and mr^- notation of figure 8.22:

$$\frac{mr^+}{mr^-} = \frac{[(1 + X)(\varepsilon^c - 1) + \varepsilon^n](\varepsilon^c + \varepsilon^n)}{[(1 + X)(\varepsilon^c + \varepsilon^n)](\varepsilon^c + \varepsilon^n - 1)} \tag{6}$$

where ε^c is the elasticity taken positively of each customer's demand for the good with respect to the retail price (all customers are assumed to have identical demand functions), ε^n is the elasticity taken positively of the equilibrium size of the clientele with respect to the retail price (i.e. the elasticity of the function $n(P)$), $X = (n_0/n(P))(rT - 1 + e^{-rT})/(1 - e^{-rT})$ and r is the retailer's rate of discount.

The customer market effect, that is the slow buildup of the size of the clientele in response to a decrease in retail price, is captured by the parameter X. If there is no customer market effect then $T = 0$ and $X = 0$ (strictly speaking, as $T \to 0$, $X \to 0$), implying by (6) that, in keeping with a non-customer market, $mr^+/mr^- = 1$. For $rT > 0$ it follows that $X > 0$ and $mr^+/mr^- < 1$. The slower the buildup of clientele in response to a decrease in retail price and /or the greater the retailer's rate of discount, the larger is the size of the discontinuity in the marginal revenue curve.

The parameter T can be related to the frequency with which a potential customer checks the retail prices offered by each potential supplier. For example if each potential customer checks the offers of all potential suppliers once a year then T is equal to one year. Any retailer will, after maintaining a lower price for one year, have been checked by all potential customers and will have achieved the new equilibrium size of clientele as given by $n = n(P)$.

In this model, if the elasticity of clientele with respect to retail price is infinite then the discontinuity disappears, even if $rT > 0$. However the presumption that retailers have some market power and thus face an $\varepsilon^n < \infty$ is reasonable. Spatial considerations alone suggest $\varepsilon^n < \infty$.

Customer markets and a range of equilibrium rates of voluntary unemployment

The stickiness of prices expected for a customer market implies, at the macroeconomic level, a range of equilibrium rates of unemployment. The easiest way to see this is to divide the firms of an economy up into two groups, retailers and producers. The producers employ labour and sell their output to retailers at the wholesale price, labelled P^W. The retailers sell this output to customers at the retail price, P. Retailers sell in customer markets. which means that customers tend to patronise particular retailers. The effect of retailing in customer markets is that the retail price is sticky relative to the wholesale price. The discontinuity in the marginal revenue curve implies a range of wholesale prices consistent in equilibrium with a particular retail price. Thus the ratio of retail to wholesale prices will lie somewhere within a range of values.

Assuming, for simplicity, that producers are perfectly competitive in selling to retailers, producers will set employment at the level where wholesale price (P^w) times the marginal product of labour (MPL) is equal to the money wage (wP). w is the consumption real wage, the real wage in terms of consumer purchasing power. P is the retail price. From this behaviour at the level of individual firms, at the aggregate level the profit maximising employment level is determined by the condition

$$P^w MPL = wP. \tag{7}$$

Workers in supplying labour are concerned about retail prices, the prices they have to pay for the goods they consume. The real wage which determines people's labour supply decision is the money wage deflated by P. The condition for the profit maximising level of employment, (7), can be expressed in terms of the consumption real wage (w) by dividing both sides by P. This gives

$$w = MPL \times \left(\frac{P^w}{P}\right). \tag{8}$$

In figure 8.26 two curves of $MPL \times (P^w/P)$ are shown. One of them, labelled $MPL \times (P^w/P)_{\text{MIN}}$, is based on the ratio of wholesale to retail prices being at its minimum possible level. This occurs if, for each retailer, the marginal cost curve intersects the marginal revenue curve at the bottom of the discontinuity, that is at mr^+ in figure 8.24. Also, shown on figure 8.26 are the SPL curve, the supply price of labour curve, and the VL curve. The latter curve determines the number of people in the labour force who are voluntarily unemployed at any moment in time. The horizontal distance between the VL curve and the SPL curve determines the voluntarily chosen level of unemployment. Notice that, as drawn in figure 8.26, the distance between the VL curve and the SPL curve decreases as the real wage increases. This reflects the presumption that people choose to be unemployed less frequently and for shorter periods if the real wage, the opportunity cost of unemployment, is high. With the ratio of wholesale to retail prices of $(P^w/P)_{\text{MIN}}$ the level of full employment can be seen in figure 8.26 to be L_1^{FE}, the size of the labour force is N_1 and the equilibrium level of unemployment is $(N_1 - L_1^{FE})$. This level of unemployment is an

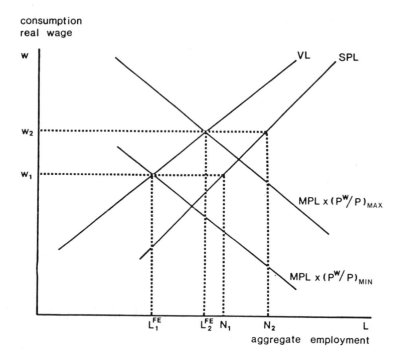

Figure 8.26   The range of equilibria with a competitive labour market

equilibrium level because it is the amount of unemployment chosen voluntarily at the equilibrium real wage of w_1.

Now imagine an expansion in aggregate demand that shifts the demand curves facing each retailer to the right. To keep things simple assume that this expansion in demand is an increase in government spending, spread across the retailers. The high demand increases sales and the retailers buy more from the producers. This pushes up the wholesale prices. Assume that the demand expansion is of the size which leads to the marginal cost curve at each shop intersecting the marginal revenue curve at the top of the discontinuity, at mr^- in figure 8.24. Under this assumption retail prices are not changed but the ratio of wholesale to retail prices increases to $(P^w/P)_{MAX}$. This increase will shift the $MPL \times (P^w/P)$ curve to $MPL \times (P^w/P)_{MAX}$ in figure 8.26. The new level of full employment will be L_2^{FE} with an equilibrium level of unemployment of $N_2 - L_2^{FE}$ and an equilibrium real wage of w_2. The equilibrium real wage being higher than the initial wage, the equilibrium level of unemployment is lower.

The two equilibrium levels of unemployment shown in figure 8.26 are the largest $(N_1 - L_1^{FE})$ and the smallest $(N_2 - L_2^{FE})$. All the other equilibrium

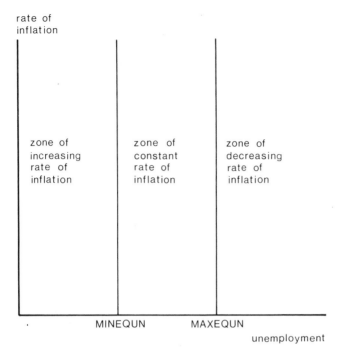

Figure 8.27   Inflation and the range of equilibria

levels of unemployment will lie in between these two bounds. A smaller increase in aggregate demand would have caused a smaller increase in the price ratio (P^w/P), a smaller upward shift in $MPL \times (P^w/P)$ and would have induced a smaller decrease in the equilibrium level of unemployment. Note that the size of the range of equilibrium rates of unemployment in this model depends on the slope of the VL curve relative to the slope of the SPL curve. The flatter the VL curve relative to the SPL curve, that is the larger the effect of the real wage on the rate of voluntary unemployment, the larger is the range of equilibrium rates of unemployment.

The Phillips curve with a range of equilibrium rates of unemployment

When the rate of unemployment is at an equilibrium rate there are no disequilibrium forces in the labour market tending to alter the rate of inflation. In figure 8.27 the long-run Phillips curve for the case of a range of equilibrium rates of unemployment is shown. For rates of unemployment between MINEQUN, the minimum equilibrium rate of unemployment (which would be the rate of unemployment generated by the level of

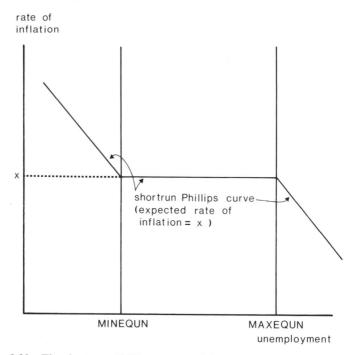

Figure 8.28   The short-run Phillips curve and the range of equilibria

unemployment of $N_2 - L_2^{FE}$ in figure 8.26, this rate arising if the price ratio (P^w/P) is at its maximum level) and MAXEQUN, the maxiumum equilibrium level of unemployment (generated when the price ratio (P^w/P) is at its minimum level inducing a level of unemployment equal to $N_1 - L_1^{FE}$ in figure 8.26) the rate of inflation is constant. If the rate of unemployment is pushed below MINEQUN then there will be an excess demand for labour which will lead to an increasing rate of inflation, while a rate of unemployment greater than MAXEQUN will lead to a decreasing rate of inflation.

The equilibrium rate of unemployment will not be disturbed by an inflationary environment. Suppose, for example, that retailers believe that their customers expect retail prices to rise by $x\%$. Then each retailer can raise his or her price by $x\%$ without dislodging any customers. Producers will be able to raise both wholesale prices and wages by $x\%$. Both real wages, that is w and wP/P^w, will remain constant, implying that the level of employment and the rate of unemployment remain constant. Of course, to maintain the level of output in an inflationary economy the nominal level of aggregate demand has to be increased to maintain the real level of aggregate demand at a constant level.

With a range of equilibrium unemployment rates the short-run Phillips curve will be horizontal within the range, between MINEQUN and MAXEQUN. In figure 8.28 a short-run Phillips curve based on an expected rate of inflation of $x\%$ is shown. It is horizontal at rates of unemployment in the range from MINEQUN and MAXEQUN and downward sloping outside of this range.

The theory of fluctuations in the rate of unemployment represented in figure 8.26 has two major deficiencies. Firstly, in this theory it is voluntary unemployment which fluctuates. In practice the fluctuations in unemployment appear to be of an involuntary nature. It is layoffs, not quits, which explain the rise in unemployment in recessions. Furthermore, in recessions people find it difficult to get jobs. Secondly, the theory suggests a fairly strong procyclical movement in real wages which is inconsistent with the acyclic behaviour observed in practice. As figure 8.19 shows, in the 1930s in the UK real wages did not fall. Nor, in the 1930s in the UK, does the non-decreasing rate of inflation suggest the existence of attempts by workers and firms to reduce wages. It is not the case that, in the 1930s, the exercise of market forces to reduce real wages through the bidding down of money wages was frustrated by a falling price level. Instead the real wage outcomes in the 1930s appear to be equilibrium outcomes and thus their lack of a strong procyclic pattern is not consistent with the theory represented in figure 8.26.

Subsequent sections of the chapter will discuss whether a satisfactory theory of the range of unemployment can be created with the help of some of the existing theories of involuntary unemployment. The discussion will use the mechanism, derived above from the determination of retail prices in customer markets, whereby changes in the level of aggregate demand can shift the marginal product of labour curve when drawn in consumption real wage/employment space. The theories of involuntary unemployment will be assessed by comparing the cyclic pattern of real wages predicted by each of these theories with the acyclic pattern observed in reality.

Trade unions and the cyclic behaviour of real wages

The theory of the economic behaviour of a trade union is based on the idea that the union aims to maximise an objective function. There are several ways of specifying this objective function. The exact specification will influence the cyclic behaviour of the real wage predicted by the theory. If the objective function includes the utility of unemployed union members then the wage will tend to be procyclic. If, on the other hand, the objective function does not include the utility of either the unemployed union members or the utility of members likely to become unemployed then the wage will tend to be acyclic. A union whose objective function includes the interests of the unemployed will be called an 'open trade union' whilst a union who only cares for members with secure employment will be called an 'insider-dominated trade union'.

The open trade union

The open trade union is assumed to give an equal weight to the interest of all its members, whether employed or unemployed, and to place no restrictions on the number of its members. It has an 'open-door' policy to new members in that the interest of the new members are given an equal weight with those of existing members. To specify this union's objective it is useful to follow the proposal of Layard and Nickell (1990) which applies the concepts of bargaining theory in Bishop (1964) and Binmore, Rubinstein and Wolinsky (1986) to the trade union and firm bargain. The union consists of m members. At the time of bargaining, n_0 are employed at the firm. The remaining $(m - n_0)$ are engaged in the best alternative to working at the firm, from which they receive a utility flow of $\bar{U}$. This alternative allows people to resume work at the firm if a job becomes available for them after a bargain is made. The alternative could be subsisting on unemployment benefits or working in a job which is considered inferior to working in the firm. After bargaining, the real wage in terms of consumer purchasing power at the firm is w and the level of employment is n. The $(m - n)$ members who fail to gain employment at the firm then turn to alternative activities from which they receive a utility flow of $\bar{U}$. These alternative activities may involve a period on unemployment benefits and the employment in an alternative job. Layard and Nickell (1990) implicitly assume that $\bar{U} = \bar{\bar{U}}$. Given this framework, the union's utility after bargaining is

$$W = n\{U(w) - D\} + (m - n)\bar{U} \qquad \text{for } n \leq m \qquad (9)$$

and

$$W = m\{U(w) - D\} \qquad \text{for } n > m$$

where D measures the disutility of work and $U()$ is the concave utility function of each member. It will be assumed that the level of demand is not high enough to cause $n \geq m$. If bargaining breaks down then there is no employment at the firm and the utility level to the union is $\bar{W}$, given by (with s representing income if on strike):

$$\bar{W} = n_0 U(s) + (m - n_0)\bar{U}. \qquad (10)$$

It is useful to define $U(x^O) = \bar{U} + D$, where x^O will be called 'layoff pay for the open trade union'; it refers to the income equivalent of not being employed by the firm after the completion of negotiations plus the disutility of work. By subtracting (10) from (9), the net payoff to the union is:

$$W - \bar{W} = n\{U(w) - U(x^O)\} + m(\bar{U} - \bar{\bar{U}}) + n_0[\bar{\bar{U}} - U(s)]. \quad (11)$$

It simplifies the subsequent analysis to assume, following Layard and Nickell (1990), that $\bar{U} = \bar{\bar{U}} = U(s)$. Making this assumption the net payoff to the union becomes simply the first term on the right-hand side of (11), that is, $n\{U(w) - U(x^O)\}$.

Three models of an open trade union can be distinguished. These are the simple monopoly union model, in which the union sets the wage, the right-to-manage or wage bargaining model, in which the union bargains with the firm over the wage, and the efficient bargains model, in which the union bargains with the firm over the wage and the level of employment. As shown in Creedy and McDonald (1991) (and, more briefly, in the appendix of this chapter, pp. 147–9) these three models predict the wage to be a mark-up over layoff pay, that is

$$w = k^O x^0 \quad (12)$$

where the size of k^O depends, in a particular way in each of the three models, on the nature of the union members' utility function, the firm's revenue function and the power of the union. If the union members' utility function and the firm's revenue function are both of constant elasticity then k^O is a constant. We will concentrate on a special version of this benchmark case in which the utility function is linear and the revenue function has constant elasticity. This special version stresses the important role of the cyclic behaviour of x^0 in determining the cyclic behaviour of real wages.

For the open union x^O is defined by $U(x^O) = \bar{U} + D$ where $\bar{U}$ is the utility flow of those who fail to gain employment at the firm after the wage bargain is concluded. To determine $\bar{U}$ follow the approach of Layard, Nickell and Jackman (1991, p. 145). Consider an unemployed worker. At the end of a period of unemployment the worker collects the unemployment benefit, which is set at the proportion b of the economy-wide real wage, w^A, and receives the benefits from household activities, the income equivalent of which is h. With probability $1/I$ the worker will get a job in the next period, where I is the expected duration of unemployment. If unsuccessful in getting a job the worker is unemployed in the next period with the same prospects as in the first period. Under these assumptions and writing V_e for the present value of a job, V_u, the present value of being unemployed, is given by

$$V_u = \frac{1}{1+r}[bw^A + h + I^{-1}V_e + (1 - I^{-1})V_u] \qquad (13)$$

where r is the discount rate. If the worker gets a job then the probability of losing the job and entering unemployment is $1/J$ where J is the expected duration of a job. Given this and assuming the real wage from the job attained is w^A, V_e is given by

$$V_e = \frac{1}{1+r}[w^A - D + J^{-1}V_u + (1 - J^{-1})V_e]. \qquad (14)$$

Substituting (14) into (13) and rearranging yields

$$x^0 = rV_u + D = \psi(h + D) + (1 - \psi(1 - b))w^A \qquad (15)$$

where

$$\psi = (r + J^{-1})/(r + J^{-1} + I^{-1}).$$

If, in the aggregate, the number of jobs acquired by the unemployed $(= (N - L)/I)$ is equal to the number of jobs vacated by the employed $(= L/J)$ then the rate of unemployment will be constant. By this reasoning, a constant rate of unemployment implies

$$I = \frac{u}{1-u}J \qquad (16)$$

where $u(= (N - L)/N)$ is the rate of unemployment. In what follows J is treated as exogenous. From this process of determination of I, it follows that:

$$\psi = \frac{r + J^{-1}}{r + (Ju)^{-1}}. \qquad (17)$$

According to the theories of the open trade union, (12) and (15) imply that the wage negotiated by a particular trade union is

$$w = k^O\{\psi(h + D) + (1 - \psi(1 - b))w^A\}. \qquad (18)$$

Assuming that all firms in the economy are identical and face identical unions, the economy-wide wage, w^A, will equal the wage negotiated by a particular union, w. Using $w^A = w$, (18) becomes

$$w = \frac{k^O\psi(h + D)}{1 - k^O(1 - \psi(1 - b))}. \qquad (19)$$

Using (17) to substitute out ψ, the relation between real wages and unemployment implied by the theory of the open trade union is

$$w = \frac{(h + D)}{[1 - b - (1 - (k^O)^{-1})(rJ + u^{-1})(rJ + 1)^{-1}]}. \qquad (20)$$

consumption
real wage

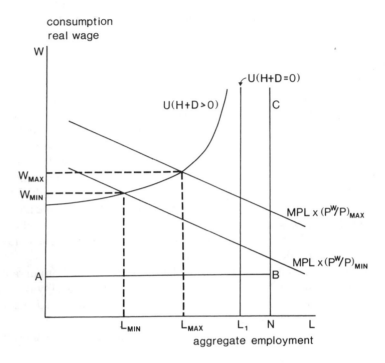

Figure 8.29 The range of equilibria and the cyclical pattern of real wages with an open trade union

We will call this relation the union wage schedule for the open trade union. If $(h + D)$ is positive then (20) determines a positive relation for the union wage schedule. In figure 8.29, the curve labelled $U(h + D > 0)$ depicts equation (20) with $(h + D) > 0$. This curve is concave from above, being flat at low levels of employment and approaching verticality as employment approaches a critical level. At levels of employment greater than this critical level, the ease with which those laid off can get a job induces a wage–wage spiral. The implied rate of unemployment is too low to act as a break on the wage demands of an open trade union. This critical level of employment is calculated by setting the denominator of the right-hand side of (20) to zero, solving for u, the rate of unemployment, and then, with this value of u and the value of the labour supply given by the vertical section of the supply price of labour curve, calculating the implied level of employment. Note that with $(h + D) > 0$ the supply price of labour curve has a right-angle shape. In figure 8.29 the example of the supply price of labour curve with $(h + D) > 0$ is shown by ABC.

Assuming that retail prices are determined in customer markets, consider the size of the range of equilibrium rates of unemployment and the cyclic nature of the behaviour of real wages. In figure 8.29 both of the two extreme labour demand curves, that is $MPL \times (P^w/P)_{MIN}$ and $MPL \times (P^w/P)_{MAX}$, intersect the $U(h + D > 0)$ curve in the relatively flat part of that curve. This implies a relatively large range of equilibrium rates of unemployment and a relatively small degree of procyclicality of the real wage. As argued on p. 114, this combination of outcomes is realistic. However, this is not the only possibility implied by the theory of the open trade union. Instead it is possible that the curve labelled $u(h + D > 0)$ is much lower relative to the labour demand curves than depicted in figure 8.29. For example, a reduction in the value of $(h + D)$ implies, by (20), a downward shift in the $U(h + D > 0)$ schedule which implies in turn that the two extreme labour demand curves intersect the $U(h + D > 0)$ curve on a steeper part of that curve. This would imply a smaller range of equilibrium rates of unemployment and a larger degree of procyclicality of the real wage.

With $(h + D) > 0$ the model suggests that the range of equilibrium rates of unemployment will be greater and the degree of procyclicality of real wages smaller the larger is h, D, b and k^o and the smaller is r and J. These results follow from (20) since differentiation of (20) shows that increasing the values of h, D, b, k^o or decreasing the values of r and J will shift the $U(h + D > 0)$ curve upwards.

In discussing a macroeconomic model with trade union wages setting, Layard, Nickell and Jackman say

Events which alter the price of consumption relative to value added have no effect on the level of equilibrium unemployment. They simply change the numeraire of the Nash maximand. The result is that unemployment is unaffected and wage earners bear the cost in proportion to their incomes . . . These results are very important because they deny the existence of 'real wage resistance' (Layard, Nickell and Jackman, 1991, p. 108).

In the framework here, the Layard, Nickell and Jackman result relies on assuming that $h + D = 0$, that is the sum of the value of household activities and the disutility of work is equal to zero. With $h + D = 0$ equation (20) becomes

$$u = \frac{k^o - 1}{[rJ(1 - bk^o) + (1 - b)k^o]} \tag{21}$$

and in this special case the theory of the open trade union determines a unique equilibrium rate of unemployment. This case implies, as shown in figure 8.29, where the vertical curve labelled $U(h + D = 0)$ depicts equation (21), that even with the shifts in the marginal product of labour in consumption real wage/employment space allowed by the existence of customer markets, the equilibrim rate of unemployment will be unique. It should be added that this case is inconsistent with the cyclical behaviour of inflation and real wages described on p. 114 above. With a unique equilibrium rate of unemployment determined by (21), a high rate of unemployment would cause decreasing inflation and would put downward pressure on real wages.

The model in this section yields a more realistic pattern of real wages and inflation if $h + D$ is assumed to be positive. Furthermore casual observation suggests that the the value of household activities and the disutility of work are indeed positive. However the analysis here has not analysed the determination of the values of h or D. An extension of the analysis to include this would be desirable.

The insider-dominated trade union

A number of authors, especially Oswald (1984), Lindbeck and Snower (1989), Blanchard and Summers (1986) and Carruth and Oswald (1987), have emphasised the idea that the union's objective is based on the utility of the employed 'insiders'. If the group of insiders corresponds to those in employment then, as discussed in McDonald and Solow (1984) and McDonald (1989), there is a 'travelling' kink in the indifference curve that is always at the current level of employment. A problem with this approach is that the travelling kink leads to somewhat irregular patterns of wage behaviour. For example, changes in the demand for labour can have large effects on wages with no effect on employment; such a pattern is not usually observed. Blanchard and Fischer (1989, pp. 448–51) provide an analysis which shows in a neat way how a union dominated by all employed insiders may agree to a very flexible real wage to maintain a rigid level of employment.

An alternative objective which while recognising the insider–outsider distinction, that is the dominance in wage determination of the interests of insiders over the interests of outsiders, does not imply large and irregular changes in real wages with little change in employment is based on a sub-group of the employed who face little risk of layoff, rather than on all those employed by the firm. This may be called the 'insider-dominated union' in contrast with the 'insider' model above. The model of the insider-dominated union is discussed in McDonald (1991b). One situation which will lead to an insider-dominated union is where layoffs are determined by seniority and union wage decisions are made by a median voter; see Oswald (1985) and Farber (1986). The objective for an insider-dominated union is the net gain from working of each of the identical members of the dominant inside group who face no risk of unemployment, that is:

$$W = U(w) - D. \tag{22}$$

This objective applies for all levels of employment greater than m^d, the size of the dominant insider group. It will be assumed that the bargained outcome yields employment levels greater than m^d. One case for which this assumption is guaranteed to hold is the median voter case with the franchise equal to the level of employment. If negotiations break down, each insider gets utility $U(s)$ and the objective function takes the value $\bar{W} = U(s)$. Thus the payoff to the insider-dominated union is given by:

$$W - \bar{W} = U(w) - D - U(s). \tag{23}$$

It is shown in McDonald (1991b) (see also Creedy and McDonald, 1991 and, more briefly, the appendix to this chapter, pp. 147–9) that the wage negotiated with an employer by an insider-dominated trade union can be expressed as a mark-up, k^I, over layoff pay for the insider-dominated trade union, x^I; that is

$$w = k^I x^I \tag{24}$$

where x^I is defined by $U(x^I) = U(s) + D$. Thus the cyclical behaviour of real wages depends, as in the case of an open trade union, on the cyclical behaviour of layoff pay. However the definition of layoff pay for the insider-dominated trade union differs from the definition of layoff pay for an open trade union. This difference yields a difference in the cyclic behaviour of the real wage.

When on strike an individual may receive the income equivalent of domestic activities, h, plus strike income paid by the union, y^s, or may find and take temporary employment. Assuming the probability of an individual on strike finding and taking temporary employment is c/I and the temporary employment pays a real wage of w^A, the value of strike pay is given by

$$s = (c/I)(w^A - D) + (1 - (c/I))(h + y^s) \quad \text{with } 0 \le c < 1. \tag{25}$$

It seems realistic to argue that c is very low, perhaps zero, for all but the longest strikes. Setting the wage received from temporary employment at the economy-wide average of w^A is probably an overstatement. For strike income, y^s, it may be argued that, because the union member 'owns' the union, strike income should not be included in the definition of s. Whether workers are that rational is debatable. Assuming y^s equal to zero will not affect the subsequent argument.

Using the definition of strike pay in (25), the wage negotiated by a particular insider-dominated union will be

$$w = k^I\{(c/I)(w^A - D - h - y^s) + h + y^s + D\}. \tag{26}$$

In general equilibrium $w^A = w$, implying, with the use of (16) to replace I by u, that the wage will be

$$w = \frac{k^I(u(c + J) - c)(h + y^s + D)}{u(ck^I + J) - k^Ic}. \tag{27}$$

If c is equal to zero then

$$w = k^I(h + y^s + D) \tag{28}$$

and the behaviour of the wage is acyclic. If c is positive then the union wage schedule for the insider-dominated trade union has a concave-from-above shape similar to the union wage schedule for the open trade union. However numerical simulation using plausible values for the parameters suggests a union wage schedule for the insider-dominated union which is flatter over most of its range than the union wage schedule for the open trade union. This implies that with retail prices set in customer markets the insider-dominated union yields a larger range of equilibria and a lower degree of procyclicality of the real wage than the open trade union.

Trade unions and wage relativities

There is a large amount of evidence which suggest that individual unions may be concerned with the wages of their members relative to the wages of some or all other workers. Many people appear to be concerned about how they rate relative to other people. Comparing one's position with the position of other people is part of human nature. Am I more beautiful than you? Is he less clever than her? Do I earn more wages than my neighbour? Feelings about relative wages can be strong, and can affect wages. Including this concern for wage relativities will change the union's objective and may change the cyclic behaviour of the real wage, compared with the two models, the open union and the insider-dominated union, discussed above.

Bhaskar (1990) has incorporated a concern for relative wages into the objective function of a union. In this incorporation Bhaskar goes further than simply allowing for a concern with relative wages. He embodies in the union's objective function a special feature, a discontinuity which, Bhaskar argues, is a reasonable reflection of the nature of concern by people with relative wages. In our notation, Bhaskar specifies the utility function of a union member as

$$U = U(w, w/w^A) \tag{29}$$

with

$$\partial U(..)/\partial w = U_1 > 0$$

and

$$\partial U(..)/\partial(w/w^A) = U_2 > 0.$$

The derivative, U_2, is specified to be discontinuous at $w = w^A$. At $w = w^A$ the left-hand derivative with respect to relative wages, written $\underline{U}_2$, is greater than the right-hand derivative, written $\bar{U}_2$. To support this discontinuity, Bhaskar cites two strands of empirical research.

The first is of social psychologists testing equity theory, which suggests that workers' morale and effort is related to how well they are paid relative to a norm. Studies have generally found a positive relationship between pay and effort, but this appears more pronounced when workers are paid less than the norm. Akerlof (1984, p. 82) summarises the evidence: 'Not all of these studies reproduce the result that "overpaid" workers will produce more, but, as might be expected, the evidence appears to be strongest for the withdrawal of services by workers who are led to believe that they are underpaid'.

Support for the non-differentiability assumption also comes from the studies of decision making under uncertainty by experimental psychologists such as Kahneman and Tversky (1979). An important finding, replicated in many experiments, is that agents use a frame of reference for evaluating outcomes. Outcomes are not perceived neutrally, but rather as involving gains or losses from a reference point. Agents tend to be risk-averse when evaluating gains but risk-taking in evaluating losses, and in addition 'the value function' (defined on monetary outcomes) 'is steeper for losses than for gains' (p. 279). Since the reference point in wage setting is likely to be the wages paid to other workers, this gives rise to a utility function which is non-differentiable at this point. Note that this assumption is significantly weaker than Trevithick's (1976) formalisation of Keynes' arguments, where labour supply is assumed to be a discontinuous function of the money wage (Bhaskar, 1990, p. 61).

The discontinuity in the effect of relative wages on utility produces a discontinuity in the trade union's indifference curves and leads to a range of equilibrium rates of unemployment. For the open trade union, the net payoff becomes

$$W - \bar{W} = n\{U(w, w/w^A) - U(x^o)\}. \tag{30}$$

The union's indifference curves have a kink at $w = w^A$. In figure 8.30 a union indifference curve when w^A has the value w_1^A is shown as $UIC(w^A = w_1^A)$. The kink is at $w = w_1^A$. Assuming, as in the simple monopoly union model, that the wage is set by the union and the firm responds by setting employment, a wage equal to w_1^A will be the union's optimal wage demand. Employment will be equal to n_1. This outcome will

consumption
real wage

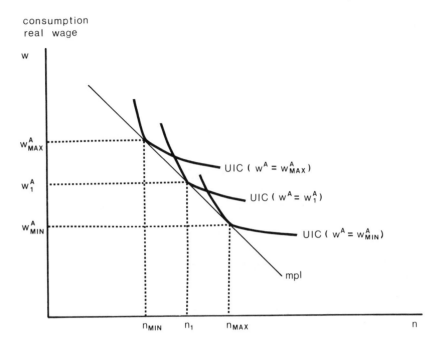

Figure 8.30   The range of equilibria with wage relativities

be a general equilibrium because the union's optimal wage is equal to the economy-wide wage. However it is possible that a different value of w^A will induce a different general equilibrium outcome. Consider the wage of w^A_{MAX} in figure 8.30. This wage places the kink in the union indifference curves at w^A_{MAX}, as shown by the indifference curve $UIC(w^A = w^A_{MAX})$ in figure 8.30. With an economy-wide wage of w^A_{MAX} the union's optimal wage demand is w^A_{MAX}, with an employment level of n_{MIN}. The economy-wide wage of w^A_{MAX} is the highest wage consistent with general equilibrium. At this wage the right-hand derivative of the union indifference curve is tangential with the marginal product of labour schedule. An economy-wide wage greater than w^A_{MAX} will shift the kink to a higher wage but will leave the union's optimal wage demand at w^A_{MAX}. Thus a higher economy-wide wage than w^A_{MAX} will not be a general equilibrium.

   An economy-wide wage equal to w^A_{MIN} is the lowest wage consistent with general equilibrium. As shown in figure 8.30, at this wage the left-hand derivative of the indifference curve, the curve $UIC(w^A = w^A_{MIN})$, is tangential with the marginal product of labour curve.

   The slope of a union indifference curve at a particular pair of values of w

and n will be steeper the lower is x. From this property it follows that the size of the range of equilibrium levels of employment will be smaller the more procyclical is layoff pay.

As the demonstration using figure 8.30 suggests, the discontinuity in capturing the union member's concern for relativities implies a range of equilibrium levels of employment even if the marginal product of labour curve drawn in consumption real wage/employment space is fixed. Thus with this particular objective for a trade union, customer market analysis is not necessary to generate a rage of equilibria. With a fixed marginal product of labour curve the real wage will be, as suggested by figure 8.30, countercyclical. Countercyclicality of the real wage may be argued to be inconsistent with the evidence. However if capital accumulation or imperfect competition is allowed, this countercyclicality will be slight or may even disappear.

If a customer market effect is present then the marginal product of labour curve in consumption real wage/employment space can be shifted by aggregate demand. Thus the combination of the customer market effect and the Bhaskar relativity effect will generate an acyclic real wage even if layoff pay is procyclic.

The size of the range of equilibria predicted by the Bhaskar relativity effect will be greater the less procyclic is layoff pay, the greater the difference between the $\bar{U}$ and $\underline{U}_2$ and if a customer market effect is added. It is the only trade union theory discussed here which can yield, without the addition of other features such as customer market setting of retail prices, a range of equilibria. How important the Bhaskar theory is depends on the size of the difference between $\bar{U}_2$ and $\underline{U}_2$. But what determines the size of this difference is a primitive assumption, not explained at present by the theory. By contrast, the size of the discontinuity in the marginal revenue curve predicted by customer market analysis is not a primitive assumption but can, as shown on pp. 123-4 above, be modelled.

Non-unionised workers and the cyclic behaviour of real wages

A weakness of relying on the behaviour of trade unions to explain the cyclical patterns of wages, prices and real wages is that in most economies not all workers are unionised. Indeed major sectors of most economies are not unionised. Furthermore in the UK, for example, in the 19th century, when trade union membership was low, the cyclical pattern of wages, prices and real wages did not differ markedly from the behaviour in the 20th century, when a larger proportion of the workforce was unionised. Phillips (1958) superimposed the data for inflation and unemployment for 1913 to 1948 on to the Phillips curve estimated using data from 1861 to 1913. The

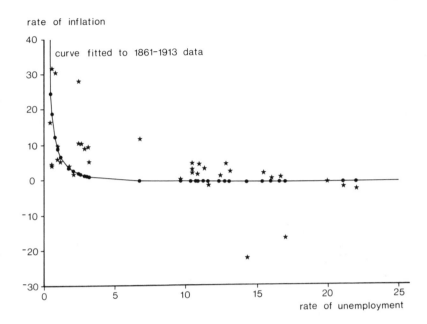

Figure 8.31   Inflation and unemployment, UK, 1913–48
Sources: As in Phillips (1958); the equation for the Phillips curve is based on
1861–1913 data, which is $\dfrac{\Delta\omega}{\omega} = 0.9 + 9.638u^{-1.394}$ where ω = money wage rate,
u = unemployment rate

result of this exercise is shown in figure 8.31. The later data fits the earlier curve well. Given how well the later data fits the earlier curve it appears that the inflation–unemployment relation had not changed, even although the coverage of workers in unions had changed markedly. Even the patterns of inflation and unemployment in the charts of the individual trade cycles throughout the nineteenth century, reported in Phillips (1958), are very similar. The flat section of the Phillips curve at high rates of unemployment is evident in both the 19th and the 20th century. For the consumption real wage an acyclic pattern can be discerned for the years in the 19th century when trade union membership was relatively small. Figure 8.32 shows the relation between the consumption real wage and the rate of unemployment for the UK for the period 1860–1918. The acyclic pattern of the consumption real wage is striking, especially for the fluctuations in unemployment in 1860–4, 1865–71, 1875–82, 1890–3 and 1900–13.

In this section theories of involuntary unemployment which do not rely on the organisation of workers into trade unions are discussed.

consumption real wage

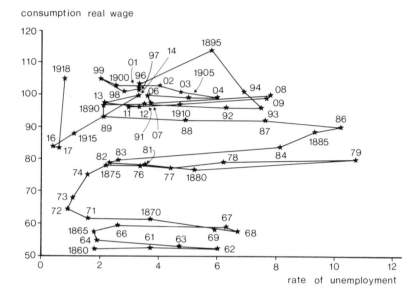

Figure 8.32   Consumption real wage and unemployment, UK, 1860–1918
Sources: Consumption real wage: Phelps Brown and Hopkins (1950)
Unemployment: Feinstein (1972)

Wage bargaining and specific human capital

In McDonald (1990, ch. 6) it is argued that the efficient bargains model of a
trade union can be interpreted as describing the behaviour of a non-
unionised group of workers who are anxious to protect their share of the
rents that are earned from the exploitation of their specific human capital.
The key assumption of the model, that workers act as a group in reacting to
wages and employment offered by the firm, may hold even if there is not a
formal trade union to coordinate the workers. Social pressure by members
of the group on potential undercutters may be sufficient to prevent anyone
from undercutting the wage which maximises the group's interest. To exert
social pressure the workers need to act as a group. If they act as a group they
may seek to pursue the group's welfare. As emphasised in McDonald (1990,
pp. 87–9), it is the maximisation of the group's objective that can generate
involuntary unemployment.

   This line of argument is consistent with Lindbeck and Snower's (1988)
point that insider power may be exerted without insiders being organised
by a union. The key requirement is the sharing with the employer of rents
from specific human capital. It should be added that the relativity model of

Bhaskar (1990), described above, may also, on the basis of this argument, be applied to non-unionised groups of workers.

Efficiency wage setting

The theory of efficiency wages predicts that firms will set wages at above market-clearing levels, thus causing involuntary unemployment, in order to induce efficiency from their workers. Yellen (1984) places into four categories the various reasons why payment of wages which are high relative to income if laid off can encourage a higher level of efficiency. If the benefits from working are higher, then this can (1) discourage shirking, (2) reduce turnover, (3) attract a higher quality job applicant and/or (4) raise morale.

Following the efficiency wage approach, postulate that the efficiency of each employee is positively related to real wages in terms of consumer purchasing power *less* the disutility of work ($v = w - D$) and negatively related to the flow per period of utility if laid off, $\bar{v}$. Then the efficiency function is written

$$e = e(v, \bar{v}), e_v > 0, e_{\bar{v}} < 0, e(v, \bar{v}) = 0 \text{ at } v = \hat{v} > 0, \qquad (31)$$

where $\hat{v}$ is a particular value of v. $\bar{v}$ will be identified with the value per period of being unemployed as defined for the open trade union model, that is from (13) and (14)

$$\bar{v} = \psi(h + D) + (1 - \psi(1 - b))w^A - D \text{ with}$$
$$\psi = (r + J^{-1})/(r + (Ju)^{-1}). \qquad (32)$$

This definition of $\bar{v}$ is consistent with the shirking model and the turnover model because in both of those models the benchmark used to assess the benefit of working with the firm is the income prospects for the worker if laid off or if he or she quits. By using this definition of $\bar{v}$ here, the comparison of the efficiency wage theory with the trade union models is facilitated.

Assume that efficiency enters the firm's production function as a multiplicative factor on employment n, so that

$$q = f(en), f' > 0, f'' < 0 \qquad (33)$$

where q is output. The producing firm sets its money wage, ω, and employment, n, to maximise profits; that is,

$$\max \pi = P^w q - \omega n \qquad (34)$$

subject to

$$q = f(en), \ e = e(v, \bar{v}), \ v = (\omega/P) - D \qquad (35)$$

where P^w is the producer price. It is assumed in (34) that competition between producers in selling to retailers is sufficiently strong for producers to regard the price they receive from retailers as fixed. The fact that the objective in (34) is the nominal value of profits does not introduce money illusion on the part of the producers into the analysis. Although producers, like workers, are interested in the real value of profits, since the decisions of an individual producer will not affect the price level, maximising the nominal value of profits will lead to the same decision as maximising the real value of profits, irrespective of the general price level. That is, dividing both sides of (34) by the aggregate price level to generate an expression for the real value of profits will not affect the first-order conditions, whatever the level of prices in the aggregate.

The first-order conditions for (34) can be written as

$$P^w e f'(en) = \omega, \tag{36}$$

$$\frac{\partial e(v, \bar{v})}{\partial v} \frac{(v + D)}{e(v, \bar{v})} = 1. \tag{37}$$

(36) sets the marginal revenue product of a natural unit of labour equal to the money wage. (37) is well known from Solow (1979). It sets the elasticity of efficiency with respect to the consumer real wage less the disutility of working equal to unity.

From the Solow condition and assuming an economy composed of many identical firms the efficient value of the real wage can be related to the aggregate rate of unemployment. To obtain this relation, which will be called the efficiency wage schedule, assume the following specific functional form for the efficiency function:

$$e = (v - \bar{v})^{\phi} \qquad \text{with } 0 < \phi < 1, \tag{38}$$

from which the Solow condition implies

$$v = (\bar{v} + \phi D)(1 - \phi)^{-1} \tag{39}$$

From the definitions of v and $\bar{v}$, the efficiency wage schedule is

$$w = \frac{(h + D)}{[1 - b - \phi(rJ + u^{-1})(rJ + 1)^{-1}]}. \tag{40}$$

In the efficiency wage model of Shapiro and Stiglitz (1984) the analogous curve to the efficiency wage schedule is the curve they label the NSC (the no-shirking constraint).

The equilibrium rate of unemployment occurs where the efficiency wage schedule cuts the marginal product of labour curve drawn in consumption real wage/employment space. Two such equilibria are shown in figure 8.33

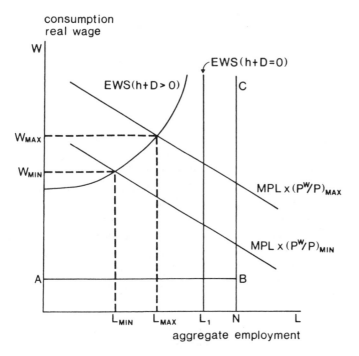

Figure 8.33   The range of equilibria and the cyclical pattern of real wages with efficiency wages

for two values of the retail/wholesale price ratio. These are the minimum and maximum values of the price ratio consistent with customer market analysis. They define maximum and minimum equilibrium rates of unemployment, the rates at the extremes of the range of equilibria.

The efficiency wage schedule has the same shape as the union wage schedule for the open trade union. Equation (40) is equation (20), the equation of the union wage schedule for the open trade union, with $(1 - \phi)^{-1}$ substituted for k^o. Thus the same comments made above for the open union about the size of the range of equilibrium rates of unemployment and the degree of procyclicality of real wages apply also to the case of efficiency wages. This similarity is due to the same definition of layoff pay used in the two models.

The efficiency wage theory can yield an acyclic pattern of real wages if the efficiency function is kinked at the equilibrium wage. Such a kink could be defended by the argument used by Bhaskar to justify a kink in the trade union's objective function. Bhaskar, in arguing for the relative wage effect, appealed to the description in Akerlof (1984) (quoted on p. 138 above) of the apparent tendency of workers to produce less if they believe they are underpaid. Akerlof's purpose in describing this evidence was to provide support for the morale-based version of the efficiency wage theory. Thus there is some support for a kinked efficiency function with the position of the kink depending on a wage relativity.

Conclusion

Empirical evidence provides many counter-examples to the proposition that high unemployment causes decreasing inflation. Instead any tendency for high unemployment to cause decreasing inflation appears to be temporary. In many recessions the rate of inflation stops decreasing even while the rate of unemployment is still high. The temporary effect of unemployment in causing decreasing inflation is illustrated most dramatically on pp. 105–13 above with data from 13 economies from between the two world wars. That data shows many examples of unemployment persisting at high levels for periods of 8 years in 10 economies and 13 and 20 years in two economies without causing decreasing inflation. (In the other economy, Germany, unemployment recovered a little sooner.)

The temporary nature of effect of high unemployment in causing decreasing inflation suggests that states of high unemployment are equilibrium outcomes. Because of this suggestion, the concept of a range of equilibrium rates of unemployment appears to be a closer description of reality than the concept of a natural rate of unemployment. In this chapter several models with a range of equilibrium rates of unemployment are discussed.

In the models described in this chapter, the existence of a range of equilibrium rates of unemployment relies on a discontinuity in the firm's marginal revenue curve or a kink in the utility functions of workers. A discontinuity in a firm's marginal revenue curve can be caused by the frequency of search by customers being less than their frequency of purchase, as shown by customer market analysis. Observation of people's behaviour suggests that the frequency of search is indeed relatively low. Furthermore empirical studies have found the behaviour of prices to be sticky in the way implied by the existence of a discontinuity in the marginal revenue curve. The relatively smaller fluctuations of retail prices compared with wholesale and producer prices is the most obvious empirical pattern that is consistent with a discontinuous marginal revenue curve for retailers. A kink in a worker's utility function can arise if a worker is concerned about the size of his or her wage relative to the wages of other workers. However to get a kink the concern for relativities has to have a special feature. That feature is a greater loss of utility if one's wage falls below the wage of others compared with the size of the gain in utility caused by an increase in one's wage above the wage of others. Whilst it seems undeniable that wage relativities are important to people, whether this concern is of the nature to yield a kinked utility function is not so obvious. There is some empirical evidence for this cited by Bhaskar (1990).

The range of equilibrium rates of unemployment implied by a discontinuity in the firm's marginal revenue curve or by a kink in the utility functions of workers is not a temporary phenomenon. The theories imply that any rate of unemployment within the range can persist as an equilibrium rate forever. Neither the discontinuity nor the kink will disappear in the long run. If a downward shift in a firm's marginal cost curve does not induce the firm to cut price immediately, because of the difficulty of attracting new customers, then it will not induce the firm to cut price later. If customers search infrequently then it is difficult for the firm to gain new customers, whenever the firm tries. Similarly, if a decline in layoff pay does not induce the trade union to settle immediately for a lower wage, because of the union's greater loss of utility from a lower wage compared with its gain from a higher wage, then it will not induce the union to settle later for a lower wage.

In addition to the temporary nature of the downward effect on inflation of high rates of unemployment, empirical evidence also shows the real wage to follow a roughly acyclic pattern. The literature fails to find a strong procyclic or countercyclic pattern to real wages. Given this acyclic pattern of real wages, a requirement for a reasonable model of the range of equilibria is that it has the property of an acyclic real wage. The combination of retailing in customer markets and the Bhaskar wage relativity effect yields a perfectly acyclic real wage. If the Bhaskar wage relativity effect is excluded then the insider-dominated trade union model yields a real wage pattern which is less procyclic than the pattern implied by the open trade union model or the efficiency wage model.

At present the models of the range of equilibria are in an early stage of development. They offer the prospect of explaining the most puzzling aspects of macroeconomic behaviour. This prospect cannot be assayed without further theoretical development and econometric investigation.

Appendix: the wage mark-up in the four union models

Writing the maximisation problem in the following form embraces the four models of union behaviour described in this chapter, that is the three open union models (simple monopoly union, wage bargaining and efficient bargains) and the insider-dominated union model:

$$\max_{\{w,n,\lambda\}} \Gamma = [n^\sigma\{U(w) - U(x^i)\}]^\Phi[R(n) - wn]^{1-\Phi} + \lambda\{w - R'(n)\} \tag{A1}$$

with

$\sigma = 1, i = O, \lambda \neq 0, \Phi = 1$ for the simple monopoly union

$\sigma = 1, i = O, \lambda \neq 0, 0 \leq \Phi \leq 1$ for wage bargaining

$\sigma = 1, i = O, \lambda = 0, 0 \leq \Phi \leq 1$ for efficient bargains

$\sigma = 0, i = I, \lambda \neq 0, 0 \leq \Phi \leq 1$ for the insider-dominated union

w is the consumption real wage, n is employment, $x^i, i = 0, I$, is layoff pay as defined on pp. 131 and 136 of the chapter, $R(n)$ is the firm's concave revenue function and Φ is the union's power parameter measuring the power of the union.

The first-order conditions can be written:

$$\frac{\partial\Gamma}{\partial w} = 0 \text{ implies } \frac{\Phi w U'(w)}{U(w) - U(x^i)} - (1 - \Phi)\frac{wn}{R(n) - wn} = \frac{-w\lambda}{V} \tag{A2}$$

$$\frac{\partial\Gamma}{\partial n} = 0 \text{ implies } \frac{\Phi w\sigma}{R''(n)n} + \frac{(1 - \Phi)w(R'(n) - w)}{R''(n)(R(n) - wn)} = \frac{w\lambda}{V} \tag{A3}$$

and

$$\frac{\partial\Gamma}{\partial\lambda} = w - R'(n) = 0 \text{ if } \lambda \neq 0 \tag{A4}$$

where

$$V = [n^\sigma\{U(w) - U(x^i)\}]^\Phi[R(n) - wn]^{1-\Phi} \tag{A5}$$

From the first-order conditions (A2)–(A4), and defining

$$\varepsilon^i = \frac{wU'(w)}{U(w) - U(x^i)} \text{ for } i = 0, I, \tag{A6}$$

the wage is determined for the four union models by the four following equations. Simple monopoly union:

$$\varepsilon^O = \frac{-R'(n)}{nR''(n)} \tag{A7}$$

Wage bargaining:

$$\varepsilon^O = \frac{1 - \Phi}{\Phi}\left[\frac{R(n)}{nR'(n)} - 1\right]^{-1} - \frac{R'(n)}{nR''(n)} \tag{A8}$$

Efficient bargains:

$$\varepsilon^O = \left\{ \frac{\Phi}{(1-\Phi)} \frac{R(n)}{nR'(n)} + 1 \right\} \left[\frac{\Phi}{(1-\Phi)} \left\{ \frac{R(n)}{nR'(n)} - 1 \right\} \right]^{-1} \qquad (A9)$$

Insider-dominated union:

$$\varepsilon^I = \frac{(1-\Phi)}{\Phi} \left[\frac{R(n)}{nR'(n)} - 1 \right]^{-1} \qquad (A10)$$

By specifying constant elasticity forms for the utility function and the revenue function, that is

$$U(w) = \frac{w^{1-r}}{1-r} \qquad \text{with } r \geq 0 \qquad (A11)$$

and

$$R(n) = An^\alpha \qquad \text{with } A > 0, 0 < \alpha < 1, \qquad (A12)$$

expressions for the mark-up of wages over layoff pay can be derived. These are:

Simple monopoly union:

$$w = [\alpha + r(1-\alpha)]^{1/(r-1)} x^O \qquad (A13)$$

Wage bargaining:

$$w = \left[\frac{\alpha + \Phi(1-\alpha)}{\alpha + r\Phi(1-\alpha)} \right]^{1/(1-r)} x^O \qquad (A14)$$

Efficient bargains:

$$w = \left[\frac{\Phi + \alpha(1-\Phi)}{\alpha + r\Phi(1-\alpha)} \right]^{1/(1-r)} x^O \qquad (A15)$$

Insider-dominated union:

$$w = \left[\frac{(1-\Phi)\alpha}{\alpha - \Phi + r\Phi(1-\alpha)} \right]^{1/(1-r)} x^I. \qquad (A16)$$

In each of the four cases, the mark-up is constant given that r, α and Φ are constant.

A fuller account of this synthesis of trade union models is given in Creedy and McDonald (1991).

Notes

I would like to thank Jeff Borland and Robert Solow for comments on an earlier draft, Charles Feinstein, Paul Klemperer, Steve Nickell, Andrew Oswald and Simon Wren-Lewis for some helpful discussions and Eugene Choo for research assistance. Some of the work on this chapter was done during my visit to the Institute of Economics and Statistics at Oxford University, and I would like to thank the people at the Institute for their hospitality.

1 For a critical discussion of some other alternative theories to the natural rate theory, especially theories of multiple equilibria and theories of hysteresis, see McDonald (1990, ch. 2).

2 There are a number of papers in which switching costs are discussed, see Klemperer (1990) for a survey. Switching costs are the costs faced by a purchaser in changing his or her supplier. By deterring search, switching costs can induce the sticky price behaviour of the customer market. The exact relation between switching costs and customer market analysis remains to be explored.

References

Akerlof, G.A., 1984. 'Gift Exchange and Efficiency Wage Theory: Four Views', *American Economic Review, Papers and Proceedings*, 74, 79–83

Bhaskar, V., 1990. 'Wage Relativities and the Natural Range of Unemployment', *Economic Journal*, 100, 60–6

Binmore, K., Rubinstein, A. and Wolinsky, A., 1986. 'The Nash Bargaining Solution in Economic Modelling', *Rand Journal of Economics*, 17(2), 176–88

Bishop, R., 1964. 'A Zeuthen–Hicks Theory of Bargaining', *Econometrica*, 32, 410–17

Blanchard, O.J. and Fischer, S., 1989. *Lectures on Macroeconomics*, Cambridge, MA: MIT Press

Blanchard, O.J. and Summers, L.H., 1986. 'Hysteresis and the European Unemployment Problem', in R. Cross (ed.), *Unemployment, Hysteresis and the Natural Rate Hypothesis*, Oxford: Basil Blackwell

Carruth, A.A. and Oswald, A.J., 1987. 'On Union Preferences and Labour Market Models: Insiders and Outsiders', *Economic Journal*, 97, 431–45

Creedy, J. and McDonald, I.M., 1991. 'Models of Trade Union Behaviour: A Synthesis', *Economic Record*, 67 (December), 346–59

Farber, H.S., 1986. 'The Analysis of Union Behaviour', in O.C. Ashenfelter and R. Layard (eds.), *Handbook of Labor Economics*, Amsterdam: North-Holland, 1039–89

Feinstein, C.H., 1972. *National Income, Expenditure and Output of the United Kingdom, 1855–1965*, Cambridge: Cambridge University Press

Gordon, R.J., 1988. 'Back to the Future: European Unemployment Today Viewed from America in 1939', *Brookings Papers on Economic Activity*, 1, 271–312

Kahneman, D. and Tversky, A., 1979. 'Prospect Theory: an Analysis of Decision under Risk', *Econometrica*, 47, 263–91

Klemperer, P., 1990. 'Competition when Consumers have Switching Costs: An Overview', The 1990 *Review of Economic Studies* Lecture

Layard, R. and Nickell, S.J., 1990. 'Is Unemployment Lower if Unions Bargain over Employment?', *Quarterly Journal of Economics*, 55(3), 773–87

Layard, R., Nickell, S.J., and Jackman, R., 1991. *Unemployment: Macroeconomic Performance and the Labour Market*, Oxford: Oxford University Press

Lebergott, S., 1964. *Manpower in Economic Growth*, New York: McGraw-Hill.

Lindbeck, A. and Snower, D.J., 1989. *The Insider–Outsider Theory of Employment and Unemployment*, Cambridge, MA: MIT Press

Lucas, R.E. and Rapping, L.A., 1969. 'Real Wages, Employment, and Inflation', *Journal of Political Economy*, 77 (September/October), 721–54

1972.'Unemployment in the Great Depression: Is There a Full Explanation?', *Journal of Political Economy*, 80, 186–91

Maddison, A., 1991. *Dynamic Forces in Capitalist Development: A Long-run Comparative View*, Oxford: Oxford University Press

Manning, A., 1990. 'Imperfect Competition, Multiple Equilibria and Unemployment policy', *Economic Journal*, 100 (Supplement), 151–62

McDonald, I.M., 1989. 'The Wage Demands of a Selfish, Plant-Specific Trade Union', *Oxford Economic Papers*, 41, 506–27

1990. *Inflation and Unemployment: Macroeconomics with a Range of Equilibria*, Oxford: Basil Blackwell

1991a. 'The Setting of Retail Prices in a Customer Market', *Economic Record*, 66 (December), 322–8

1991b. 'Insiders and Trade Union Wage Bargaining', *Manchester School of Economics and Social Studies*, 59 (December), 395–407

McDonald, I.M. and Solow, R.M., 1984. 'Union Wage Policies: Reply', *American Economic Review*, 74, 759–61

McDonald, I.M. and Spindler, K.J., 1987. 'An Empirical Investigation of Customer Market Analysis: A Microfoundation for Macroeconomics', *Applied Economics*, 19, 1149–74

McDonald, I.M. and Suen, A., 1992. 'On the Measurement and Determination of Trade Union Power', *Oxford Bulletin of Economics and Statistics*, 54, 209–24

Okun, A., 1981. *Prices and Quantities: A Macroeconomic Analysis*, Washington, DC: Brookings Institution

Oswald, A.J., 1984. 'On Union Preferences and Labour Market Models: Neglected Corners', Institute for International Economic Studies, paper 296, University of Stockholm

1985. 'The Economic Theory of Trade Unions: An Introductory Survey', *Scandinavian Journal of Economics*, 87, 160–93

Phelps, E.S., 1985. *Political Economy: An Introductory Text*, New York: W.W. Norton

Phelps, E.S. and Winter, S.J., 1970. 'Optimal Price Policy under Atomistic Competition', in E.S. Phelps (ed.), *Microeconomic Foundations of Employment and Inflation Theory*, New York: W.W. Norton and London: Macmillan, 309–37

Phelps Brown, E.H. and Hopkins, S.V., 1950. 'The Course of Wage Rates in Five Countries', *Oxford Economic Papers*, 2, 226–79

Phillips, A.W., 1958. 'The Relationship between Unemployment and the Rate of Change of Money Wage Rates in the United Kingdom, 1861–1957', *Economica*, 25 (November), 283–99

Rees, A., 1970. 'On Equilibrium in Labour Markets', *Journal of Political Economy*, 78 (March/April), 306–10

Sachs, J.D. and Larrain, B.F., 1993. *Macroeconomics in the Global Economy*, New York: Harvester Wheatsheaf

Scitovsky, T., 1952. *Welfare and Competition: The Economics of a Fully Employed Economy*, London: Unwin University Books

Shapiro, C. and Stiglitz, J.E., 1984. 'Equilibrium Unemployment as a Worker Discipline Device', *American Economic Review*, 74 (June), 433–44

Sibly, H., 1922a. 'Asymmetric Information Flows in Customer Markets', *Bulletin of Economic Research*, 44(4), 323–41

    1992b. 'The Timing of Search in Customer Markets', University of Tasmania, mimeo

    1992c. 'On the Economics of Customer Markets', University of Melbourne, PhD thesis

Solow, R.M., 1979. 'Another Possible Source of Wage Stickiness', *Journal of Macroeconomics*, 1, 79–82

Trevithick, J., 1976. 'Money Wage Inflexibility and the Keynesian Supply Function', *Economic Journal*, 86, 327–32

Yellen, J.L., 1984. 'Efficiency Wage Models of Unemployment', *American Economic Review, Papers and Proceedings*, 74, 200–5

9 Hysteresis revisited: a methodological approach

Bruno Amable, Jérôme Henry, Frédéric Lordon, and
Richard Topol

It is somehow logical that economists have been tempted to use the concept
of hysteresis in the field of unemployment theory since its apparent
properties seem to fit rather well with the employment dynamics of the
1980s. Roughly speaking, if the rise of unemployment can easily be related
to the 'low growth context' of the 1970s, it is more difficult to account for
the persistence of high unemployment during the recovery of the 1980s,
especially in Europe. This puzzle suggests that one should go beyond the
'traditional' reversible dynamical tools of economic theory. In this
perspective, the concept of hysteresis and its properties of 'remanence'
appear very appealing.

The economic literature confirms this particular interest of unemployment theory for the concept of hysteresis (Blanchard and Summers, 1986,
1988; Sachs, 1987; Layard, Nickell and Jackman, 1991).[1] The frequency of
its uses calls for an examination of the concept in itself, abstracted from its
actual economic content, and from a more formal point of view. This effort
is all the more desirable since the uses of the term entail some difficulties.

Actually the precision and general nature of the definitions of this
concept borrowed from physics vary greatly from one author to another,
and their status is uncertain. For instance, Blanchard and Summers (1986)
explained that they did not intend necessarily to abide by the definition that
they gave in a footnote. Still more disturbing is the fact that the definitions
do not, for the most part, coincide from one text to another.

Given this context, the use of the term 'hysteresis' raises two problems.
To begin with, the use of a term that is ill-defined, or not defined at all, is a
source of difficulty when it comes to interpretation. While an author is free
to use the term that corresponds to the concept he wishes to employ, he
must nevertheless be able to provide a precise definition of that term; and
the way in which that term is used must correspond unambiguously to that
definition.

Second, the fact that the different definitions of hysteresis, from one
author to another, or from one text to another, do not coincide can cause
confusion simply by virtue of the fact that the same term is used for different

purposes within the same discipline, in this case economics. We wish to underscore the idea that the concept of hysteresis refers to a set of formal properties, independently of the various phenomenologies within which they are liable to be encountered (magnetism, ferro-electricity, physical mechanics, various fields of economics, etc.). The present-day problem regarding the uses of the concept of hysteresis in economics is that, in addition to the legitimate diversity of economic fields within which it might find application, the formal structures employed are fundamentally heterogeneous (see Cross, 1993). Thus, the models of Blanchard and Summers (1986) and Baldwin and Krugman (1989), for example, are both described as exhibiting hysteresis, whereas they differ fundamentally in both structures and formal properties.

In fact, the use of the term 'hysteresis' in the economic literature revolves around two relatively vague ideas: on the one hand, '*dependence on the path followed*', whereby the equilibrium state of a system depends on the transition towards equilibrium; on the other, the '*permanent effects of transitory actions*', in which a system retains the traces of past external influences on it even after those influences have ceased to apply. The vagueness of these characterisations has given rise to various derivations, as a result of which the term hysteresis has been applied to phenomena that are structurally very different. Consequently, there appears to be a need for clarification. Rather than starting a sterile controversy over vocabulary, this chapter aims to identify and classify, according to their relative 'richness', the different kinds of processes that can be related to some extent to these properties. For that purpose, reference will be made to formal representations of hysteretic models developed by mathematicians (Krasnosel'skii and Pokrovskii, 1989; Mayergoyz, 1986, 1991). By highlighting the formal properties of hysteresis as they originally appear in physics, they allow us to show, by way of comparison, how phenomena characterised by zero root dynamics (ZRD)[2] have weaker properties (Amable, Henry, Lordon and Topol, 1994).

This comparison allows us to sketch a first taxonomy where 'strong hysteresis' appears as a set of rich dynamic properties, while zero root processes should rather be qualified in terms of persistence. This chapter will reach its target if it helps to reveal another meaning to hysteresis, more faithful to its origins, overlooked by economists due to the focus on ZRD, and carrying a set of formal properties that can be of great help in the analysis of economic facts.

The first section presents very briefly the constructive method through which strong hysteresis can be obtained. Starting from a 'weak hysteresis operator' at the micro level, an aggregation procedure makes strong hysteresis emerge at the macro level. The second section is devoted to a presentation of the dynamical properties of ZRD, in the case of the equilibrium rate of unemployment. The third section establishes the comparison between strong hysteresis and ZRD and states their structural differences, while arguing that persistence properties come from a degeneracy of the dynamics.

Two forms of hysteresis

Formal approaches developed by mathematicians (Krasnosel'skii and Pokrovskii, 1989; Mayergoyz, 1986, 1991) have sought to abstract hysteresis from the particularities of the different areas of science where it may be bound, and consider it as a class of phenomena. A mathematical modelling of hysteresis requires the consideration of a system subject to an external action, i.e. an *input–output system*. Hysteresis is defined as a particular type of response of the system when one modifies the value of the input: *the system is said to exhibit some remanence when there is a permanent effect on output after the value of the input has been modified and brought back to its initial position.* In what follows, such a change in the input value will be referred to as a '*loading–unloading*'. Since the value of the output is altered after such a 'loading–unloading', the present state of the system depends on the history of the input. The richness of this history varies with the form of hysteresis. Two forms of hysteresis, namely weak and strong, are distinguished and their relationship with each other is discussed.

The weak form of hysteresis

An initial illustration of these ideas may be provided in the generic form of the fold catastrophe associated with weak hysteresis, which represents a first step towards characterising the strong form of hysteresis. In such a framework, an underlying dynamics possesses a multiplicity of equilibria, partially overlapping (figure 9.1). The number of equilibria varies according to the value taken by a control. The value of the equilibrium magnitude, x, can therefore be assimilated to the output of an input–output system, while the control is assimilated to the input.

Such a structure is neither exotic nor pathological, but more and more frequent through various fields in economic theory: Roberts (1980) derives it in a monopolistic competition framework, Dixit (1992) in investment theory, Dixit (1989), Baldwin and Krugman (1989) and Amable, Henry, Lordon and Topol (1991) in foreign trade. To refer to unemployment theory, Cross (1991) suggests that the behaviour of an agent on the labour

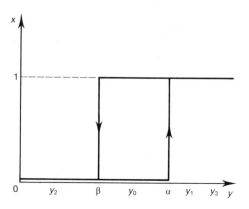

Figure 9.1

market could exhibit a very similar structure. The worker's situation is represented by an elementary input–output system. The input corresponds to the economic activity level, y, while the output, x, is binary and takes value 1 if the worker is employed or 0 if he is unemployed (figure 9.1b).

Referring to Cross (1991) for the economic background of this model, we would like to emphasise the formal properties of such a general input–output system. Such a system possesses, albeit in a weak form, the properties referred to in the Introduction:

1 The history of the system matters because of the local multiplicity of equilibria (output). For a value of the input between β and α, there is an indeterminacy concerning the output. It may either be zero or one according to whether the system is 'out' or 'in'. It is therefore necessary to know the history of the system in order to assess its position. However, this history simply boils down to the initial value of the input and the number of times the system has switched positions.

2 There exists a remanence effect. Consider a change in the value of the input from y_0 to y_1 and back (figure 9.1). If initially out, the system will switch in when the value of the input passes α, and will stay in when the input decreases back to y_0. Nevertheless, it must be noted that a change in the value of the input from y_2 to y_0 or y_2 to y_1 and back will bring the system back to its initial position, possibly via another path.

3 The remanence, if any, is independent of the magnitude of the change in the input. If the system is initially out, a change from y_0 to y_3 and back will produce the same remanence as a change from y_0 to y_1 and back.

The strong form of hysteresis

The crux of the mathematical formalisations[3] of strong hysteresis such as those of Krasnosel'skii and Pokrovskii (1989) or Mayergoyz (1986, 1991) is an aggregation of a large number of heterogeneous elements, or 'elementary hysteretic operators' in the terminology of Mayergoyz, such as the one presented above.

An economic example of such a procedure is given in Amable, Henry, Lordon and Topol (1991, 1992a), where a model of strong hysteresis is built in foreign trade theory. Cross (1991) uses the same method starting from an elementary input–output system related to a single worker on the labour market.

Apart from its various economic contents, the aggregation procedure presents the following formal characteristics. Each elementary input/output operator,[4] referred to as an hysteron hereafter,[5] can be represented by a point in the (β, α) plane. An heterogeneous population of hysterons is considered on a triangle T defined by the 45° line and extremum values of $\alpha = 0$ and $\alpha = y$, and characterised by a density $\mu(\alpha,\beta)$ (figure 9.2).

It can be shown that the representative points of the hysterons which are in belong to a domain S^I, while those which are out are in the domain S^O (Amable, Henry, Lordon and Topol, 1992a). The interface L between these two non-overlapping domains is a staircase line whose vertices have β and α coordinates that correspond respectively to the sequence of the past minima and maxima of the input. An increase in the input will have the hysterons whose α is below the new input value switch in, which brings about a new horizontal line to the staircase separation line L (figure 9.3). A decrease in the input makes the hysterons whose β is above the new input value switch out, which gives a new vertical line to L (figure 9.4).

The history which is stored by a hysteretic system consists of the sequence of the past extrema of the input. As a matter of fact, an increase in the input over the past maxima that lie under the current maximum will wipe out the part of the staircase line corresponding to those past values (figure 9.5). The same wiping-out property applies when the input is decreased below some past minima. Therefore, the history is a sequence of increasing minima and decreasing maxima of the input.

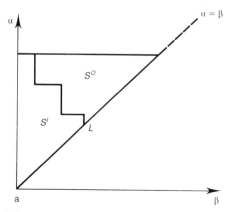

Figure 9.2

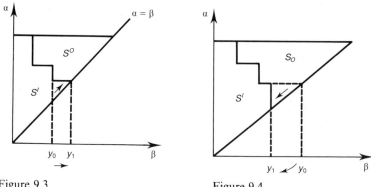

Figure 9.3   Figure 9.4

Knowing what the distribution of the hysterons either in or out is, according to the past changes in the value of the input, it is possible to determine the volume of aggregate output.[6] Since the hysterons which are out correspond to a zero output, the aggregate output is determined solely by the hysterons which are in, i.e. whose representative points belong to the domain S^I.

At time t, the aggregate output $X_A(t)$ reads:[7]

$$X_A(t) = \iint\limits_{S^I_{(t)}} \mu(\alpha,\beta)d\alpha d\beta. \tag{1}$$

The properties of the aggregate output $X_A(t)$ go beyond the properties of the weak form of hysteresis. In general terms, the strong form of hysteresis is characterised by the following:

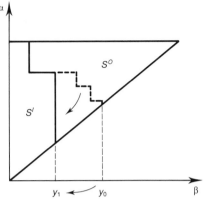

Figure 9.5

1 The current output of the system depends on a much richer history than in the weak form of hysteresis. History now consists of the sequence of the extrema of the input that have not been wiped out.
2 A much wider class of 'loading–unloading' produces a remanence effect. Actually, every 'loading–unloading' which involves an increase in the value of the input over the last local maximum or a decrease below the last local minimum will produce a remanence.
3 By contrast to the weak form of hysteresis, the remanence depends on the magnitude of the 'loading–unloading'.

In that case, following Mayergoyz (1986), we may say that a system is hysteretic if '*the input–output relationship is non-linear multibranch, the transitions from branch to branch occurring each time the input reaches an extremum*'.

The relationship between aggregate output and the input is represented by the curve in figure 9.6, which is deduced from the interface L shown in figure 9.2. The aggregate output will depend on the history of past extrema of the inputs, and any increase of the input over the previous maximum followed by a return to its initial value will produce a remanence: the final volume of output will exceed the initial one.

Micro and macro behaviour

The strong form of hysteresis presented above involves a non-trivial transition from heterogeneous micro elements to a macro aggregate. Indeed, the macro behaviour is not a mere reproduction of the micro behaviour. This claim is illustrated by the comparison between the

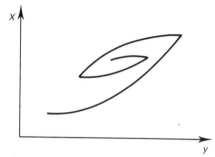

Figure 9.6

properties of the aggregate output, i.e. the properties of the strong form of hysteresis, and the properties of the individual hysteron, i.e. the weak form of hysteresis.

In fact, hysteretic non-linearities such as exposed above are based on:

(a) The existence of elements possessing two stable equilibria for some range of the input.
(b) The aggregation of elements that are heterogeneous with respect to the input thresholds within which there exist two stable equilibria.

The qualitative change in the micro–macro transition is a direct consequence of the aggregation over a set of heterogeneous hysterons.

Actually, a structural break may be associated to the hysteresis phenomenon. This structural break is elementary in the weak form, where it corresponds to the jump of the system between the two stable equilibria. The break is much more sophisticated in the strong form of hysteresis: the relationship between aggregate output and the input is altered at every turning point in the input. Since the aggregate output is a function of the number of elements which are in, the relationship depends on the history of the input, or more precisely on the values of its extrema.

Zero and unit roots: an improper use of the concept of hysteresis

The characteristic properties of hysteresis, namely 'dependence on the history of inputs' and 'remanence', have given rise to more or less wide divergences from their fundamental meaning. The term 'hysteresis' is often mentioned in connection with dynamic models characterised by zero eigenvalue for continuous time (Sachs, 1985, 1987; Van de Klundert and Van Schaik, 1990) or by unit roots for discrete time (Blanchard and Summers, 1986). The properties of these models bear only an approximate and distant relation to those of hysteresis. The shifts of meaning and analogical deformations are described in what follows.

Deterministic multivariate systems and 'path dependence'

Some economic models lead to a problem of equilibrium indeterminacy, within a linear differential system of the type:

$$\dot{Y} = AY - Z \tag{2}$$

where Y is a vector of dimension n and Z is a vector of exogenous variables. A is not full rank, i.e. has some zero eigenvalues.

Sachs (1985, 1987) presents a model that leads to a three-equation system of this type. The components of Y are the rate of unemployment, the rate of inflation and the non-accelerating inflation rate of unemployment (NAIRU). The first equation is a Phillips curve according to which the inflation rate, denoted P, varies with the gap between the current rate of unemployment, U, and the NAIRU, U^*. The second equation models the trade-off between unemployment and inflation, derived from the loss function of the government, say with an equal weight on both objectives. Sachs adds to these two standard equations an error correcting adjustment of the NAIRU to the current rate of unemployment. The addition of this last equation makes A exhibit a zero root. The system of Sachs is similar to:

$$\dot{P} = U^* - U \tag{3}$$

$$U^* = g(U - U^*) \tag{4}$$

$$\dot{U} = P - U \tag{5}$$

The general result (see Giavazzi and Wyplosz, 1985) with such systems is that the steady state is no longer unique, because A is singular. If one notes its rank $r, r < n$, the resolution of $A\,Y = Z$, presents an indeterminacy whose order $n - r$ represents the dimension of the continuum sub-space of the equilibria. As noted by Giavazzi and Wyplosz (1985), this indeterminacy can be dispelled, and one can show that the equilibrium reached, selected from within the continuum, depends on the initial conditions and the adjustment parameters. In the degenerate case where A possesses no eigenvalues different from zero, the economy would not move at all from any given initial position. Applied to Sachs' model, the locus of equilibria would be a line $(U^* = P = U)$. The equation of this line can be derived from the transformed system in the eigenvectors base. It is the first direction associated to the zero eigenvalue. Its projection in the (NAIRU, inflation) diagram is a line $(P = U^*)$, as shown in figure 9.7.

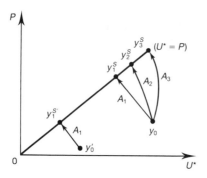

Figure 9.7

From any given initial state $y_0(U_0, P_0)$, the economy, if stable,[8] would converge to a point on the line of equilibria, denoted y_1^s. The final steady state is entirely determined by the initial conditions and the A matrix. The selected equilibrium is determined by the first intersection between the continuum of equilibria and the trajectory, which depends on the adjustment speed parameters which determine its curvature (see figure 9.7 for various A matrices). But for any given A, the final steady state depends only on y_0, which means that only initial conditions matter. What is represented as the 'dependence of equilibrium on the approach trajectory' is therefore merely a by-product of a simple property of dependence on initial conditions.

Such dependence did not exist in the case of a single equilibrium. Indeed, a single-equilibrium dissipative system 'loses the memory' of the initial conditions, since the stationary state, when stable, attracts all of the trajectories from any point in the phase space (figure 9.8).

Another interpretation of the multiple equilibria property might have added to the confusion between zero root dynamics and hysteresis: the 'permanent effect of transitory shock'. Consider an initial equilibrium with zero rates of inflation and unemployment (natural or current): point O in figure 9.9. Any exogenous transitory shock – which means a shock applied only once – on inflation or unemployment would instantaneously displace the economy to y_0, for instance. The adjustment dynamics of the system would then lead the economy to a final non-zero inflation and unemployment steady state in y^s. The NAIRU would have changed in the process: the steady state would be a new one, which implies a new 'natural' rate of unemployment. Had the A matrix been non-singular, a transitory exogenous shock would have left no long-run impact on the economy,

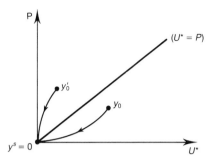

Figure 9.8

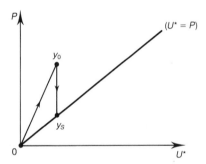

Figure 9.9

which would have come back to the zero inflation and unemployment point. The NAIRU would have stayed constant, equal to zero.

This characteristic of the zero eigenvalue dynamics allows to speak of 'persistence'. Yet, this phenomenon has little in common with the type of memory kept in hysteretic systems.

Persistence of unemployment and hysteresis: the unit root approach

According to Lindbeck (1992), 'Persistence may be understood either as slow dynamic adjustment or as a change in the equilibrium rate itself under the influence of the previous path of unemployment. In the empirical analysis, it is difficult perhaps impossible to distinguish between these alternative interpretations of persistence.'

It is nevertheless true that in the empirical – or even in some theoretical – work on unemployment persistence, 'hysteresis' is yet very often said to occur when there is a unit root in a discrete stochastic univariate or multivariate linear system. Though there might well be an observational equivalence between close-to-unity and unit roots, the long-run behaviours of both processes do drastically differ. The analysis of these differences are similar to the conclusions drawn from the deterministic framework.

For instance, consider the kind of wage–price spiral to be found in Layard, Nickell and Jackman (1991) as a theoretical benchmark, according to which there are two independent deterministic equations, identified as a price and a wage equation, for the real wage denoted WP:

$$WP = b.U + c.Q + cp \qquad \text{(P)}$$
$$WP = -d.U - d'.dU + c.Q + cw \qquad \text{(W)}$$

where cp and cw are constant, all other coefficients are positive.

Unemployment, denoted U, affects prices, for it is a proxy for excess activity effect on the mark-up behaviour. It enters (W) too, through the wage bargaining. Changes in unemployment, denoted dU, are supposed, for the sake of simplicity, to appear only in (W). The productivity trend, denoted Q, determines the reservation wage in (W) and is a component of unit labour cost in (P).

In their discussion of hysteresis, Layard, Nickell and Jackman (1991) always use it in connection with parameters d' or $b + d$. 'Pure hysteresis' occurs when the latter is zero and 'partial hysteresis' when the former is non-zero. But their system is mainly static, apart from the change in unemployment, which makes it difficult to link it to the dynamic considerations usually at work when dealing with persistence.

The deterministic system we started with can be turned into a stochastic process, a vector autoregressive (VAR) model in discrete time. To obtain the VAR representation, express the first-difference variables on the left-hand side with respect to the lagged ones on the right-hand side of the system.

In order to assess the consequences of such characteristics on the equilibrium of the empirical system, namely on the existence of a NAIRU (or NAWRU): (i) derive, through (P) − (W), the expression of the change in unemployment, which appears to be an error correction equation; (ii) add such a similar ECM dynamics for real wage, so that the current wage will not always equal the optimal wage; and (iii) also assume the productivity trend to be stochastic (or to follow a random walk with drift). The dynamic stochastic system then may read, omitting constants and lags:

$$\Delta Q = u$$
$$\Delta U = [(b + d)/d'].U + v$$

$$\Delta\text{WP} = -g.(\text{WP} - b.\text{U} - c.\text{Q}) + w = -g.(\text{WG}) + g.b.\text{U} + w$$

where WG is similar to a wage gap; u, v and w are i.i.d. disturbances. In the more general case, the lagged differences of variables would also be on the right-hand side, so that the discrete time system would read:

$$(1 - \text{L}).X = A(\text{L}).X,$$

where $A(\text{L})$ is a polynomial matrix, L is the lag operator and $A(1) = A$. This is of course similar to the previous continuous time system. The corresponding $A(1)$ matrix is by definition the impact matrix, which sums up the effects of variables in levels or of permanent changes in variables. The matrix $A(1)$ is the long-run transition matrix of the trivariate system, it is the value of the polynomial expression in L = 1, which is tantamount to considering a long-run equilibrium in the levels of the three variables, with all variables held at a constant level. This matrix is equal to:

0	0	0
0	$(b + d)/d'$	0
$g.c$	$g.b$	$-g.$

This stochastic system can be estimated and analysed in terms of cointegration and stochastic trends (see for instance Johansen, 1988). The implications of such an analysis is yet strictly equivalent to those derived from the deterministic counterpart, i.e. depends on the rank of the transition matrix $A(1)$, which is found when solving for x the equation:

$$0 = x.(x - g).[x - (b + d)/d'] = |x.\text{Id} - A(1)|.$$

The number of zero eigenvalues in $A(1)$ measures its rank deficiency. By construction it is also the number of unit roots in $A(\text{L})$. In the current model, the roots of the equation are obvious, so therefore is the dynamic of the system under study.

Whatever the coefficients, there is indeed at least one stochastic trend, or unit root, corresponding to the exogenous productivity trend (see the first row in the matrix above). The unemployment rate is stationary, or converges towards a unique equilibrium level, provided $b + d$ is non-zero. There is finally a cointegrating relation between the real wage and productivity, provided g is non-zero. In this case, i.e. with only one stochastic trend, for any given level of productivity, there will exist a unique equilibrium in the levels of real wage and unemployment, which is the NAWRU when productivity grows at a constant rate.

It is remarkable that d' does not play any part in this analysis: it is purely a part of the short-run or adjustment dynamic, which is by definition not relevant at all in terms of the long-run equilibria of the system.

It is also obvious that if, on the contrary, g is equal to zero, there is another stochastic trend in the model. In fact, the real wage will then follow its own random trend, with no relation to productivity although the rate of unemployment is stationary: there is no NAIRU. This case is not mentioned in Layard, Nickell and Jackman (1991) since they do not take into account the dynamic adjustment of the real wage to its optimal level.

Similarly, were b and d to sum up to zero, the unemployment rate would also follow a stochastic trend, leading to a process of the type described in Blanchard and Summers (1986). Thus, no stationary unemployment – or no constant NAIRU – could appear. This would be a case of 'pure hysteresis' according to Layard, Nickell and Jackman (1991): the real wage will steadily follow productivity and unemployment, but these latter two variables will follow two independent random walks.

The locus of long-run equilibria, i.e. the solution of the system with all stochastic disturbances set to zero and the three variables set to some given initial values (long-run equilibrium requires 'an extended period with no exogenous shocks' according to Engle and Granger, 1991) then depends on the rank of $A(1)$. Because productivity is non-stationary, $A(1)$ is never a full-rank matrix and the locus of equilibria is never reduced to a single point. It is nevertheless sufficient to study the lower part of A, since productivity is an exogenous variable, to know the influence of initial conditions on the final state of the system (see Mosconi and Giannini, 1992, for a general analysis of such systems).

If the productivity trend is the only stochastic trend (the usual basic system), the initial values of both unemployment and real wage do not matter. One single NAWRU exists and the real wage will end on an equilibrium path, which is unique and depends only on the deterministic part of productivity, since there is a unique equilibrium wage gap. But if the unemployment rate is non-stationary too ($b + d = 0$) its initial value would also determine the path of the real wage, but still independently of the initial value of the wages. Finally, if the real wage does not follow an error correction process, there is no long-run equilibrium at all for any of the variables, and all final values would depend on initial conditions. In all these cases, the dependence of long-run values on initial conditions *is strictly that found in the deterministic system, which means there is no 'path-dependence' either.* The NAWRU exists if and only if there is no unit root except in the productivity trend.

Another history: about the 'history of shocks'

Up to now, we have considered the final equilibria consistent with any given set of initial values. Even in terms of response to shocks, the discussion of the behaviour of our system is indeed very similar to the point just made, since a once-and-for-all shock is equivalent in terms of its consequences to a change in the initial conditions. Such shocks would persist on the system only on the variable associated to a stochastic trend (or similarly when the long-run equilibrium depends on the initial value of this variable). In the basic system, shocks would not persist on unemployment nor on the wage gap, though they would on both productivity and real wage.

Of course, when submitted to i.i.d. shocks at any time t, the current state of our system would depend on all past values of the shocks (the so-called 'history of shocks'). But this is true of all dynamic stochastic systems, with a non-zero adjustment lag. The only interesting property of such systems is not that current unemployment or real wage is not equal to its equilibrium value, but if they *would* be an equilibrium and *how soon it would be reached* if there were no shocks any longer. Besides, when accounting for shocks at any time t, one must also study the variance of the variables, i.e. the confidence interval around the equilibrium mean values. For instance, in the basic system, the variance of productivity and that of real wage do increase continuously but the variance of the wage gap is constant. It is strictly equivalent to assess that shocks on productivity persist on real wage but not on the wage gap.

Remanence or persistence?

For a system possessing unit roots, shocks would cumulate forever without progressively vanishing. Indeed, Blanchard and Summers (1986) identify their particular brand of 'hysteresis' with the existence of a unit root in their univariate system. Yet, to keep such a perfect memory of shocks is not sufficient to justify the use of the term hysteresis.

There are two main reasons for this point; they both deal with the two characteristics mentioned by Mayergoyz (1991), namely the *'non-linear'* and *'multibranch'* aspects of the hysteresis dynamics.

If one wanted at all costs to establish a link between zero eigenvalue dynamics and hysteresis, one would need to take the comparison to its conclusion. Indeed a first shock followed by a second one of the same intensity in the opposite direction takes the univariate system back to its initial level, whatever the intensity of the shock. On the contrary, a system with hysteresis would exhibit remanence subject to this kind of impulse.[9] There lies a major difference between persistence and hysteresis. The response to impulses is a linear function, which is not the case for a system exhibiting hysteresis.[10] This remark is not restricted to univariate systems. Indeed, one may state the following proposition:

Proposition 1
Consider a dynamical system such as that of equation (2), where $RkA = r < n$, the system being in an equilibrium position. A shock on the system followed by a second one of the same intensity in the opposite direction will bring the system back to its initial position.

Proof
See Appendix 1, p. 174.

Proposition 2
Consider a dynamical system such as that of equation (4), where $RkA = r < n$, the system being in an equilibrium position. A shock on the constant Z followed by a second one of the same intensity in the opposite direction will bring the system back to its initial position.

Proof
See Appendix 2, p. 177.

Therefore, one may state that systems with zero eigenvalues or unit roots cannot exhibit remanence effects.

The lack of remanence in unit root systems also occurs with the so-called 'asymmetric persistence' mentioned in the insider–outsider model. For instance, Huizinga and Schiantarelli (1992) say that

Lindbeck and Snower argue that their model generates 'asymmetric persistence' in the sense that when a large negative shock is followed by a positive one of same magnitude, the economy ends up with a level of *n* lower than the initial one (since the smaller group of Insiders that remains sets a high wage). However, it is equally true that if a large positive shock is followed by a negative one of equal magnitude, the final level of employment is higher than the original one. The asymmetry is therefore symmetric.

Actually, the theoretical gap between hysteresis and zero root dynamics has empirical implications, too. Simulations of a hysteretic system prove that there is not even an observational equivalence between a unit root system and a system with strong hysteresis (Amable, Henry, Lordon and Topol, 1992b, 1994). In the case of a white noise input, most of the outputs have no unit root, but with a random walk input, the input–output relation does not exhibit a stable (cointegrated) pattern in most cases.

Non-stationary econometrics based on cointegration would fail to capture the parameters of a strong hysteresis data generating process.

But in our view, the problem lies in the very principle of equating a shock to the system with a parametric 'loading–unloading'. As pointed out on p. 155 above, one can only meaningfully speak of hysteresis in the case of a system for which one can clearly distinguish a state variable, or several state variables, and an input, i.e. a control parameter, representative of an external action upon the system. Going back to the illuminating image of the potential curves suggested by Blanchard and Summers (1986), one can show – albeit contrary to the authors' intentions – that an exogenous shock to the system on the one hand and a parametric 'loading–unloading' of the input on the other imply very different types of problem.

Shock to the system versus parametric loading–unloading

First, and as a metaphor, it is actually convenient to envisage the stationary state of a dynamics as the minimum of a certain potential $v(x)$.[11] The 'standard' case of a linear system with a single equilibrium corresponds to a single-bottom potential curve (figure 9.10). Blanchard and Summers (1988) propose that hysteretic phenomena be conceived in terms of configurations in which the potential curve presents not one but several, or even an infinity, of local minima. The first of these two cases (figure 9.11) in fact corresponds to a non-linear model with a (discrete and finite) multiplicity of equilibria. The second case, which is an extreme case of the former (figure 9.12), corresponds to a 'flat-bottom' potential curve, in other words to the existence of a continuum of equilibria characteristic of a zero root dynamics.

In the first case (figure 9.11), the change of equilibrium requires a sufficiently substantial shock to allow it to breach the 'potential barrier' separating the two attractors. In other words, the system must be sufficiently distanced from E to allow it to pass into the domain of attraction of F. In the case of a 'flat-bottom' potential curve characteristic of a zero root dynamics (figure 9.12), any shock will modify the equilibrium of the system. But in either case, the external action takes the form of a direct shock to the system, or more accurately to its state variables, whereas the very structure of the dynamic, the shape of its potential curve, is left invariant.

Hysteresis and structural change in the dynamics

A very different kind of phenomenon is involved in the weak form of hysteresis associated with the fold catastrophe, for instance. Here, the action exerted from the outside consists in modifying the value of a

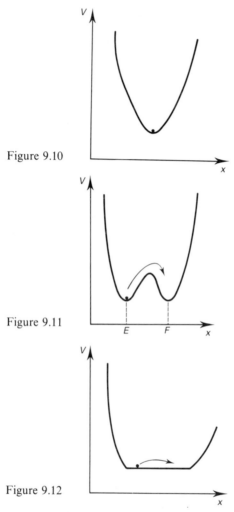

Figure 9.10

Figure 9.11

Figure 9.12

parameter λ, akin to a change in the value of the input for the input–output system considered on p. 155 above, which entails a structural change in the 'conflict between attractors' (Thom, 1972; Haken, 1977). If the system does move from one equilibrium to another, it is no longer as the result of an external impulse enabling it to cross a potential barrier (which may be zero in the case of a zero root dynamics). It is because a structural modification alters the shape of the potential curve and eliminates one of its minima, leaving the system no option but to move towards the remaining attractor (figures 9.13, 9.14, 9.15). Bringing the parameter (or the input) back to its initial value (figure 9.16) undoubtedly produces a structural deformation

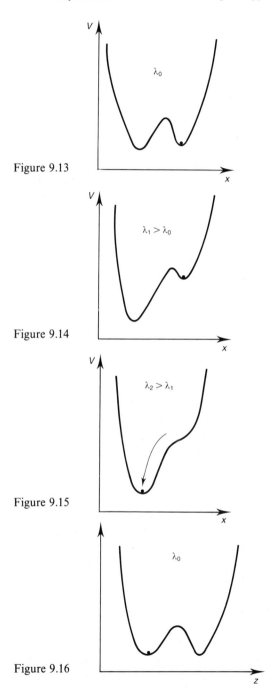

Figure 9.13

Figure 9.14

Figure 9.15

Figure 9.16

that is the exact reverse of the potential curve, but the system remains the captive of attractor F ('maximum delay convention', Thom, 1972) such that the 'loading–unloading' may leave a remanent effect.

This crucial difference between these formal structures should shed some light upon the gap between formalisation and interpretations with respect to the idea of structural change. We would like to emphasise that the most satisfactory way for structural change to make sense, formally speaking, is intimately linked with modifications of the parameters of the model, in this case the parameter λ of the dynamical system. Actually it is quite obvious that only a change in a parameter may cause a modification of the formal characteristics of a dynamics, mainly the number and stability of the equilibria. This is quite visible in the potential curve metaphor where a change in a parameter may imply the vanishing of an equilibrium. More generally hysteresis, as already seen, comes from micro structure where the variation of a control parameter (the input) leads to the disappearance of an equilibrium and the jump towards a lower or upper one. Such an event refers exactly to what we call 'a structural change in the formal characteristics of the dynamics'.

On the contrary effects manifested by zero root dynamics have nothing to do with such modifications in the formal characteristics of the dynamics. They arise because of the special nature of the equilibrium locus: a continuum. The latter remains unchanged during the shock-and-persistence phenomenon described on p. 167 above. However, a confusion may arise from the fact that some of the state variables of these zero root models are sometimes interpreted as 'structural' economic variables. This is particularly the case in Sachs' model where the NAIRU, taken as a 'structural characteristic' of the economy, is endogenous. There, the structural change is purely semantic and does not refer at all to the characteristics of the dynamics which are fundamentally invariant. Persistence effects thus come from a shock on the state variables (on 'the economy') which affects neither the set of equilibria nor their stability properties. The economic magnitude to which pertains an interpretation in terms of 'structural change' is a state variable in models with zero root dynamics.[12] It must be an external parameter in the case of hysteresis, even in its weak form. Although Sachs' story on the NAIRU may be found economically relevant,[13] it is totally neutral with respect to the formal characteristics of the dynamics. By contrast, hysteresis phenomena are crucially linked with the existence of structural change of the dynamics itself.

Zero root versus hysteresis: global versus local structural instability

More generally and to overcome the limits of the potential curve metaphor, the difference between zero root and hysteretic dynamics refers in last resort to the distinction between (respectively) global and local structural instability. A dynamical system is structurally unstable as soon as it possesses a stationary state in which at least one eigenvalue has a zero real part (Hirsch and Smale, 1974). It is globally structurally unstable if this property holds, whatever the values of the parameters. As a matter of fact, the essential formal property behind zero root dynamics is global structural instability.

This formal characteristic of Sachs' model from which the persistence property stems unfortunately leads to its mathematical rejection. Indeed, it is well known that the global structural instability of a model is quite unsatisfactory. The weakest perturbation of the functional form of its equations makes its dynamical properties drastically changed: Sachs' continuum disappears into an ordinary equilibrium. This lack of robustness is obviously a major drawback for a model. Incidentally, this crucial objection, formulated long ago for instance against Goodwin's model (1967), should apply to all the zero root or unit root models.

On the contrary, local structural instability is a much more attractive property. The eigenvalue's real part vanishes only for some particular values of the parameters.[14] Far from these critical values the dynamics is structurally stable. A modification in a parameter value is therefore quite a remarkable event when crossing such thresholds: it implies a structural change in the formal characteristics of the dynamics[15] such as, in the weak form of hysteresis, the vanishing of an equilibrium and the sudden jump toward another one.

Conclusion

The evolution of employment over the last decade has puzzled economists. According to the models they used, an increase in unemployment brought about by a negative shock should have vanished after the occurrence of a positive shock of an equal magnitude. The persistence of a high unemployment rate in Europe in spite of a recovery called for an explanation that could not easily be given by the traditional models. Some adjustment lags could of course explain why the return to the initial unemployment rate could be very slow, but they could hardly account for the observed persistence. Some economists have argued that unemployment could follow a random walk so that there existed no tendency to return to equilibrium after a shock. This explanation has been labelled hysteresis

(Blanchard and Summers, 1986) and several models have been developed in this spirit in either discrete or continuous time.

The present chapter aimed to show that such models could not be considered as exhibiting hysteresis, the latter being defined as a particular type of response of a system (remanence) after a certain change in the value of the control. Zero root dynamics models do not qualify for such a description, two opposite shocks of the same magnitude bring the system back to its initial position. Their persistence properties come from a kind of degeneracy of the dynamics which supports them. Besides, such models cannot capture the idea of formal structural change and at the same time must deal with serious mathematical objections.

The use of mathematical models allows us to distinguish several forms of hysteresis (weak and strong) corresponding either to a micro or macro level. Such a formalisation can be applied to various fields of economics where the individual behaviour leads to overlapping multiple equilibria. For instance, investment decisions under uncertainty in the presence of fixed costs (Dixit, 1989) leads to a behaviour which is formally similar to an elementary hysteretic operator. A system characterised by an heterogeneity of such elementary operators can exhibit strong hysteresis, characterised by its formal properties of remanence and dependence of the system on the past value of the control.

Such a modelling approach has been used in foreign trade theory (Amable, Henry, Lordon and Topol, 1991) and unemployment (Cross, 1991). Some models (Bentolila and Bertola, 1990) have stressed the importance of fixed hiring and firing costs in explaining unemployment. The approach is in some sense parallel to the macroeconomic literature that deals with the behaviour of the aggregate in the presence of micro heterogeneity (Caplin and Spulber, 1987; Caballero and Engel, 1990, 1993). These latter papers emphasise the smoother behaviour of the aggregate contrasting with the 'lumpy' micro behaviour. It must be noted though that if a hysteretic system does behave more smoothly than a hysteron, aggregation does not bring about a vanishing of the formal remanence and 'historical' properties observable at the micro level, but rather a strengthening of them.

Appendix 1: Lack of remanence in linear systems

Proof of proposition 1

Two shocks on the system of the same magnitude in opposite directions bring the system back to its initial position.

We consider the following dynamical system:

$$\dot{Y} = AY - Z. \tag{A1}$$

Y is a $(n \times 1)$ vector of endogenous variables, Z a $(n \times 1)$ vector of exogenous variables and A is a singular $(n \times n)$ matrix, $Rk\, A = r < n$. To keep things simple, we assume that it is possible to write A as:

$$A = V\Lambda V^{-1} \tag{A2}$$

where Λ is a diagonal matrix containing the eigenvalues of A. A more general case would involve resorting to Jordan-form matrices.

The matrix is partitioned so that the $d = n - r$ zero eigenvalues appear first.

$$\Lambda = \begin{pmatrix} 0 & | & 0 \\ 0 & | & \Lambda_r \end{pmatrix}.$$

Λ_r is a $(r \times r)$ diagonal sub-matrix containing the (negative) non-zero eigenvalues of A. After the transformation $X = V^{-1}Y$, the dynamical system is:

$$\dot{X} = \Lambda X - V^{-1}Z. \tag{A3}$$

The steady state is thus defined as:

$$X^* = \Lambda^+ V^{-1}Z \tag{A4}$$

where Λ^+ is the generalised inverse of Λ. The existence of a solution requires that the first d elements of $V^{-1}Z$ be zero. Indeed, with A singular, a solution to $AY = Z$ exists only when Z is restricted to the sub-space spanning the column vectors of A. The diagonalised system is thus:

$$\dot{X} = \Lambda(X - X^*). \tag{A5}$$

Transforming the system back and taking a particular solution allows to express $Y(t)$:

$$Y(t) = V\Lambda^+ V^{-1}Z + Ve^{\Lambda t}V^{-1}(Y(0) - V\Lambda^+ V^{-1}Z) \tag{A6}$$

The function $e^{\Lambda t}$ becomes asymptotically the matrix E such that:

$$E = \begin{pmatrix} I_d & | & 0 \\ 0 & | & 0 \end{pmatrix}$$

and I_d is a $(d \times d)$ identity sub-matrix. The steady state solution is thus:

$$Y^* = V\Lambda^+ V^{-1}Z + VEV^{-1}(Y(0) - V\Lambda^+ V^{-1}Z) \tag{A7}$$

which can also be written as:

$$Y^* = V[(I - E)\Lambda^+]V^{-1}Z + VEV^{-1}Y(0).\tag{A8}$$

We suppose now that the system is initially at rest in Y_1^*, defined as:

$$Y_1^* = V[(I - E)\Lambda^+]V^{-1}Z + VEV^1Y(0).\tag{A9}$$

A shock is applied to the system, which now finds itself instantaneously out of equilibrium in Y_2, defined as:

$$Y_2 = Y_1^* + \Theta\tag{A10}$$

where Θ is a $(n \times 1)$ vector of shocks. The new equilibrium corresponding to this new initial condition is:

$$Y_2^* = V[(I - E)\Lambda^+]V^{-1}Z + VEV^{-1}Y_2\tag{A11}$$

or:

$$Y_2^* = V[(I - E)\Lambda^+]V^{-1}Z + VEV^{-1}[V(I - E)\Lambda^+V^{-1}Z + VEV^{-1}Y(0) + \Theta]$$

since $E (I - E) = 0$, one has:

$$Y_2^* = V[(I - E)\Lambda^+]V^{-1}Z + VEV^{-1}Y(0) + VEV^{-1}\Theta.\tag{A12}$$

Applying the same shock in reverse displaces the system in Y_3, with:

$$Y_3 = Y_2^* - \Theta\tag{A13}$$

the system will thus reach a new equilibrium:

$$Y_3^* = V[(I - E)\Lambda^+]V^{-1}Z + VEV^{-1}Y_3\tag{A14}$$

or:

$$Y_3^* = V[(I - E)\Lambda^+]V^{-1}Z + VEV^{-1}[V(I - E)\Lambda^+V^{-1}Z + VEV^{-1}Y(0) + VEV^{-1}\Theta - \Theta]$$

which can be written as:

$$Y_3^* = V[(I - E)\Lambda^+]V^{-1}Z + VEV^{-1}Y(0) = Y_1^*.\tag{A15}$$

Therefore, two shocks of opposite signs bring the system back to its initial position, there is no remanence.

Appendix 2: The case of shocks to the constant

Proof of proposition 2

Two shocks on the constant of the same magnitude in opposite directions bring the system back to its initial position.

A shock is now applied to the (vector of) constants. We suppose that the system is at rest at its equilibrium Y_1^*:

$$Y_1^* = V[(I - E)\Lambda^+]V^{-1}Z + VEV^{-1}Y(0) \qquad (A16)$$

A shock is applied to Z. The system finds itself instantaneously out of equilibrium at Y_1^*, while a new equilibrium-subspace is defined, after the appropriate transformation, by:

$$X^* = \Lambda^+ V^{-1}Z' \qquad (A17)$$

where $Z' = Z + \Theta$. The system will reach a new steady state Y_2^*:

$$Y_2^* = V[(I - E)\Lambda^+]V^{-1}Z' + VEV^{-1}Y(0). \qquad (A18)$$

The same shock is now applied in reverse. The new equilibrium sub-space is the same as before the shock. The new steady state for the system is Y_3^*:

$$Y_3^* = V[(I - E)\Lambda^+]V^{-1}Z + VEV^{-1}Y(0) = Y_1^*. \qquad (A19)$$

Therefore, two shocks of the same magnitude in opposite directions applied to the constant bring the system back to its initial position. There is no remanence.

Notes

1 However, it should be noted that its generality allows the concept of hysteresis to be used in various fields of economic theory such as foreign trade (Baldwin and Krugman, 1989; Dixit, 1989; Amable, Henry, Lordon and Topol, 1992a, 1992b) or investment theory (Dixit, 1992).

2 A unit root in discrete time.

3 Mathematical approaches aim at reproducing hysteresis loops independently of phenomenology. On the other hand, there exist physical formalisations of hysteresis based on a particular phenomenology. For instance, Maugin (1990) constructed a phenomenological model of magnetic hysteresis which is not based on the procedure of aggregation of heterogeneous elements described here.

4 For example, an exporting firm in Amable, Henry, Lordon and Topol (1991), a single worker in Cross (1991).

5 Following the terminology of Mayergoyz (1991).

6 Recall that 'aggregate output' refers here to a general input–output macro system.

7 The choice of a binary hysteron in the present example does not restrict the generality of the method. Any functional relationship between input and output is compatible with it provided there exists a partial overlapping (multiplicity of equilibria).

8 Which requires negative real part eigenvalues.

9 For an hysteretic system, one must consider a 'loading' (a variation in the input) followed by an 'unloading' (a change of the same magnitude in the opposite direction).

10 This misinterpretation might have stemmed from the famous 'hysteresis (closed) loop' graph, which is only a response to a very particular case of 'loading–unloading'.

11 The idea of a potential is not merely a metaphor but absolutely rigorous for single-dimensional dynamics, which can always be considered as derived from a gradient.

12 The NAIRU in Sachs (1987).

13 Or may not be found relevant at all, but this is not the point here.

14 Local structural instability means that the critical parameters are located in a set of measure zero in the parameter space. This set is referred to as the bifurcation state.

15 The flows before and after the crossing of the bifurcation set are no longer topologically equivalent.

References

Amable, B., Henry, J., Lordon, F. and Topol, R., 1991. ' "Strong" Hysteresis: an Application to Foreign Trade', *Working Paper*, 9103, Paris: OFCE

1992a. 'Hysteresis: What it is and What it is not', *Working Paper*, CEPREMAP, 9216

1992b. 'Hysteresis Versus Unit Root or can Non-linear Remanence be Equal to Linear Persistence?', INRA–Banque de France–CEPREMAP–OFCE, mimeo

1994, 'Strong Hysteresis versus Zero-root Dynamics', *Economics Letters*, 44, 43–7

Arthur, B., Ermoliev, Y.M. and Kaniovski, Y.M., 1987. 'Path-dependent Processes and the Emergence of Macro-structure', *European Journal of Operational Research*, 30, 294–303

Baldwin, R. and Krugman, P., 1989. 'Persistent Effect of Large Exchange Rate Shocks', *Quarterly Journal of Economics*, 104(4), 635–54

Bentolila, S. and Bertola, G., 1990. 'Firing Costs and Labour Demand: How Bad is Eurosclerosis?' *Review of Economic Studies*, 57, 381–402

Blanchard, O. and Summers, L., 1986. 'Hysteresis in Unemployment', *NBER Working Paper*, 2035

1988. 'Beyond the Natural Rate Hypothesis', *American Economic Review*, 78(2) (May), 182–7

Caballero, R. and Engel, E., 1990. 'Dynamic (S,s) Economies', *Econometrica*, 59(6), 1659–86

1993. 'Heterogeneity and Output Fluctuations in a Dynamic Menu-cost Economy', *Review of Economic Studies*, 60, 95–119

Caplin, A. and Spulber, D., 1987. 'Menu Costs and the Neutrality of Money', *Quarterly Journal of Economics*, 102(4), 703–25

Cross, R., 1991. NAIRU: Not An Interesting Rate of Unemployment, Strathclyde University, mimeo

1993. On the Foundations of Hysteresis in Economic Systems, *Economics and Philosophy*, 9(1) (Spring), 53–74

Dixit, A., 1989. 'Hysteresis, Import Penetration and Exchange Rate Pass-through', *Quarterly Journal of Economics*, 104(2), 205–28

1992. 'Investment and Hysteresis', *Journal of Economic Perspectives*, 6(1), 107–32

Engle, R. and Granger, C. (eds), 1991. *Long-Run Economic Relationships: Readings in Cointegration*, Oxford: Oxford University Press

Giavazzi, F. and Wyplosz, C., 1985. 'The Zero Root Problem: A Note on the Dynamics of the Stationary Equilibrium in Linear Models', *Review of Economic Studies*, 52(2), 353–7

Goodwin, R., 1967. 'A Growth Cycle', in S. Feinstein (ed.), *Capitalism, Socialism and Economic Growth*, Cambridge: Cambridge University Press

Haken, H., 1977. *Synergetics: An Introduction*, Berlin: Springer Verlag

Hirsch, M. and Smale, S., 1974. *Differential Equations, Dynamical Systems and Linear Algebra*, New York: Academic Press

Huizinga, F. and Schiantarelli, F., 1992. 'Dynamic and Asymmetric Adjustment in Insider–outsider Models', *Economic Journal*, 102(415), 1451–66

Johansen, S., 1988. 'Statistical Analysis of Cointegrating Vectors', *Journal of Economic Dynamics and Control*, 12(1/2), 231–54

Krasnosel'skii, M.A. and Pokrovskii, A.V., 1989. *Systems with Hysteresis*, Berlin: Springer-Verlag

Layard, R., Nickell, S.J. and Jackman, R., 1991. *Unemployment: Macroeconomic Performance and the Labour Market*, Oxford: Oxford University Press

Lindbeck, A., 1992. 'Macroeconomic Theory and the Labor Market', *European Economic Review*, 36(2/3), 209–35

Maugin, G., 1990. 'Thermodynamics of Hysteresis', in S. Sienutycz and D. Salamon (eds.), *Non-Equilibrium Thermodynamics*. New York: Taylor & Francis

Mayergoyz, I.D., 1986. 'Mathematical Models of Hysteresis', *IEEE Transactions on Magnetics*, 22(5), 603–8

1991. *Mathematical Models of Hysteresis*, Berlin: Springer-Verlag

Mosconi, R. and Giannini, C., 1992. 'Non-Causality in a Cointegrated System: Representation Estimation and Testing', *Oxford Bulletin of Economics and Statistics*, 54(3), 399–417

Roberts, K., 1980. 'The Limit Points of Monopolistic Competition', *Journal of Economic Theory*, 22, 256–78

Sachs, J., 1985. 'High Employment in Europe. Diagnosis and Policy Implications', Harvard, mimeo

1987. 'High Employment in Europe. Diagnosis and Policy Implications', in Claes Henrie (ed.), *Unemployment in Europe*, Stockholm: Timbro

Thom, R., 1972. *Structural Stability and Morphogenesis*, Reading, MA: W.A. Benjamin

Van de Klundert, T. and Van Schaik, B., 1990. 'Unemployment Persistence and Loss of Productive Capacity: A Keynesian Approach', *Journal of Macroeconomics*, 12(3), 363–80

10 Is the natural rate hypothesis consistent with hysteresis?

Rod Cross

Hysteresis effects are distinct in that they remain after the initial causes are removed. The term itself is derived from the Greek ὑστερέω, meaning to come later, and was first coined for the explanation of scientific phenomena by the physicist James Alfred Ewing (1881a). The initial application was to the thermo-electric properties of metals when subjected to stress by loading and unloading, the more celebrated application being to the behaviour of electromagnetic fields in ferric metals (Ewing, 1881b, 1885, 1893). The non-hysteretic account of electromagnetic fields in Maxwell's equations had the property that the application of a once-off magnetising force would have no remaining effect on field characteristics once the force was removed. Ewing's studies revealed that this was not the case for ferric metals, and the term 'hysteresis' was coined to describe this phenomenon (see Cross and Allan, 1988; Cross, 1993).

The standard definition of the natural rate of unemployment (Phelps, 1967; Friedman, 1968) as depending on 'the actual structural characteristics of the labour and commodity markets, including market imperfections, stochastic variability in demands and supplies, the cost of gathering information about job vacancies and labour availabilities, the costs of mobility, and so on' (Friedman, 1968, p. 8) does not in itself preclude hysteresis: temporary shocks affecting actual unemployment, for example, could have permanent effects on the 'structural characteristics of labour and commodity markets', and consequently on the natural rate. The preclusion of hysteresis comes instead from the specification of factors which do *not* affect the natural rate, this set covering nominal magnitudes including the level of nominal demand: '[the] crucial element is that nominal magnitudes must be sharply distinguished from real magnitudes, and that nominal magnitudes in and of themselves cannot determine real magnitudes' (Friedman, letter to the author, 2 November 1990). Thus the natural rate hypothesis applies the classical proposition of monetary neutrality to unemployment, and in doing so yields the policy ineffectiveness proposition that aggregate demand policy measures cannot change the sustainable or equilibrium rate of unemployment.

The 1980s brought an apparent refutation of the natural rate hypothesis: 'structural characteristics' indicated, if anything, a downward shift in the natural rate, but the rate of unemployment consistent with steady inflation rose sharply in many countries. This led investigators to introduce a phenomenon which was termed 'hysteresis' into the natural rate framework. The present chapter points out that this phenomenon was not hysteresis, and that hysteresis is not consistent with the natural rate hypothesis.

The rest of the chapter is organised as follows. The first section offers brief account of how the natural rate hypothesis re-interpreted the Phillips curve relationship between inflation and unemployment. The second section reviews a standard model used to estimate the influence of 'structural characteristics of labour and commodity markets' on the natural rate. The third section refers to the problems encountered by this model and outlines how a phenomenon which was termed 'hysteresis', but which was nothing more than the *persistence* of deviations from the natural rate, was introduced in an attempt to reconcile the natural rate hypothesis with the evidence. The fourth section points out what hysteresis actually implies for time paths for equilibrium unemployment, and sketches how the hysteretic properties of *remanence* and *selective memory* arise (see also chapter 9 in this volume). The fifth and final section draws out the implications for time paths of equilibrium unemployment.

The Phillips curve

Natural rate models quickly supplanted Phillips curve models as explanations of inflation–unemployment interaction. The complaint was that Phillips curve models assumed money illusion, a complaint that is not upheld by Phillips' own account of the reasoning behind the famous curve:

a third factor influencing the rate of change of money wage rates is the rate of change of retail prices operating through cost of living adjustments in wage rates . . . assuming that the value of imports is one fifth of national income, it is only at times when the annual rate of change of import prices exceeds the rate at which wage rates would rise as a result of the competitive bidding by employers by more than five times the rate of increase of productivity that cost of living adjustments become an operative factor in increasing the rate of change of money wage rates (Phillips, 1958, pp. 283–4).

Natural rate (NR) models also reinterpreted the Phillips curve as a disequilibrium relationship arising from unexpected changes in the rate of inflation. Here, again, Phillips' own procedure in estimating the Phillips curve has been neglected: 'a second factor influencing the rate of change of money wage rates might be the rate of change of the demand for labour, and so of unemployment' (Phillips, 1958, p. 283). Instead of fitting the Phillips curve to the annual observations 1861–1913 on the rate of change of money wages rates ($\dot{w}$) and unemployment (u), Phillips fitted the curve to the average values of $\dot{w}$ and u for six intervals on u:

since each interval includes years in which unemployment was increasing and years in which it was decreasing the effect of changing unemployment on the rate of change of wage rates tends to be cancelled out by this averaging, so that each cross gives an approximation to the rate of change of wages which would be associated with the indicated level of unemployment if unemployment were held constant at that level (Phillips, 1958, p. 290).

It is difficult to see what the purpose of this procedure could be other than to estimate a $\dot{u} = 0$ locus, where the dot indicates a time derivative. Thus the Phillips curve itself can be seen as a quasi-equilibrium locus for $\dot{u} = 0$ (see Desai, 1975), and not the disequilibrium relationship which appears through the lens of the natural rate hypothesis. There is no particular reason why the position or shape of the Phillips curve should be invariant from one period to another (see Desai, 1975; Alogoskoufis and Smith, 1991, for evidence), and seen in this light the original Phillips curve provides an alternative rather than an adjunct to the natural rate account of equilibrium unemployment.

Symbolically, Phillips' own curve can be expressed as:

$$\dot{w} = f[u \mid \dot{u} = 0, \dot{p}_w < m^{-1}\dot{\pi}] \tag{1}$$

where $\dot{p}_w$ is the rate of change of world prices expressed in domestic currency, m is the proportion of goods open to international competition, and $\dot{\pi}$ is productivity growth. Taking time derivatives implies:

$$\ddot{w} = f[\dot{u} \mid \ddot{u} = 0, \ddot{p}_w < m^{-1}\ddot{\pi}]. \tag{2}$$

This suggests that changes in the rate of inflation ($\ddot{w} \neq 0$) are driven by *changes* in unemployment ($\dot{u} \neq 0$) rather than by the *level* of unemployment relative to the natural rate ($u - u^*$), as the natural rate hypothesis would suggest. Different monetary regimes, and different $I(1)$ or $I(2)$ processes for the price level (see Alogoskoufis and Smith, 1991), would shift the way the $\dot{p}_w$ variable conditions the quasi-equilibrium locus, as would changes in productivity growth.

Natural rate models

Early models of the natural rate (Phelps, 1967, 1970) were based on specifications of labour market turnover or search. There are now a wide variety of specifications of how the natural rate 'structural characteristics of labour and commodity markets' affect equilibrium time paths for unemployment (see Nickell, 1990, for a survey). Correspondingly, despite Friedman's view that it is not possible to 'know what the "natural" rate is . . . we have as yet devised no method to estimate accurately and readily the natural rate of either interest or unemployment' (Friedman, 1968, p. 7), there is a huge empirical literature on the importance of various 'structural characteristics' in explaining changes in the natural rate (see Bean, 1992a, for a survey). Despite this outpouring of research effort various combinations of 'structural characteristics' have singularly failed to explain why the unemployment rates consistent with steady inflation have risen in many countries since the 1960s. In what follows the problems encountered by the natural rate hypothesis are illustrated by reference to the NAIRU literature on unemployment in the UK.

The NAIRU is an acronym for the 'non-accelerating inflation rate of unemployment'. Despite the terminology, the NAIRU is 'fundamentally of the natural rate type . . . exogenous demand-side factors do not influence the equilibrium . . . in the long run the unemployment rate always reverts' (Layard, Nickell and Jackman, 1991, pp. 10, 16, 369). The need for a new term arose because it was felt that the natural rate 'smacks of inevitability', though Friedman had emphasised that 'by using the term "natural" rate of unemployment [he did] not mean to suggest that it is immutable and unchangeable . . . on the contrary, many of the market characteristics that determine its level are man-made and policy-made' (Friedman, 1968, p. 9). More curious is the acronym itself: taken literally the NAIRU implies $\ddot{p} \leq 0$, where p is the log of the price level. Yet the NAIRU is a synonym for the natural rate, so the acronym should imply $\ddot{p} = 0$, e.g. CIRU (constant inflation rate of unemployment): it is the price level, not the rate of inflation, which neither accelerates nor decelerates. To avoid confusion the natural rate terminology is used in the following discussion.

The NAIRU/natural rate model of equilibrium unemployment is derived from an imperfect competition specification of the 'structural characteristics of labour and commodity markets'. The natural rate equilibrium emerges from a 'battle of the mark-ups', being the rate of unemployment which reconciles price- and wage-setting behaviour (see Blanchard, 1986). The price, wage and aggregate demand equations in the Layard–Nickell version of this model (Layard, Nickell and Jackman, 1991, p. 378) can be written as:

$$p - w = \alpha_0 - \alpha_1 u + \alpha_2(p - p^e) - \alpha_3(k - l) \tag{3}$$

$$w - p = \beta_0 - \beta_1 u + \beta_2(p - p^e) + z + \alpha_3(k - l) \tag{4}$$

$$y = x - p. \tag{5}$$

Here p is the price level, w the money wage level, u is unemployment, p^e is the expected price level, k and l are the capital stock and labour force, z is a vector of wage pressure variables, y is aggregate demand, x is a vector of variables affecting aggregate demand, all variables are measured in logarithms. The rate of inflation is assumed to follow a unit root process, $\Delta p = \Delta p_{-1} + \varepsilon$, price level expectations being geared to this process, so that $p^e = p_{-1} + \Delta p_{-1}$ and $p - p^e = \Delta^2 p$, where Δ is the difference operator. The natural rate equilibrium condition is $p - p^e = \Delta^2 p = 0$. Imposing this condition and adding equations (1) and (2) yields the natural rate equilibrium:

$$u^* = \frac{\alpha_0 + \beta_0 + z}{\alpha_1 + \beta_1}. \tag{6}$$

Thus, assuming parameter constancy, the time path for equilibrium unemployment u_t^* is driven by the time path of the wage pressure z_t, and is independent of the x variables affecting the level of aggregate demand. A more general formulation of this imperfect competition model would allow capital intensity $(k - 1)$ and productivity (π) to affect the natural rate (see Blanchard, 1990), but such effects are ruled out a priori in the Layard–Nickell model.

The 'structural characteristics' which drive the natural rate in this model are wage pressure variables of the socioeconomic type. The main variables included in this vector z have been measures of trades union power (TUP) in wage bargaining; the characteristics of the unemployment benefits (UB) system; and mismatch (MM) between the skills required in job vacancies and skills of the unemployed. Estimates of the significance and importance of these variables differ widely between empirical studies (see Cromb, 1993, for a survey). The broad pattern in post-1945 UK data is that the z variables tracked the upward drift in unemployment from the mid-1960s to the late 1970s reasonably well, but that they pointed to a reduction in the natural rate in response to the supply-side approach to unemployment policy in the 1980s. The steady inflation or equilibrium rate of unemployment ($\ddot{p}$ was approximately zero in the UK, 1983–7), however, rose sharply in the 1980s, refuting this account of equilibrium unemployment in qualitative as well as quantitative terms. A popular line of further investigation was to see if changes in the 'wedge' between the prices paid by consumers (p_c) and the prices received by firms (p_F) could rescue the model. Thus measures of tax rates (t), world prices (p_w) and exchange rates (er) were included in the z vector as measures of real wage resistance, though it is not clear that the underlying theory of price- and wage-setting behaviour implies a long-run role for such effects (see Barrell, 1993). The estimates of the size and significance of such real wage resistance effects again differ widely between studies (see Cromb, 1993), but the broad thrust was an inability to explain the upward shift in u_t^* during the 1980s.

Given the Duhem problem it is always possible that a hypothesis can be rescued from refutation by amendment of auxiliary hypotheses. Recent natural rate models have widened the set of 'structural characteristics of labour and commodity markets' beyond the wage pressure and resistance variables identified in the Layard–Nickell model. Productivity, changes in the capital stock arising from movements in real interest rates and oil prices, and demographic effects are amongst the 'structural characteristics' investigated (see Bean, 1992b; Phelps, 1992).

While the jury remains out, the question arises of whether it would be wise to abandon the natural rate hypothesis in order to construct an account of equilibrium unemployment which is consistent with the evidence. The distinguishing feature of the natural rate hypothesis is that which is excluded: nominal variables, such as the level of aggregate demand, affect actual but not equilibrium unemployment. It can be argued that this distinction between the determinants of actual and equilibrium unemployment has encountered too much embarrassment to be tenable:

this dichotomy did not fit the experience of the 1980s, in which a sharp, aggregate demand induced increase in unemployment had been followed by an increase in equilibrium unemployment . . . the increase in unemployment is attributed to a variety of supply and demand factors, with supply factors dominating the scene in the 1970s and demand factors . . . [in] the early 1980s . . . these original factors have in large part disappeared but unemployment has not (Blanchard, 1990, pp. 72, 84).

Blurring the dichotomy

As Keynes remarked, 'the ideas of economists and political philosophers, both when they are right and when they are wrong, are more powerful than is commonly understood' (Keynes, 1936, p. 383). The power of the natural rate hypothesis comes from the same source as classical doctrine. In the case of the Layard–Nickell NAIRU/natural rate model the evidential inconsistencies revealed in the 1980s led not to the abandonment of the hypothesis but to its relegation to the very long run. As it happens, this was in line with a neglected aspect of Friedman's version of the hypothesis, in which he speculated that 'a full adjustment to the new rate of inflation takes as long as for interest rates, say, a couple of decades' (Friedman, 1968, p. 11). The basic idea is that there is an equilibrium rate of unemployment in the medium term which violates the natural rate hypothesis in that it is partly determined by the nominal variables, such as aggregate demand, which affect actual unemployment. The obvious question is whether this medium-term time path for equilibrium unemployment is consistent with convergence to a long-run natural rate equilibrium path. The Layard–Nickell model asserted that such convergence holds: 'there is short-term "hysteresis", in the sense that past events affect the current short-run NAIRU – but there is no long-term "hysteresis": there is a unique long-run NAIRU . . . in the end the unemployment rate always reverts' (Layard, Nickell and Jackman, 1991, p. 10). There are similarities here with the attempted accommodation of Keynesian economics within the neoclassical synthesis model of the 1950s.

The possibility that natural rate equilibria could be affected by 'hysteresis' was first raised by Phelps: 'the transition from one equilibrium to the other tends to have long lingering effects on the labour force, and these effects may be discernible on the equilibrium rate of unemployment for a long time . . . the natural rate . . . at any future date will depend on the course of history in the interim . . . such a property is often called hysteresis' (Phelps, 1972, p. xxiii). The 'hysteresis' amendment to the Layard–Nickell model is outlined in Nickell (1987) and Layard and Nickell (1987), and works as follows: an increase in actual unemployment leads to an increase in long-term unemployment, the proportion of the unemployed who have been out of work for longer than, say, a year; the long-term unemployed are disenfranchised from the labour market, and cannot exert downward pressure on wages; this change in the 'structural characteristics' of the labour market reduces the downward pressure on wages arising from any given level of unemployment, raising the equilibrium rate of unemployment, the rate which reconciles wage- and price-setting behaviour.

The proportion of the long-term unemployed (R) increases, after a short time lag, in response to increases in unemployment, so a crude way of capturing this 'hysteresis' effect is via Δu. This leads to a reformulation of the price and wage equations as:

$$p - w = \alpha_0 - \alpha_1 u - \alpha_{11}\Delta u + \alpha_2(p - p^e) - \alpha_3(k - l) \qquad (7)$$

$$w - p = \beta_0 - \beta_1 u - \beta_{11}\Delta u + \beta_2(p - p^e) + z + \alpha_3(k - l). \qquad (8)$$

Imposing the steady or anticipated equilibrium condition $p - p^e = \Delta^2 p = 0$ yields:

$$um^* = \frac{(\alpha_1 + \beta_1)u^* + (\alpha_{11} + \beta_{11})u_{-1}}{\alpha_1 + \beta_1 + \alpha_{11} + \beta_{11}}. \qquad (9)$$

Thus in the medium term equilibrium unemployment (um^*) is a weighted average of the natural rate (u^*) and the previous period's actual unemployment (u_{-1}) or, more generally, the dynamics of unemployment. The natural rate hypothesis in this domain applies only when $\Delta u = 0$ as well as

$p = p^e = \Delta^2 p = 0$. Here there is an interesting comparison with the original Phillips curve which yields a negative, non-linear relationship between inflation and unemployment when the $\Delta u = 0$ or $\dot{u} = 0$ condition is applied (see (1) above).

Several problems arise with this 'hysteresis' model of equilibrium unemployment. First is the identification problem. Specifications of wage bargaining, or of the opportunity cost of working, suggest that the exogenous variables in the wage equation should also appear in the price equation (see Bean, 1992a). This raises the problem of whether such 'structural' equations can be identified, or whether the wage equation is the price equation stood on its head, and vice versa (see Sims, 1982). This problem does not arise in the quasi-equilibrium reduced form of the original Phillips curve.

Second is the problem of level and change of unemployment effects in the price and wage equations. If there is no level of unemployment effect, i.e. $\alpha_1 = \beta_1 = 0$ in (9) above, the equilibrium rate of unemployment becomes simply $um^* = u_{-1}$, and the natural rate of unemployment is no longer defined by the z 'structural characteristics'. Some investigators have found significant effects from the change in unemployment, but level effects which are not significantly different from zero (e.g. Alogoskoufis and Smith, 1991, for the UK, 1857–1957). This suggests that the level of unemployment effects required for the natural rate of unemployment to exist in empirical models are fragile, and sensitive to the way the wage or price equations are specified. Again there is an interesting contrast with the original Phillips curve in which it is the change in unemployment that drives changes in the rate of inflation (see (2) above).

A third issue is whether the presence of a non-natural rate medium-term equilibrium is consistent with convergence to a long-run natural rate equilibrium. What is required is a demonstration that a stable, unique long-run equilibrium exists, and is determined by 'structural characteristics' which are immune to changes in nominal variables such as aggregate demand, and to changes in actual unemployment. At an analytical level, allowing equilibrium unemployment to be partly determined by actual unemployment can produce an unstable natural rate equilibrium (see Cross, 1987). At an empirical level, the existence requirement is that u is cointegrated with the z deep 'structural characteristics', and that long-term unemployment does not have a separate long-run effect. The most exhaustive study to date failed to find plausible cointegration relationships between u and z for the UK, 1954–89 (Darby and Wren-Lewis, 1993). Unemployment is a bounded variable, so it must be $I(0)$ over very long time periods. Over longish periods, such as post-1945, however, unemployment displays the persistence characteristics of an $I(1)$ variable. The challenge for proponents of the natural rate hypothesis is to find a vector of z variables which is $I(0)$ in the very long run, but $I(1)$ for long periods, and cointegrates with u over such long periods. Without such a demonstration the natural rate remains an article of faith rather than a hypothesis whose equilibrium claims are supported by the evidence.

A fourth issue, which is expanded on in the next section of this chapter, is whether the presence of 'hysteresis' in equilibrium unemployment is consistent with the natural rate hypothesis. It turns out that the 'hysteresis' in the NAIRU/natural rate model is not hysteresis at all, but instead a form of *persistence* of deviations from the natural rate equilibrium path (see chapter 9 in this volume). The basic problem here is that the NAIRU/natural rate model is a linear model with 'representative' agents, whereas hysteresis is a property of non-linear models with heterogeneous agents. In a linear system, 'hysteresis' arises in the special case of a unit root/zero root solution to difference/differential equations (see Giavazzi and Wyplosz, 1985; Wyplosz, 1987). The implications of this linear form of 'hysteresis' for the NAIRU/natural rate model can be illustrated by using equations (7) and (8) above to write unemployment as:

$$u_t = A + Bu_{t-1} + Cz_t + D\epsilon_t \tag{10}$$

where

$$
\begin{aligned}
A &= (\alpha_0 + \beta_0)(\alpha_1 + \alpha_{11} + \beta_1 + \beta_{11})^{-1} \\
B &= (\alpha_{11} + \beta_{11})(\alpha_1 + \alpha_{11} + \beta_1 + \beta_{11})^{-1} \\
C &= (\alpha_1 + \alpha_{11} + \beta_1 + \beta_{11})^{-1} \\
D &= (\alpha_2 + \beta_2)(\alpha_1 + \alpha_{11} + \beta_1 + \beta_{11})^{-1}
\end{aligned}
$$

and

$$\epsilon = p - p^e.$$

When both level and rate of change effects of unemployment on price- and wage-setting are significant we have $0 < B < 1$, and imposing the natural rate equilibrium conditions of $p - p^e = \Delta^2 p = 0$ and $\Delta u = 0$ yields:

$$u_t^* = \frac{A + Cz_t}{1 - B}. \tag{11}$$

If the level effects are insignificant, however, $\alpha_1 = \beta_1 = 0$ gives $B = 1$, and u_t^* now becomes, for $p_T - p_T^e = 0$ and $\Delta u_T = 0$:

$$u_T^* = u_0 + AT + C \sum_{i=0} z_{T-i} + D \sum_{i=1} \epsilon_{T-i}. \tag{12}$$

Thus the whole history of past shocks to actual unemployment determines the equilibrium rate of unemployment. The Layard–Nickell model assumes 'partial hysteresis' (Layard, Nickell and Jackman, 1991, p. 336), so ruling out the $B = 1$ case of 'pure hysteresis'. So what is termed 'hysteresis' is not actually hysteresis, not even in the way 'hysteresis' appears in linear systems.

Hysteresis is a non-linear phenomenon

In physics, from which the term derives, hysteresis is a non-linear phenomenon. In economics linear models have been the rule rather than the exception, so this is how a bastardised, linear version of 'hysteresis' came to be imported into natural rate models. Analysis of the implications of non-linear hysteresis for the behaviour of economic systems is still at a rudimentary stage. Cross (1993) sketches the implications for how aggregate output responds to shocks, Amable *et al.* (1991) analyse the way international trade responds to exchange rate changes, and Cross (1994) provides an application to asset switching. This work falls short of providing a full account of agent and market interaction. The general mathematical properties of systems with hysteresis have, however, been elucidated by Krasnosel'skii and his associates (Krasnosel'skii and Pokrovskii, 1983, 1989), and permit a sketch of the likely implications of non-linear hysteresis for time paths for equilibrium unemployment.

Applied to unemployment, the key components of a hysteresis explanation are: the existence of some non-linearity in the way employment or unemployment responds to shocks to the economic system; and heterogeneity in the way different firms, workers or other relevant agents respond to the shocks. The implications of these seemingly innocuous postulates are far-reaching. The equilibrium unemployment rate no longer, as in the natural rate hypothesis, returns to the *status quo ante* once a temporary shock is reversed, but instead displays *remanence*: this means that the new equilibrium will not be the same as the old, but will remain displaced. The other major implication is that the equilibrium rate of unemployment *retains a selective memory* of past shocks: it neither forgets all past shocks, as in the natural rate hypothesis; nor does it, like the elephant, remember all past shocks, as in the case of the linear version of hysteresis in (12) above. The *selective memory* property is such that only the *non-dominated extremum values* of shocks affect the equilibrium path, the dominated values being erased from the memory bank. This means that the global maximum of the shocks experienced, and any relevant decreasing sequence of local maxima, along with the global minimum and any increasing sequence of local minima, help shape the equilibrium path. Thus the last major expansionary and contractionary shocks will continue to affect the present equilibrium, their effects being

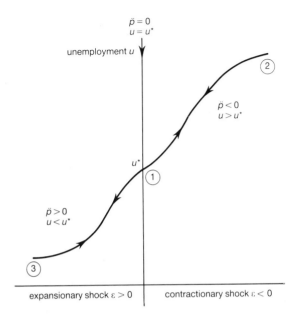

Figure 10.1   The natural rate hypothesis

modified by the influence of subsequent (non-dominated) local extrema. This implies that shocks arising from changes in nominal variables can, by way of the selective memory process, shape the equilibrium path for unemployment. This is a direct contradiction of the natural rate hypothesis, and so hysteresis is not a phenomenon which can be accommodated within the natural rate framework or, more generally, within the classical doctrine of neutrality.

The contrast between the hysteresis and natural rate accounts of equilibrium unemployment is illustrated in figures 10.1 and 10.2. The horizontal axis represents temporary shocks (ϵ) to aggregate demand, contractionary to the right, expansionary to the left. The vertical axis measures unemployment. Points on the vertical axis itself represent equilibrium rates of unemployment: the absence of contractionary or expansionary shocks, $\epsilon = 0$, means that the rate of inflation will be correctly anticipated and unchanging, i.e. $\dot{p} = 0$. To the right of the vertical axis contractionary shocks lead to $u > u^*$ and $\dot{p} < 0$; to the left, the expansionary shocks lead to $u < u^*$ and $\dot{p} > 0$. Figure 10.1 illustrates the case of the natural rate hypothesis, with the natural rate equilibrium u^* being independent of the shocks arising from nominal variables. A contractionary shock arising from, say, a restrictive monetary policy will

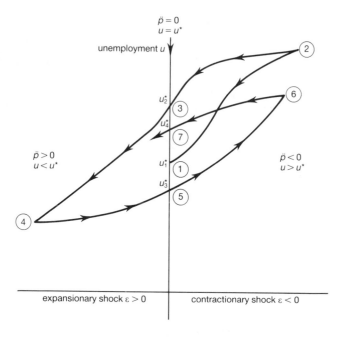

Figure 10.2   The hysteresis hypothesis

lead to an increase in actual unemployment along the trajectory ① to ②: this leads to a fall in the rate of inflation, and, eventually, a retreat back from ② to ① as the level of real demand recovers. Symmetrically, in the case of an expansionary shock the trajectory ① to ③ will be followed until the path is reversed once the rise in the rate of inflation reverses the initial expansionary effect on the level of real demand. *Contra* the Old Testament, the system does not pass this way only once.

Figure 10.2 illustrates what happens to equilibrium unemployment in the presence of hysteresis. Taking the same starting point u_1^* as in figure 10.1, the imposition of a contractionary shock leads unemployment to rise, and the rate of inflation to fall, along the trajectory ① to ②. The recovery of real demand in this case, however, sees a return to the equilibrium rate of unemployment u_2^* along the trajectory ② to ③. The equilibrium unemployment rate is higher because the system remembers the extremum value of this contractionary shock. A subsequent expansionary shock would see unemployment fall and the rate of inflation rise along the trajectory ③ to ④. Once the level of real demand starts to fall back the system returns along the trajectory ④ to ⑤ to u_3^*. This equilibrium unemployment rate is lower than u_2^* because the system remembers the extremum value of the expansionary

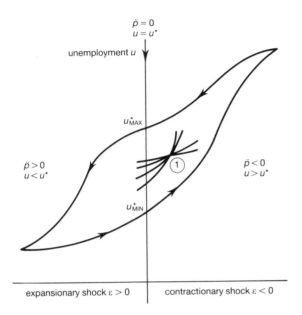

Figure 10.3   Multiple trajectories

shock experienced. And so on. As Heraclitus said, you don't put your foot into the same stream twice.

Figure 10.3 illustrates the possible trajectories of unemployment under hysteresis. Because unemployment is a bounded variable there are upper and lower limits to unemployment, the equilibrium counterparts of which are labelled u^*_{MAX} and u^*_{MIN}. Within the loop describing the largest variations in actual unemployment feasible, there are a potentially infinite number of trajectories which could be followed by actual, and hence, equilibrium unemployment in response to any given shock. The particular trajectory followed will be determined by the selective memory of non-dominated extremum values (of shocks experienced) at the particular point in time.

The analytics of the microeconomic processes underlying the hysteresis selective memory property can be illustrated by considering the hiring and firing practices of firms who respond differently to some common aggregate shock. Because of fixed costs of adjustment, firms respond discontinuously to the shocks experienced (see Hamermesh, 1989, for the case of the demand for labour and Caballero and Engel, 1992, for a review of the general literature on discontinuous adjustment). Each firm requires an aggregate

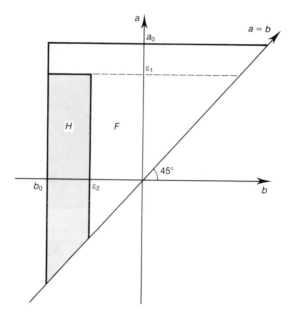

Figure 10.4   The effects of temporary shocks

demand shock of $\in \geq a$ to induce it to hire labour, and an aggregate demand shock $\in \leq b$ to induce it to fire labour. Thus shocks within the range $b < \in < a$ lead to inertia. Across the cross-sectional distribution of firms the different switching values from an infinite set of hysteresis operates F_{ab}. Introduce a weight function $g(a, b)$, which attaches weights to the switching values according to the contribution of firms with such switching values to total employment, and aggregate employment can be written as:

$$n_t = \iint\limits_{a \,\geq\, b} g(a,b) F_{ab} \in_t dadb \qquad (13)$$

where n_t is aggregate employment.

The way the remanence and selective memory properties of hysteresis arise is illustrated in figure 10.4, which uses the half-plane diagram of Mayergoyz (1991). The switching points $a \geq b$ are points on or above the line $a = b$. The boundary condition is that the weight function $g(a, b)$ is equal to zero outside the right-angled triangle with vertex (a_0, b_0). The initial condition is that $\in_0 < b_0$, so initially all firms are firing labour. A particular sequence of shocks is illustrated in figure 10.5. The expansionary

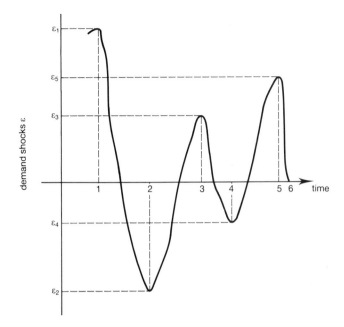

Figure 10.5   A sequence of shocks

shock ϵ_1 leads forms with a $\leq \epsilon_1$ to hire labour, those with $a > \epsilon_1$ continue to fire labour. This serves to divide firms into two sets, H and F, of hirers and firers respectively, the division corresponding to a horizontal line drawn at ϵ_1 in figure 10.4. A subsequent contractionary shock ϵ_2 will lead firms with $b \geq \epsilon_2$ to fire labour, firms with $b < \epsilon_2$ continuing to hire labour. The division between the set of firms hiring labour, H, and firing labour, F, is illustrated in figure 10.4, having a vertex (ϵ_1, ϵ_2).

A subsequent contractionary shock, ϵ_3, and expansionary shock, ϵ_4, traces out the staircase between the sets H and F illustrated in figure 10.6, the vertices being (ϵ_1, ϵ_2), (ϵ_3, ϵ_2) and (ϵ_3, ϵ_4). So far, because of the declining and increasing sequences of expansionary and contractionary shocks respectively, aggregate employment depends on all the extremum values experienced. The memory wiping-out process can be illustrated with respect to the effects of an expansionary shock ϵ_5. As illustrated in figure 10.6 this erases the (ϵ_3, ϵ_4) vertex of the staircase, generating a new staircase line with vertices (ϵ_1, ϵ_2) and (ϵ_5, ϵ_2). Thus the ϵ_5 shock serves to erase dominated extremum values from the memory bank. Thus if the aggregate demand shock disappears to $\epsilon_6 = 0$, the 'equilibrium' level of employment n_6^* will retain a selective memory of the non-dominated extremum values

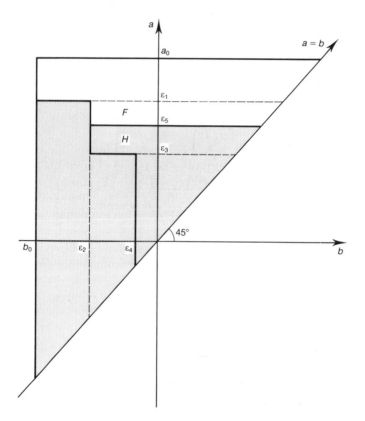

Figure 10.6   The wiping-out process

experienced. If $u \simeq \bar{n} - n$, where $\bar{n}$ and n are the logs of labour 'supply' and 'demand' respectively, the implication is that the equilibrium rate of unemployment u_t^* will retain a selective memory of the aggregate demand shocks experienced.

The above is but an illustration of how the hysteresis properties of *remanence* and *selective memory* arise. These properties are likely to arise in a wider class of economic models which have non-linear relationships and heterogeneous agents (see Krasnosel'skii and Pokrovskii, 1989, for the mathematics of the general case).

Implications

The natural rate hypothesis has been highly influential in conditioning thought about what determines, and what can be done about, unemployment. Politicians and their advisers in the UK and elsewhere have 'distilled their frenzy' from the hypothesis, drawing the message that, over a time horizon short enough to be relevant to policy, only 'supply-side' measures could be effective in achieving a sustainable reduction in unemployment. Expansionary aggregate demand policies, according to the hypothesis, would not yield a sustainable reduction in unemployment, and contractionary demand policies to reduce the rate of inflation can be pursued without any lasting adverse effects on unemployment and the real economy. The outcome of the pursuit of this 'natural rate' policy strategy has, however, been higher, not lower, unemployment. In an attempt to save the hypothesis, proponents of the natural rate introduced a form of persistence of deviations of actual from equilibrium unemployment which was termed 'hysteresis', postulating that the natural rate would still be a strong attractor for actual unemployment in the long run. The question then is one of whether the presence of 'hysteresis' is consistent with the natural rate hypothesis.

Critics have argued that this 'hysteresis' amendment has produced a theory which is no longer a natural rate hypothesis: 'a theory that allows the natural rate to trundle along after the actual rate is not a natural rate theory' (Blinder, 1987, p. 132); 'a natural rate that hops around from one triennium to another under the influence of unspecified forces, including past unemployment rates, is not "natural" at all . . . "epiphenomenal" would be a better adjective' (Solow, 1987, p. S33). The present chapter has argued, along such lines, that the presence of hysteresis produces a time path for equilibrium unemployment which is inconsistent with the natural rate hypothesis. This conclusion follows from the recognition that hysteresis is a property of non-linear systems with heterogeneous micro elements. Such systems retain a memory of the non-dominated extremum values of shocks experienced, including temporary shocks to aggregate demand. Thus equilibrium unemployment rates are shaped, *inter alia*, by nominal variables, which contradicts the natural rate hypothesis.

The implication for the explanation of equilibrium unemployment is that any cointegration vectors between unemployment and 'structural characteristics of labour and commodity markets' will be shifted by the non-dominated extremum values of shocks experienced. A given vector of 'structural characteristics' z_t can be associated with a wide range of equilibrium unemployment rates, the particular equilibrium being determined by the shocks experienced. Thus the equilibrium rate of unemployment in the UK at the time of writing will be higher because of the contractionary shocks of 1979–81 and 1990–1, and lower because of the expansionary shocks of 1988–9. The implication is that any cointegration vector which attracts actual unemployment will have kinks or ratchets corresponding to the non-dominated extremum values of shocks experienced in these periods.

The policy implication is that aggregate demand policies can shift the equilibrium rate of unemployment both upwards and downwards. The broad negative association between equilibrium unemployment and inflation captured in the original Phillips curve is reintroduced, but in the form of a series of trajectories rather than a single curve. The particular trajectory taken, and the reduction of equilibrium unemployment that can be 'bought' by any given increase in steady inflation, will depend on the inherited memory of shocks. History, or at least some of it, is not bunk. Thus the answer to the question posed in the title of this chapter is 'no': the natural rate hypothesis is not consistent with hysteresis.

References

Alogoskoufis, G.S. and Smith, R., 1991. 'The Phillip Curve, the Persistence of Inflation and the Lucas Critique: Evidence from Exchange Rate Regimes', *American Economic Review*, 81, 1254–75

Amable, B., Henry, J., Lordon, F. and Topol, R., 1991. ' "Strong" Hysteresis: an Application to Foreign Trade', *Working Paper*, 9103, Paris: OFCE

Barrell, R., 1993. 'Internal and External Balance: the Layard, Nickell and Jackman Approach to the NAIRU and External Balance', *Journal of Economic Studies*, 20(1/2), 73–86

Bean, C.R., 1992a. 'European Unemployment: A Survey', Centre for Economic Performance, *Discussion Paper*, 71 (March), London: LSE

1992b. 'Identifying the Causes of British Unemployment', paper given to the *European Unemployment Programme Conference*, Chelwood Gate

Blanchard, O.J., 1986. 'The Wage–Price Spiral', *Quarterly Journal of Economics*, 101, 543–66

1990. 'Unemployment: Getting the Questions Right and Some of the Answers', in J.H. Drèze and C.R. Bean, *Europe's Unemployment Problem*, Cambridge, MA: MIT Press

Blinder, A.S., 1987. 'Keynes, Lucas and Scientific Progress', *American Economic Review*, 77(2), 130–6

Caballero, R.J. and Engel, E.M.R.A., 1992. 'Microeconomic Adjustment Hazards and Aggregate Dynamics', *NBER Working Paper*, 4090, Cambridge, MA: NBER

Cromb, R., 1993. 'A Survey of Recent Econometric Work on the NAIRU', *Journal of Economic Studies*, 20(1/2), 27–51

Cross, R., 1987. 'Hysteresis and Instability in the Natural Rate of Unemployment', *Scandinavian Journal of Economics*, 89(1), 71–89

1993. 'On the Foundations of Hysteresis in Economic Systems', *Economics and Philosophy*, 9(1) (Spring), 53–74

1994. 'The Macroeconomic Consequences of Discontinuous Adjustment:

Selective Memory of Non-Dominated Extrema', *Scottish Journal of Political Economy*, 41(2), 212–21

Cross, R. and Allan, A., 1988. 'On the History of Hysteresis', in R. Cross (ed.), *Unemployment, Hysteresis and the Natural Rate Hypothesis*, Oxford: Blackwell

Darby, J. and Wren-Lewis, S., 1993. 'Is there a Cointegrating Vector for UK Wages?', *Journal of Economic Studies*, 20.1/2, 87–115

Desai, M., 1975. 'The Phillips Curve: a Revisionist Interpretation', *Economica*, 42, 1–19

Ewing, J.A., 1881a. 'The Effects of Stress on the Thermoelectric Quality of Metals', *Proceedings of the Royal Society of London*, 32, 399–402

1881b. 'On the Production of Transient Electric Currents in Iron and Steel Conductors by Twisting Them When Magnetised or by Magnetising Them When Twisted', *Proceedings of the Royal Society of London*, 33, 21–3

1885. 'Experimental Researches in Magnetism', *Philosophical Transactions of the Royal Society of London*, 176II, 523–640

1893. *Magnetic Induction in Iron and Other Metals*, London: D. Van Nostrand

Friedman, M., 1968. 'The Role of Monetary Policy', *American Economic Review*, 58(1) (March), 1–17

Giavazzi, F. and Wyplosz, C., 1985. 'The Zero Root Problem: a Note on the Dynamics of the Stationary Equilibrium in Linear Models', *Review of Economic Studies*, 52(2), 353–7

Hamermesh, D.S., 1989. 'Labour Demand and the Structure of Adjustment Costs', *American Economic Review*, 79(4), 674–89

Keynes, J.M., 1936. *The General Theory of Employment, Interest and Money*, New York: Harcourt Brace and London: Macmillan

Krasnosel'skii, M.A. and Pokrovskii, A.V., 1983. *Sistemy s Gisteresisom*, Moscow: Nauka

1989. *Systems with Hysteresis*, Berlin: Springer-Verlag

Layard, R. and Nickell, S.J., 1987. 'The Labour Market', in R. Dornbusch and R. Layard (eds), *The Performance of the British Economy*, Oxford: Oxford University Press

Layard, R., Nickell, S. and Jackman, R., 1991. *Unemployment: Macroeconomic Performance and the Labour Market*, Oxford: Oxford University Press

Mayergoyz, I.D., 1991. *Mathematical Models of Hysteresis*, Berlin: Springer-Verlag

Nickell, S.J., 1987. 'Why is Wage Inflation in Britain So High?', *Oxford Bulletin of Economics and Statistics*, 49, 103–28

1990. 'Unemployment: a Survey', *Economic Journal*, 100(401), 391–439

Phelps, E.S., 1967. 'Phillips Curves, Expectations of Inflation and Optimal Unemployment over Time', *Economica*, 34(3) (August), 254–81

et al., 1970. *Microeconomic Foundations of Employment and Inflation Theory*, New York: W.W. Norton and London: Macmillan

1972. *Inflation Policy and Unemployment Theory*. London: Macmillan

1992. 'A Review of Unemployment; Macroeconomic Performance and the Labour Market', *Journal of Economic Literature*, 30, 1476–90

Phillips, A.W., 1958. 'The Relation between Unemployment and the Rate of

Change of Money Wage Rates in the United Kingdom, 1861–1957', *Economica*, 25 (November), 283–99

Sims, C.A., 1982. 'Policy Analysis with Econometric Models', *Brookings Papers on Economic Activity*, 1, 107–52

Solow, R.M., 1987. 'Unemployment: Getting the Questions Right', *Economica*, 53, S23–34

Wyplosz, C., 1987. 'Comments', in R. Layard and L. Calmfors (eds.), *The Fight against Unemployment*, Cambridge, MA: MIT Press

III

Empirical tests and macro models

11 The natural rate hypothesis and its testable implications*

Hashem Pesaran and Ron Smith

Introduction

The natural rate hypothesis (NRH) was introduced by Phelps (1967) and by Milton Friedman in his 1967 Presidential Address to the American Economic Association (1968). Friedman's version of the hypothesis is based on the Wicksellian concept of the 'natural' rate, and broadly speaking postulates that it is impossible to *permanently* reduce (increase) the realised or the 'market' rate of unemployment below (or above) its 'natural' level. The natural rate of unemployment, which plays a central role in the formulation of the natural rate hypothesis, is defined by Friedman (1968, p. 8) to be

the level that would be ground out by the Walrasian system of general equilibrium equations, provided there is imbedded in them the actual structural characteristics of the labor and commodity markets, including market imperfections, stochastic variability in demands and supplies, the cost of gathering information about job vacancies and labor availabilities, the costs of mobility, and so on.

According to this definition the natural rate of unemployment is not a constant or an immutable rate, but is determined by a host of market and non-market factors. It is influenced by government policy towards legal minimum wage rates, costs of searching for new employments, labour mobility, technological innovations and many other factors that have direct bearings on the workings of the labour and capital markets. Friedman's primary reason for introducing this concept, as with Wicksell before him, was an attempt to 'separate the real forces from the monetary forces' that impinge on the market rate of unemployment. Whether such a separation is possible or can be made operational in a meaningful manner lies at the heart of the theoretical and empirical debates over the natural rate hypothesis that have ensued ever since. Like most theories in economics, the natural rate hypothesis, by postulating that the deviation of the market rate of unemployment from its 'natural rate' is determined by the 'unexpected' changes in the rate of price inflation ('surprises'), involves two important types of unobservable, namely the natural rate itself and the expected rate of price inflation. To give it empirical content requires making some auxiliary assumptions about the determinants of the natural rate of unemployment, and the way inflation expectations are formed. Friedman assumed adaptive expectations and derived a long-run policy ineffectiveness conclusion; later writers, particularly Lucas, Sargent and Wallace (hereafter LSW), assumed rational expectations (RE), in linear models and derived short-run policy ineffectiveness conclusions.

In this chapter we wish to review some of the empirical issues associated with attempts to estimate and test the LSW version of the natural rate hypothesis–rational expectations model, examining in particular the model used by Barro (1977, 1978) and Barro and Rush (1980) in which deviations from the natural rate are explained in terms of a distributed lag of money supply surprises. In the second section we discuss alternative formulations of the natural rate hypothesis.[1] Empirical examination of the natural rate hypothesis requires proxy measures of the natural rate itself in terms of observed determinants. There has been considerable work on providing explanations of observable determinants of the natural rate of unemployment, and we review these in the third section. The rest of the chapter emphasises the natural rate of output, which despite playing a central role in the Lucas supply curve, has not been investigated as systematically. We discuss three issues. First, if output is trend stationary and the natural rate of output can be represented by a deterministic trend, then, as the fourth section shows, the model used by Barro and others does not constitute a valid representation of the LSW natural rate hypothesis–rational expectations model.[2] Secondly, if output is difference stationary as is widely believed, then as the fifth section shows, the standard Barro-type regressions can be spurious, and there will be important implications for the natural rate of output if the LSW model holds, which have been ignored in the literature. Thirdly, if the economy is described by a Keynesian model with an optimising government, the resulting reduced form equations for output will be indistinguishable from the equations used by the proponents of the natural rate hypothesis, unless the theory specifies observable differences between government target levels of output and the natural rate. This argument is set out in the sixth section. Not only do these three considerations cast doubt on conventional attempts to test the natural rate hypothesis, they suggest that it may be impossible to test the hypothesis at all, unless the theory provides a fairly precise formulation of the determinants of the level of output, or employment, which would be 'ground out by the Walrasian system'.

Although the proponents of the LSW natural rate hypothesis models have largely moved on to real business cycle and other models, the issues raised by the natural rate hypothesis controversy are still important.

Determining the impact of government policy, anticipated or unanticipated, on output and employment remains a central theoretical and empirical question in economics. The reasons that Barro (1989, p. 3) gives for abandoning the 'surprise' model are that: information lags did not seem important; the relationship of price shocks and money supply surprises to output or employment seemed to be weak or non-existent and that it was difficult within this model to reproduce features of the economy such as the strong procyclical behaviour of investment and the fact that consumption and leisure (unemployment) tend to move in opposite directions. This explanation does not seem convincing. All the empirical evidence against the 'surprise' model was available and was pointed out at the time when the proponents were developing the new classical model. In particular, it was pointed out at the time that the implication of the LSW model was that the natural rate of output had to move procyclically in a way that was inconsistent with the theory. The transition seems to have been driven by quite different theoretical considerations: the demands of a research agenda directed by the desire to explain how intertemporal substitution by an optimising representative agent within a neoclassical (endogenous) growth model could provide an explanation of output fluctuations. Ironically, this involved the proponents moving from models where the unanticipated component of money drove the cycle, to models à la Kydland and Prescott (1982, 1988) where money had no role at all and the cycle was driven by real technology shocks.

Alternative formulations of the natural rate hypothesis

As a way of providing some background, let us begin with Friedman's rationale for explaining deviations of the market rate of unemployment from its natural rate in terms of unexpected inflation. This is based on a particular characterisation of the clearing process in the labour market. Suppose that workers and firms bargain over nominal wages, but care about *real* wages. At the beginning of each period both workers and firms form expectations of the price level over the duration of the contract and base their decisions on 'expected' real wages. However, if expectations are not fulfilled and if prices turn out to be higher than expected, firms initially will expand output and employment to take advantage of the lower real wages as compared to the level of real wages which had been expected at the beginning of the period. But this initial increase in output will be temporary, and sooner or later will be reversed as workers experience the fall in real wages and start to renegotiate their nominal wages at the end of the period. The market rate of unemployment can only be kept below its natural rate by further and further increases in the rate of inflation. In cases where inflation is fully anticipated, all contracts will be in real terms and the equilibrium in the labour market will be unaffected by the rate of inflation. Hence, Friedman argued that only unanticipated inflation can have real effects. Similar arguments were also advanced by Phelps (1967,1970). A simple version of the natural rate hypothesis can be written as

$$u_t - u_t^* = -\alpha(\pi_t - \pi_t^e) + \varepsilon_t, \qquad \alpha > 0, \tag{1}$$

where

u_t = the 'market' rate of unemployment
u_t^* = the natural rate of unemployment
π_t = the rate of inflation
π_t^e = the expected rate of inflation formed at time $t - 1$
ε_t = zero mean serially uncorrelated supply shocks.

Apart from the supply shocks, the deviation of the market rate from the natural rate is determined solely in terms of the expectations errors, $\pi_t - \pi_t^e$. To keep the market rate permanently below the natural rate requires a *systematic* downward bias in the formation of inflation expectations.

The natural rate hypothesis can also be derived from an inflation-augmented version of the Phillips curve. Consider, for example, the model

$$\pi_t - \pi_{t-1} = -\alpha^{-1}(u_t - u_t^*) + \beta(\pi_t^e - \pi_{t-1}) + \varepsilon_t, \tag{2}$$

where u_t^* now stands for the non-accelerating inflation rate of unemployment (NAIRU). The natural rate hypothesis is then equivalent to the hypothesis that $\beta = 1$ (see, for example, Tobin, 1970).

The new classical formulation of the natural rate hypothesis differed from Friedman in two important respects: the assumption that inflation expectations are formed adaptively was replaced by the rational expectations hypothesis (REH), and the focus of the theoretical analysis was shifted from the inflation-augmented Phillips curve to the 'aggregate' supply function. (See, for example, Lucas, 1972, 1973; Sargent and Wallace, 1973, 1975; Barro, 1976.) Sargent and Wallace, for example, consider the following simple version of the aggregate supply function:

$$y_t - y_t^* = \gamma(\pi_t - \pi_t^e) + \xi_t, \qquad \gamma > 0, \tag{3}$$

where y_t is a measure of aggregate output (in logarithm) and y_t^* is the logarithm of the natural level output corresponding to u_t^*, the natural rate of unemployment. In some models of aggregate supply, such as the 'island' model discussed by Lucas (1973), the coefficient γ is not a constant but is inversely related to the conditional variance of π_t.

The precise specification of the aggregate supply function is important.

Lucas (1972), for example, basing his analysis on an intertemporal substitution framework, obtains the following forward-looking version:

$$y_t - y_t^* = \gamma(\pi_t - \pi_{t+1}^e) + \xi_t, \qquad \gamma > 0, \tag{3a}$$

where the expectations of π_{t+1} formed at t and not the current expectations, π_t^e, enters the supply equation. Despite their apparent similarities, (3) and (3a) have different policy implications under the rational expectations hypothesis. Writing (3a) as

$$y_t - y_t^* = \gamma(\pi_t - \pi_t^e) - \gamma(\pi_{t+1}^e - \pi_t^e) = \varepsilon_t,$$

it is clear that unlike the standard formulation of the natural rate hypothesis given by (3), the intertemporal version (3a) predicts an inverse relationship between the deviations of output from its natural level and the acceleration in the inflation rate (i.e. $\pi_{t+1} - \pi_t$), even if inflation is perfectly anticipated.

The natural rate theorists tended to be rather vague about how the natural rate hypothesis based on the aggregate supply function was linked to the natural rate of unemployment. One possibility, implicitly entertained in the literature, would be to start with an aggregate production function and obtain the derived demand for employment (in logarithm), e_t, as deviations from its natural level, e_t^*:

$$e_t - e_t^* = \lambda(y_t - y_t^*) + \eta_t, \lambda > 0$$

where the 'residual' term, η_t, is intended to capture the differential effects of other variables. It then readily follows that

$$(n_t - e_t) - (n_t - e_t^*) = -\lambda(y_t - y_t^*) - \eta_t,$$

where n_t is the (logarithm) of the exogenously given labour supply, and establishes an inverse relationship between the deviations of the market rate of unemployment from its natural rate, and the deviations of output from its natural rate.[3] This is unsatisfactory because the size of the cyclical response of unemployment to output (the so-called Okun's law) is estimated to be quite different from the estimates that arise using the production function interpretation of the assumed relationship between output and unemployment.

The natural rate hypothesis on its own does not rule out short- or even medium-term trade-offs between inflation and unemployment. For example, when inflation expectations are formed adaptively, expectations consistently lag behind the actual rate of inflation when inflation is rising and only adjust to it very gradually. The natural rate hypothesis altered the terms on which macroeconomic policy concerning inflation and unemployment was conducted, but still left room for an activist unemployment policy. The view was, however, challenged by the rational expectations theorists such as Lucas, Sargent and Barro, who following Muth (1961) argued that 'rational' agents in forming their expectations are unlikely to make systematic mistakes and therefore it is not possible to systematically 'fool' the public about the future rates of inflation. For a general discussion of the rational expectations hypothesis and the information assumptions that underlie it see, for example, Pesaran (1987). The combination of the natural rate hypothesis and the rational expectations hypothesis yields the rather startling policy invariance result of Sargent and Wallace (1975), namely that systematic, anticipated monetary policy has no effect on the mean of output or employment, though it does affect the variance. The argument is set out formally below.

However, as is now well understood, the policy ineffectiveness proposition is fragile in the sense that small changes to the specification of the form of the aggregate supply function or policy rule (though not the IS/LM structure) render the proposition invalid. For instance, replacing the Sargent–Wallace supply function (3) by the Lucas supply function (3a) causes policy to have an impact. Policy can be made effective by introducing non-linearities (e.g. allowing the policy feedback rule to have a multiplicative component), by introducing lags in the adjustment of wages and prices, or by giving the government an informational advantage over the agents which allows it to respond more rapidly than private sector expectations (by using automatic stablilisers, for instance). Pesaran (1984) discusses some simple cases of policy non-neutrality. As King (1993, p. 75) points out 'incorporating rational expectations simply alters the operation of a macroeconomic model: it can act to either raise or lower the potency of macroeconomic policy'.

Under the rational expectations hypothesis, the simple formulations of the natural rate hypothesis given by (1) or (3) imply that $u_t - u_t^*$ or $y_t - y_t^*$ should have mean zero and be serially uncorrelated. However, both u_t and y_t are highly serially correlated and it must therefore be the case that variations in u_t (or y_t) are largely mirrored by variations in the natural rate of unemployment (or output). But it is not clear how one could account for such procyclical variations in the natural rate of unemployment or output. Faced with these realities some authors such as Lucas (1973) and Sargent (1973, 1976a) have modified the natural rate hypothesis to read

$$u_t - u_t^* = -\alpha(\pi_t - \pi_t^e) + \sum_{i=1}^{m} \lambda_i(u_{t-i} - u_{t-i}^*) + \varepsilon_t,$$

or in its aggregate supply form

$$y_t - y_t^* = \gamma(\pi_t - \pi_t^e) + \sum_{i=1}^{n} \theta_i(y_{t-i} - y_{t-i}^*) + \xi_t,$$

where u_t^* and y_t^* are now treated as trends, representing demographic and technological changes in the economy. The disturbances ε_t and ξ_t are introduced to account for the effect of other non-systematic influences on unemployment and output. These modifications of the natural rate hypothesis are capable of explaining the observed serial correlations in output and unemployment, but can introduce long lags between expectations errors and output changes which are often difficult to rationalise theoretically. One possible rationale for the presence of such lags has been provided by Lucas (1975), in the context of a general equilibrium model with 'information lags' and serially correlated shocks to the capital stock. However, the importance of such information lags in economies where information on money supply figures and price indices are made available on a weekly or a monthly basis is highly questionable (see, for example, McCallum, 1989 and Gordon, 1990). We discuss the implications of the serial correlation of output and unemployment in more detail on p. 216 below.

Determinants of the natural rate of unemployment

As was emphasised in the Introduction, nothing in Friedman's definition of the natural rate of unemployment suggested that it would be a constant, rather it would be determined by a host of market and non-market factors. However, in empirical tests, for example by Barro, the natural rate of unemployment was proxied by a constant plus some demographic effects, while the natural rate of output was proxied by a deterministic trend plus some fiscal policy influences. However, given the big swings in unemployment in Europe and the US that have been observed over the past 25 years any empirical natural rate model needs to provide explanations of why equilibrium unemployment has shown such procyclical movements, or it needs to explain why adjustment to a constant equilibrium rate is so slow (the persistence of unemployment is so high). Any test of the natural rate hypothesis will have to begin from a tight specification of how equilibrium unemployment is determined. In this section we shall use some examples from the recent literature to indicate the difficulty in using current theory to provide such a tight specification. There is a vast literature devoted to trying to explain unemployment (Nickell, 1990 provides a survey), and we will provide only a brief discussion.

The first difficulty is that there is controversy about the appropriate notion of 'equilibrium'. Some theories assume that equilibrium means market clearing, and hence, in equilibrium they regard all unemployment as voluntary. Others view equilibrium as a state where expectations are fullfilled and individuals have no reason to choose to act differently. To them the labour market need not clear, and some workers may be involuntarily unemployed even in equilibrium. A third strand emphasises the existence of multiple history dependent equilibria, with the possibility that the economy may switch between full employment and underemployment equilibria.

Traditional search theories provide an explanation of voluntary unemployment. Firms have vacancies and there is some 'matching technology' which turns vacancies into offers to the unemployed. Structural change and low mobility of labour (e.g. because of the nature of the housing market) can mean that vacancies are not turned into offers to the unemployed. The individuals observe a distribution of wage offers over time and become employed if a particular offer is greater than their reservation wage; or more generally if the expected value of the offer is greater than the expected value of continuing to search. Anything that changes the distribution of vacancies, the matching technology, or the distribution over individuals of the reservation wage will change the equilibrium (or the natural) unemployment rate. For instance, in some of these theories, higher interest rates will increase labour supply by reducing the reservation wage because the expected value of the potentially higher paid jobs obtained by continued search will be less. While 'searching' the unemployed are likely to lose skills, reducing their attractiveness to employers. This can feed back onto the demand for labour. High unemployment, as a result of a demand shock, say, means that average duration of unemployment increases, the average quality of the unemployed pool declines, so firms make fewer offers. Pissarides (1992) provides a model of this process.

Many theories treated unemployment benefits as a major determinant of the reservation wage; assuming that higher benefits raise the expected value of continuing to search and thus the reservation wage. Atkinson and Micklewright (1991) provide a critical review of such explanations, emphasising the importance of the institutional detail of real insurance and assistance schemes and the importance of there being three (or more) rather than two states: employed, unemployed or out of the labour market. For instance, unemployment benefit increases labour supply because it makes being in the labour market more attractive. It may also increase the attractiveness of taking a job offer, because eligibility for insurance often depends on the contribution record which is acquired through employment. Some schemes also have important demand-side effects, encouraging temporary layoffs by employers, for example.

Of course, many of the unemployed do not get any job offers at all, despite being willing to work for less than the prevailing wage rate. There are a range of theoretical explanations of why an economy may show equilibrium involuntary unemployment of this sort. Insider–outsider models attribute it to the bargaining power held by the incumbent workforce, who would be expensive to replace. In efficiency or incentive wage models each firm is driven to set its wages above the market-clearing level to create an inducement for its employees to behave in less costly ways, e.g. expend more effort or shirk less. The firm cannot monitor effort completely, but the higher wage and the threat of unemployment if caught shirking create incentives for the workers to supply the cost minimising amount of effort. While these theories provide a plausible account of the existence of involuntary unemployment, they are less successful in providing an explanation of the movement in the unemployment rate. Increased insider power, a deterioration in the monitoring technology or an increased demand for on-the-job leisure by workers do not seem plausible explanations for the increased unemployment of the 1980s. Phelps (1992) provides a general equilibrium model with incentive wages in the labour market which examines the interaction with the goods and capital markets. In this model, higher real interest rates depress the derived demand for labour and increase equilibrium unemployment. This model also has the feature that increased consumer (or government) demand is contractionary. Other models emphasise movements in the wedge created by taxes and relative prices between the real product wage, relevant to employers, and the real consumption wage, relevant to workers.

A different strand of work has moved 'beyond the natural rate hypothesis', with Blanchard and Summers (1988) emphasising 'fragile' or multiple equilibria in the labour market. There are a variety of reasons why the firm and worker curves in wage–employment space may intersect more than once or coincide (or be very close together) over a range of outcomes. In most of these models, which may involve imperfectly competitive firms, possibly facing non-convex production technologies, bargaining with organised workers, the curves are not traditional labour demand and supply curves. If there is a multiplicity of equilibria, labour market institutions may influence the particular equilibrium that is chosen, and there has been a range of work on the way that the degree of centralisation of labour market bargaining influences unemployment (e.g. Rowthorn, 1992).

This rather brief review of the alternative theories clearly brings out that the determinants of the natural rate, or equilibrium unemployment, are likely to be complex and not well approximated by the sort of ad hoc measures used in the traditional tests of the natural rate hypothesis. The direct attempts at establishing empirical support for the natural rate–rational expectations hypothesis by Barro (1977, 1978), Barro and Rush (1980), Attfield, Demery and Duck (1981a, 1981b) and others have been controversial: Mishkin (1982), Leiderman (1980), Gordon (1982), Pesaran (1982, 1988), Bean (1984), Rush and Waldo (1988), and McAleer and Mackenzie (1991). The disputes have centred on: the proxies used for the natural rate of unemployment, for example, how to allow for demographic factors and wartime conscription; the treatment of expectations, in particular the information set used to form conditional expectations; dynamic specification, in particular lag lengths; econometric issues associated with the treatment of 'generated regressors' like the unanticipated money supply; and the specification of the alternative models against which the natural rate hypothesis is tested.

Dynamic specification of natural rate models

In this section, we shall derive the testable implications of the LSW hypothesis and show that the Barro (1977, 1978) and Barro and Rush (1980) models which have been the basis of most tests of the 'surprise' version of the natural rate hypothesis cannot be rationalised theoretically, even if the LSW model which is supposed to underlie them is accepted.

Our starting point is Sargent and Wallace's (1975) new classical macroeconomic model set out below. This specifies aggregate supply, aggregate demand, money demand and expectations formation

$$y_t - y_t^* = a(p_t - p_t^e) + \xi_{t1}, \tag{4}$$

$$y_t = b_0[r_t - (p_{t+1}^e - p_t^e)] + b_1 g_t + \xi_{t2}, \tag{5}$$

$$m_t - p_t = c_0 y_t + c_1 r_t + \xi_{t3}, \qquad (c_0 > 0, c_1 < 0) \tag{6}$$

and

$$p_{t+1}^e = E(p_{t+1} | \Omega_{t-1}), \qquad p_t^e = E(p_t | \Omega_{t-1}), \tag{7}$$

where Ω_t denotes the information available at time t, and at least contains all the current and past values of output, y_t; prices, p_t; interest rates, r_t; money supply, m_t; and government expenditure, g_t. In this version of the model, it is assumed that y_t^* can be predicted exactly and that all the disturbances are non-autocorrelated, independently distributed random variables with zero means and constant variances. The assumption of the non-autocorrelation of the disturbances will be relaxed below.

Taking mathematical expectations of both sides of (4)–(6) conditional on Ω_{t-1} we obtain:

$$y_t^e = y_t^*, \tag{8}$$

$$y_t^e = b_0[r_t^e - (p_{t+1}^e - p_t^e)] + b_1 g_t^e, \tag{9}$$

$$m_t^e - p_t^e = c_0 y_t^e + c_1 r_t^e, \tag{10}$$

where $r_t^e = E(r_t | \Omega_{t-1})$, $g_t^e = E(g_t | \Omega_{t-1})$, etc. Now subtracting these relations from their corresponding equations in (4)–(6) yields the following system of equations only involving *unanticipated* magnitudes of endogenous and exogenous variables:[4]

$$\nabla y_t = a\nabla p_t + \xi_{t1}, \tag{11}$$

$$\nabla y_t = b_0\nabla r_t + b_1\nabla g_t + \xi_{t2}, \tag{12}$$

$$\nabla m_t - \nabla p_t = c_0\nabla y_t + c_1\nabla r_t + \xi_{t3}, \tag{13}$$

where the operator ∇ transforms a variable into its unanticipated value; for example, $\nabla p_t = p_t - p_t^e$. Now assuming that

$$b_0 + a(b_0c_0 + c_1) \neq 0,$$

and solving for unanticipated output in terms of unanticipated changes in monetary and fiscal policies we get

$$\nabla y_t = \gamma_{11}\nabla m_t + \gamma_{12}\nabla g_t + v_{t1}, \tag{14}$$

where

$$\gamma_{11} = ab_0/D > 0, \ \gamma_{12} = ac_1b_1/D > 0, \tag{15}$$

$$v_{t1} = (b_0\xi_{t1} + ac_1\xi_{t2} - ab_0\xi_{t3})/D, \tag{16}$$

$$D = b_0 + a(b_0c_0 + c_1) < 0. $$

Finally, since by (9) the rational expectations of output and its natural rate coincide, (14) can be written as:

$$y_t - y_t^* = \gamma_{11}(m_t - m_t^e) + \gamma_{12}(g_t - g_t^e) + v_{t1}. \tag{17}$$

An important modification of the LSW model which plays a crucial role in statistical tests of the natural rate–rational expectations hypothesis involves generalising (4) to include lagged values of output relative to its natural level:

$$y_t - y_t^* = a(p_t - p_t^e) + \sum_{i=1}^{m} \lambda_i(y_{t-i} - y_{t-i}^*) + \xi_{t1}. \tag{4a}$$

This specification is most favourable to the natural rate–rational expectations hypothesis and is adopted here merely to derive testable implications for the LSW model that are not readily refuted as a result of the observed persistence of the rate of unemployment and the strong observed serial correlation of output.

Taking expectations of both sides of (4a) conditional on the available information at time $t - 1$, and noting that y_t^* is assumed to be perfectly predictable we obtain:

$$y_t^e = y_t^* + \sum_{i=1}^{m} \lambda_i(y_{t-i} - y_{t-i}^*), \tag{8a}$$

which replaces (8) as the full information measure of capacity output. Subtracting (8a) from (4a) takes us back to (11) which, together with (12) and (13), results in a reduced form relation given by (14). Now using (8a) in (14) yields the following generalisation of (17):

$$y_t - y_t^* = \sum_{i=1}^{m} \lambda_i(y_{t-i} - y_{t-i}^*) + \gamma_{11}\nabla m_t + \gamma_{12}\nabla g_t + v_{t1}, \tag{18}$$

where γ_{11}, γ_{12} and v_{t1} are defined as before by (15) and (16).

Assuming (18) to be stable, it can also be written in the form of a distributed lag relation between the deviations of output from its natural rate and current and lagged values of the unanticipated changes in m_t and g_t. But such a transformation, depending on the strength of serial correlation in output, can generate a high degree of serial correlation in the disturbances of the resultant distributed lag relation. Furthermore, this residual autocorrelation cannot be eliminated no matter what autocorrelation patterns are assumed for the structural disturbances ξ_{t1}, ξ_{t2} and ξ_{t3}, and the reduced form error, v_{t1}. This follows directly from the fact that any autocorrelation of the structural disturbances will also be incorporated into the rational expectations solutions of the endogenous variables given by (8a), (9) and (10), and thus removes any autocorrelation in the disturbances of (11)–(13) which underlies the derivation of (14), and hence (17). This in turn means that the disturbances in (18) will always contain a serially uncorrelated component, irrespective of the pattern of autocorrelation that may be assumed for the structural disturbances in (4a), (5) and (6). To give a formal proof of this result we reformulate the LSW model by assuming that its disturbances follow general-order autoregressive schemes.

$$y_t - y_t^* = a(p_t - p_t^e) + \sum_{i=1}^{m} \lambda_i(y_{t-i} - y_{t-i}^*) + u_{t1}, \tag{19}$$

$$y_t = b_0[r_t - (p_{t+1}^e - p_t^e)] + b_1 g_t + u_{t2}, \tag{20}$$

$$m_t - p_t = c_0 y_t + c_1 r_t + u_{t3}. \tag{21}$$

The disturbances are now assumed to follow the autoregressive processes

$$u_{ti} = R_i(L)u_{t-1,i} + \xi_{ti}, \qquad \text{for } i = 1, 2, 3 \tag{22}$$

where $R_i(L)$ is a polynomial in the lag operator, $(Lu_{ti} = u_{t-1,i})$, and the ξ_{ti}s are serially uncorrelated. Again taking expectations of both sides of (19)–(21), conditional on Ω_{t-1} we obtain:

$$y_t^e - y_t^* = \sum_{i=1}^{m} \lambda_i(y_{t-i} - y_{t-i}^*) + R_1(L)u_{t-1,1}, \tag{23}$$

$$y_t^e = b_0[r_t^e - (p_{t+1}^e - p_t^e)] + b_1 g_t + R_2(L)u_{t-1,2},$$

$$m_t^e - p_t^e = c_0 y_t^e + c_1 r_t^e + R_3(L)u_{t-1,3}.$$

Subtracting these results from their corresponding relations given by (19)–(21), and utilising (22) once again we get relations (11)–(13) which yield the solution given by (14). Now using (23) in (14) to solve for y_t^e we finally obtain:

$$\Lambda(L)(y_t - y_t^*) = \gamma_{11}\nabla m_t + \gamma_{12}\nabla g_t + v_{t1} + R_1(L)u_{t-1,1}, \tag{24}$$

where v_{t1} is defined by (16), and

$$\Lambda(L) = 1 - \sum_{i=1}^{m} \lambda_i L^i.$$

Now assuming that (19) is stable,[5] (24) can be written as the following general distributed lag relation:

$$(y_t - y_t^*) = \Lambda^{-1}(L)(\gamma_{11}\nabla m_t + \gamma_{12}\nabla g_t) + w_t, \tag{25}$$

where, using (22) it is easily shown that

$$w_t = \frac{\theta_1 + (1 - \theta_1)R_1(L)}{\Lambda(L)[1 - R_1(L)]}\xi_{t1} + \Lambda^{-1}(L)[\theta_2\xi_{t2} + \theta_3\xi_{t3}], \tag{26}$$

where θ_1, θ_2 and θ_3 are the coefficients of ξ_{t1}, ξ_{t2} and ξ_{t3} in (16), respectively. Clearly, even if $\Lambda(L)$ or $R_1(L)$ is chosen in such a way as to make the first term on the right-hand side of (26) non-autocorrelated, the rest of the terms in (26) will necessarily be autocorrelated. It is *not* possible to derive from LSW-type models a distributed lag relation such as (25) which does not have autocorrelated disturbances.

It is worth noting that modifications of the aggregate demand function (5) and the money market equilibrium condition (6) to include lagged values of *any* variable in the information set will have no consequence for (24) or the distributed lag relation (25). Furthermore, it is not difficult to show that generalisation of (4) by

$$y_t - y_t^* = \sum_{i=0}^{m} \alpha_i(p_{t-i} - p_{t-i}^e) + \xi_{t1}, \tag{4b}$$

where $p_{t-1}^e = E(p_{t-i}|\Omega_{t-i-1})$, cannot resolve the problem of autocorrelation in the disturbances of the distributed lag relation between deviations of output from its natural rate and current and lagged unanticipated money, utilised by Barro (1977, 1978). Often serially correlated residuals are taken as an indication of mis-specification. In this case, the theory implies serial correlation. So the fact that the annual equations estimated by Barro, which take the form (25), do not show serial correlation is thus *prima facie* evidence against the theory.

Time series models of the natural rate

Since the original tests of natural rate theories, the importance of the time series structure of economic variables for inference has become more widely recognised. Since the time series structures of output and unemployment are somewhat different, we will discuss the cases separately.

Most natural rate models for output assumed that it was stationary around a deterministic trend. However, the bulk of the evidence suggests that it is better to regard the first differences of output as stationary; it is difficult to reject the hypothesis that output has a unit root or is integrated of order one. There is now a substantial econometric literature on the subject. If output is difference stationary, rather than trend stationary, this has two implications for conventional attempts to test the natural rate hypothesis. First, models which proxy the natural rate by a deterministic trend, as is commonly done, can give rise to spurious output equations in the sense that their residuals will be non-stationary. The left-hand side variable, the level of output is difference stationary, but the right-hand side contains only a deterministic trend and money supply surprises, which are stationary by construction. None of the normal properties of least squares applies to spurious regressions; for instance as the sample size grows the R^2 goes to unity even if the variables are independent.

In this section, we shall examine the implications of the issues discussed above for output equations estimated on quarterly US data of the type considered by Barro and Rush (1980).[6] Barro-type equations take the form:

$$y_t = y_t^* + A(L)(m_t - m_t^e) + w_t, \tag{27}$$

where $A(L)$ is a polynomial lag operator, and w_t is a random disturbance term. In Barro and Rush (1980, p. 36, table 2.1) various estimates of this equation are given. The natural rate is proxied by an intercept, various government spending measures and a time trend. Up to 10 lags of the residual from an equation explaining money supply growth by its own lags and some fiscal policy variables are included. The Barro–Rush (hereafter BR) results are very robust, in the sense that it is very easy to replicate the qualitative features of the BR results, even on different samples and using different variables in the money supply equation and different fiscal influences as determinants of the natural rate. Long lags of unanticipated money are highly significant (albeit using standard errors which are incorrect because of the generated regressor problem), and as the argument of pp. 212–16 predicts the output equations exhibit a substantial degree of residual serial correlation. Our estimates of a Barro-type surprise equation for output correcting for second-order residual serial correlation, reported in the appendix (pp. 222–7), give coefficients on the lagged disturbances (1.30 and −0.37) that are similar to those reported by BR: 1.22 and −0.42.

If output has a unit root, as seems very likely, then the BR regression is spurious, in the sense that the error term is not merely serially correlated but is integrated of order unity. BR were aware of this problem and attempted to test for a unit root in the residuals using a likelihood ratio test (n. 13, p. 34) which, as they note, is inappropriate if the null hypothesis is true. On replicated Barro-type equations using more recent data, Augmented Dickey–Fuller (ADF) tests do not reject the null hypothesis that the residuals have a unit root. The Barro-type output equations, appear to be approximating the high-order (and probably non-stationary) serial correlation in the disturbances by a long moving average of white noise terms – unanticipated money – which would not be statistically significant if the non-stationarity of output series was allowed for directly.

The discussion of pp. 212–16 suggests that the appropriate form of the LSW specification for empirical analysis is given by:

$$y_t = y_t^* + B(L)(y_{t-1} - y_{t-1}^*) + a(m_t - m_t^e) + v_t, \tag{28}$$

where only current money supply surprises are included together with lagged values of $y_t - y_t^*$. It should be noted that this equation does not suffer from the generated regressor problem, because only the current value of the residual (unanticipated money) appears as a regressor.

If an equation like (28) is estimated, with a deterministic trend as a proxy for the natural rate, the coefficient of the lagged dependent variable is close to unity as one would expect if output is difference stationary. However, if output is difference stationary the natural rate of output must also be difference stationary, and thus cannot be measured by a deterministic trend. It must also be cointegrated with output with a unit coefficient. To provide a coherent natural rate model requires specifying a proxy for the natural rate which is difference stationary. One possibility, which has not been used in this context though it has been used by real business cycle theorists, is to use the cumulated Solow residuals as a measure of technology and a determinant of the natural level of output. This is an interesting area for future research.

Whereas output seems to have a unit root or to have a root that is close enough to unity that it behaves like an I(1) variable, the position with regard to unemployment is more ambiguous. Since the unemployment rate is bounded between zero and unity one would expect it to be I(0) and on long time series this appears to be the case. The ADF(1) statistic without trend (with critical value in parentheses) for the UK over 1857–1987 is −3.49 (−2.88) and for the US over 1892–1987 is −3.58 (−2.89). However over the period 1950–87 ADF tests, with and without trends, up to order 4 all fail to reject the unit root for the UK; and in the US only the ADF(1) with trend rejects a unit root at −3.59 (−3.53).

These tests confirm what is apparent from a plot of the unemployment rate. Over a century it shows no trend, but over the postwar period it shows a clear upward trend and great persistence (hysteresis) in both the US and UK. The fact that over the last 40 years unemployment appears I(1) is strong evidence against any theory in which the natural rate is a constant. Theories which allow the natural rate to vary over time need to consider determinants that are I(1), and cointegrate with the unemployment rate over the postwar period, yet are I(0) over the longer period. There are a large number of possible candidates – e.g. real interest rates, wedge effects, benefits, measures of structural mismatch, union power – some of which were discussed on pp. 209–12. Such variables have been included in a variety of labour market models, which are usually systems rather than single equations. However, there is little consensus about the relative importance of these variables because of the sensitivity of the results to the usual problems of specification, measurement, aggregation, etc. Although such systems will deliver an estimate of the natural rate or NAIRU, they are not designed as tests of the natural rate hypothesis itself, which is used as an organising equilibrium concept. Testing the theory itself will be difficult without some agreement on the main determinants of the equilibrium.

Rather than reviewing the large empirical literature on determinants of unemployment, we shall turn to another inherent difficulty associated with testing the natural rate–rational expectations hypothesis, namely the identification problem that arises because of possible policy endogeneity.

Endogenous policy, and tests of the natural rate–rational expectations hypothesis

The striking result of the natural rate–rational expectations hypothesis is the ineffectiveness of anticipated policy to influence output or unemployment. In this section, we wish to emphasise a potential pitfall in any attempt to use reduced form estimates of the sort used by the proponents of the natural rate–rational expectations hypothesis to test for the effectiveness of policy. It is quite possible for policy to be effective, but for estimated equations to exhibit what are apparently new classical features. The problem can best be illustrated by a parable. Imagine that you are on the bridge of a ship navigating turbulent waters, being swept by wind and currents. You can observe the captain, who is wildly swinging the helm and ordering changes in speed, and the course, which is steady. These observations are consistent with two hypotheses. First, the steering has no effect, and the ship continues on its steady course despite all the captain's actions. Secondly, the captain's actions are effectively offsetting the impact of the elements, maintaining a steady course despite the buffeting of the wind and currents. From the observations on actions and outcomes alone there is no guarantee that one is able to discriminate between the two hypotheses. To discriminate one needs more information on the structure of the problem: independent information on the forces that were affecting the ship's course and on the impact of the rudder and the engine on the ship's course in the absence of winds and currents.

Responsive control, endogenous government economic policy, raises the same type of identification problems. Observations on policy measures and outcomes alone are unlikely to identify the impact of policy. In this section we set out a policy model where the government has two sets of instruments, but at any one time uses only one of the instrument sets. We also examine what happens when the government shifts reliance from one set of instruments to another. Although the basic argument made here is not new, it goes back at least to Goldfeld and Blinder (1972), its implications do not seem to have been widely appreciated.

Suppose that the economic system is characterised by the dynamic model:

$$y_t = Ay_{t-1} + B_1 x_{1t} + B_2 x_{2t} + Cz_t + u_t, \tag{29}$$

where y_t is an m vector of endogenous variables, x_{1t} and x_{2t} are k and s vectors of policy instruments, z_t is a r vector of exogenous non-policy variables, and u_t an m vector of serially uncorrelated disturbances with zero means. A, B_1, B_2 and C are coefficient matrices with appropriate dimensions. Suppose that the government's target for y_t is y_t^*. Since the government is likely to want to stabilise the economy around some feasible long-run trends for the endogenous variables, the government's targets may be difficult to distinguish from standard proxies for their natural rates. The distinction between the instruments could arise because of possible separation of powers over the control of the instruments (e.g. an independent central bank) or because the government attaches large political costs to changing, say, x_{2t}.

Assume that the instrument set that the government is prepared to change is x_{1t}, and suppose that the government has enough instruments, i.e. $k = m$, and B_1 is of full rank. Conditional on the available information, which we continue to denote by Ω_{t-1}, the optimal policy for period t is given by:

$$\mathbf{x}_{1t}^* = \mathbf{B}_1^{-1}(\mathbf{y}_t^* - \mathbf{A}\mathbf{y}_{t-1} - \mathbf{B}_2\mathbf{x}_{2t}^e - \mathbf{C}\mathbf{z}_t^e), \tag{30}$$

where $\mathbf{z}_t^e = E(\mathbf{z}_t | \Omega_{t-1}), \mathbf{x}_{2t}^e = E(\mathbf{x}_{2t} | \Omega_{t-1})$, etc. Therefore, substituting this result in (29) we have

$$\mathbf{y}_t^* = \mathbf{A}\mathbf{y}_{t-1} + \mathbf{B}_1\mathbf{x}_{1t}^* + \mathbf{B}_2\mathbf{x}_{2t}^e + \mathbf{C}\mathbf{z}_t^e. \tag{31}$$

Subtracting (31) from (29) now yields:

$$\mathbf{y}_t - \mathbf{y}_t^* = \mathbf{B}_2(\mathbf{x}_{2t} - \mathbf{x}_{2t}^e) + \mathbf{C}(\mathbf{z}_t - \mathbf{z}_t^e) + \mathbf{u}_t. \tag{32}$$

If $\mathbf{y}_t$ were the scalar output, $\mathbf{x}_{1t}$ was a measure of fiscal policy and $\mathbf{x}_{2t}$ money supply growth, the result would have exactly the same form as the LSW natural rate equation, with the difference that $\mathbf{y}_t^*$ would be interpreted as government's output target, rather than the natural rate. An interesting feature of this formulation is that if the government switches to targeting $\mathbf{x}_{2t}$, say the money supply, and $\mathbf{B}_2$ is also of full rank, the equation becomes:

$$\mathbf{y}_t - \mathbf{y}_t^* = \mathbf{B}_2(\mathbf{x}_{1t} - \mathbf{x}_{1t}^e) + \mathbf{C}(\mathbf{z}_t - \mathbf{z}_t^e) + \mathbf{u}_t. \tag{33}$$

Thus while the government is using fiscal policy to control output, fiscal policy has no effect on deviations of output from target, but unexpected money supply shocks do; while the situation is reversed if the government starts targeting the money supply.

We can relax the strong assumption that the $\mathbf{B}_1$ and $\mathbf{B}_2$ are of full rank and assume that the government has a quadratic loss function:

$$\mathbf{L} = (\mathbf{y}_t - \mathbf{y}_t^*)'\mathbf{Q}(\mathbf{y}_t - \mathbf{y}_t^*),$$

and controls $\mathbf{x}_{1t}$. Then optimal policy is:

$$\mathbf{x}_{1t}^* = (\mathbf{B}_1'\mathbf{Q}\mathbf{B}_1)^{-1}\mathbf{B}_1'\mathbf{Q}(\mathbf{y}_t^* - \mathbf{A}\mathbf{y}_{t-1} - \mathbf{B}_2\mathbf{x}_{2t}^e - \mathbf{C}\mathbf{z}_t^e). \tag{34}$$

Substituting $\mathbf{x}_{1t}^*$ for $\mathbf{x}_{1t}$ in (29), after some algebra, we have:

$$\mathbf{y}_t - \mathbf{y}_t^* = \mathbf{H}\mathbf{A}\mathbf{y}_{t-1} - \mathbf{H}(\mathbf{y}_t^* - \mathbf{B}_2\mathbf{x}_{2t}^e - \mathbf{C}\mathbf{z}_t^e) + \mathbf{B}_2(\mathbf{x}_{2t} - \mathbf{x}_{2t}^e) +$$
$$\mathbf{C}(\mathbf{z}_t - \mathbf{z}_t^e) + \mathbf{u}_t, \tag{35}$$

where

$$\mathbf{H} = \mathbf{I} - \mathbf{B}(\mathbf{B}'\mathbf{Q}\mathbf{B})^{-1}\mathbf{B}'\mathbf{Q}.$$

Thus, when the government has inadequate instruments, it cannot fully offset anticipated shocks. If the government switched policy instruments from $\mathbf{x}_{1t}$ to $\mathbf{x}_{2t}$, an equation of exactly the same form would result, but with $\mathbf{x}_{2t}$ replaced by $\mathbf{x}_{1t}$.

Whether or not with complete control, or with partial control of the economy under a quadratic loss function, the instruments that are used to control the endogenous variables explicitly influence the deviations $\mathbf{y}_t$ from its target value, y_t^*, the unanticipated shocks to non-controlled exogenous variables do influence the deviations from target.

A pure Keynesian model in which the government is optimally controlling a sub-set of instruments will produce a reduced form that, in the absence of fairly precise models of the natural rate or target output levels, is likely to be empirically indistinguishable from a new classical model. Given that the government is likely to wish to stabilise the economy around equilibrium levels of the variables, and that its information set is likely to be similar to that used to form private sector expectations in natural rate–rational expectations models, natural rates and government targets and private and public sector expectations will be observationally equivalent. Up to now we have assumed that the government was able to control x_{1t} exactly. If it could not, then a term $\mathbf{B}_1(x_{1t} - x_{1t}^*)$ would also appear in the equation. If the government is not responding optimally, i.e. setting the policy instruments exogenously with respect to the feedback rules, then the reduced form will be given by (29) and the actual values of the policy instruments will determine outcomes.

Rather similar arguments apply to lagged values of policy variables and, on this basis, Buiter (1984) argues that tests of Granger causality shed no light on the effectiveness of policy. However, as Granger (1989) argues, if we have information on variations in the government's target, and the shocks that it is trying to stabilise against, namely the zs, then it would be possible to identify the true forces determining the outcomes. In general, however, the empirical models of the natural rate–rational expectations hypothesis, and the Keynesian models of output determination may prove to be difficult to distinguish in practice.[7]

Concluding remarks

This chapter has emphasised how any evaluation of the testable implications of the natural rate hypothesis, or any other economic hypothesis, is crucially dependent on the detailed theoretical structure of the model which provides the information needed for specification of the determinants of 'unobservables' that are invariably included in theoretical economic models. The logic of the argument under rational expectations is that the natural rate would be highly correlated with the actual rate and exhibit the same time series properties. There is no reason, within the natural rate theory itself, to expect this to be the case. Proponents then had to try to develop arguments which got around this difficulty. The discussion in the fourth section above showed how the equation normally used to test policy ineffectiveness was not consistent with the theory upon which the policy ineffectiveness conclusion was based. The fifth section showed that if output

Table 11A.1 *Augmented Dickey–Fuller tests for unit roots* (*sample 1954:1–1990:4*)

	Variables			
	y	g	r	m
Order of ADF				
0	−1.39	−2.14	−2.49	−4.30
1	−2.10	−2.41	−3.10	−2.70
2	−2.42	−2.59	−2.20	−2.71
3	−2.15	−2.78	−2.94	−2.64
4	−2.03	−2.81	−2.63	−2.63

Trends were included in all cases. The 95% critical value of the ADF tests is −3.4407.

was difference stationary (had a unit root or was integrated of order one), the traditional equations used to test the natural rate hypothesis would be spurious unless the proxies for the natural rate were also difference stationary and cointegrated with output. The sixth section showed that a reduced form equation of exactly the new classical form would be generated in a Keynesian world with an optimising government, and that the proxies used to model the government's output targets were likely to be indistinguishable from the proxies used commonly in empirical analysis of the natural rate hypothesis.

Any test of the natural rate hypothesis will be dependent on a clear theoretical specification which links the natural rate itself to observables.

Appendix: Some new econometric evidence on 'surprise' equations for US GNP

This appendix provides details of the empirical evidence on 'surprise' equations for output, summarised in the text. These equations explain the logarithm of output over the period 1954:1–1990:2, which avoids the Korean War and the problems, discussed in the literature, associated with the treatment of conscription. The data come from the USGNP.FIT tutorial file distributed with Microfit 3.0. This gives US quarterly data for the period 1947:1–1990:4. Of the series we use, all variables except the interest rate are in logarithms. To establish the order of integration, Augmented Dickey–Fuller (ADF) tests, up to order 4, were applied to all the variables. Table 11A.1 gives the ADF statistics. Over this sample and according to ADF tests, the hypotheses that output, y, government spending g, and the nominal interest rate, r, are $I(1)$ clearly cannot be

Table 11A.2 *Alternative estimates of surprise output equations (sample 1954:1–1990:4)**

	Barro-type equations		Lucas–Sargent–Wallace-type equation
	(1)	(2)	(3)
DMR	0.27	0.28	0.27
	(0.59)	(1.73)	(1.71)
DMR(-1)	0.42	0.46	0.12
	(0.91)	(1.71)	(0.76)
DMR(-2)	0.78	0.85	0.37
	(1.71)	(2.36)	(2.35)
DMR(-3)	0.95	1.01	0.11
	(2.06)	(2.38)	(0.68)
DMR(-4)	1.19	1.07	0.16
	(2.65)	(2.25)	(1.00)
DMR(-5)	1.08	0.97	0.05
	(2.36)	(1.98)	(0.29)
DMR(-6)	1.11	0.81	0.06
	(2.45)	(1.70)	(0.38)
DMR(-7)	1.02	0.65	0.05
	(2.18)	(1.51)	(0.28)
DMR(-8)	1.06	0.53	0.09
	(2.26)	(1.42)	(0.53)
DMR(-9)	1.02	0.53	0.18
	(2.19)	(1.91)	(1.1)
DMR(-10)	0.49	0.10	-0.29
	(1.04)	(0.59)	(-1.79)
Constant	4.90	6.17	0.47
	(23.92)	(17.55)	(2.92)
$T \times 100$	0.53	0.65	0.05
	(23.34)	(15.75)	(2.9)
g	0.38	0.15	0.14
	(10.60)	(2.51)	(2.59)
$g(-1)$			-0.20
			(-2.30)
$g(-2)$			0.09
			(1.71)
$y(-1)$			1.25
			(15.52)
$y(-2)$			-0.35
			(-4.43)
$\rho 1$		1.30	
		(15.76)	

Table 11A.2 (continued)

| | Barro-type equations | | Lucas–Sargent–Wallace-type equation |
	(1)	(2)	(3)
$\rho 2$		-0.37	
		(-4.48)	
R^2	0.99340	0.99917	0.99922
$SEE(\times 100)$	2.633	0.918	0.904
$\chi^2_{SC}(4)$	125.80	6.23	3.51
	[0.000]	[0.176]	[0.476]
$\chi^2_{FF}(1)$	2.54	5.55	0.03
	[0.111]	[0.018]	[0.868]
$\chi^2_N(2)$	0.84	6.91	5.95
	[0.658]	[0.032]	[0.051]
$\chi^2_H(1)$	0.46	0.12	0.002
	[0.499]	[0.726]	[0.964]

*The dependent variable is the logarithm of output y, g is the logarithm of government expenditure, DMR is the residual from an equation explaining the change in log money supply reported in the text. The figures in round brackets are t-ratios, and those in square brackets are rejection probabilities. The equations in columns (1) and (3) are estimated by least squares, the equation in column (2) by the Cochrane–Orcutt method allowing for second-order residual serial correlation. SEE is the standard error of regression, $\chi^2_{SC}(4)$, $\chi^2_{FF}(1)$, $\chi^2_N(2)$, and $\chi^2_H(1)$ are chi-squared statistics (with the degrees of freedom in brackets) for tests of residual serial correlation, functional form mis-specification, non-normal errors, and heteroscedasticity.

rejected. For money, m, the ADF rejects the null hypothesis of a unit root when no lagged changes are included. However, once the lagged changes are included the null hypothesis of a unit root cannot be rejected, at conventional levels of significance.

The equation used to predict the changes in the logarithm of money supply is:

$$\Delta m_t = 0.003 + 0.701\Delta m_{t-1} - 0.317\Delta r_{t-1} + DMR_t,$$
$$ (5.48) \quad (13.99) \qquad (-6.23)$$

$$\bar{R}^2 = 0.6089, \qquad SEE = 0.00528, \qquad \text{Durbin} - h = -0.971,$$

$$\chi^2_{SC}(4) = 5.637, \; \chi^2_{FF}(1) = 4.96, \; \chi^2_N(2) = 32.65, \; \chi^2_H(1) = 10.99$$
$$\phantom{\chi^2_{SC}(4) =} [0.228] \qquad\quad [0.0263] \qquad\quad [0.000] \qquad\quad [0.000]$$

To generate adequate lagged values of money supply surprises for inclusion in the Barro-type output equations, the money supply growth equation is estimated over the period 1951:3–1990:4. DMR is the unpredicted component of money supply growth, used in the regressions below. SEE is the standard error of regression, $\chi^2_{SC}(4)$, $\chi^2_{FF}(1)$, $\chi^2_N(2)$, and $\chi^2_H(1)$ are chi-squared statistics (with degrees of freedom in brackets) for tests of residual serial correlation, functional form mis-specification, non-normal errors, and heteroscedasticity. This equation fails tests for functional form, normality and heteroscedasticity. The difficulties of explaining US money supply data are well known. But the results below are generally robust to changing the specification of the equation determining DMR.

The logarithm of income is then explained by an intercept, current and 10 lags of DMR, log government spending and a time trend. This is the same form as is given in column 3 of table 2.1 in Barro and Rush (1980). For comparability with their results we use the conventional estimates of the standard errors, though these are not appropriate with generated regressors like lagged surprises. Appropriate standard errors are provided below. The results given in column (1) of table 11A.2 broadly match those of Barro and Rush despite the difference in sample; in particular the long distributed lag of money supply surprises is significant according to conventional tests. The equation also shows massive serial correlation. Following Barro and Rush the equation is re-estimated allowing for second-order serial correlation of the residuals. This corresponds to column 5 of table 2.1 in Barro and Rush (1980). The pattern of serial correlation they report (coefficients of 1.22 and -0.42) is very similar to our estimates of 1.29 and -0.37, shown in column (2) of table 11A.2. This high level of residual serial correlation suggests that the results should be treated with caution, as they could be spurious.

If output is trend stationary, the natural rate can be regarded as a trend disturbed by fiscal shocks. But if output is difference stationary, g and y are required to cointegrate for this equation to make sense; DMR is $I(0)$ by construction. There is no reason to expect this to be the case and, in fact, g and y do not seem to cointegrate, whether a deterministic trend is allowed for or not. The ADF(3), the order closest to rejecting the unit root in the residual of the cointegrating relation between y and g (with a deterministic trend), is -3.15 compared to a critical value of -3.85. The Johansen procedure gives conflicting results depending on the order chosen for the vector autoregressive (VAR) specification. At orders 1 to 3 and 8, both the test based on the maximal eigenvalue and the one based on the trace of the stochastic matrix reject cointegration. At order 4 the eigenvalue test does not reject one cointegrating vector but the trace test does. At orders 5, 6 and

Table 11A.3 *Alternative estimates of surprise equations for the growth rate of output (sample 1954:1–1990:4)**

	(1)	(2)
Intercept	0.005	0.005
	(4.72)	(4.80)
$\Delta y(-1)$	0.30	0.30
	(3.73)	(3.77)
Δg	0.09	0.09
	(1.68)	(1.73)
DMR	0.12	0.13
	(0.81)	(0.89)
DMR(-1)	0.14	0.15
	(0.95)	(1.08)
DMR(-2)	0.29	0.29
	(1.93)	(2.04)
DMR(-3)	-0.05	-0.05
	(-0.32)	(-0.33)
DMR(-4)	0.02	0.03
	(0.17)	(0.18)
$\bar{R}^2$	0.12	0.12
$SEE(\times 100)$	0.9400	0.9477
$\chi^2_{SC}(4)$	3.16	
	[0.532]	
$\chi^2_{FF}(1)$	1.19	
	[0.276]	
$\chi^2_{N}(2)$	6.79	
	[0.034]	
$\chi^2_{H}(1)$	0.578	
	[0.447]	

*See the note to table 11A.2 for variable definitions and other notations. Column (1) reports the least squares estimates, and column (2) the maximum likelihood estimates obtained by jointly estimating the money supply and output equations imposing the rational expectations cross-equation restrictions. The figures in round brackets are the t-ratios, and those in square brackets are rejection probabilities.

7 neither reject cointegration. The strongest evidence for cointegration is at order 6 where the test statistics for the null hypothesis of no cointegrating vectors are: eigenvalue 16.31 (14.07), trace 16.64 (15.41). The appropriate 95% critical values are given in brackets. On balance, despite the conflicting test statistics, it seems likely that this constitutes a spurious regression.

Column (3) of table 11A.2 gives the estimates, when the model is reformulated in the correct LSW form, i.e. including lagged output terms. There is then no need for a correction for residual serial correlation, and the surprise terms are only individually significant at lag 2. The pattern of coefficients on y and g suggests that a first-difference model is appropriate, as we would expect given that y and g do not cointegrate. Table 11A.3 gives the results for a first-difference model, using a shorter distributed lag of surprises. The first column gives the OLS estimates and the second column gives the maximum likelihood estimates which impose the cross-equation restrictions between the output and money supply equations and provide asymptotically correct standard errors. Using a system's estimator has virtually no effect on the coefficient estimates but reduces the standard errors, raising the t ratios. Again, only the lag 2 surprise term is significant.

Notes

Hashem Pesaran is grateful to the ESRC and the Isaac Newton Trust of Trinity College for partial financial support. Both authors are grateful to Rod Cross and David Miles for comments on earlier versions of this paper.
1 This section draws on Pesaran (1984, 1993).
2 This section is an extended version of the argument presented very tersely in the appendix to Pesaran (1982).
3 Note that $n_t - e_t = -\log(1 - u_t)$, which is approximately equal to u_t, the rate of unemployment. Similarly, $n_t - e_t^* = -\log(1 - u_t^*) \approx u_t^*$.
4 This method of solving for the unanticipated change in the values of a rational expectations model presumes that a rational expectations solution exists. In this case a non-explosive solution for price and nominal interest expectations exists if the conditional expectations of m_{t+i} and g_{t+i} taken with respect to the information set exist and b_0 is non-zero.
5 The necessary and sufficient condition for the stability of the aggregate supply function is that the roots of $\Lambda(L)$ and $1 - R_1(L)$ should all lie outside the unit circle.
6 We only summarise the main features of the results here and give further details in an appendix (p. 222). These are easily replicated, e.g. using the data from the USGNP.FIT tutorial file distributed with Microfit 3.0 (Pesaran and Pesaran, 1991).
7 The discussion of the observational equivalence of the neoclassical and Keynesian models in this section should be distinguished from the general problem of observational equivalence debated by Nelson (1979), McCallum (1979), Sargent (1976, 1979) and others in the literature.

References

Atkinson, A.B. and Micklewright, J., 1991. 'Unemployment Compensation and Labor Market Transitions: a critical review', *Journal of Economic Literature*, 29, 1679–1727

Attfield, C.L.F., Demery, D. and Duck, N.W., 1981a. 'Unanticipated Monetary Growth, Output and the Price Level: UK 1946–1977', *European Economic Review*, 16, 367–85

1981b. 'A Quarterly Model of Unanticipated Monetary Growth, Output and the Price Level in the UK 1963–1978', *Journal of Monetary Economics*, 8, 331–50

Barro, R.J., 1976. 'Rational Expectations and the Role of Monetary Policy', *Journal of Monetary Economics*, 2, 1–33

1977. 'Unanticipated Money Growth and Unemployment in the United States', *American Economic Review*, 67, 101–15

1978. 'Unanticipated Money, Output and the Price Level in the United States', *Journal of Political Economy*, 86, 549–80

1989. 'Introduction', in R.J. Barro (ed.), *Modern Business Cycle Theory*, Cambridge, MA: Harvard University Press

Barro, R.J. and Rush, M., 1980. 'Unanticipated Money and Economic Activity', in S. Fischer (ed.), *Rational Expectations and Economic Policy*, Chicago: University of Chicago Press for the National Bureau of Economic Research

Bean, C.R., 1984. 'A Little Bit More Evidence on the Natural Rate Hypothesis from the U.K.', *European Economic Review*, 25, 279–92

Blanchard, O. and Summers, L.H., 1988. 'Beyond the Natural Rate Hypothesis', *American Economic Review, Papers and Proceedings*, 78 (*May*), 182–7

Buiter, W.H., 1984. 'Granger Causality and Policy Ineffectiveness', *Economica*, 51, 151–62

Friedman, B.M. and Kuttner, K.N., 1992. 'Money, Income, Prices and Interest Rates', *American Economic Review*, 82, 472–92

Friedman, M., 1968. 'The Role of Monetary Policy', *American Economic Review*, 58 (March), 1–17

Goldfield, S. and Blinder, A., 1972. 'Some Implications of Endogenous Stabiliz-ation Policy', *Brookings Papers on Economic Activity*, 585–640

Gordon, R.J., 1982. 'Price Inertia and Policy Ineffectiveness in the United States, 1890–1980', *Journal of Political Economy*, 90 (December), 1087–117

1990. 'What is New-Keynesian Economics?', *Journal of Econometric Literature*, 28, 1115–71

Granger, C.W.J., 1989. 'Causality, Cointegration and Control', *Journal of Economic Dynamics and Control*, 12, 551–9

King, R.G., 1993. 'Will the New Keynesian Macroeconomics Resurrect the IS–LM Model?', *Journal of Economic Perspectives*, 8, 67–82

Kydland, E.F. and Prescott, E.C., 1982. 'Time to Build and Aggregate Fluctu-ations', *Econometrica*, 50, 1345–70

1988. 'The Workweek of Capital and its Cyclical Implications', *Journal of Monetary Economics*, 21, 343–60

Leiderman, L., 1980. 'Macroeconometric Testing of the Rational Expectations and Structural Neutrality Hypothesis for the United States', *Journal of Monetary Economics*, 6, 69–82

Lucas, R.E. Jr., 1972. 'Expectations and the Neutrality of Money', *Journal of Economic Theory*, 4(2), 103–24

1973. 'Some International Evidence on Output–inflation Tradeoffs', *American Economic Review*, 63(3) (June), 326–34

1975. 'An Equilibrium Model of the Business Cycle', *Journal of Political Economy*, 83, 1113–44

McAleer, M. and Mackenzie, C.R., 1991. 'Keynesian and New Classical Models of Unemployment Revisited', *Economic Journal*, 101 (May), 359–81

McCallum, B.T., 1979. 'On the Observational Inequivalence of Classical and Keynesian Models', *Journal of Political Economy*, 87, 395–402

1989. 'Real Business Cycle Models', in R.J. Barro (ed.), *Modern Business Cycle Theory*, Cambridge, MA: Harvard University Press

Mishkin, F.S., 1982. 'Does Anticipated Monetary Policy Matter? An Econometric Investigation', *Journal of Political Economy*, 90 (February), 22–51

Muth, J.F., 1961. 'Rational Expectations and the Theory of Price Movements', *Econometrica*, 29, 315–35

Nelson, C.R., 1979. 'Granger Causality and the Natural Rate Hypothesis', *Journal of Political Economy*, 87, 390–4

Nickell, S.J., 1990. 'Unemployment: a survey', *Economic Journal*, 100, 391–439

Pesaran, M.H., 1982. 'A Critique of the Proposed Tests of the Natural Rate – Rational Expectations Hypothesis', *Economic Journal*, 92 (September), 529–54

1984. 'The New Classical Macroeconomics: a Critical Exposition', in F. van der Ploeg (ed.), *Mathematical Methods in Economics*, New York: Wiley, 195–215

1987. *The Limits to Rational Expectations*, Oxford: Basil Blackwell

1988. 'On the Policy Ineffectiveness Proposition and a Keynesian Alternative: a Rejoinder', *Economic Journal*, 98 (June), 504–8

1993. 'The Natural Rate Hypothesis', in P. Newman, M. Milgate and J. Eatwell (eds), *The New Palgrave Dictionary of Money and Finance*, London: Macmillan

Pesaran, M.H. and Pesaran, B., 1991. *Microfit 3.0: An Interactive Econometric Software Package*, Oxford: Oxford University Press

Phelps, E.S., 1967. 'Phillips Curves, Expectations of Inflation and Optimal Unemployment Over Time', *Economica*, 34 (August), 254–81

1970. 'The New Microeconomics in Employment and Inflation Theory', in E.S. Phelps *et al.*, *Microeconomic Foundations of Employment and Inflation Theory*, New York: W.W. Norton and London: Macmillan

1992. 'Consumer Demand and Equilibrium Unemployment in a Working Model of the Customer-market Incentive Wage Economy', *Quarterly Journal of Economics*, 107, 1003–32

Pissarides, C., 1992. 'Loss of Skill During Unemployment and the Persistence of Unemployment Shocks', *Quarterly Journal of Economics*, 107, 1371–91

Rowthorn, R.E., 1992. 'Centralisation, Employment and Wage Dispersion', *Economic Journal*, 102, 506–23

Rush, M. and Waldo, D., 1988. 'On the Policy Ineffectiveness Proposition and a Keynesian Alternative', *Economic Journal*, 98 (June), 498–503

Sargent, T.J., 1973. 'Rational Expectations, the Real Rate of Interest and the Natural Rate of Unemployment', *Brookings Papers on Economic Activity*, 429–72; correction of errors, 799–800

1976a. 'A Classical Macroeconomic Model for the United States', *Journal of Political Economy*, 84 (April) 207–37

1976b. 'The Observational Equivalence of Natural and Unnatural Rate Theories of Macroeconomics', *Journal of Political Economy*, 84, 631–40

1979. 'Causality, Exogeneity, and Natural Rate Models: Reply to C.R. Nelson and B.T. McCallum', *Journal of Political Economy*, 87, 403–9

Sargent, T.J. and Wallace, N., 1973. 'Rational Expectations and the Dynamics of Hyperinflation', *International Economic Review*, 14, 328–50

1975. 'Rational Expectations, the Optimal Monetary Instrument and the Optimal Money Supply Rule', *Journal of Political Economy*, 83, 241–55

Tobin, J., 1970. 'The Wage Price Mechanism', in O. Eckstein (ed.), *The Econometrics of Price Determination Conference*, Washington: Board of Governors of the Federal Reserve System

12 Non-linear dependence in unemployment, output and inflation: empirical evidence for the UK

David Peel and Alan Speight

Introduction

Two competing views dominate the recent theoretical literature on the nature of the relationship between cyclical fluctuations and the long-run steady states of the key macroeconomic aggregates. On the one hand, the 'natural rate hypothesis' (NRH) holds that the decisionmaking of rational agents depends only on relative price movements with market clearing ensuring self-stabilisation of the economic system on a natural real equilibrium, about which cyclical variation will occur if agents cannot perfectly distinguish relative from general price movements. Consequently, demand management policies which seek to maintain a position away from the natural equilibrium will only affect nominal variables in the long run.[1] In contrast, the 'hysteresis hypothesis' holds that actual changes in real magnitudes themselves alter underlying natural rates such that transitory shocks have permanent effects, implying 'path dependence' in the dynamics of the economic system in the sense that the steady state equilibrium is determined by how it is arrived at. Equilibria under hysteresis are therefore ephemeral, and the notion of a 'natural' rate tenuous. Moreover, policy actions which cause actual changes are capable of exerting real as well as nominal long-run effects.[2]

More formally, hysteresis may be defined as occurring 'when there are two quantities M and N such that cyclic variations of N cause cyclic variations of M . . . [and] the changes of M lag behind those of N . . . the value of M at any point of the operation depends not only on the actual value of N, but on all the preceding changes (and particularly on the immediately preceding changes) of N . . .'.[3] Theoretically, such effects are most simply rationalised on the basis of factors which prevent equilibrating wage reductions in response to rising unemployment. In particular, it has been argued (e.g. Blanchard and Summers, 1986, 1987) that 'insiders' (the employed, union members, etc.) are able to negotiate wage settlements which maintain their employment, without concern for the employment prospects of 'outsiders' (the unemployed, non-unionised labour, etc.). Adverse supply shocks which reduce labour demand and increase unemployment will then reduce the number of insiders, who subsequently form a smaller empowered group determining wages at the next negotiation round. As a consequence, a temporary negative shock may cause a permanently higher level of unemployment. Such hysteresis will be reflected in a 'unit root' in the autoregressive representation of unemployment (see below). Similarly, adverse demand shocks which reduce the capital stock may cause unemployment that is 'persistent' over time (but may not be fully permanent) as firm closures and capital scrapping are not readily reversible, and unemployment converges only slowly on its long-run equilibrium (i.e. exhibits sluggish mean reversion).[4] More generally, as Krasnosel'skii and Pokrovskii (1983, 1989) have demonstrated, hysteresis will be exhibited by any system containing a non-linear relationship, since that system's current behaviour will then depend selectively on past shocks.[5]

Given the foregoing, the time series properties of unemployment, output and inflation, and the nature of their interdependence, are of central importance to the natural rate–hypothesis debate. This chapter therefore appraises these properties and extends extant empirical work in several directions, using monthly data for the UK over the floating/target zone exchange rate period, 1972:07–1993:02. In particular, we test for the presence of non-linearity in these series and appraise the adequacy of a range of explicit time series representations of such non-linearity, including bilinear and threshold autoregressive models. The latter class of models are of particular interest given their ability to parameterise asymmetric path dependence with respect to past behaviour of differing magnitude and sign, as well as their ability to accommodate equilibria that follow fixed cycles rather than converging on a fixed point.

The remainder of the chapter is organised as follows. The second section discusses the connection between hysteresis and presence of a unit root, provides tests for unit roots in our series, and discusses the power of such tests. Given a number of considerations, this debate gives reason to question the conclusiveness of such tests, and we therefore proceed to examine non-linear time series representation of our series. These models and their properties are outlined in the third section, while the fourth section describes the tests of model adequacy we employ. Our empirical results are presented in the fifth section. The sixth and final section summarises our findings and draws some conclusions.

Non-stationarity and unit root testing

The linkage between hysteresis and a unit root in unemployment is easily demonstrated using the simple Phillips curve relating the actual inflation rate π_t, the divergence of actual unemployment from its natural rate, u_t and u_t^* respectively, and expected inflation at time t, π_t^e,

$$\pi_t = \alpha_0 - \alpha_1(u_t - u_t^*) + \alpha_2\pi_t^e. \tag{1}$$

Imposing homogeneity ($\alpha_2 = 1$) and characterising the dependence of the current natural rate on the past realisation of unemployment as:

$$u_t^* = \alpha_3 + \alpha_4 u_{t-1} \tag{2}$$

yields

$$u_t = \alpha_5 + \alpha_4 u_{t-1} + \alpha_6(\pi_t^e - \pi_t) \tag{3}$$

where $\alpha_5 = (\alpha_0/\alpha_1) + \alpha_3$ and $\alpha_6 = (1/\alpha_1)$. For $\alpha_4 = 1$ in (2) realised unemployment changes lead to equivalent changes in the natural rate, and (3) describes a (drifting) random walk in u_t; i.e. u_t possesses a unit root for $\alpha_4 = 1$.

The above is easily generalised to a stochastic setting in keeping with the standard unit root testing framework using the distinction between trend stationary (TS) and difference stationary (DS) processes emphasised by Nelson and Plosser (1982). Both cases may be nested in the general model:

$$u_t = \mu + \beta t + \alpha u_{t-1} + v_t \tag{4}$$

where β is the time trend coefficient and v_t is a stationary cyclical component with zero mean and variance, σ^2. For the polar TS case ($\alpha = 0$), secular non-stationary growth is due to secular trend, while for the DS case ($\beta = 0, \alpha = 1$), u_t is integrated of order 1, denoted $I(1)$, requiring to be differenced once to induce stationarity. Such a process has no tendency to return to trend, and its magnitude at any point is the sum of its past cyclical behaviour:

$$u_t = u_0 + \mu_t + \Sigma_t v_t. \tag{5}$$

In contrast with the TS case, the non-secular component here is non-stationary, having increasing variance $t\sigma^2$, implying the presence of a unit root in u_t.

In recent years a number of tests of the null hypothesis of a unit root in autoregressive representations of the form (4) have been developed, following that initially proposed by Dickey and Fuller (1979, 1981). A common motivation for test development has been to recognise and appropriately accommodate potentially serially correlated residuals in the underlying autoregression. The Augmented Dickey–Fuller (ADF) procedure, for example, is appropriate in the presence of autoregressive moving average (ARMA) error processes of unknown order (Said and Dickey, 1984) given the inclusion of a number of lagged differences in the dependent variable sufficient to render the error process uncorrelated. As an alternative approach, Phillips and Perron (1988) have proposed a non-parametric correction to the Dickey–Fuller (DF) procedure to deal with a broad class of serial correlation types, and MA errors which the ADF procedure may not be able to accommodate in particular. However, it has been demonstrated that although size distortions of the Phillips–Perron statistics are small in the presence of MA errors displaying positive autocorrelation, size distortions become large for negatively autocorrelated MA errors (Phillips and Perron, 1988; Park and Choi, 1988; Schwert, 1989). Additionally it has been shown that of these procedures, in the presence of autoregressive (AR) errors, the ADF procedure is reasonably well-behaved whilst Phillips–Perron test statistics suffer serious size distortions (DeJong et al., 1992a). Further, Campbell and Perron (1991) have argued that the ADF test possesses greater power in the small samples typical of postwar data. The choice of test procedure in any given application cannot therefore be made independently of the error structure associated with the test autoregression or the sample size available. We therefore report both ADF and Phillips–Perron statistics for our three UK series: namely, the unemployment rate, the log of industrial production, and the inflation rate calculated as the difference in the log of the retail price index.[6]

As reported in table 12.1, ADF statistics fail to reject the null of non-stationarity in the levels of all series, but clearly do reject the same null in the differences of all series except unemployment, where there is some indication that the first difference may also be non-stationary. Phillips–Perron $Z(\hat{\alpha})$, $Z(t\hat{\alpha})$ and $Z(\alpha^*)$ test statistics confirm non-stationarity in the levels of all series at standard significance levels for 'window' sizes of both 4 and 12 (see notes to table 12.1). For unemployment and log industrial production $Z(\varnothing_3)$ and $Z(\varnothing_2)$ statistics further suggest the exclusion of both drift and trend from the test autoregressions.[7] In contrast, drift and trend cannot be excluded from the inflation test autoregression (even at the 1% level) and $Z(t\alpha^*)$ and $Z(\varnothing_1)$ reject the presence of a unit root in π, and the joint hypothesis of unit root and zero drift, respectively. However, for a non-zero trend coefficient these statistics are of low power, their sampling distribution being inappropriate. All test statistics reject non-stationarity in the first difference of all series, except in test $Z(\varnothing_1)$ under $l = 12$ for differenced unemployment. However, the power of this test of both unit root and zero drift given the exclusion of a significant trend is questionable. On balance we are therefore encouraged to interpret these statistics as suggesting that unemployment and log industrial production are $I(1)$ processes following random walks, while inflation is an $I(1)$ process described by a drifting random walk about trend.

Table 12.1 *Unit root tests*

| | | Phillips–Perron statistics | | | | | | | | | | | | |
| | ADF | l=4 | | | | | | | l=12 | | | | | | |
		$Z(\tilde{\alpha})$	$Z(t\tilde{\alpha})$	$Z(\emptyset_3)$	$Z(\emptyset_2)$	$Z(\alpha^*)$	$Z(t\alpha^*)$	$Z(\emptyset_1)$	$Z(\tilde{\alpha})$	$Z(t\tilde{\alpha})$	$Z(\emptyset_3)$	$Z(\emptyset_2)$	$Z(\alpha^*)$	$Z(t\alpha^*)$	$Z(\emptyset_1)$
U	-3.160(4)	-1.74	-0.93	0.44	0.15	-0.89	-0.69	0.19	-3.84	-1.39	0.96	1.20	-1.96	-1.02	1.08
ΔU	-2.578(2)	-58.50	-5.93	17.32	11.55	-58.50	-5.93	30.38	-98.43	-7.37	26.98	17.99	-98.54	-7.37	3.43
y	-2.590(1)	-15.39	-2.80	3.86	2.57	-4.09	-1.49	2.64	-21.09	-3.29	5.37	5.45	-5.43	-1.75	5.40
Δy	18.399(0)	-279.70	-18.58	170.40	113.60	-279.70	-18.58	188.80	-272.20	-18.59	170.50	113.70	-272.00	-18.59	206.00
π	-0.741(3)	-1.17	-1.07	16.45	58.79	-1.50	-5.70	99.24	-1.43	-1.09	11.73	41.34	-1.52	-4.86	70.63
$\Delta \pi$	-6.951(1)	-174.80	-11.38	64.03	42.68	-143.70	-9.85	37.46	-208.50	-11.97	71.09	47.39	-211.90	-11.34	4.73
5% critical values	3.422	-21.80	-3.41	6.25	4.68	-14.10	-2.86	4.59	-21.80	-3.41	6.25	4.68	-14.10	-2.86	4.59

Notes: U denotes the unemployment rate, y the log of industrial production, π the differenced log of the retail price index, and Δ the difference operator. ADF is the Augmented Dickey–Fuller test of $\alpha_1 = 0$ in $\Delta x_t = \alpha_0 + \alpha_1 x_{t-1} + \sum_{j=1}^{p} \gamma_j \Delta x_{t-j} + u_t$, where the number in parentheses is the value of p necessary to render $\hat{u}_t$ 'white'. The Phillips–Perron statistics reported follow the notation of Perron (1989) as follows: in $x_t = \mu + \beta(T - T/2) + \alpha x_{t-1} + v_t$, tests $Z(\tilde{\alpha})$ and $Z(t\tilde{\alpha})$ are of $\alpha = 1$, $Z(\emptyset_3)$ is of $(\mu, 0, 1)$ versus (μ, β, α), and $Z(\emptyset_2)$ is of $(0, 0, 1)$ versus $(\mu, 0, 1)$. In the regression $x_t = \mu + \alpha x_{t-1} + u_t$, $Z(\alpha^*)$ and $Z(t\alpha^*)$ are tests of $\alpha = 1$, and $Z(\emptyset_1)$ is of $(0, 1)$ vs. (μ, α). Formulas for the transformed test statistics are given in Perron (1989). Estimates of the error variances associated with these Z tests are constructed from the estimated residuals as $(1/T) \sum_{t=1}^{T} \hat{\varepsilon}_t^2 + \sum_{s=1}^{l} w(s, l) \sum_{t=s+1}^{T} \hat{\varepsilon}_t \hat{\varepsilon}_{t-s}$, where $w(s, l)$ is a 'window' and l a truncation parameter determining window size. See text and Perron (1989) for further details.

It may be tempting to conclude from the above that our series, and the unemployment rate in particular, exhibits hysteresis. However, a number of caveats must be borne in mind. Apart from the problem of test statistic selection, the standard null hypothesis in unit root tests is that of integration, implying the need for strong evidence against the null in order for a TS representation to be favoured, and several studies have indeed drawn attention to the potential low power of such tests in discriminating against TS alternatives (Schwert, 1989; Christiano and Eichenbaum, 1990; DeJong and Whiteman, 1991; DeJong et al., 1992a, 1992b), particularly in the presence of MA residual structure (Phillips and Perron, 1988; Schwert, 1989; Park and Choi, 1988; DeJong et al., 1992b), and to the low information content in typically relatively short macroeconomic time series (Cochrane, 1988; Diebold and Rudebusch, 1989; Christiano and Eichenbaum, 1990; Sowell, 1992). Indeed, studies which adopt the null hypothesis of trend stationarity (possibly segmented) against the alternative of integration, are often unable to reject that null (Kwiatowski, Phillips and Schmidt, 1991; DeJong and Whiteman, 1991; Rappaport and Reichlin, 1989; Perron, 1989). Such difficulties are compounded in the analysis of the unemployment rate, since any bounded series must exhibit stationarity in a sufficiently long (possibly infinite) run of data. The statistical non-stationarity of the postwar unemployment rate might therefore be regarded as a small-sample result. Given these difficulties, it does not seem feasible to claim evidence of a unit root or not as conclusive in determining a series as hysteretic or not. Rather, given that hysteresis is the natural consequence of non-linear systems, we examine the evidence for such non-linearity, and the appropriate time series representation of such non-linearity where present. The models and tests employed are described in the following sections.

Non-linear time series models

As is well known, in the context of any (known or unknown) linear structural model, any stationary endogenous variable (or its stationary transform), say y_t, can be given a univariate time series representation. Specifically an autoregressive moving average, ARMA (p, q), representation (or autoregressive integrated moving average ARIMA (p, d, q) representation, where differencing d times is required to induce stationarity), which may be expressed as:[8]

$$\alpha(L)y_t = \beta(L)e_t \tag{6}$$

where $\alpha(L)$ and $\beta(L)$ are polynomials of orders p and q in the lag operator, L (i.e. $L^d x_t = x_{t-d}$). Rearranging (6):

$$y_t = a_0 + \sum_{i=1}^{p} a_i y_{t-i} + \sum_{j=0}^{q} b_j e_{t-j} \qquad (7)$$

for $t = r + 1, \ldots, r = \max(p, q)$, where appropriate p and q in specific applications of ARMA modelling are established by satisfaction of the requirement that $\{e_t\}$ be 'white': $E(e_t) = \bar{e}$; $\mathrm{Var}(e_t) = \sigma_e^2 < \infty$; $\mathrm{Corr}(e_t, e_{t-i}) = 0$. However, this general ARMA (p, q) representation is inappropriate in circumstances where the true underlying structural process generating y_t is non-linear in parameters of variables. To see this, note that where $\alpha(L)$ is invertible, the general ARMA (p, q) representation also has the $\mathrm{MA}(\infty)$ representation:

$$y_t = \alpha^{-1}(L)e_t = \gamma(L)e_t = g + \sum_{j=0}^{\infty} g_j e_{t-j}. \qquad (8)$$

Linearity then holds in (8) when the $\{e_t\}$ in this $\mathrm{MA}(\infty)$ representation are strictly independent random variables (Priestley, 1981). Therefore, the zero autocorrelation property of white disturbances to an ostensibly correctly specified ARMA process does not ensure linearity, since independence of those disturbances is further required.

Conditional heteroscedasticity

One characterisation of non-linearity in conditional variance that has enjoyed widespread application in recent empirical work is the AutoRegressive Conditional Heteroscedasticity (ARCH) model (Engle, 1982) and its generalisations. The characteristic feature of the ARCH model is persistence and possible clustering in conditional variance, and it has been given various interpretations, including: (i) the ability of past volatility to explain current volatility (irrespective of the sign of change) especially in financial data (Engle and Bollerslev, 1986); (ii) due to random coefficients in the associated (ARMA) regression model (Tsay, 1987); or (iii) due to the non-coincidence of calendar and 'business cycle time' (i.e. 'time deformation', Stock, 1987).

The simple qth order, ARCH (q), model for e_t (the error in the linear processes above) is formally defined in terms of its conditional distribution as (Engle, 1982):

$$e_t = \varepsilon_t h_t; \; h_t^2 = \varnothing_0 + \varnothing(L)e_t^2 = \varnothing_0 + \sum_{i=1}^{q} \varnothing_i e_{t-i}^2 \qquad (9)$$

where $\varnothing_0 > 0$ and $\varnothing_i \geq 0, \Sigma_q \varnothing_i < 1$ for $i > 0$, and the $\{e_t\}$ are i.i.d. random variables with standard normal distribution: $E(\varepsilon_t) = 0$, $\mathrm{Var}(\varepsilon_t) = 1.$[9]

On both theoretical and practical grounds, a popular extension of the ARCH model involves introducing lagged dependent variables into (9) to yield the Generalised-ARCH, or GARCH (q_1, q_2), model (Bollerslev, 1986):

$$h_t^2 = \varnothing_0 + \sum_{i=1}^{q_1} \varnothing_i y_{t-i}^2 + \sum_{i=1}^{q_2} \psi_i h_{t-i}^2 \tag{10}$$

where $\varnothing_0 > 0, \varnothing_i \geq 0, \psi_i > 0$ for all i, and $\Sigma_q \varnothing_i + \Sigma_p \psi_i < 1$. Recursive substitution reveals that the GARCH model is equivalently an infinite-order ARCH model with exponentially decaying weights, and therefore clearly encompasses ARCH, providing a parsimonious representation for the potentially infinite Wold decomposition of (linear) h_t^2 (Brock, Hsieh and Le Baron, 1991, hereafter BHL). Further, Drost and Nijman (1990) have demonstrated that the temporal aggregation of high frequency ARCH processes results in GARCH processes at low frequency for both stock and flow variables.[10] However, as noted by Engle (1982) and Weiss (1986), an alternative interpretation of GARCH effects in the residuals of linear models is as an indicator of non-linearity in the conditional mean of the underlying regression model. Two such models are described in the following sub-sections.

Bilinear models

Most generally, non-linear models are of the Volterra series expansion form, involving quadratic, cubic and higher components:

$$y_t = g + \sum_{j=0}^{\infty} g_j e_{t-j} + \sum_{j=0}^{\infty} \sum_{k=0}^{\infty} g_{jk} e_{t-j} e_{t-k} + \sum_{j=0}^{\infty} \sum_{k=0}^{\infty} \sum_{l=0}^{\infty} g_{jkl} e_{t-j} e_{t-k} e_{t-l} + \cdots \tag{11}$$

An obvious difficulty in applying non-linear models of such general form, given finite time series, lies in the plethora of parameters $\{g\}$. However, it has been shown (Brockett, 1976; Sussman, 1977) that such general models can be approximated with an arbitrary degree of accuracy in finite samples by so-called 'bilinear' (BL) models (Granger and Andersen, 1978). In the absence of MA terms, BL (p, m, n) models are of the general form:

$$\alpha(L)y_t = \delta(L)y_t e_t \tag{12}$$

or, rearranging:

$$y_t = a_0 + \sum_{i=1}^{p} a_i y_{y-i} + \sum_{i=0}^{m} \sum_{j=0}^{n} d_{ij} y_{t-m} e_{t-n} + e_t \tag{13}$$

where the e_t are again required to be independent random variables. The bilinear form thus clearly provides a direct generalisation of the linear ARMA form. Indeed, Weiss (1986) has demonstrated that ARMA–ARCH processes can be mistakenly identified when the true process is BL. The BL model also provides a convenient example of inappropriate ARMA modelling in the presence of non-i.i.d. disturbances. For example, consider the case where $\{e_t\}$ is identified as white in an ARMA model but has the true non-linear (BL) generating process:

$$e_t = \eta_t + \varnothing \eta_{t-1} \eta_{t-2} \tag{14}$$

where η_t is an independent process with constant mean and finite variance. That e_t would have been correctly identified as white may be verified from its autocovariance function:

$$E(e_t e_{t+s}) = E(\eta_t \eta_{t+s} + \beta \eta_{t-1} \eta_{t-2} \eta_{t+s} + \beta \eta_t \eta_{t+s-1} \eta_{t+s-2} + \beta^2 \eta_{t-1} \eta_{t-1-2} \eta_{t+s-1} \eta_{t+s-2}) = 0, \tag{15}$$

suggesting that there is no remaining model structure to fit when, in fact, the non-linear structure of e_t might be exploited to improve on linear ARMA forecasts. That is, by exploiting $e_{t+1} = \beta \eta_t \eta_{t-1}$.

As with GARCH models, the bilinear form may also be motivated as an approximation to an underlying time-varying parameter linear model. For example, the simple model $y_t = a_0 + a_1 y_{t-1} + e_t$, where $a_1 = \bar{a} + v_t$, can be re-expressed as $y_t = a_0 + \bar{a} y_{t-1} + v_t y_{t-1} + e_t$.

Threshold autoregressive models

Another class of non-linear model, also possessing finite parameters, 'threshold autoregressive' (TAR) models, has been developed by Tong (1983, 1990). Such models allow the parameters of a linear model to vary according to the values of a finite number of lags in some conditioning variable, z_t. Such TAR models may be regarded as 'piecewise-linear' approximations to more general kth-order non-linear autoregressions of the form $y_t = f(y_{t-1}, y_{t-2}, \ldots, y_{t-k}) + e_t$. TAR models may therefore be motivated along the same lines as GARCH and BL models. We consider two variants within this general class of non-linear threshold models.

The sub-set of TAR models known as Self-Exciting (SETAR) models assume the conditioning variable to be the dependent variable itself, and have the general form:

$$y_t = a_{j0} + a_j(L) y_t + e_{jt} \qquad \text{for } y_{t-dj} \mathcal{E} R_j \text{ and } j = 1, \ldots, J \tag{16}$$

where R denotes the real line, $a_j(L)$ denotes a polynomial in the lag operator of order p_j, there are J 'regimes' which are defined according to whether the value of y with 'delay parameter' (lag) d_j lies above or below the various threshold values r_j, and the e_t are again independent random variables. Alternatively, (17) may be expressed as (Tong, 1990):

$$y_t = a_0^j + \sum_{i=1}^{p_j} a_i^j y_{t-i} + e_t^j \qquad \text{for } y_{t-d_j} \varepsilon R_j \qquad (17)$$

where the e_t^j are heterogeneous white noise sequences with zero mean and finite variances each being independent of one another. The system in (17) may then be summarised in terms of the number of regimes and the lengths of the AR processes characterising those regimes as SETAR $(J; pj)$. A simple one-threshold two-regime autoregressive model with first-order AR lag structure in both regimes would therefore be SETAR $(2; 1, 1)$:

$$y_t = \begin{cases} a_{10} + a_{11}y_{t-1} + e_{1t} & \text{if} \quad y_{t-d} < R \\ a_{20} + a_{22}y_{t-1} + e_{2t} & \text{if} \quad y_{t-d \geqslant r_1} \end{cases} \qquad (18)$$

SETAR models therefore reduce to linear AR models when $J = 1$. SETAR models also possess the interesting property of being able to accommodate equilibrium 'limit cycles' in the sense of solutions which have an asymptotic periodic form.

Various extensions of the SETAR model are possible. In particular, there is no *a priori* reason why a TAR model should consist solely of univariate autoregressions partitioned on the basis of an indicator function defined over the dependent variable only. An obvious generalisation of (4) therefore admits the vector of additional 'exogenous' explanatory variables, Z_t, yielding the threshold vector autoregressive system conditioned on past movements in (elements of) Z_t:

$$y_t = a_0^j + \sum_{i=1}^{p_j} a_i^j y_{t-j} + \sum_{i=0}^{s_j} B_i^j Z_{t-i} + e_t^j \qquad \text{for } wZ_{t-d_j} \varepsilon R_j \qquad (19)$$

where B_i is the matrix of coefficients associated with the vector Z_{t-i}, and in addition to being i.i.d., the $\{e_t^j\}$ are assumed to be independent of $\{Z_t\}$. Where the Z_t in (19) are indeed exogenous, the threshold model is termed 'open-loop' (TARSO) (Tong, 1990). In the simple case where Z_t comprises a single variable, z_t, the model in (19) is summarised as TARSO $[J; (p_1, s_1), \ldots, (p_J, s_J)]$. For the simple case $Z_t = z_t$, if both $(y_t z_t)$ and (z_t, y_t) are described by TARSO processes, the joint process is termed a closed loop TAR (TARSC).

Tests of model adequacy

A recurring issue in the previous section is the requirement that the disturbances to a correctly specified process be i.i.d., departures from i.i.d.

indicating neglected structure. In appraising the adequacy of fitted models it is therefore necessary to conduct tests for such departures.

Brock, Dechert and Scheinkman (1987, hereafter BDS) propose a statistic that may be used to test for departures from i.i.d. This statistic, developed from the theory of U-statistics (Serfling, 1980), is based upon the 'correlation integral' (Grassberger and Procaccia, 1983) and defined as follows. Convert the series of scalars comprising the time series e_t into a number of shorter series with overlapping entries. That is, construct the series of 'm'-histories:

$$e_t^m = (e_t, e_{t+1}, \ldots, e_{t+m-1}) \tag{20}$$

where m is termed the 'embedding dimension'. The 'distance', $\mathcal{E}$, between two m-histories can then be measured as

$$\mathcal{E}_{t,s}^m = \max(1 \leq i \leq m) |e_{t-i}^m - e_{s-i}^m|. \tag{21}$$

The correlation integral, C, is then defined as the cumulative distribution function of $\mathcal{E}^m$, and the BDS statistic is defined for m, $\mathcal{E}$ and sample size T, as:

$$BDS(m, \mathcal{E}) = T[C_m(\mathcal{E}) - C_1(\mathcal{E})^m]/\sigma_m(\mathcal{E}) \sim_{t \to \infty} N(0, 1) \tag{22}$$

where $\sigma_m^2(\mathcal{E})$ denotes the large sample variance of the data for which formulae are provided by BDS (1987) and Hsieh (1989). As BDS and BHL (1991) demonstrate, the BDS statistic is asymptotically normally distributed and applicable to model residuals in the sense of being robust to nuisance parameters, as well as distributions exhibiting skewness and kurtosis, and has high power against a wide range of linear and non-linear alternatives to i.i.d. However, Monte Carlo simulations conducted by BHL suggest that the finite sample distribution of the BDS statistic does not approximate asymptotic normality for sample sizes under 500, and that the asymptotic distribution does not very well approximate the BDS statistic applied to the standardised residuals of ARCH and GARCH models. On the other hand, the Engle (1982) ARCH test has low power and the BDS test has high power in detecting GARCH models where h_t^2 depends on its own past in a non-linear manner (BHL, 1991). For this reason we employ both the Engle ARCH and BDS statistics as diagnostics of functional mis-specification. Given our finite data set we also follow the recommendations of BHL in: (i) reporting BDS diagnostics for embedding dimensions of $m = 2, 3, 4, 5$ and distances $\mathcal{E} = \sigma, \sigma/2$, and (ii) using the quantiles they report from their small sample simulations as guidance to the actual sizes for our BDS statistics.

Non-linear model estimates

Following the approach of Brock and Sayers (1988), we consider the performance of AR models prior to their generalisations to the bilinear BL and TAR non-linear forms described on pp. 238–40.[11] Table 12.2 reports a range of diagnostics applied to the residuals of the most parsimonious AR processes fitted to the (mean-adjusted) unemployment rate, U',[12] the differenced unemployment rate ΔU, the rate of growth of industrial production, Δy, and the differenced inflation rate, $\Delta \pi$. These models require that the variables being modelled are (stationary transforms of non-) stationary processes. Given the results of our second section above, and that our priors are strongly in favour of difference stationarity in aggregate series we are nevertheless urged to exercise caution with respect to the unemployment rate, and it is for this reason that we therefore consider both the level (mean-adjusted) and first difference of that rate.

Whilst not reported in full, employing AIC criteria, these specifications are, respectively, AR(5), AR(4), AR(1) and AR(3). For these models reported diagnostics include measures of residual variance, skewness and kurtosis, the Ljung–Box test for up to twelfth-order autocorrelation, first- and fourth-order ARCH tests, and BDS(m, $\mathcal{E}$) tests for non-linear residual structure ($m = 2, \ldots .5$, $\mathcal{E} = \sigma, \sigma/2$).

Whilst all linear AR processes eliminate residual autocorrelation, residual ARCH effects are significant for both Δy and $\Delta \pi$. For Δy, BDS statistics strongly suggest that such effects are due to non-linearity in conditional mean. Non-linearity is also indicated by BDS statistics for U' and ΔU. However, for Δy and $\Delta \pi$ BDS statistics are marginally significant, suggesting the presence of ARCH effects rather than non-linearity in $\Delta \pi$. We therefore estimate AR–GARCH specifications for both these series, in the case of $\Delta \pi$ along the lines established by Engle (1982). In both cases AR–GARCH processes yield i.i.d. residuals on the basis of insignificant BDS statistics.

Bilinear model estimates

Given the non-linearity detected in the residuals of linear AR models on the basis of BDS test statistics, we proceed to investigate the appropriateness of the non-linear model candidates described on pp. 238–9 as representations of that non-linearity and competitors to the AR–GARCH models identified for Δy and $\Delta \pi$. Estimated coefficients and residual diagnostics for BL models are reported in table 12.3. In the notation of p. 244, the most parsimonious models on the basis of AIC criteria are, for U', ΔU, Δy and $\Delta \pi$ respectively, BL(5, 2, 1), BL(4, 1, 1), BL(1, 5, 1) and BL(3, 3, 2). Note that

Table 12.2 *Residual diagnostics for linear AR(p) models*

Series	Model	Variance	Skewness	Kurtosis	LB_{12}	A_1	A_4	BDS (m_ε)							
								$(2,\sigma)$	$(2,\sigma/2)$	$(3,\sigma)$	$(3,\sigma/2)$	$(4,\sigma)$	$(4,\sigma/2)$	$(5,\sigma)$	$(5,\sigma/2)$
U'	AR(5)	52.52	0.04	2.88	8.01	0.97	5.26	12.60	7.46	12.12	8.66	11.54	9.34	11.09	9.75
ΔU	AR(4)	53.64	0.06	2.93	9.66	0.90	5.26	1.15	10.19	1.08	16.15	0.76	20.82	0.86	23.66
Δy	AR(1)	2.56	−0.36	7.01	14.86	12.96	18.10	5.30	4.36	5.15	4.08	4.84	4.75	4.33	5.11
Δy	AR-GARCH	1.00	−1.11	8.84	12.41	0.90	3.44	1.34	0.99	1.39	1.30	1.34	1.70	0.96	1.93
$\Delta \pi$	AR(3)	0.18	0.61	4.69	18.36	4.14	10.00	2.84	2.95	2.78	2.35	3.52	2.78	3.72	3.13
$\Delta \pi$	AR-GARCH	1.00	0.51	4.18	17.97	0.03	6.65	0.87	1.22	1.05	0.91	1.82	1.41	2.15	1.69
5% critical values					21.03	3.84	7.78	−2.15	−2.64	−2.17	−2.92	−2.17	−3.37	−2.18	−4.11
								2.27	2.98	2.37	3.23	2.39	3.84	2.56	4.98

Notes: U' denotes the mean-adjusted unemployment rate, ΔU the differenced unemployment rate, Δy the growth rate of industrial production, and $\Delta \pi$ the differenced inflation rate. Reported diagnostics are measures of residual variance, skewness and kurtosis. LB_{12} is the Ljung–Box test for up to twelfth-order autocorrelation. A_1 and A_4 are Engle (1982) tests for first- and fourth-order ARCH effects respectively, and BDS (m, ε) is the BDS (1987) test for non-i.i.d. residuals where m denotes 'embedding dimension' and ε 'distance'. Critical values for the BDS test are the 95% quantiles reported by BHL from simulations for 250 observations (1991, table C1). See text for further details.

Table 12.3 Bilinear models

Estimates

Series	Model	a_0	a_1	a_2	a_3	a_4	a_5	d_{11}	d_{21}	d_{31}	d_{41}	d_{51}	d_{12}	d_{22}	d_{32}
U'	BL(5,2,1)	0.001	1.136	0.209	−0.099	−0.080	−0.170	0.705	−0.734	—	—	—	—	—	—
ΔU	BL(4,1,1)	0.001	0.153	0.351	0.251	0.146	—	0.709	—	—	—	—	—	—	—
Δy	BL(1,5,1)	0.072	−0.159	—	—	—	—	0.004	−0.088	−0.010	−0.031	−0.151	—	—	—
$\Delta \pi$	BL(3,3,2)	−0.004	0.372	0.221	0.096	—	—	0.010	1.060	−1.19	—	—	−0.405	0.880	−0.317

Residual diagnostics

Series	Model	Variance	Skewness	Kurtosis	LB_{12}	A_1	$A4$	$(2,\sigma)$	$(2,\sigma/2)$	$(3,\sigma)$	$(3,\sigma/2)$	$(4,\sigma)$	$(4,\sigma/2)$	$(5,\sigma)$	$(5,\sigma/2)$
								\multicolumn{8}{c}{BDS $(m\,\mathcal{E})$}
U'	BL(5,2,1)	51.45	0.05	2.74	7.70	0.50	4.52	1.26	1.16	1.92	4.69	2.51	7.16	3.05	8.40
ΔU	BL(4,1,1)	52.95	0.06	2.93	9.02	0.65	3.85	0.86	5.09	1.18	11.73	1.32	16.61	1.62	18.80
Δy	BL(1,5,1)	23.34	−0.62	7.09	18.10	3.01	3.44	2.48	2.15	3.06	3.08	3.07	3.25	2.81	2.70
$\Delta \pi$	BL(3,3,2)	0.16	0.61	4.21	14.59	1.61	6.76	2.65	2.49	2.88	2.67	3.42	3.35	3.63	3.09
5% critical values					21.03	3.84	7.78	−2.15 2.27	−2.64 2.98	−2.17 2.37	−2.92 3.23	−2.17 2.39	−3.37 3.84	−2.18 2.56	−4.11 4.98

Notes: As table 12.2. Additionally BL denotes a bilinear with associated parameter estimates as given in equation (13). See p. 238 of the text for further details.

only for $\Delta\pi$ does interaction between the lagged dependent variable and the lagged error extend beyond a single lag. The upper panel of table 12.3 reports the coefficient estimates for these models (associated t-ratios are not reported due to the inability to derive standard errors appropriate for the BL form). Of particular interest is the near-unit coefficient on the first lag in the U' equation, which lends support to the proposition that the unemployment rate is indeed difference stationary. The performance of all BL models appears satisfactory from an ARCH test perspective. However, BDS statistics suggest remaining non-linear structure for all series, despite reductions in those statistics relative to their linear model counterparts. Whilst the bilinear models fitted and the extent of the reduction in residual variance they offer provides further evidence of non-linearity in the conditional means of our series, those models do not provide a completely satisfactory representation of that non-linearity. Additionally, despite its usefulness as a close approximation to a broad range of non-linear forms, the BL form is not readily interpreted in economic terms, and with respect to hysteresis in particular. We therefore turn to the potentially more interesting class of threshold models.

Threshold autoregressive model estimates

SETAR model estimates and residual diagnostics are reported in table 12.4. As noted earlier, these models are clearly capable of capturing the selective path dependence characteristic of hysteretic systems. Moreover, this selective path dependence may be asymmetric for past movements of greater and lesser magnitude, and of differing sign.

The results reported in table 12.4 indicate that for U', ΔU, Δy, and $\Delta\pi$ respectively, on the basis of AIC criteria, appropriate models are SETAR $(2; 4, 5)$, SETAR $(3; 4, 3, 2)$, SETAR $(2; 5, 5)$ and SETAR $(2; 3, 1)$. These specifications are also satisfactory in terms of the partitioning of the overall sample across regimes, and further notable reductions in residual variance over earlier BL models. These models also reveal some interesting features concerning the degree of persistence and the nature of the equilibria possessed by the series examined.

In the presence of a unit root in unemployment, stochastic shocks become fully embodied in u_t, lasting indefinitely and implying a unitary degree of persistence; i.e. they are permanent. More generally, for $\alpha \neq 1$ and where stationarity of v_t in (4) implies a Wold representation, $v_t = \lambda(L)w_t$,[13] first differencing yields the stationary process:

$$\Delta u_t = \rho + \lambda(L)w_t \tag{23}$$

where $\lambda(1)$ is widely interpreted as reflecting the degree of persistence in u_t;

Table 12.4 Threshold models

Estimates

Series	Model	Threshold	a_0^j	a_1^j	a_2^j	a_3^j	a_4^j	a_5^j	n	P
U^r	SETAR(2;4,5)	$U^r_{t-3} \le 0.2235$	0.0271 (0.0148)	1.2547 (0.0861)	0.2333 (0.1385)	-0.3015 (0.1382)	-0.1821 (0.0888)	—	129	n/a
		$U^r_{t-3} > 0.2235$	-0.0191 (0.0169)	1.0601 (0.0898)	0.1545 (0.1320)	0.1358 (0.1322)	-0.1034 (0.1310)	-0.2445 (0.0867)	119	n/a
ΔU	SETAR(3;4,3,2)	$\Delta U_{t-3} \le -0.0065$	0.0451 (0.0211)	0.1754 (0.1110)	0.1891 (0.1101)	0.4976 (0.1693)	0.3631 (0.1130)	—	68	—
		$-0.0065 < \Delta U_{t-3} \le 0.1487$	-0.0032 (0.0085)	0.1512 (0.0818)	0.4660 (0.0753)	0.4396 (0.1337)	—	—	143	—
		$\Delta U_{t-3} > 0.1487$	0.0515 (0.0354)	0.4370 (0.1476)	0.2651 (0.1510)	—	—	—	37	3.36
Δy	SETAR(2;5,5)	$\Delta y_{t-1} \le 1.7834$	0.1081 (0.0990)	-0.1478 (0.0713)	-0.0526 (0.0621)	0.0957 (0.0626)	0.0719 (0.0591)	0.1332 (0.0536)	227	1.11
		$\Delta y_{t-1} > 1.7834$	0.4118 (1.2273)	-0.4022 (0.4093)	-0.3731 (0.3177)	-0.3090 (0.2198)	-0.3880 (0.3099)	-0.9120 (0.3651)	21	—
$\Delta \pi$	SETAR(2;3,1)	$\Delta \pi \le 0.1464$	-0.0403 (0.0362)	0.3638 (0.0732)	0.0291 (0.1164)	0.1966 (0.0665)	—	—	176	2.44
		$\Delta \pi > 0.1464$	0.1436 (0.0778)	0.4760 (0.1089)	—	—	—	—	72	1.91

Residual diagnostics

Series	Model	Variance	Skewness	Kurtosis	LB^1_2	A_1	A_4
U^r	SETAR(2;4,5)	50.08	-0.04	2.88	9.40	0.13	0.78
ΔU	SETAR(3;4,3,2)	51.33	0.04	2.66	9.87	1.23	3.78
Δy	SETAR(2;5,5)	2.26	-0.29	7.81	11.35	1.97	3.63
$\Delta \pi$	SETAR(2;3,1)	0.18	0.48	3.93	14.89	1.10	5.18
5% critical values					21.03	3.84	7.78

BDS $(m, \mathcal{E})$

Series	Model	$(2,\sigma)$	$(2,\sigma/2)$	$(3,\sigma)$	$(3,\sigma/2)$	$(4,\sigma)$	$(4,\sigma/2)$	$(5,\sigma)$	$(5,\sigma/2)$
U^r	SETAR(2;4,5)	0.53	1.36	0.08	4.04	0.19	7.05	0.51	9.72
ΔU	SETAR(3;4,3,2)	-0.38	-4.64	-0.25	-2.86	-0.58	1.01	-0.48	4.39
Δy	SETAR(2;5,5)	2.99	2.84	2.76	3.27	2.59	3.25	2.49	4.05
$\Delta \pi$	SETAR(2;3,1)	1.71	1.75	0.71	0.44	0.64	-0.29	0.35	-1.04
5% critical values		-2.15	-2.64	-2.17	-2.92	-2.17	-3.37	-2.18	-4.11
		2.27	2.98	2.37	3.23	2.39	3.54	2.56	4.98

Notes: As table 12.2. Additionally, SETAR denotes a self-exciting threshold autoregressive model with associated parameters as given in equation (17). See p. 239 of the text for further details.

i.e. the response of the long-run forecast of u_t to the shock w_t (Beveridge and Nelson, 1981):

$$\lim_{k \to \infty} [E(u_{t+k} | \Omega_t) - E(u_{t+k} | \Omega_{t-1})] = \lambda(1)w_t \tag{24}$$

where E denotes the expectations operator and Ω the information set. Measures of the degree of persistence have therefore been interpreted as measures of the degree of hysteresis in systems which do not yield permanent dependence on past behaviour.

The final column of table 12.4 reports measures of the degree of persistence in u, y and π implied by the AR processes comprising the SETAR models reported. For those AR processes, these measures are calculated quite simply as

$$P^j = \left(1 - \sum_{i=1}^{pj} a_i^j\right)^{-1} \tag{25}$$

for $|\Sigma_i a_i^j| < 1$. Where the latter does not hold, the AR process is unstable, and not listed. For π, a positive shock has a greater long-run impact during regimes of falling rather than rising inflation. For y, shocks during recessionary regimes are near-permanent, marginally exceeding unity. However, the expansionary AR process is unstable, tending to revert to the contractionary regime. For U, shocks occurring during episodes of rising unemployment have a more than three-fold long-run impact, whilst the other two regimes are again unstable.

Some explanation for the latter result is provided by simulation of the disturbance-free model (the 'skeleton' of the model as termed by Tong, 1990). An interesting property of SETAR models is their ability to accommodate limit cycle equilibria, in the sense of a stable equilibrium cycle rather than stable limit point. Such an equilibrium characterises the SETAR models for unemployment reported in table 12.4, and figures 12.1 and 12.2 depict simulations of the skeletons of these models for U' and ΔU respectively.

As discussed on p. 240, AR models may be generalised to include additional explanatory variables and threshold conditioning on such variables. The results from estimating such models in the trivariate context of U or ΔU, with Δy and $\Delta \pi$, where successful, are reported in table 12.5. In particular, such models with Δy and $\Delta \pi$ as the dependent variables proved unsatisfactory relative to the SETAR models discussed above, and are therefore reported for U' and ΔU only. Also reported for comparative purposes are VAR models of which TARSO models may be viewed as generalisations.

As the residual diagnostics for VAR specifications reveal, although

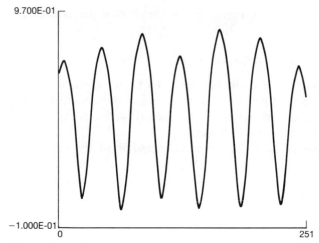

Figure 12.1 Simulation of the noise-free SETAR 'skeleton' for the mean-adjusted UK unemployment rate; see table 12.4 and the text for further details

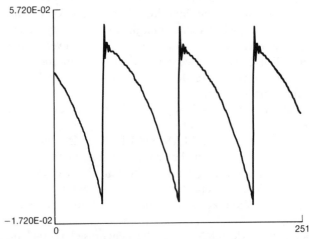

Figure 12.2 Simulation of the noise-free SETAR 'skeleton' for the differenced UK unemployment rate; see table 12.4 and the text for further details

ARCH tests are insignificant, structure remains in VAR residuals on the basis of BDS statistics. However, this structure is removed by a TARSO model conditioned on the growth rate of industrial production. Interestingly, these TARSO forms do not involve lagged terms in either inflation or output, such effects being fully accommodated by conditioning on Δy. Such conditioning also proves most parsimonious around a zero growth rate in industrial production suggesting strong asymmetry in unemployment over the business cycle. Whilst not reported in table 12.5, the AR processes comprising the TARSO model for ΔU imply persistence measures of over 7 and 12 for regimes of ouput contraction and expansion respectively.

Finally, we appraise the extent of interdependence between the series analysed by examining the extent to which shocks to each series, as proxied by the residuals from linear AR and non-linear SETAR model residuals, are correlated, and Granger-cause each other. The results of this exercise are reported in table 12.6. With the exception of the association between U', ΔU and Δy, these correlations are zero at standard levels of significance. The negative correlation between unemployment and output growth bolsters the TARSO results of table 12.5, which are further confirmed by evidence of significant causality moving from the residuals of output growth models to unemployment model residuals.

Summary and conclusions

There has been much debate in recent years as to whether the key macroeconomic aggregates, and unemployment in particular, converge on well-defined equilibria, or exhibit hysteresis in the sense of path dependence, possible due to non-linearity in the underlying data generating process. To date, attempts to resolve the issue empirically have typically focused on tests for unit roots in such series, as a test of the presence of hysteresis. However, concerns regarding the power of such tests, particularly in small samples, cast doubt on their conclusiveness.

The primary purpose of this chapter is therefore to document the key time series features of unemployment and related series. In particular, following initial unit root tests, including ADF and Phillips–Perron tests, we report evidence of non-linear structure in the residuals of the most parsimonious linear AR models fitted to unemployment (both mean-adjusted and differenced), the growth rate in industrial production and the differenced inflation rate. We then proceed to implement a number of time series models as candidate representations of this non-linearity, including AR–GARCH, bilinear (BL) and threshold autoregressive (TAR: both self-exciting, SETAR, and multivariate, TARSO) models.

Non-linearity in the growth rate in industrial production and the differenced inflation rate can be adequately represented by AR–GARCH forms. While BL and SETAR models provide competing parsimonious representations of these series they fail to eliminate all residual structure. We therefore conclude that AR–GARCH processes characterise these processes. In contrast, neither the mean-adjusted nor differenced unemployment rate may be satisfactorily modelled as AR–GARCH processes. BL

Table 12.5 *Multivariate models*

Estimates

Series	Model	Threshold	a_0^i	a_1^i	a_2^i	a_3^i	a_4^i	a_5^i	b_1^i	b_2^i	b_3^i	n
U'	VAR	—	0.0074 (0.0048)	1.1308 (0.0639)	0.1660 (0.0970)	−0.0401 (0.0980)	−0.0689 (0.0969)	−0.1910 (0.0634)	−0.0089 (0.0029)	−0.0061 (0.0030)	−0.0079 (0.0029)	248
U'	TARSO	$\Delta y_{t-1} < 0$	0.0153 (0.0071)	1.5335 (0.0784)	−0.2455 (0.1478)	−0.2912 (0.0776)	—	—	—	—	—	121
		$\Delta y_{t-1} \geq 0$	−0.0074 (0.0061)	0.9690 (0.0791)	0.5018 (0.1221)	0.0059 (0.1332)	−0.4791 (0.0802)	—	—	—	—	127
ΔU	VAR	—	0.0076 (0.0048)	0.1438 (0.0670)	0.3018 (0.0625)	0.2530 (0.0618)	0.1788 (0.0635)	—	−0.0092 (0.0029)	0.0063 (0.0030)	0.0081 (0.0029)	248
ΔU	TARSO	$\Delta y_{t-1} < 0$	0.0159 (0.0071)	0.5333 (0.0788)	0.2925 (0.0780)	—	—	—	—	—	—	121
		$\Delta y_{t-1} \geq 0$	−0.0079 (0.0061)	−0.0222 (0.0790)	0.4646 (0.0759)	0.4758 (0.0804)	—	—	—	—	—	127

Residual diagnostics

Series	Model	Variance	Skewness	Kurtosis	LB_{12}	A_1	A_4	BDS (m, ε) $(2,\sigma)$	$(2,\sigma/2)$	$(3,\sigma)$	$(3,\sigma/2)$	$(4,\sigma)$	$(4,\sigma/2)$	$(5,\sigma)$	$(5,\sigma/2)$
U'	VAR	49.20	−0.01	2.82	6.34	0.30	3.75	0.08	3.08	0.62	5.13	1.54	8.64	2.01	9.14
U	TARSO	47.72	0.11	2.95	11.97	0.30	0.97	−0.01	0.90	−0.01	2.15	−0.24	3.04	−0.24	5.37
ΔU	VAR	50.09	−0.01	2.87	7.03	0.48	3.41	0.68	5.04	0.86	9.47	1.47	15.19	2.14	20.50
$\Delta U'$	TARSO	48.50	0.09	2.95	11.14	0.29	1.45	0.56	−0.71	0.54	1.02	0.41	2.95	0.38	4.51
5% critical values					21.03	3.84	7.78	−2.15 / 2.27	−2.64 / 2.98	−2.17 / 2.37	−2.92 / 3.23	−2.17 / 2.39	−3.37 / 3.54	−2.18 / 2.56	−4.11 / 4.98

Notes: As table 12.4. For model details see p. 245 of the text.

Table 12.6 *Cross-model residual correlations and causality tests*

Linear AR models

	Correlations				Granger causality tests			
	ΔU	U'	Δy	$\Delta\pi$	ΔU	U'	Δy	$\Delta\pi$
ΔU	1.00	0.99	−0.15	0.07	—	—	5.32* 1.94	0.92 0.74
U'	—	1.00	−0.14	0.04	—	—	5.06* 1.88	0.55 0.56
Δy	—	—	1.00	−0.03	1.94 1.38	1.49 1.09	—	—
$\Delta\pi$	—	—	—	1.00	0.92 1.79	1.45 1.94	—	—

Non-linear SETAR model residuals

	Correlations				Granger causality tests			
	ΔU	U'	Δy	$\Delta\pi$	ΔU	U'	Δy	$\Delta\pi$
ΔU	1.00	0.93	−0.14	0.07	—	—	2.72* 2.25*	1.03 0.77
U'	—	1.00	−0.14	0.03	—	—	2.89 1.82	0.19 0.31
Δy	—	—	1.00	−0.04	0.60 1.01	0.90 0.89	—	0.74 0.99
$\Delta\pi$	—	—	—	1.00	1.08 1.31	1.97 1.35	0.51 0.85	—

Notes: As table 12.4. Additionally, Granger causality tests are of the null that the residuals of models for variables listed on the vertical are *not* caused by the residuals of models for variables listed on the horizontal. These tests are conducted for lag lengths of 3 and 15, and an asterisk denotes statistically significant rejection of the null at the 5% level.

forms provide reasonable descriptions of these series, strongly supporting the presence of non-linearity in unemployment, but again fail fully to eradicate non-linearity in the residual structure. SETAR models also provide convenient representations of non-linearity in unemployment, and are therefore supportive of path dependence and dynamic asymmetry in unemployment. Such models also suggest that the long-run equilibrium for unemployment is described, not by a stable limiting point, but by a stable cyclical motion, i.e. a 'limit cycle'. While these models are also unable completely to remove non-linear residual structure, the generalisation of TAR models to the TARSO form, entailing the dependence of unemployment on its own past behaviour and that in industrial production, with thresholds conditioned on the sign of industrial production growth, do yield i.i.d. residuals. Estimates from such a model for the differenced unemployment rate also suggest that, were regime processes to hold indefinitely shocks to unemployment during episodes of output contraction have a seven-fold long-run impact on the unemployment rate, whilst shocks occurring during expansion have a twelve-fold long-run impact. However, we are unable to find any evidence of non-linear interaction amongst any other pairings of our series.

Notes

1 See, for example, Lucas (1973).
2 See Cross (1988).
3 Ewing (1885, p. 524), quoted in Cross (1993, p. 154).
4 A similar argument may be couched in terms of the human capital stock. See Hargreaves-Heap (1980).
5 In the simplest example, non-linearity may be induced by imposing floors and ceilings on the potential range of variation in a system. For instance, exogenous fluctuations may have diminishing effects on employment and output as the productive potential and output floor are approached respectively. For an elaboration of this point see Cross (1993).
6 Source: Datastream. All series are seasonally adjusted, except the retail price index. We therefore seasonally adjust the generated inflation rate using a seasonal MA12 process and 11 seasonal dummies, together with a dummy for the outlier observation of 79:07. Results reported below proved qualitatively similar in the absence of this dummy. This adjustment does not therefore appear to unduly influence our results, and estimates are only reported for the adjusted data. Further details are available on request.
7 Except for industrial production on $Z(\emptyset_2)$ and $Z(\emptyset_1)$ tests under $l = 12$ at the 5%, but not the 1% level.
8 Stationarity implies fixity of mean, variance and autocorrelation (autocovariance) in y_t:

$$E(y_t) = \bar{y}; \text{var}(y_t) = E(y_t - \bar{y})^2 = \sigma_y^2 < \infty;$$
$$\text{corr}(y_t, y_{t-i}) = \text{cov}(y_t, y_{t-i})/\text{var}(y_t) = E[(y_t - y)(y_{t-i} - \bar{y})]/\text{var}(y_t)$$

9 Non-negativity in $\emptyset$ ensures a non-negative variance, while the unit sum of $\emptyset_i$ renders y_t 'wide-sense stationary'.

10 For surveys of further generalisations of ARCH modelling, see Nijman and Palm (1991) and Bollerslev, Chou and Kroner (1992).

11 Initial investigations of ARMA processes indicated the insignificance of MA terms.

12 $U' = U - 6.7632411$.

13 Assuming $w_t \sim (0, \sigma_w^2)\Sigma_j \lambda_j^2 < \infty$ and $\pi\lambda(1) = \Sigma_j\lambda_j \neq 0$.

References

Beveridge, S. and Nelson, C.R., 1981. 'A New Approach To the Decomposition of Economic Time Series into Permanent and Transitory Components with Particular Attention to Measurement of the 'Business Cycle', *Journal of Monetary Economics*, 7, 151–74

Blanchard, O. and Summers, L., 1986. 'Hysteresis and the European Unemployment Problem', in S. Fischer (ed.), *NBER Macroeconomics Annual*, vol. 1 (September), Cambridge, MA: MIT Press

1987. 'Hysteresis in Unemployment', *European Economic Review*, 31, 288–95

Bollerslev, T., 1986. 'Generalized Autoregressive Conditional Heteroskedasticity', *Journal of Econometrics*, 31, 307–27

Bollerslev, T., Chou, R.Y. and Kroner, K.F., 1992. 'ARCH Modeling in Finance: A Review of the Theory and Empirical Evidence', *Journal of Econometrics*, forthcoming

Brock, W., 1986. 'Distinguishing Random and Deterministic Systems: Abridged Version', *Journal of Economic Theory*, 40, 168–95

1987. 'Notes on Nuisance Parameter Problems in BDS Type Tests for i.i.d', Madison: University of Wisconsin, unpublished manuscript

Brock, W. and Sayers, C., 1988. 'Is the Business Cycle Characterized by Deterministic Chaos?', *Journal of Monetary Economics*, 22, 71–90

Brock, W., Dechert, W.D. and Scheinkman, J., 1987. 'A Test for Independence Based on the Correlation Dimension', University of Wisconsin, *Economics Working Paper*, SSRI-8702

Brock, W., Hsieh, D.A. and LeBaron, L., 1991. *Nonlinear Dynamics, Chaos and Instability*, Cambridge, MA: MIT Press

Brockett, R.W., 1976. 'Volterra Series and Geometric Control Theory', *Automatica*, 12, 167–72

Campbell, J.Y. and Perron, P., 1991. 'Pitfalls and Opportunities: What Macro-economists Need to Know about Unit Root Tests', *NBER Working Paper*, 100, Cambridge, MA: NBER

Christiano, L.J. and Eichenbaum, M., 1990. 'Unit Roots in Real GNP: Do We Know, and Do We Care?', *Carnegie–Rochester Conference Series on Public Policy*, 32, 7–62

Cochrane, J.H., 1988. 'How Big is the Random Walk in GNP?', *Journal of Political Economy*, 96, 893–920

Cross, R. (ed.), 1988. *Unemployment, Hysteresis and the Natural Rate Hypothesis*, Oxford: Basil Blackwell

1993. 'On the Foundations of Hysteresis in Economic Systems', *Economics and Philosophy*, 9(1) (Spring), 53–74

DeJong, D.N. and Whiteman, C.H., 1991. 'Reconsidering Trends and Random Walks in Macroeconomic Time Series', *Journal of Monetary Economics*, 28, 221–54

DeJong, D.N., Nankervis, J.C., Savin, N.E. and Whiteman, C.H., 1992a. 'Integration Versus Trend Stationarity in Time Series', *Econometrics*, 60, 423–33

1992b. 'The Power Problems of Unit Root Tests in Time Series with Autoregressive Errors', *Journal of Econometrics*, 53, 323–43

Dickey, D.A. and Fuller, W.A., 1979. 'Distribution of the Estimators for Autoregressive Time Series with a Unit Root', *Journal of the American Statistical Association*, 74, 427–31

1981. 'Likelihood Ratio Statistics for Autoregressive Time Series with a Unit Root', *Econometrica*, 49, 1057–72

Diebold, F.X. and Rudebusch, G.D., 1989. 'Long Memory and Persistence in Aggregate Output', *Journal of Monetary Economics*, 24, 189–209

Drost, F.C. and Nijman, T.E., 1990. 'Temporary Aggregation of GARCH processes', Tilburg University, *CentER Discussion Paper*, 9066

Engle, R.F., 1982. 'Autoregressive Conditional Heteroscedasticity with Estimates of the Variance of United Kingdom Inflation', *Econometrica*, 50, 987–1007

Engle, R.F. and Bollerslev, T., 1986. 'Modeling the Persistence of Conditional Variances', *Econometric Reviews*, 5, 1–50

Ewing, J.A., 1885. 'Experimental Researches in Magnetism', *Philosophical Transactions of the Royal Society of London*, 176II, 523–640

Granger, C.W.J. and Anderson, A.P., 1978. *An Introduction to Bilinear Time Series Models*, Göttingen: Vandenhoeck & Ruprecht

Grassberger, P. and Procaccia, I., 1983. 'Measuring the Strangeness of Strange Attractors', *Physica D*, 9, 189–208

Hargreaves-Heap, S.P., 1980. 'Choosing the Wrong "Natural" Rate: Accelerating Inflation or Decelerating Employment and Growth?', *Economic Journal*, 90, 611–20

Hsieh, D.A., 1989. 'Testing Nonlinear Dependence in Daily Foreign Exchange Rates', *Journal of Business*, 62, 339–68

Hsieh, D.A. and LeBaron, B., 1988. 'Finite Sample Properties of the BDS Statistic', Chicago: University of Chicago, mimeo

Krasnosel'skii, M.A. and Pokrovskii, A.V., 1983. *Sistemy s Gisteresisom*, Moscow: Nauka

1989. *Systems with Hysteresis*, Berlin: Springer-Verlag

Kawitowski, D., Phillips, P.C.B. and Schmidt, P., 1991. 'Testing the Null of Stationarity Against the Alternative of a Unit Root: How Sure Are We that Economic Time Series Have a Unit Root?', *Cowles Foundation Discussion Paper*, 979

Lucas, R.E. Jr., 1973. 'Some International Evidence on Output–Inflation Tradeoffs', *American Economic Review*, 63(3), 326–34

Mayergoyz, I.D., 1985. 'Hysteresis Models from the Mathematical and Control Theory Points of View', *Journal of Applied Physics*, 57.8.2B, 3803–5

1991. *Mathematical Models of Hysteresis*, Berlin: Springer-Verlag

Nelson, C.R. and Plosser, C.I., 1982. 'Trends and Random Walks in Macroeconomic Time Series: Some Evidence and Implications', *Journal of Monetary Economics*, 10, 139–62

Nijman, T.E. and Palm, F.C., 1991. 'Recent Developments in Modeling Volatility in Financial Data', Tilburg University, *CentER Discussion Paper*, 9168

Park, J.Y. and Choi, B., 1988. 'A New Approach to Testing for a Unit Root', Cornell: Cornell University, mimeo

Perron, P., 1989. 'Trends and Random Walks in Macroeconomic Time Series: Further Evidence from a New Approach', *Journal of Economic Dynamics and Control*, 12, 297–332

Phillips, P.C.B. and Perron, P., 1988. 'Testing for a Unit Root in Time Series Regression', *Biometrika*, 75, 335–46

Priestley, M.B., 1981. *Spectral Analysis and Time Series*, London: Academic Press

Rappaport, P. and Reichlin, L., 1989. 'Segmented Trends and Nonstationary Time Series', *Economic Journal*, 99, 168–77

Said, S.E. and Dickey, D.A., 1984. 'Testing for unit roots in autoregressive moving-average models with unknown order', *Biometrika*, 71, 599–607

Schwert, G.W., 1989. 'Tests for Unit Roots: A Monte Carlo Investigation', *Journal of Business and Economic Statistics*, 7, 147–60

Serfling, R., 1980. *Approximation Theorems of Mathematical Statistics*, New York: Wiley

Sowell, F., 1992. 'Modeling Long-Run Behaviour with the Fractional ARIMA Model', *Journal of Monetary Economics*, 29, 277–302

Stock, J.H., 1987. 'Measuring Business Cycle Time', *Journal of Political Economy*, 95, 1240–61

Sussmann, H.J., 1977. 'Existence and Uniqueness of Minimal Realisations of Non-linear Systems – I: Initialised Systems', *Journal of Mathematical Systems Theory*, 10, 263–84

Tong, H., 1983. 'Threshold Models in Nonlinear Time Series Analysis', *Lecture Notes in Statistics*, 21, New York: Springer-Verlag

1990. *Non-linear Time Series: A Dynamical System Approach*, Oxford: Clarendon Press

Tsay, R.S., 1987. 'Conditional Heteroskedastic Time Series Models', *Journal of the American Statistical Association*, 82, 590–604

Weiss, A.A., 1986. 'ARMA Models with ARCH Errors', *Journal of Time Series Analysis*, 5, 129–43

13 Prices, wages, and employment in the US economy: a traditional model and tests of some alternatives

Albert Ando and Flint Brayton

Introduction

In our earlier paper (Ando, Brayton and Kennickell, 1991) we reported on the performance of the price–wage sector of the MPS model (one of the models maintained at the Board of Governors of the Federal Reserve System) between the late 1960s and 1990 and supplemented the analysis with a series of tests designed to check if the specification of this part of the model was missing any direct effects of the money supply on the movements of prices and wages.

We have two purposes in writing the present chapter. First, listening to the reaction from readers of our earlier paper, it is evident that we have failed to communicate our basic message, especially the theoretical framework underlying our empirical results.[1] By taking advantage of the parallel work of Layard and Nickell (Layard and Nickell, 1985 and 1986, hereafter LN) and constrasting our formulation with theirs, we hope to clarify the basic features of both structures. Our second objective is to elaborate and reinforce our earlier empirical results, embedding our price–wage equations in a somewhat broader context, offering alternative algebraic formulations of the same hypotheses to demonstrate their robustness, extending the time period covered and improving our statistical procedures slightly.

In the second section of this chapter, we show what these two formulations say about the behaviour of wages, prices and employment on the steady state growth path. In the third section, we proceed to review the dynamic adjustment processes and also the ability of our formulation to account for the pattern of actual data in the US. In the fourth section, we pick up some ideas from LN and test their relevance against US data, as well as some other hypotheses incorporating alternative views of how prices and wages are determined, especially those associated with a more direct role for the money supply.

Theoretical background

Optimal capital–output ratio and price–wage frontier

Simplified MPS formulation

We must take note of two basic assumptions at the outset. First, we share with LN a view that firms face oligopolistic markets for their products and that they can set the price of output, although the ability of individual firms to set output price is narrowly limited.

For many firms, the output market can probably be characterised as monopolistically competitive, and therefore the output price must be very close to minimised average cost. For other firms in a genuinely oligopolistic market, insofar as they produce goods having common features and share a similar production technology, the minimised average cost must be similar. They also share the knowledge that, if they set their product price much higher than the minimised average cost in an attempt to extract exceptionally large oligopoly rents, then they face the threat that a new firm may enter the market and undercut their price. If this is the environment in which most firms operate, then a reasonable approximation to their pricing policy is to start with the description of their minimised average cost, and then to enrich it by considering factors that may affect the size of the mark-up. Given the assumption that the production function is homogeneous of degree one in labour and capital and that it is common to all firms competing in the market, we may identify the minimised average cost for some arbitrarily given output and assume that the cost minimising factor proportions remain the same for any other given level of output. We can then consider the price–setting behaviour of firms in two distinct stages. We can first model their determination of the minimised total average cost and associated factor proportions for a given output and factor prices. We can then analyse determination of the mark-up and the dynamic adjustments of the price to changes in environment in a separate analysis.

Our second critical assumption is about the nature of capital. Based on persistent evidence in our estimation of the investment function, starting with work of Bischoff (1971) and continuing to the one reported below, we believe that capital goods, at least producer's equipment, are 'putty-clay' in nature. That is, before installation, production possibilities faced by a firm can be described by a flexible production function and any factor proportion is possible to accommodate relative factor prices. However, once equipment is put in place, it is no longer possible to change factor proportions insofar as this particular equipment is concerned. Nor is it possible to take advantage of new technology developed *after* the equipment is put in place by upgrading the equipment to improve its productivity. This has a number of implications both on the form and interpretation of several equations.

Let us begin by considering a 'stripped down' case of the firm's optimisation problem given by the following:

$$\min_{E,I} \beta(E, I; XCA) = WE + RI \tag{1}$$

$$\text{subject to: } XCA = f(Ee^{\gamma t}, I) \tag{2}$$

f is assumed to be homogeneous of degree one in $Ee^{\gamma t}$ and I. (2) may be specialised to:

$$XCA = f = B\left[a(Ee^{\gamma t})^{\frac{\sigma-1}{\sigma}} + (1-a)I^{\frac{\sigma-1}{\sigma}} \right]^{\frac{\sigma}{\sigma-1}}. \tag{2'}$$

(The definitions of symbols are collected in appendix 1 (p. 285).)

Most of the discussions below use the CES production function (2') rather than (2) both because it is a particularly easy case to analyse, and because we have reasonable empirical support for the hypothesis that aggregate production possibilities before equipment is put in place can be approximated by the CES production function. Indeed, the Cobb–Douglas function is acceptable for most purposes. We will, however, have an occasion to make use of the CES formulation rather than the Cobb–Douglas to clarify some technical points.

For the problem at hand, we assume that the decisionmaker who is responsible for capital investment and for output price takes factor prices, W and R, as given. It is important to be clear about the nature of the production function f. It is an *ex ante* description of the production possibilities associated with new investment currently undertaken, not a description of the relationship among total output, total capital stock and total employment for the firm or for the industry. Such a description of the total production process must recognise that there exists a whole series of capital with different vintages which require different labour inputs for a given output. We will discuss the implications of this structure for the labour demand equation on pp. 270–1 below. It should be noted here, however, that the non-malleable nature of capital makes it necessary to look forward at least as long as the currently acquired capital is expected to remain, and that the length of life of equipment is determined by the timing of when the labour cost of producing one unit of output with equipment in question becomes greater than the total cost of producing the same output using new equipment incorporating the then newest technology and the then prevailing prices.[2]

The Lagrange function of this problem is given by

$$L = \beta + \lambda(XCA - f) \tag{3}$$

where λ, the Lagrange multiplier, can be interpreted as the cost of increasing the requirement XCA by one unit at the point of the minimum; in other words, λ is the minimised total unit cost. If the market for output is perfect, then the price of output, P, must be equal to λ. We assume, however, that the market for output is oligopolistic with some restrictive features as discussed above, so that the price of output is expected to be characterised by a mark-up on the minimised unit cost, that is,

$$P = \mu\lambda \tag{4}$$

where μ is the mark-up factor. We will discuss factors affecting the size and the movement of μ over time later, but for the moment let us suppose that μ is constant and exogenous. Then the first-order conditions for the optimum in the CES case are:

$$\frac{I}{XCA} = B^{\sigma-1}(1 - \alpha)^\sigma \left(\frac{P}{\mu R}\right)^\sigma \tag{5a}$$

$$\frac{Ee^{\gamma t}}{XCA} = B^{\sigma-1}\alpha^\sigma \left(\frac{P}{\mu We^{-\gamma t}}\right)^\sigma \tag{5b}$$

or

$$\frac{\mu We^{-\gamma t}}{P} = B^{\frac{\sigma-1}{\sigma}}\alpha \left(\frac{XCA}{Ee^{\gamma t}}\right)^{\frac{1}{\sigma}} \tag{5b'}$$

and

$$\frac{Ee^{\gamma t}}{I} = \left(\frac{\alpha}{1 - \alpha}\right)^\sigma \left(\frac{R}{We^{-\gamma t}}\right)^\sigma. \tag{5c}$$

The Cobb–Douglas case can be obtained by equating σ to unity in (5a), (5b), and (5c). (5a) serves as the starting point for the definition of the optimal capital output ratio, and hence of the investment equation. It may be noted that the ratio R/P involves the price of output, P, and hence the argument appears circular. But this is not really so, because $R/P = (\rho + \delta)\dfrac{P^I}{P}$, and hence it involves the relative price P^I/P, which can be taken as given for our purposes here.

(5b), on the other hand, can be rewritten in the form

$$P = \mu W e^{-\gamma t} \frac{B^{\frac{\sigma-1}{\sigma}}}{\alpha} \left(\frac{Ee^{\gamma t}}{XCA}\right)^{\frac{1}{\sigma}} \tag{5bb}$$

and it can be thought of as the pricing equation for output by firms. Note that the ratio $(Ee^{\gamma t}/XCA)$ is uniquely determined once the ratio (I/XCA) is determined by equation (5a). Hence, (5bb) makes the real wage rate a function of the mark-up factor, the productivity trend, a parameter of the production function and the user cost of capital $(\rho + \delta)(P^I/P)$.[3] (5bb) with $(\rho + \delta)(P^I/P)$ substituted for $Ee^{\gamma t}/XCA$ is sometimes referred to as 'the price–wage frontier'.

Comparison with the Layard–Nickell formulation
    While we realise that LN have restated their formulation several times in the literature, we find it most convenient to base our interpretation of their formulation on their two relatively early papers dating from 1985 and 1986.

LN take the capital stock as exogenously given, and under the assumption of fully malleable capital, they jointly derive the employment equation and the pricing rule for output. Indeed, their employment equation and the pricing rule for output are the same equation in the steady state, differing only in dynamics. In this section we focus our attention on their pricing rule.

While we find the reasoning leading to their pricing rule given as (19) in (LN, 1985) and (6c) in (LN, 1986) somewhat difficult to follow, these equations are identical to our (5bb) above.[4] While (5bb) is specialised to the CES production function, it is nothing but the proposition that the wage rate should be equal to the marginal value product of labour adjusted for the mark-up, and so is (6c) in (LN, 1986).[5] In their 1985 paper, LN argued that this rule was the result of profit maximisation with respect to the output price, but in their 1986 paper they de-emphasised the profit maximisation story, in our opinion correctly.

A problem arises in the empirical implementation of this equation by LN. Abstracting from short-run dynamics, their estimated equation for price is given by

$$\ln \frac{P}{W} = \frac{1}{0.456}\left[-4.18 + 0.0381G - 0.486\ln\left(\frac{I}{L}\right)\right] \tag{6}$$

where G is a set of demand variables (LN, 1986, table 5), L is the labour force rather than employment, but for the purposes of looking at the equilibrium properties of the system, the difference between E and L could be compounded into the constant. We have

$$\frac{I}{E} = \frac{I}{XCA} \frac{XCA}{E}$$

and the optimal capital–output ratio, $\left(\dfrac{T}{XCA}\right)^*$ is a function of $\dfrac{\mu R}{P}$. Let us consider the case in which the price of I is proportional to the price of XCA, and the real rate of interest and all other factors entering R are constant. In that case, $\left(\dfrac{I}{XCA}\right)^*$ is constant and hence we have

$$\ln \frac{P}{W} = \text{const.} + 1.067\ln \frac{E}{XCA}. \tag{6a}$$

In other words, at a fixed cost of capital, any increase in labour productivity results in an increase in the real wage rate with an elasticity of 1.067. In such a world, if the productivity of labour continues to rise as we hope it would, then the share of labour income in total value added will continually rise, because the real wage rate is rising faster than the rate of increase of productivity per man-hour. Thus, LN's price equation is inconsistent with the existence of a steady state growth path. Since they restrict the steady state elasticity of I/E with respect to P/W to be the same in the price equation and in the labour demand equation, their labour demand equation is also inconsistent with the existence of a steady state growth path.

Since LN's estimated elasticity of 1.067 is barely significantly different from 1.0, we assume that they could have restricted it to unity without changing their result significantly. On the other hand, if they wanted to give their data the possibility of generating the elasticity of the optimal labour–output ratio with respect to the real wage rate different from unity, they could have easily based their estimates more explicitly on the CES production function with labour–augmenting technical progress.

The basis for such a reformulation is given by equation (5b) or (5bb) above. Recasting it in the form that LN use in their empirical work, we have, for a given cost of capital,

$$\ln \frac{W}{P} = \text{const.} + \frac{1}{\sigma}\ln \frac{XCA}{E} + \left(1 - \frac{1}{\sigma}\right)\gamma t. \tag{6b}$$

(6b) is different from (6a) only by the presence of the last term, $\left(1 - \dfrac{1}{\sigma}\right)\gamma t$. But this is the term that ensures the proper homogeneity, making it possible for the system to have productivity growth while maintaining constant shares of total value added between capital and labour. When σ goes to one – the Cobb–Douglas case – the coefficient of $\ln(XCA/E)$ becomes unity while at the same time the last term vanishes. One cannot let the coefficient of $\ln(XCA/E)$ deviate from unity while ignoring the emergence of the last term. This is also an easy modification to implement empirically, since the constraint is linear. LN report that they attempted to introduce a productivity trend term in their estimation equation but its estimated coefficient was always insignificant.[6] There should be no question of significance, since only one independent coefficient needs to be estimated between two independent variables, $\ln(X/E)$ and γt, if γ has been estimated elsewhere. Alternatively, σ might be estimated, for example, in the investment equation, then introduced here so that γ can be estimated here. Estimation of these two equations together, on the other hand, is fairly difficult because of critical non-linearity in such a system.[7]

The Phillips curve

Traditional MPS formulation
Since Phillips (1958) observed the relationship between the rate of change of the nominal wage rate and the rate of unemployment, a number of different interpretations of this relationship have been offered, but we prefer to view it as a description of a particular equilibrating process in the labour market. Let us begin our discussion by observing that, when Phillips worked on this topic, the most popular formulation of price dynamics was the one proposed by Samuelson (1947) which posited that the rate of change of a price is an increasing function of the excess demand for the corresponding good. We may assume that what Samuelson meant by 'price' was the price of the good in question relative to the price index of some basic basket of goods.

In the context of the aggregate labour market, taking the relative price of labour as the ratio of the nominal wage rate to some general price index and the unemployment rate as an indicator of excess demand (supply) in the labour market, the Samuelson hypothesis can be written as,

$$\Delta(W/P^c)/(W/P^c) = \phi(u) \tag{7}$$

or

$$\Delta W/W = \phi(u) + \Delta P^c/P^c. \tag{7a}$$

If the price term in (7a) is interpreted as the expected rate of inflation, then it can be immediately viewed as the expectations-augmented Phillips curve. In what follows, in order to keep our exposition as simple as possible, we replace the term $(\Delta P^c/P^c)$ by $(\Delta P^c/P^c)_{-1}$.[8] The separation of the wage and price terms in (7a) recognises that, in the context of the structure of the labour market in the US, actions of employers and employees determine the nominal wage rate, not the real wage. Neither employers nor employees in a particular market have much control over an aggregate price measure such as P^c. This point is important in the comparison of our formulation with that of LN.

In the original Samuelson formulation, which referred to a specific commodity such as corn, the rate of change of the price becomes zero at the point where the excess demand is zero. When the formulation is applied to the wage rate and the labour market, the situation is more complex. Equilibrium in the labour market, defined as the level of u that is consistent with a 'stationary' relationship between W and P^c, may depend on factors such as the relative bargaining power of employers and employees, the generosity of unemployment insurance benefits compared with potential earnings, and shifts in the demographic composition of the labour force.

In further elaborating the specification of the Phillips curve, two 'wedges' between price variables that are of interest to workers and firms need to be considered. One is the difference between the total cost to the firm of employing a worker relative to workers' take-home pay. The wage rate W is defined as total compensation inclusive of employer contributions to social insurance representing the total hourly cost of employing a worker. The wage rate that matters to employees, on the other hand, is likely to exclude certain items, especially employment taxes on employers. In the American context, the latter include employer contributions to the social security system (including Medicare) and to the unemployment insurance programme. We assume, therefore, that when contribution rates on these items are increased, some fraction of such increases will show up as an increase in W with only a partial reduction in take-home pay.

The second wedge represents any divergence of consumption prices from product prices. An explicit relationship between these prices is needed because (7a) involves P^c while we have only explained P in (5bb). We will make use of the definition:

$$P^c C = PX + P^{IM}IM \tag{8}$$

and the approximation

$$\Delta P^c / P^c = (\Delta P/P) + (P^{IM}IM/P^cC)[(\Delta P^{IM}/P^{IM}) - (\Delta P/P)] \tag{9}$$

where P^{IM} is the price of intermediate inputs, including domestic and imported raw materials such as oil and agricultural products, and C, X, and IM are consumption expenditure, value added and intermediate inputs in base year prices. The relationship is exact if the ratio IM/C is constant over time.[9]

Finally, suppose that, for whatever reason, the difference between the actual value of the real wage rate, W/P, and its equilibrium value, $(W/P)^*$, defined by (5b), turns out to be unusually large. It seems reasonable, under such conditions, that the adjustment process for P can be seen as too slow and that the participants in the labour market would also attempt to adjust W to correct for this situation. This may be especially true in economies in which institutional indexation of wages is prominent.

All these considerations imply that the simple Phillips curve (7a) should be modified to include several additional variables, resulting in:

$$\Delta W/W = \phi(u^w) + (\Delta P/P)_{-1} + \theta_1(\Delta T/W) + \theta_2(B^u/W)_{-1} \qquad (7b)$$
$$+ \theta_3[(\Delta P^{IM}/P^{IM}) - (\Delta P/P)]_{-1} + \theta_4[(W/P) - (W/P)^*]_{-1}$$

where θs are parameters to be estimated, u^w is a demographically weighted unemployment rate,[10] T is the dollar amount of employment taxes collected per hour, and B^u is unemployment insurance benefits. Other variables have been previously defined.

Along the steady state growth path, the wage equation simplifies to

$$\Delta W/W = \phi(u^W) + (\Delta P/P)_{-1} + \theta_2(B^u/W). \qquad (7b')$$

A second structural relationship between P and W is given by the price equation (5bb). Since we are focusing our attention here on the steady state growth path, let us replace E_t/XCA_t in (5bb) by $(E_0/XCA_0)e^{\gamma t}$ and then take the time derivative of (5bb), holding μ constant along the growth path:

$$\Delta P/P = (\Delta W/W) - \gamma. \qquad (5bb')$$

Substitution of (5bb') into (7b') yields the necessary condition for constant wage inflation:

$$\phi(u^W) - \gamma + \theta_2(B^u/W) = 0. \qquad (10)$$

The unemployment rate that satisfies (10) is defined as the 'natural' rate of unemployment and denoted by u^*.[11]

We complete the discussion of the Phillips curve by noting that, because the response of both the demand and supply of labour to the level of the real wage rate is quite weak in the short run, the level of the unemployment rate may be taken as given for the purposes of analysing short-run wage–price behaviour at the macroeconomic level. With regard to labour supply, accumulated evidence in the US indicates that primary workers – those who are between 25 and 60 years old and the main income earners for their families – are not very responsive to variations in the real wage rate. That is, they tend to remain in the labour force under most conditions. On the other hand, secondary workers tend to be quite responsive positively to their own wage rate, but they are also responsive negatively to the wage rate of primary workers. Since the aggregated wage rate is an average of the wage rates for both groups, we find that the participation rate of workers does not respond much to the aggregate wage rate.

With regard to the effect of the real wage on labour demand, we must remember that the stock of capital available to firms is a collection of vintage capital. The real wage rate is equated to the marginal value product of labour associated with the newest vintage, and the same nominal wage must be paid to labour working with all vintages of capital. The price of output is also determined on the basis of the cost associated with the newest vintage, as described in the preceding section. The cost of using older equipments, other than maintenance expenses, is a 'sunk cost' and not relevant for current decisions. Thus, so long as the gross labour cost of using older vintage machines is less than the price of output and sufficient demand for output exists, production with the older vintages will be undertaken. The price of output *less* gross labour cost defines the residual rent for older vintage equipment, and the present value of current and future rents determines the market value of this capital. The only effect of the real wage rate on the demand for labour is associated with the decision to utilise or not to utilise the least efficient vintage of capital. After utilising various vintages of capital in order of efficiency, if the demand for output is such that firms can sell more output, they must compare the potential revenue associated with the next vintage of machines, and the cost of labour for operating them. If the real wage rate is such that the net revenue after the wage payment is still positive, firms will utilise these marginal machines, otherwise they will not utilise them. It is generally expected that firms do not face this type of decision because their investment policy should have ensured that there should be enough efficient machines to meet the demand without utilising really inefficient machines. The short-run effect of the real wage rate on the demand for labour, therefore, is expected to be quite small. We present some evidence for this proposition on pp. 274–5 below.

Layard–Nickell formulation of wage rate determination
As in the case of the price-setting behaviour of firms, the basic framework that LN use to describe wage-setting behaviour in the labour market contains some parallel considerations to the one we have used in formulating the Phillips curve in the MPS model. They both describe responses of the wage rate to excess demand (supply) in the labour market, that is, the interaction between the behaviour of firms and that of workers. We believe, on the other hand, that the differences between the two formulations are much more basic in this case than in the case of the price-setting equation. Let us begin by introducing the LN formulation

explicitly. The basic formulation remains the same in their 1985 and 1986 papers, and it is given by

$$(l - g\psi)(\ln W - \ln P) = (\ln P^e - \ln P) + g_0 + g_1(\ln L - \ln N)$$
$$+ g_2(\ln K - \ln L) + g_3 Z + g_4 \gamma t + g_5 G \qquad (11)$$

where ψ is the lag operator.

In both 1985 and 1986 papers, empirical estimates of parameters in (11) were based on the above equation with one modification ($\ln L - \ln N$ is replaced by $\ln u$, where u is the unemployment rate) and some restrictions on parameters ($g = 0$, $g_4 = 0$, and g_2 is set to be equal to the coefficient of I/L in (6) in equilibrium). Given that g is restricted to be zero, this equation determines the level of the real wage rate, and it plays an entirely different role from the Phillips curve which determines the rate of change of the nominal wage rate.[12]

Before we attempt to understand the nature of this equation, we wish to note one mechanical point, the same one we raised with regard to LN's pricing equation, recast in the form of equation (6b) above. In the pricing rule, we pointed out that if the coefficient $(1/\sigma)$ of $\ln(K/L)$ is not equal to unity, then the equation must contain an additional term $\left(1 - \dfrac{1}{\sigma}\right)\gamma t$ in order to maintain the homogeneity implied by the production function and to ensure that it is possible for the labour share of total value added to remain constant. Exactly the same argument holds here, and since LN have imposed the restriction that the coefficient of $\ln(K/L)$ must be the same with the opposite sign here as in the pricing equation, their estimates of the wage equation are not consistent with the implications of the homogeneous production function.[13]

In spite of a fairly lengthy discussion by LN, we find this equation rather difficult to interpret. One possible interpretation is that it is the supply function of labour, but then the variable like K, which belongs strictly to firms who employ workers, does not belong in this equation. We offer here one possible interpretation, although it will leave some puzzles in its economic motivation. Suppose that we write the supply equation of labour as:

$$\ln L = l_0 + l_1 \ln(W/P) + \ln LT + ZS \qquad (12)$$

where LT is the size of all potential workers in the economy, for instance, civilian, non-institutional population of working age, ZS is the set of all other variables that may affect the participation rate, and l_is are numerical parameters. That is, (12) represents the participation behaviour of workers.

Let us take LN's labour demand equation (LN, 1986, (17) and table 4) and write its steady state implication as

$$\ln N = n_0 + n_1(W/P) + \ln K + ZD \qquad (13)$$

where ZD represents all variables in LN's demand for labour equation (in its steady state form) other than the one explicitly shown in (13) above, and n_is are parameters.

By subtracting (13) from (12), we have

$$\ln L - \ln N = (l_0 - n_0) + (l_1 - n_1)\ln(W/P) + \ln LT - \ln K + ZS$$
$$- ZD. \qquad (14)$$

Solving (14) for $\ln(W/P)$, we finally have

$$\ln(W/P) = \frac{1}{(l_1 - n_1)}[-(l_0 - n_0) + \ln(K/LT) + \qquad (14a)$$

$$(\ln L - \ln N) - ZS + ZD].$$

(14a) has almost the same form as LN's wage equation (LN, 1986, (23) and table 6), except that LN replaced $\ln L - \ln N$, or its approximation u, with $\ln u$, thus making it impossible to match coefficients, especially the requirement that the coefficients of $\ln(K/LT)$ and $(\ln L - \ln N)$ should both be $[1/(l_1 - n_1)]$. If (14a) provides the proper interpretation, then LN's requirement that the coefficient of $\ln K/L$ in their wage equation equal the reciprocal of the (steady state) coefficient of $\ln W/P$ in their labour demand equation is equivalent to saying that the supply of labour is not responsive to the real wage rate. In the case of the US we have argued that this is not a bad assumption, but we wonder if LN meant to impose such a restriction.

Equation (14) may be thought of as a reduced form equation which gives the maintainable level of the unemployment rate for a hypothetical value of the real wage rate, given other exogenous variables. If, in addition, we take the real wage rate to be given by the price–wage frontier defined on p. 257–60 and in (6*) in n. 7, then (14) is consistent with the system that we have outlined as representing the structure for prices and wages in the MPS model, except that the relationship between P and P^c must be made explicit.

In writing this relationship in the form of (14a) rather than in (14), LN appear to assert that the real wage may be set at a value different from that given by (6*) in n. 7. LN may mean to suggest that workers and employers bargain between them to determine the sharing of the mark-up, while accepting the basic real wage rate before the mark-up given by the price–wage frontier (6*). If this is their intention, there is little difficulty in integrating those features of the labour market with which LN are concerned with the optimising behaviour of firms.[14] On the other hand, if LN's formulation calls for participants in the labour market to impose the real wage rate different from that given by (6*) which cannot be accommodated by a redistribution of the mark-up, then such a model must face all the difficulties outlined in n. 4 above. We do not believe that the short-run optimisation scheme of the type outlined in n. 4 can be a basis for explaining dynamic pattern of the real wage rate over a long period of time, and for generating an estimate of basic equilibrium concepts such as the natural rate of unemployment.

Empirical implementation of producer behaviour in the MPS model and tests of some popular propositions

Some general comments

In this section, we report the empirical implementation of four equations discussed in the second section above, namely, the investment equation for producer equipment, the manhours equation (demand for labour), the pricing rule for the output by firms, and the Phillips curve. These four equations are the collection of equations minimally needed to describe the mechanism generating the price–wage behaviour and the level of employment in the MPS model. They must be supplemented by a few semi-definitional equations, approximately in the form of (8) and (9), in order to relate specific prices needed elsewhere to the value added price index determined by our main pricing equation.[15]

These equations have been a part of the MPS model for more than 20 years, and they have gone through a series of reformulations, although their basic form has not been changed significantly. Most of the changes have to do with forms of dynamic adjustments, but in our experience respecifications of this sort do not affect the behaviour of the system much, provided that they are so formulated to preserve the steady state properties of each equation.

To give ourselves an opportunity to check on this proposition and for purposes of exposition, we have reported in this chapter formulations of the equations in question that are somewhat different in their adjustment processes from those used in the model itself. We simply report here that in no case does the change create significant differences in the behaviour of the system as a whole both in terms of its steady state properties and also in its dynamic behaviour. We now proceed to summarise empirical findings for each of four basic equations.

Estimation of the basic equations

Investment in producer equipment

The starting point of the investment equation is (5a) (p. 259), which gives the optimal capital–output ratio as a function of the ratio of minimised average cost (which is equal to the output price divided by the mark-up factor) to the gross rental price of capital. We observe two simplifications. First, in repeated estimations of the investment equation over many years, we have never found σ to be significantly different from unity. We therefore conclude that the relevant production function here is Cobb–Douglas, and assume that σ is in fact unity. Second, gross rent, R is simply equal to $P^I(\rho + \delta)$ in the absence of various fiscal interventions, but it can become a fairly complex expression once taxes and subsidies are introduced. Fortunately, however, almost all of these fiscal interventions contribute to the definition of the cost of capital through a complex multiplicative factor to R. We will therefore rewrite (5a) as

$$\frac{I}{XCA} = A(1 - \alpha)\left[\frac{P}{\mu P^I(\rho + \delta)}F(\tau)\right] = Av \qquad (5a')$$

where $F(\tau)$ is the summary measure of fiscal intervention on the cost of capital, and we denote the optimal capital–output ratio by v. Because some variables, especially prices, are measured in arbitrary units, we need the scale factor, A.

For estimation, XCA is moved to the right-hand side and lags are introduced to reflect the time it takes for firms to recognise needs for new investment, to design the appropriate equipment corresponding to the best available technology and relative prices, to order such equipment and then to wait for its delivery. The second reason for lags is that the relevant addition to capacity on which investment should be based is the needed addition in a future period, while we must approximate it in terms of currently available information. Traditionally, double distributed lags originally proposed by Bischoff have been used:

$$\sum_{i=0}^{T} b_i XCA_{t-i}v_{t-i-1} + \sum_{i=1}^{T} c_i XCA_{t-i}v_{t-i}.$$

We will work, however, with a somewhat different form here. We may rewrite (5a') by dividing gross investment into a net addition to capacity, ΔXC, and replacement of depreciating capacity, δXC_{-1}, and express the steady gross investment, I^*, as

$$I^* = Av\Delta XC + Av\delta XC_{-1}. \qquad (5aa)$$

Note that the constant A is added to take account of the arbitrary scale of

Table 13.1 *Tests of alternative dynamics in some key equations*

Equation	Additional variable	Coefficient[a]
Employment[b]	$[\ln W - \ln P - \ln(X/E)^*]_{-1}$	-0.006
		(0.33)
Wage[c]	$[\ln W - \ln P - \ln(X/E)^*]_{-1}$	-0.002
		(0.11)
Investment[d]	$\sum_{i=0}^{11} a_i X B_{-i-1} \Delta v_{-i}$	-0.006^e
		(0.14)

[a] t-statistics are reported in parentheses.
[b] See (19) (p. 271) and discussion on pp. 273–4.
[c] See (22) (p. 273) and discussion on pp. 273–4.
[d] See (15) (this page) and discussion immediately following it.
[e] Coefficient sum. An F-test of the joint significance of the set of lags has a p value of 0.78.

price indices. The empirical investment equation expresses investment in terms of current and lagged values of the variables on the right-hand side of (5aa), with capacity output being approximated by moving averages of actual output:

$$I = \sum_{i=0}^{17} A1_i \Delta X B_{-i} v_{-i-1} + \sum_{i=1}^{18} A2_i \delta_{-i} X B_{-i} v_{-i}$$
$$\Sigma A1_i = 0.35(6.0); \ \Sigma A2_i = 0.13(33.5). \tag{15}$$

Sample period: 1967:1–1991:4; $\bar{R}^2 = 0.995$; $se = 4.81$.

Detailed estimation results are given in appendix 2 (p. 287).[16]

The putty-clay assumption is imposed on (5aa) and (15) by the absence of the term $XC_{-1}\Delta v$ which would reflect investment undertaken to change the capital intensity on existing vintages. In (5aa) and (15), changes in relative factor prices only affect investment to the extent that firms are undertaking gross additions to capacity. We have undertaken a test of whether or not the term $XC_{-1}\Delta v$ contributes significantly to the explanation of I. If it is added to (15) as another distributed lag, it is clearly insignificant as reported in table 13.1.

Demand for employment

Given that the nature of capital is putty-clay, labour demand in the short run is determined by an approximation to the labour requirements associated with the sum of the fixed coefficient production technologies for the existing vintages of capital, used in order of efficiency, to produce the output required. With the assumption that the *ex ante* production function is Cobb–Douglas, in time t, the manhours required to produce output asssociated with capital of vintage s are given by

$$\ln E(t,s) = \text{const.} + \ln X(t,s) - [(1 - \alpha)/\alpha]\ln \hat{v}(t,s) - \gamma s. \qquad (16)$$

The first argument in the parenthesis refers to the time of production, while the second argument refers to the vintage of capital used. $E(t,s)$ and $X(t,s)$, respectively, are the manhours required to utilise equipment of vintage s fully in period t, and output that can be produced using equipment of vintage s fully in period t. $\hat{v}(t,s)$ represents a weighted average of $v(t - s - \tau)$, $\tau = 1, 2, \ldots T$ where T is the same as the limit in the summation in (15).[17]

Let us construct the optimal capital–output ratio averaged across all vintages of capital in place at time t, $\bar{v}(t)$, recursively by

$$\bar{v}(t)XC(t) = (1 - \delta_t)\bar{v}(t - 1)XC(t - 1) + 0.25\hat{v}(t, o)XCA(t). \qquad (17)$$

0.25 is necessary because XCA, gross addition to capacity, is measured at an annual rate, and time is measured in quarters.

We can then show, through rather tedious algebra, that the aggregate demand for manhours in the steady state growth path can be described as

$$\ln E_t^* = \text{const.}^* + \ln X - [(1 - \alpha)/\alpha]\ln \bar{v}_t - \gamma t^{18} \qquad (18)$$

where E_t^* is the path of E_t corresponding to a stationary growth path of X_t. The basic assumption is that $\hat{v}_t$ is stationary over time, and that X_t is also stationary around $X_0(e^{(\gamma + \eta)t})$, where η is the rate of growth of the potential labour force. The same γ as in (16) holds here, but const.* is not the same as const.* in (16). The numerical value of $[(1 - \alpha)/\alpha]$ in the US is estimated to be 0.285. The estimated labour equation is specified in an error correction format, except that adjustment to $\bar{v}$ is assumed to be instantaneous as this term already is a very long weighted average of past relative prices.[19]

$$\Delta(\ln E + 0.258\ln \bar{v}) = -0.15 + 0.31\Delta(\ln E + 0.258\ln \bar{v})_{-1} \qquad (19)$$
$$\phantom{\Delta(\ln E + 0.258\ln \bar{v}) = -}(3.5) \quad (5.8)$$

$$+ 0.46\Delta\ln X - 0.00015t - 0.061(\ln E + 0.258\ln \bar{v} - \ln X)_{-1}$$
$$(13.0) \qquad\quad (3.2) \qquad\quad (3.5)$$

Sample period: 1961:1–1991:4, $\bar{R}^2 = 0.734$, se $= 0.0044$.

(19) is again shown in an abbreviated form, and detailed estimation results are given in appendix 2.

Price of the value added measure of output
The price equation is based on (5b), the first-order condition of the cost minimisation for labour input, rearranged to express the price level as a mark-up on unit labour costs. Invoking once again the Cobb–Douglas assumption, we have

$$\ln P^* = \text{const} + \ln W - \ln(E/X)^* + \mu \qquad (20)$$

where $(E/X)^*$ is the labour–output ratio excluding the effects of short-run, cyclical fluctuations, and it is constructed by taking the predicted value of E excluding short-run, cyclical terms in equation (19) and then dividing the result by X. Note that, by construction, $(E/X)^*$ has the long-run trend of γ.[20] The mark-up factor, μ, is assumed to vary with cyclical conditions and the degree of price competition from imports, represented by real terms of trade, $\mathcal{E}$.

$$\mu = \mu(u^w, \mathcal{E}).$$

The actual price equation is estimated in error correction form:

$$\Delta \ln P = 0.11 + 0.12(\ln W - \ln(E/X)^* - \ln P)_{-1}$$
$$\quad\;\; (5.3) \quad (5.6)$$

$$- \;0.001u^w_{-1} + 0.015\mathcal{E}_{-1} + \sum_{i=1}^{4} B4_i \Delta \ln P_{-i} \qquad (21)$$
$$\quad (2.7) \qquad\quad (4.2)$$

$$\sum_i B4_i = 0.26(2.3).$$

Sample period: 1963:1–1991:4; $\bar{R}^2 = 0.661$; $se = 0.0043$.

As before, the detailed estimation results are given in appendix 2. Although not shown in (21) above, the estimated equation contains dynamic terms reflecting the speed with which energy and agricultural prices are passed through to final product prices.

Phillips curve
The final equation needed in this block is the Phillips curve, which determines the nominal wage rate (total compensation per manhour). Our estimated equation is a straightforward dynamic implementation of equation (7b), except that we did not explicitly split $\dfrac{\Delta P^c}{P^c}$ into its components as in (9), nor did we introduce the term in the real wage rate $\left[\left(\dfrac{W}{P}\right) - \left(\dfrac{W}{P}\right)^*\right]$. The summary of the result is shown below as (22):

$\Delta \ln W = 0.007 - 0.002u^w + 0.25\Delta \ln W_{-1}$
     (3.2)   (5.2)   (3.0)

$$+ \sum_{i=1}^{6} B3_i \Delta \ln P^c_{-i} + \sum_{i=0}^{3} B7_i (B^u/W)_{-i} \qquad (22)$$

$\sum_i B3_i = 0.75(9.0); \sum_i B7_i = 0.03(2.1).$

Sample period 1963:1–1991:4; $\bar{R}^2 = 0.684$, $se = 0.0037$.

Here again, (22) is an abbreviated report of the result, and full estimation results are given in appendix 2. They show that the additional terms representing employer contributions to social insurance and the labour force participation of the female population are significant in explaining the inflation rate of the wage rate. The wage–price control measure, represented by a dummy variable corresponding to its introduction and removal, is marginally significant.

Tests of alternative dynamics

We have already discussed the test of the putty-clay assumption in the context of the investment equation and the result is reported in table 13.1. We see no evidence that this assumption is inconsistent with the data. Analogous tests have been performed in the course of re-estimating the investment function for producer's equipment in the MPS model whenever major revisions of data took place, and the results have always been the same. We believe, therefore, that we are on a reasonably sound basis in accepting the putty-clay hypothesis.[21]

In comparing our formulation with that of LN, a critical issue related to the question of the malleability of capital is the response of labour demand to variations in the real wage rate. We have introduced the term $(\ln W - \ln P - \ln(X/E)^*)$ into the manhours equation (19) to check whether or not the demand for labour responds to the current level of the real product wage, adjusted for average productivity, over and above the impact of the real wage on labour demand incorporated into our formulation through $\bar{v}$. As reported in table 13.1, this term is totally insignificant. This, of course, does not mean that the demand for labour does not depend on the real wage rate. It does mean that the channel through which the real wage rate affects the demand for labour goes through $\bar{v}$, and it takes a long time.

Finally, LN stressed the point that bargaining in the labour market between employers and employees determines the level of the real wage rate, in contrast to the traditional Phillips curve which assigns the role of determining movements of the nominal wage rate to the labour market. We indicated above that we do not find their argument fully convincing, but we are prepared to entertain the possibility that labour market participants pay close attention to the level of the real wage rate in bargaining about the nominal wage. To test this possibility, we have introduced into (22) the term $(\ln W - \ln P - \ln(X/E)^*)$. The result is again reported in table 13.1, and again this term proves to be totally insignificant.

We conclude, therefore, that, as far as US data are concerned, there is little evidence that the MPS formulation of the price–wage sector mis-specified the role of the real wage and its determination, nor is there any evidence that its demand function for labour is missing some additional channels through which the real wage rate affects the demand for labour.

The natural rate of unemployment

Implicit in the estimated structure of the wage and price equations (21) and (22) is the equilibrium, or natural, rate of unemployment (u^*) – the unemployment rate consistent with a constant rate of inflation. Although u^* could be defined in terms of all factors affecting wages and prices, including highly transitory ones, it is more illuminating to calculate it as a medium-run concept which excludes transitory influences on wages and prices. Based on the estimated wage and price equations, the medium-term natural rate varies over time with the demographic structure of the labour force, the rate of growth of 'permanent' productivity, and the unemployment insurance replacement ratio. Because the rate of growth of wages is specified to depend on the rate of growth of consumption prices, rather than the price of value added, the spread between the growth rates of these two prices can also be viewed as influencing the natural rate, especially if the growth rates diverge for a substantial period of time. On the other hand, short-term fluctuations of this spread, due for instance to effects of weather variations on agricultural prices, should not be included in the definition of the natural rate. Unfortunately, it is usually quite difficult to distinguish between the long-term movements of the spread from short-term fluctuations. In order to provide the maximum information, we report two measures of the natural rate, one (u_1^*) excluding the effects of the inflation spread and the second (u_2^*) including them.[22]

Both measures of the natural rate display considerably variation over time. Figure 13.1 plots u_1^* in panel (a) and the contributions to the variation in u_1^* over time of demographics, productivity growth and unemployment insurance in panel (b). Figure 13.2 plots u_2^* (panel (a)) and the additional contribution of the inflation spread (panel (b)). The general slowdown in

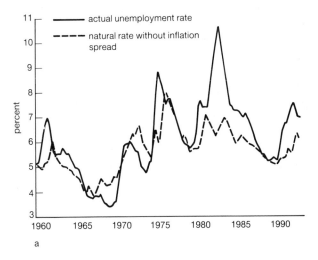

a

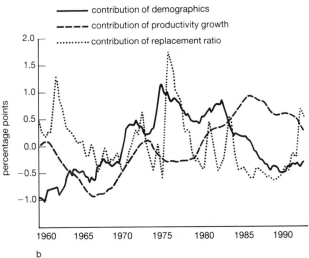

b

Figure 13.1 The natural rate of unemployment u_t^*

productivity growth has raised the natural rate over time: changing demographic structure gradually raised the natural rate from the early 1960s through the mid-1970s and slowly lowered it since. The effect of the replacement ratio is lagged, with considerable volatility at high frequencies (reflecting factors such as the legislation of temporary benefits) around a small secular downtrend. The effect of the spread between consumption and product price inflation also has tended to be erratic, although in recent

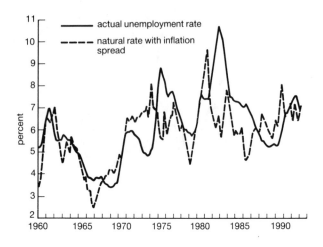

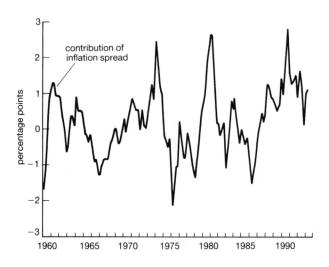

Figure 13.2   The natural rate of unemployment u_2^*

years this spread has been persistently positive, tending to raise the natural rate.

We should perhaps observe here that the magnitude of the task of explaining the movement of the natural rate from the 1960s to the present is very different in the US from the parallel task in most European countries. In the UK, for instance, it seems to have risen 6 to 9 percentage points during the past 30 years or so depending on how it is defined and measured.

In the US, on the other hand, including the inflation spread in the definition, it rose from the low of less than 5% in 1960s to the high of close to 8% in the late 1970s, and fell to roughly 6%–6.5% in the early 1990s. The maximum movement recorded is therefore some 3.5 percentage points. While the contribution by LN contains some useful suggestions which may be helpful in explaining apparently large movements of the natural rate in the UK, in order to assess the order of magnitudes of these movements and of contributions to these movements from factors considered by LN, the proper homogeneity restrictions on their basic system are essential.

A closer examination of the wage and price equations

The motivation

In discussions of macroeconomic theory and policy since the mid-1970s, it is often taken for granted that conventional macroeconomic models have failed in some way to account for the course of economic history from the 1970s to 1990s, and that one of the prime culprits is the wage–price block of these models. As Visco (1991) has shown in some detail, even among better known models, there is sufficient variation in both the specification and the estimates of these equations that their performance probably has not been uniform, and we do not know the performance of models other than the MPS model. For those of us who have followed the performance of the modified Phillips curve and associated equations in the MPS model since the 1970s, however, the perception of the failure of these equations to explain movements in wages and prices has been a puzzle, since these equations have been more stable and reliable than most other empirical macroeconomic relationships in the MPS model during the period in question.

This section provides evidence for this view. We first examine the stability of these empirical relationships and then test the hypothesis that they are mis-specified by failing to include a direct effect of the money supply on inflation. This latter question is important because, if the hypothesis is true, then even in a serious recession, the monetary authority may hesitate to follow an aggressively stimulative monetary policy if it resulted in a higher rate of growth of the money supply. On the other hand, if the money supply affects the rate of inflation only through excess demand or supply in the labour and goods and services markets, then the monetary authority may feel more inclined to follow active policies to keep the economy near the growth path consistent with the maintenance of the natural rate of unemployment, even if this causes the supply of money to grow at a rate different from some predetermined target.

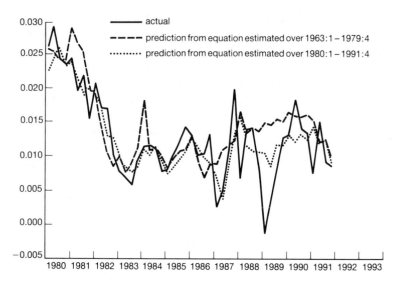

Figure 13.3   Prediction errors of the wage equation since 1980 (measured on log first difference of compensation per manhour)

Stability tests

We focus our stability tests on the beginning of the 1980s when US monetary policy shifted to a strongly anti-inflationary stance. In particular, if our formulation of adaptive inflation expectations is wrong and economic agents shifted their view of future inflation around the time of this major policy change, this should show up as evidence of instability in the MPS wage and price equations. In the case of the price equation, the hypothesis of structural stability cannot be rejected at standard significance levels (p-value of 0.12), while stability of the wage equation can be rejected (p-value of 0.04). While the evidence regarding the wage equation appears to be at odds with the claim made above, the instability has to do with very short-run dynamics, not with wage movements over periods of a year or longer. Figure 13.3 plots the actual change in compensation per hour from 1980 to 1991 along with the predictions of two versions of the wage equation, one estimated from 1963 to 1979 and the other over the 1980–94 period.[23] Figure 12.3 thus compares an out-of-sample estimate of wage growth since 1980 with an in-sample estimate. The version of the wage equation estimated through the end of 1979 actually does quite a good job of tracking the behaviour of wage inflation since 1980. Not surprisingly, the out-of-sample predictions are poorer than the in-sample ones: the root mean square error of the former is about one-third larger than the latter. But if the errors are averaged over four quarter intervals, the out-of-sample measure is only 5% larger than the in-sample measure. This suggests to us that, despite the formal statistical result, there really is no evidence of any fundamental shift in wage behaviour.

An out-of-sample simulation of inflation since 1980

The second approach to testing the robustness of the wage and price equations is through out-of-sample simulation. Figure 13.4(a) (p. 280) reports the results of such an exercise using versions of the wage and price equations estimated through the end of 1979 in a dynamic simulation starting in the first quarter of 1980 and ending in the second quarter of 1993.[24] The equations accurately track the speed of disinflation through 1982, but then underpredict somewhat through the mid-1980s, and overpredict it somewhat after the late 1980s. The root mean squared forecast error of the rate of price inflation (GDP deflator) is 2.16 percentage points while the mean forecast error is only -0.06 percentage point as the periods of underprediction and overprediction largely cancel out. For an out-of-sample simulation that is 13 years long, this performance seems rather good.

A closer examination of results shows that the prediction errors are associated to a large extent with the estimated response of the price mark-up to the real terms of trade. The version of the price equation estimated through 1979 has a coefficient on the real terms of trade that is twice the value estimated over the full sample. As a consequence, in the dynamic simulation the appreciation of the dollar in the first half of the 1980s and its subsequent depreciation lead to movements in the price mark-up – first falling and then rising – that are too large. Nonetheless, because the value of the real terms of trade is about the same at the beginning and end of the simulation period, the movements in the mark-up are offsetting.

Pagan (1989), Chong and Hendley (1986) and others have questioned the appropriateness of using dynamic simulations in evaluating the performance of a system of equations. We have already reported on p. 278 above the stability of individual equations in the system over a period of major policy changes by a more standard procedure and found that our equations do not show much instability. We supplement these sets of information by providing in figure 13.4(b) the static simulation of the same set of equations as in figure 13.4(a). That is, the only difference between figure 13.4(a) and figure 13.4(b) is that, in generating figure 13.4(b), we have utilised acutal values of lagged endogenous variables on the right-hand side

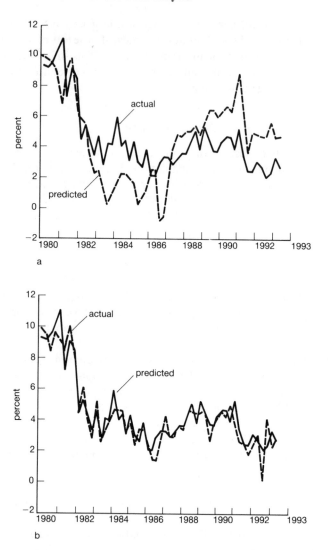

Figure 13.4   Out-of-sample simulation of wage–price sub-system (GDP implicit deflator, annual rate of change). a Dynamic simulation; b Static simulation

of equations, while in figure 13.4(a) we used lagged endogenous variables internally generated by the system. In both cases, equations were estimated using data through 1979:4, and predicted values are the simultaneous solution of equations in question.

Without getting into the technical issues of interpreting dynamic simulation errors, looking at figures 13.4(a) and 13.4(b), at least intuitively, it should be clear that it is helpful to look at them together rather than one or the other alone. Figure 13.4(b) suggests that the system performs well in extrapolation, and there is little evidence of a clear break in the structure. Figure 13.4(a), on the other hand, highlights the problem, hinting at its cause, namely, overestimation of the effects of the terms of trade.

Tests of a direct influence of money on prices

In the MPS wage and price equations, the role of monetary quantities is indirect: a change in the supply of money affects prices over time in the full model, but the causal chain extends from the supply of money to short-term nominal interest rates, to real interest rates, to the demand for output relative to supply, to the unemployment rate, and finally to wages and prices. Although this approach in which effects of money on prices and wages are indirect is similar to much of the empirical literature on US inflation, over the years a variety of inflation models have been proposed that contain a direct influence of the supply of money. Examples include the PSTAR model of Hallam, Porter and Small (1991) and Rotèmberg's (1982) adjustment cost model of price. This section provides evidence that the MPS wage and price equations are not mis-specified by omitting a direct role of money on wage and price setting.

The PSTAR model is the monetary model of inflation that has received the most attention in recent years, and it is the focus of our mis-specification tests. The monetary variable in the PSTAR model is a measure of money market disequilibrium, gap^m, equal to the log difference between $M2$ per unit of potential output and the price level:

$$gap^m = \ln M2 - (\ln GDPC + \ln PGDP) = (\ln VEL + gap^x) \quad (23)$$

where $M2$ and GDP are standard official definitions, $GDPC$ is the capacity GPD, $PGDP$ is the deflator of GDP, and VEL is the GDP velocity of $M2$. gap^x is the difference between $\ln GDP$ and $\ln GDPC$. The second equality of (23) indicates that the money gap can be expressed in terms of velocity and the output gap. gap^m is similar to what one might expect to find in a money demand equation as a measure of short-run money market disequilibrium except that potential output is used in place of actual output, and the effects of interest rates are excluded. But the differences between gap^m and short-run disequilibrium are transitory. The output gap is stationary by construction and the relevant interest rate – the difference between market interest rates and rates on $M2$ deposits – has little low frequency movement. Thus, it seems reasonable to characterise gap^m as a form of money market disequilibrium.

The PSTAR model specifies that the rate of change of inflation ($\Delta^2 p$) depends on the lagged money gap and lagged changes in inflation:

$$\Delta^2(\ln PGDP) = a_0 + a_1 gap^m_{-1} + \sum_{i=1}^{4} a_{2i}\Delta^2(\ln PDGP)_{-i}. \tag{24}$$

We also consider a second monetary model of inflation in which the rate of inflation depends on lagged inflation and lagged money growth:

$$\Delta\ln(PGDP) = b_0 + \sum_{i=1}^{4} b_{1i}\Delta\ln(PGDP)_{-i} + \sum_{i=1}^{12} b_{2i}(\ln M2)_{-i}. \tag{25}$$

Estimates of equation (24) and (25) are shown in section A of table 13.2.

The first set of tests comparing the MPS wage–price equations to these two monetary price specifications are based on the 'C test' of Davidson and MacKinnon (1981). This non-nested test estimates the regression

$$\pi = c_0 + c_1\pi^{mps} + c_2\pi^m \tag{26}$$

where π is the actual rate of inflation ($= \Delta\ln PGDP$), π^{mps} the predicted rate of inflation from the MPS model, and π^m the predicted rate of inflation from one of the monetary models.[25] Davidson and MacKinnon describe why the C test is inferior to other non-nested tests they present, but this seems to be the only test that can be implemented without serious difficulty given that the MPS specification is a multi-equation system. The non-nested test results are presented in section B of table 13.2. In each case, the estimated coefficient on the MPS inflation prediction is insignificantly different from unity, and the coefficient on the inflation prediction from the monetary model is insignificantly different from zero. Thus, the C tests show no evidence that the MPS equations are mis-specified by excluding a direct role of money on prices.

To buttress the non-nested test results, a set of regressions was estimated in which the income velocity of money – the monetary component of the money gap used in the PSTAR model – is included in the MPS wage and price equations.[26] Velocity is not significant in either equation.[27]

Some concluding remarks

In this chapter, we have attempted to present a reasonably comprehensive review of the performance of the price–wage sector of the MPS model, with the emphasis on the period starting in the late 1970s when it is presumed that a major change in the monetary and fiscal policy in the US took place. As a part of this review, we have also tried to lay out the underlying theoretical structure for factor demands of firms and their pricing

Table 13.2 *Tests for a direct effect of money on prices* (1963:1–1991:4)

A Monetary models of inflation[a]

P STAR model (24) (p. 282)

$$\Delta^2(\ln PGDP) = 0.203 + 0.040 gap^m_{-1} + \sum_{i=1}^{4} a_{21}\Delta^2(\ln PGDP)_{-i}$$
$$\quad\quad\quad\quad (4.2)\quad\quad (4.2)$$

$$\sum_i a_{2i} = -1.252$$
$$\quad\quad (4.2)$$

$\bar{R}^2 = 0.333$; $se = 0.00357$; $Durbin - H = -0.11$.

Traditional money model (25) (p. 282)[a]

$$\Delta(\ln PGDP) = -0.001 + \sum_{i=1}^{4} b_{1i}\Delta(\ln PGDP)_{-i} + \sum_{i=1}^{12} b_{2i}\Delta(\ln M2)_{-i}$$
$$\quad\quad\quad\quad (0.8)$$

$$\sum_i b_{ii} = 0.833; \sum_i b_{2i} = 0.178$$
$$\quad (12.3)\quad\quad\quad (2.0)$$

$\bar{R}^2 = 0.649$; $se = 0.00371$; $dw = 1.99$.

B Non-nested tests[b]

$$\pi = c_0 + c_1\pi^{mps} + c_2\pi^m.$$

Monetary model	c_0	c_1	c_2
1. P STAR model	0.0002	0.86	0.13
	(0.2)	(5.4)	(0.7)
2. Traditional model	0.001	0.84	0.16
	(0.1)	(6.2)	(1.1)

[a] t-statistics are shown in parentheses.
[b] The design of this set of tests and discussion of the result is given on p. 282 of the text, following (26), and in n. 25.

behaviour for output, and the hypothesis concerning the workings of the labour market leading to the wage-setting behaviour embodied in the Phillips curve. We found it useful to contrast our formulation with the more recent work of Layard and Nickell on the same subject, which has become well known, especially in the UK.

At the empirical level, we have extended the results reported in our earlier paper (Ando *et al.*, 1991) and tried to show that the relevant equations, taken individually or as a system, do not show any indication of a break or a shift in their structure at the time of the important policy rule change at the beginning of the 1980s. Equations estimated through the end of the 1970s did a reasonable job of predicting the development of the inflation pattern up to the early 1990s, except that these equations tended to overestimate the effects of the real terms of trade on the domestic prices. While this is somewhat surprising, we are observing the same phenomenon for other countries, in some cases in a rather dramatic manner.[28] We need to understand the mechanism generating this pattern better, especially because, for almost every country, trade is becoming more important over time and the interaction between domestic prices and the real terms of trade is bound to play a more significant role in determining the inflation pattern everywhere.

On the theoretical level, we found what we believe to be a slip in Layard and Nickell's formulation which makes their equations violate the homogeneity constraints. More importantly, we believe that the nature of capital is putty-clay, and we have presented some evidence for our belief. If we are even partly correct, Layard and Nickell's formulation needs reconsideration, especially the demand for labour equation. We also find their wage equation difficult to understand. Taken literally, it is in conflict with the optimisation process of firms with homogeneous production functions and its implication on the relationship between the rental rate for capital and the real product wage for labour. Layard and Nickell may have meant to describe the process in which management and labour bargain to share the oligopoly mark-up while respecting the cost structure of firms. If this was their intention, their wage equation must be reformulated substantially.

On the other hand, we have found their list of additional factors affecting the dynamic adjustment process of prices, wages and unemployment serves as a reasonable checklist, and it has led us in particular to check if there are direct effects of the deviation of the real wage rate from its equilibrium value on movements of wages and employment. In the case of the US, the results were negative, but it may be significant in other countries depending on the specific structure of the labour market in the country. Our tests of whether or not our system is mis-specified because of the absence of the direct effect of money supply on prices and wages also came out uniformly negative. In an empirical investigation in social sciences, no evidence is ever conclusive. For the description of the price–wage mechanism for the US economy and for many of the OECD countries, however, evidence presented here together with results of many preceding studies suggests that it would be more fruitful to work on revisions and improvements of existing framework rather than a radical overhaul.

Appendix 1: list of variables

A	a scale factor in the investment function
a	parameter in the production function
B	a scale factor in the production function
B^u	unemployment insurance benefits per hour
β	total factor costs of production
C	total consumption
DPW	dummy variable for price–wage control
δ	the rate of depreciation of producer equipment
E	employment in manhours
$(E/X)^*$	labour–output ratio excluding cyclical fluctuations; see p. 272 for further discussion
ε	real terms of trade
$F(\tau)$	tax and subsidy effects on the cost of capital
G	demand factors as defined by LN (1985, 1986)
GDP	gross domestic production in base year price
$GDPC$	capacity GDP
γ	the rate of labour-augmenting techincal progress per period
I	gross investment in producer equipment in constant dollars
IM	intermediate inputs, including imports and agricultural goods
K	total capital stock, used by LN (1985, 1986)
L	labour force, in manhours
LF	female labour force, number of persons
LT	total non-institutional, civilian population
λ	Lagrange multiplier in the cost minimisation by firms, minimised total average cost
M	money stock outstanding, $M2$
M^S	the supply of money
μ	the mark-up factor (a number somewhat greater than units)
P	price of value added measure of output for private, domestic nonfarm business sector
P^b	price of gross output that is, XB
P^c	price of consumption goods

P^E	price of energy
P^f	price of farm products
P^I	price of investment goods
P^{IM}	price of IM
$PGDP$	implicit deflator of GDP
π	actual rate of inflation in terms of $PGDP$
π^{mps}	prediction of the price–wage sector of MPS model for π
π^m	prediction of the monetary models for π
R	gross rent per unit of capital per period
ρ	the real rate of interest
σ	elasticity of substitution in the production function
t	time (measured quarterly with 1947:1 = 1)
T	employment tax in dollars per manhour
ΔT	changes in employment tax per manhour
u	unemployment rate (standard definition)
u^w	unemployment rate with fixed weights for components of labour force
u_1^*	the natural rate of unemployment excluding effects of the spread between inflation rates of P^c and P
u_2^*	the natural rate of unemployment including effects of the spread between inflation rate of P^c and P
v	optimal capital–output ratio
$\hat{v}(t,s)$	the weighted average of the optimal capital–output ratio relevant for capital produced in period $t - s$. See (16) and the paragraph following (16) in the text, p. 271
$\bar{v}(t)$	the average optimal capital–output ratio applicable to equipments of all vintages in use in period t. See (17) in the text, p. 271
VEL	GDP velocity of $M2$
W	rate of compensation per manhour
W^1	wage rate per manhour net of employment taxes and employee contribution to social insurance
w^e	the ratio of the value of energy input to total value added
w^f	the ratio of the value of farm products to total value added
X	value added output of the private, domestic non-farm, business output, in constant dollars
XB	gross output corresponding to X
XC	capacity output corresponding to X
XCA	gross addition to XC

Appendix 2: detailed estimation results of key equations

1 Investment equation

$$I = \sum A1_i \Delta X B_{-i} v_{-i-1} + \sum A2_i \delta X B_{-i} v_{-i}.$$

Restrictions:
$A1$: third-degree polynomial
$A2$: third-degree polynomial

Estimation technique: autoregression of order 1
Sample period: 1967:1–1991:4 (100 observations)

ρ	Std error	T-statistic
0.91983	0.036822	24.98

Sums of distributed lag coefficients

Coefficient	Sum	T-statistic
A1	0.34835	6.0404
A2	0.12518	33.473

$R^2 = -0.99537$
R^2 (corrected) $= 0.99496$
Durbin–Watson statistic $= 2.5071$
Sum of squared residuals $= 2106$
F-statistic $(9, 91) = 2172.6$
Degrees of freedom (adjusted) $= 91$
F-probability $= -8.4466E - 7$
Std error of repression $= 4.8106$

Name	Lag	Coeff.	Std error	T-statistic
A1	0	0.021372	0.0032121	6.6535
A1	1	0.028551	0.003046	9.3732
A1	2	0.033281	0.0034075	9.7672
A1	3	0.035846	0.003828	9.3641
A1	4	0.036525	0.00414	8.8225
A1	5	0.035603	0.0043268	8.2285
A1	6	0.033361	0.0044235	7.5418
A1	7	0.030081	0.0044776	6.718
A1	8	0.026044	0.0045287	5.751
A1	9	0.021534	0.0045939	4.6876
A1	10	0.016833	0.0046628	3.61
A1	11	0.012221	0.0046995	2.6006
A1	12	0.0079826	0.0046538	1.7153
A1	13	0.0043984	0.0044731	0.9833

Name	Lag	Coeff.	Std error	T-statistic
A1	14	0.0017509	0.0041205	0.42491
A1	15	$3.2211E - 4$	0.0036109	0.089204
A1	16	$3.9422E - 4$	0.0031164	0.1265
A1	17	0.0022493	0.0031748	0.70848
A2	1	0.0072908	0.0064091	1.1376
A2	2	0.0071372	0.0041562	1.7173
A2	3	0.0073301	0.0030997	2.3648
A2	4	0.0077828	0.0029021	2.6818
A2	5	0.0084086	0.0029411	2.859
A2	6	0.0091209	0.0028805	3.1664
A2	7	0.0098328	0.0026815	3.667
A2	8	0.010458	0.0024463	4.2749
A2	9	0.010909	0.0023314	4.6792
A2	10	0.0111	0.002436	4.5567
A2	11	0.010944	0.0027022	4.0499
A2	12	0.010354	0.0029754	3.4797
A2	13	0.0092432	0.0031167	2.9656
A2	14	0.0075254	0.0030675	2.4533
A2	15	0.0051137	0.0029511	1.7328
A2	16	0.0019214	0.0032768	0.58639
A2	17	-0.0021382	0.0047272	-0.45231
A2	18	-0.0071518	0.0074667	-0.95782

2 Employment equation

$$\Delta(\ln E - 0.258\ln\bar{v}) = AO + A1\Delta(\ln E - 0.258\ln\bar{v})_{-1} + A2\Delta\ln X + A3t + A4(\ln E - 0.258\ln\bar{v} - \ln X)_{-1}.$$

Estimation technique: OLS
Sample period: 1961:1–1991:4 (124 observations)

Name	Lag	Coeff.	Std error	T-statistic
A0	0	-0.14686	0.041705	-3.5214
A1	1	0.31096	0.053911	5.7679
A2	0	0.45629	0.035163	12.977
A3	0	$-1.521E - 4$	$4.6895E - 5$	-3.2434
A4	0	-0.064247	0.0184	-3.4917

$R^2 = 0.7432$
R^2 (corrected) $= 0.73457$
Durbin $- H$ statistic $= -0.8312$
Sum of squared residuals $= 0.0023374$
Std error of regression $= 0.0044319$

3 Price equation

$$\Delta \ln P = B0 + B1(\ln W - \ln(E/X)^* - \ln P)_{-1} + \sum B2_{-i} w_i^e \Delta \ln(P^E/P_{-1})_{-i}$$
$$+ B3 w^f \Delta \ln(P^f/P_{-1}) + \sum B4_i \Delta \ln P_{-i} + B5 u_{-1}^w + B6\mathcal{E}_{-1}.$$

Restrictions:
$B2$: second-degree polynomial
$B4$: second-degree polynomial

Estimation technique: OLS
Sample period: 1963:1–1991:4 (116 observations)

Name	Lag	Coeff.	Std error	T-statistic
B0	0	0.1078	0.020238	5.3266
B1	0	0.11771	0.021158	5.5633
B2	0	−0.44349	0.075722	−5.8568
B2	1	0.074673	0.058848	1.2689
B2	2	0.24027	0.055104	4.3603
B2	3	0.053312	0.084605	0.63013
B3	0	−0.54916	0.11474	−4.7862
B4	1	−0.0027032	0.081441	−0.033192
B4	2	0.15198	0.052045	2.9201
B4	3	0.14132	0.0526	2.6866
B4	4	−0.034694	0.071649	−0.48422
B5	0	−0.0010108	3.7781E − 4	−2.6754
B6	0	0.014671	0.0035089	4.1811

Sums of distributed lag coefficients

Coefficient	Sum	T-statistic
B2	−0.075229	−0.50445
B4	0.2559	2.3554

$R^2 = 0.69086$
R^2 (corrected) = 0.66142
Durbin − H statistic = 0.64866
Sum of squared residuals = 0.0019749
Std error of regression = 0.0043369

4 Wage equation

$$\Delta \ln W = BO + B1u^w + B2\Delta \ln W_{-1} + \sum B3_i \Delta \ln P^c_{-1} + B4\Delta \ln(T/W)$$
$$+ B5DPW + B6\Delta(LF/LT) + \sum B7_i(B^u/W)_{-i}.$$

Restrictions:
$B2 + \Sigma B3 = 1$
$B3$: third-degree polynomial
$B7$: first-degree polynomial

Estimation technique: OLS
Sample period: 1963:1–1991:4 (116 observations)

Name	Lag	Coeff.	Std error	T-statistic
B0	0	0.0068876	0.002139	3.2201
B1	0	−0.0019133	3.4554E − 4	−5.5373
B2	0	0.25158	0.083392	3.0169
B3	1	0.19433	0.10836	1.7935
B3	2	0.15511	0.080615	1.9241
B3	3	0.13876	0.072049	1.9259
B3	4	0.12617	0.0746	1.6913
B3	5	0.098229	0.08182	1.2005
B3	6	0.035809	0.10849	0.33005
B4	0	0.76334	0.21378	3.5707
B5	0	−0.0092389	0.0032985	−2.801
B6	0	−0.0049128	0.0030209	−1.6263
B7	0	−0.014766	0.01572	−0.93929
B7	1	−3.9734E − 5	0.0062436	−0.0063639
B7	2	0.014686	0.0061014	2.407
B7	3	0.029412	0.015551	1.8913

Sums of distributed lag coefficients

Coefficient	Sum	T-statistic
B3	0.74842	8.9747
B7	0.029293	2.0874

$R^2 = 0.71105$
R^2 (corrected) $= 0.68353$
Durbin $- H$ statistic $= -0.38265$
Sum of squared residuals $= 0.0014188$

Appendix 3: a note on the money market and the price level

This note reminds the reader of a well known property of the standard demand function for money, and explains why this property forms an important background for the effort invested in the study of the Phillips curve and its alternatives.

In the tradition of macroeconomic analysis leading up to the work by Patinkin (1965), the economy is viewed as divided into the real sector and the monetary sector, and conditions are defined for the so-called dichotomy of these two sectors under which all quantities and relative prices are determined in the real sector, and the price level is determined by the demand and supply of money. Even Milton Friedman (1971) expressed his adherence to this mental framework.

Unfortunately, this set-up, which is useful in comparative static analysis up to a point, is unlikely to work when it is applied to the dynamic process in the real economy. To see this, consider the standard demand function for money and equate it with the supply of money, and write

$$\ln M^s = m_0 + m_x \ln X + \ln P + m_r \ln \left[\rho + \left(\frac{P}{P} \right)^e \right]$$

where M^s is the supply of money, X is the measure of real income and P its price, and ρ is the real rate of interest. m_is are numerical coefficients, and we know, from the standard theory of the demand for money, that $0.5 < m_x < 1.0$, and $-0.5 < m_r < 0$.

Suppose now that, for the expected rate of inflation, $\left(\frac{\dot{P}}{P} \right)^e$, we adapt the perfect foresight assumption and let $\left(\frac{\dot{P}}{P} \right)^e = \frac{\dot{P}}{P}$. This is not unreasonable because in the equation the nominal rate of interest should be a relatively short-term rate, say for one week to three months. In the framework just outlined, this equation then is a first-order differential equation in P, because M^s is exogenously given, and X and ρ are determined in the real sector of the economy and exogenously given for this equation.

With a suitable transformation of the variable, ρ, this equation can be shown to be equivalent to a linear differential equation in P, and it is then easy to show that, for any reasonable values of parameters, it is unstable when it is solved forward, with the initial condition defined in t. In other words, if the system is started in period t with a given path of M^s, X, and ρ and an initial value of P, P will increase at an increasing rate or decline to zero, depending on the initial conditions. Thus, this set-up is incapable of determining the path of P that is reasonable.

Of course, if the first-order differential equation is unstable forward, it is stable backward. Therefore, if we have the terminal condition in a distant future and then solve the equation backward, we will have a stable path and the initial price level is well determined. This leads some analysts with rational expectations models to conclude that the stability problem does not exist here. Note, however, that if the system is solved backward, a slight change in the path of forcing variables or the terminal condition must cause a significant, though finite, shift in the price level at t. Hence, we should observe frequent and large jumps in the price level over time if this is the mechanism by which the price level is determined. This seems inconsistent with the nature of observed data on prices.

It is true that we can avoid this problem by some strong assumptions. For example, if m_r is exactly zero, so that the demand for money is independent of the rate of interest, then this problem does not arise. We believe, however, that the case we have discussed here is the reference case and points to the basic problem of why any model in which the basic price level is directly determined by the money supply is unlikely to be successful for economies with a reasonable price pattern. That is, our argument would not necessarily apply to hyperinflationary economies.

Of course, this does not mean that the money supply does not have an impact on the price level. It merely means that the causal chain is indirect and complex, and the Phillips curve and its variations is the most promising hypothesis of how such an indirect causal chain works so far available.

Notes

Views expressed represent those of the authors, and do not necessarily reflect those of the Federal Reserve Board or its staff. We wish to thank Danielle Terlizzese of the Bank of Italy for careful reading of the manuscript and many useful comments.
 1 See especially Wallis (1992). In addition to the lack of communication about our underlying framework. Wallis appears to object to our use of dynamic simulation as a measure of the performance of our system of equations. While acknowledging the technical result of Pagan (1989) on this question, we do not believe that his result makes all uses of dynamic simulations unacceptable for all purposes. We will, however, keep the use of dynamic simulations to a minimum in this chapter in order to avoid a methodological controversy and to concentrate our attention on the analysis of the mechanism determining price, wages and employment.
 2 While the formulation of the problem incorporating, in addition to the putty-clay assumption, an anticipation of relevant future events and replacement requirements can become quite complex, under a certain set of assumptions, the qualitative nature of the solution can be shown to remain unchanged

from the ones presented here. Such an analysis was worked out in some detail in Ando, Modigliani, Rasche and Turnovsky (1976).

3 In the Cobb–Douglas case, (5bb) can be reduced to

$$\alpha \frac{PXCA}{\mu} = WE$$

$PXCA/\mu$ is the total value added, so that this is nothing but the familiar propositions that with the Cobb–Douglas, the share of labour in value added is equal to the exponent of labour.

4 The basic issue here is how the capital stock was determined in the first place. Although LN say that capital stock is given in their verbal discussion, based on their algebraic presentation we are under the impression that the rental rate is taken as given and the capital stock was implicitly determined consistently with this rental rate and the demand for output. If this is so, then the price–wage frontier referred to immediately after (5bb) and explicitly derived as (6*) in n. 7 is well defined. This means that, corresponding to a given rental rate for capital and the production function, the real wage rate is uniquely determined up to the mark-up factor, as in our formulation.

On the other hand, LN may have in mind a different formulation, in which the real wage rate is determined in the labour market prior to other decisions by firms. They also take the stock of capital to be given. Since the cost of capital is presumably the 'sunk' cost in this case, the firm will accept whatever the real wage rate imposed upon it, and hire workers up to the point where the marginal value product of labour is equal to the wage rate. Since the marginal product of labour is declining (given that the capital stock is given), after paying all workers the uniform real wage, there remains residual income and this determines the quasi-rent for capital. Presumably, this is accomplished by letting the market price of capital float so that the rate of return on capital is consistent with the rate of interest, but there is nothing to ensure that the market value of capital is consistent with the replacement cost for it.

If this is what LN have in mind as the model of the firm behaviour, then the optimisation problem must be formulated in a different way from the algebraic exposition sketched in their 1986 paper. Note also that the formulation outlined in the preceding paragraph is a very short-run solution, and in order to explain the pattern of prices, wages and employment over time, a description of how the capital stock in the following period is determined is needed. But if the process of capital accumulation is to be made endogenous, the relationship between the replacement cost and the market value of capital cannot be ignored. We are thus forced back to the standard formulation we have presented in the text.

5 When factor proportions are at the point where the total unit cost is minimised, the marginal cost of producing an extra unit of output using additional labour or additional capital is the same, and they are both equal to the minimised average cost. This is not true at any other point on the product function, so that it is somewhat misleading to say that the pricing rule is a mark-up on marginal cost without specifying exactly what is meant by 'marginal cost'.

6 In other words, LN recognise that the rate of change of the productivity term belongs here as we have shown in (6b) above, but they did not seem to have realised the importance of the constraint imposed on the coefficient of $\ln(X/E)$ and that of γt by the homogeneity of the production function. If this constraint is not taken into account in estimation, and σ is reasonably close to unity as in their case, it is natural that the coefficient of γt turns out to be *statistically* insignificant. But even a very small, statistically insignificant coefficient here has a critically important role to play on the long-term properties of the model. It is not the exact numerical value but the constraint relating two coefficients that is important.

7 LN may respond that they have in mind a more general production function than a CES. Consider then a general homogeneous production function of degree one in inputs,

$$XCA = f(Ee^{\gamma t}, I)$$

and define

$$f_1 = \frac{\partial f}{\partial (Ee^{\gamma t})}; f_E = e^{\gamma t}f_1.$$

(5b) then becomes

$$\frac{uWe^{-\gamma t}}{P} = f_1(Ee^{\gamma t}, I).$$

Since f is homogeneous of degree one in $Ee^{\gamma t}$ and I, f_1 is homogeneous of degree zero and, hence,

$$\frac{\mu We^{-\gamma t}}{P} = f_1(Ee^{\gamma t}/I). \tag{6bb}$$

(6bb) is then exactly the same form as (5bb) and makes $\dfrac{\mu W}{P}$ proportional to $e^{\gamma t}$.

Note that

$$f_I(Ee, I) = f_I(Ee/I) = \frac{\mu R}{P}$$

Hence, provided that the inverse function f_I^{-1} exists, $Ee^{\gamma t}/I$ is uniquely determined for a given $\dfrac{\mu R}{P}$. By substituting the last expression into (6bb), we obtain

$$\frac{\mu We^{-\gamma t}}{P} = f_1\left[f_I^{-1}\left(\frac{\mu R}{P}\right)\right]. \tag{6*}$$

(6*) expresses $\dfrac{W}{P}$ as a function of the real interest rate. As noted in comments immediately following (5bb), (6*) is sometimes referred to as the 'price–wage frontier'.

8 The basic characteristics of the system do not change significantly if this simplification is replaced by a lengthy distributed lag, or by the assumption of perfect foresight.

9 From (8), we have

$$\Delta P^c \cong \frac{X}{C}\Delta P + \frac{IM}{C}\Delta P^{IM}; \frac{X}{C} = 1 - \frac{IM}{C}$$

so long as $\frac{IM}{C}$ is nearly constant. We then have

$$\frac{\Delta P^c}{P^c} = \frac{XP}{P^cC}\frac{\Delta P}{P} + \frac{P^{IM}IM}{P^cC}\frac{\Delta P^{IM}}{P^{IM}}$$

$$\frac{\Delta P^c}{P^c} = \left(1 - \frac{P^{IM}IM}{P^cC}\right)\frac{\Delta P}{P} + \frac{P^{IM}IM}{P^cC}\frac{\Delta P^{IM}}{P^{IM}}$$

(9a) above follows immediately.

10 That is, u^w is the unemployment rate computed keeping the demographic structure of the labour force constant as it was in the base year.

11 (10) yields u^{w*}, that is, the natural rate in terms of u^w, and the unemployment rate for various demographic groups in the labour force. We can then compute the standard definition of the unemployment rate corresponding to this solution, and designate it as u^*. See n. 22 below.

12 In their 1985 paper, LN offer a transformation of (11) which appears to be more like a conventional Phillips curve. It is given as (11a) below.

$$\ln W - \ln W_{-1} = (\ln P^e - \ln P_{-1}) + g_0 + (g - 1)(\ln W_{-1} - \ln P_{-1})$$

$$+ g_1 u + g_2(\ln K - \ln L) + \dots \text{etc.} \tag{11a}$$

We believe that (11a) has a virtue of making clear exactly what P^e has to be. It must be the expected value for P in the current period, and $\ln P^e - \ln P_{-1}$ must be the first difference from the pricing equation under the assumption of rational expectation. It then becomes critical that the homogeneity restriction discussed throughout in our review of LN be observed both in (11) and (6b), because otherwise these equations simply imply that wage inflation increases as the level of productivity in the economy increases, other things being equal.

13 Of course, in the UK, it may be that the share of labour in domestic business value added steadily increased during the sample period and LN's estimates account for the increase. But even in such a situation, it is more desirable to impose the homogeneity restriction and then to search for causes of such shifts in factor shares of income.

14 This formulation is especially plausible for economies in which a centralised bargaining between the workers and employers is effective. This is especially

true if workers and employers recognise the implications of their activities, and agree to index the basic wage rate to the value added price index rather than to the final good price index. Then the arrangement implies that income between labour and capital is set by the bargaining insofar as such sharing can be accomplished by distributing the mark-up. This appears to be the scheme followed by Japan since 1980.

15 We will refer to these equations as 'producer behaviour' equations, although they are missing two critical sets of equations for producer behaviour, namely, inventory equations and/or scheduling of output production, as well as the equations for producers' structure, while the Phillips curve is not exclusively the behaviour of producers. We cannot quite call them the supply block because the supply of saving is excluded. We find it least misleading to call them the producer behaviour equations.

16 For the simplicity of exposition all estimated equations reported in the text are abbreviated. The full results are given in appendix 2.

17 In other words, (16) may be thought of as a specific realisation of the production function (2) in period $t - s$ except that a fraction of equipments then produced had disappeared through the normal depreciation process, and that the investment equation (15) made an error in period $t - s$.

18 Because $\ln(E(v))$ is not equal to $E(\ln(v))$, (18) must be regarded as an approximation. However, if, for example, v is distributed by the log-normal distribution, and its variance is constant over time, then the equation is exact except for an adjustment needed to the constant.

19 The formulation that is actually in the MPS model differs from (19) in its dynamics and takes account of the fact that the structure of the vintage capital makes labour less and less productive as actual output increases relative to capacity, while the presence of overhead workers has the opposite effects, leading to some non-linearity in the relationship between employment and output in the short run. The dynamic behaviour of (19) and that of the equation in the model, however, appears to be very similar.

20 We may note that in (5b) we referred to the employment and output associated with the currently installed, latest vintage of capital, while in (20) we are using total employment and the value added of the private, domestic, non-farm business sector. The justification for this switch is the argument leading to the proposition that γ in (18) is the same as γ in (16).

21 A similar result was obtained in the context of the econometric model of the Bank of Italy using Italian data.

22 The formula for the first natural rate measure is

$$u_1^* = 5.66 + (u - u^w) - 522.7\Delta(X/E)^* + 15.3(B^u/W).$$

Each explanatory variable is expressed as a deviation from its mean so that the constant is the sample average of the natural rate. The second measure of the natural rate is defined as

$$u_2^* = u_1^* + 522.71\left(1/8 \sum_{i=0}^{1}\left[\left(\frac{\Delta P^c}{pc}\right) - \left(\frac{\Delta P}{P}\right)_{-i}\right]\right).$$

In order to include only persistent effects of the inflation spread on the natural rate, the spread is measured as in eight-quarter moving average.

23 The predicted values are static estimates based on the actual values of all explanatory variables.

24 The set of equations simulated consists of price and wage equations, (21) and (22), augmented with simple equations for the personal consumption deflator and the GDP deflator. In the simulations, the ratios of energy and farm prices to the GDP deflator are held at their historical values, as are other variables such as the real terms of trade and the unemployment rate.

25 The MPS inflation predictions are the one-step-ahead (i.e. static) forecasts from the wage–price block. This set of equations consists of price and wage equations, (21) and (22), augmented with simple equations for the personal consumption deflator (which appears on the right-hand side of the wage equation) and the GDP deflator (the price series explained by the monetary models). For each of these auxiliary price equations, the rate of change of the prices series depends on its own lagged values and contemporaneous and lagged growth rates of other prices in the system. To put the information structure of forecasts of the wage–price block on a comparable basis with that of the monetary models, which require information only through the prior quarter, the version of the wage–price block used in the tests also contains autoregressive equations for the energy and farm price indexes and the unemployment rate.

26 As shown above, the money gap can be decomposed into velocity and the output gap. Only velocity is included in the regressions because we are interested in whether there is a direct role of money, not if the output gap is a better cyclical measure than the corresponding variables in the wage and price equations.

27 The regressions are estimated from 1963:1 to 1991:4 with the first lag of the logarithm of $M2$ velocity added to the specifications reported in (21) and (22). Estimated velocity coefficients (t-statistics) are $0.018(1.4)$ and $-0.22(0.1)$ in the wage and price equations, respectively.

28 For example, while the lira was devalued significantly between September 1992 and January 1993, domestic inflation in Italy measured in terms of the CPI actually declined.

References

Ando, A., Brayton, F. and Kennickell, A., 1991. 'Reappraisal of the Phillips curve and Direct Effects of Survey Supply on Inflation', in L.R. Klein (ed., *Comparative Performance of U.S. Econometric Models*, New York: Oxford University Press

Ando, A., Modigliani, F., Rasche, R. and Turnovsky, S., 1976. 'On the Role of Expectations of Prices and Technological Change in an Investment Function', in L.R. Klein and E. Burmuster (eds.), *Econometric Model Performance*, Philadelphia, PA: University of Pennsylvania Press

Bischoff, C., 1971. 'The Effects of Alternative Lag Distribution', in G. Fromm (ed.), *Tax Incentive and Capital Spending*, Washingdon, CD: Brookings Institution

Chong, Y.Y. and Hendley, D., 1986. 'Econometric Evaluation of Linear Macro-Economic Models', *Review of Economics Studies*, 53, 671–90

Davidson, R. and Mackinnon, J. G., 1981. 'Several Tests for Model Specification and the Presence of Alternative Hypotheses', *Econometrica*, 49, 781–94

Friedman, M., 1971. *A Theoretical Framework for Monetary Analysis, NBER Occasional Paper*, 112, New York: Columbia University Press

Hallman, J.J., Porter, R.D. and Small, D.H., 1991. 'Is the Price Level Tied to the M2 Monetary Aggregate in the Long Run?', *American Economic Review*, 81, 841–58

Layard, R. and Nickell, S.J., 1985. 'The Causes of British Unemployment', *National Institute Economic Review*, 111 (March), 62–85

1986. 'Unemployment in Britain', *Economica*, 53, 121–69

Pagan, A., 1989. 'On the Role of Simulation in the Statistical Evaluation of Econometric Models', *Journal of Econometrics*, 40, 125–9

Patinkin, D., 1965. *Money, Interest and Prices*, New York: Harper & Row, 2nd edn

Phillips, A.W., 1958. 'The Relation Between Unemployment and the Rate of Change of Money Wage Rate in the United Kingdom 1861–1957', *Economica*, 25 (November), 283–99

Rotemberg, J.J., 1982. 'Sticky Prices in the U.S.', *Journal of Political Economy*, 90, 1187–211

Samuelson, P.A., 1974. *Foundations of Economic Analysis*, Cambridge, MA: Harvard University Press

Visco, I., 1993. 'A New Round of U.S. Model Comparison: A Limited Appraisal', in L.R. Klein (ed.), *Comparative Performance of U.S. Econometric Models*, New York: Oxford University Press

Wallis, K.F., 1992. *Comparing Macroeconometric Models: A Review Article*, ESRC Macroeconomic Modelling Bureau, *Discussion Paper*, 30 (July)

14 The natural rate in empirical macroeconomic models

Simon Wren-Lewis

Introduction

I want to argue two propositions in this chapter. The first is that the concept of a natural rate can and has played a positive role in the development of econometric macroeconomic models. The second, and more interesting from a theoretical point of view, is that in future macroeconometric models may be able to tell us about some of the important limitations of the natural rate concept.

The natural rate concept[1] is useful to econometric modellers because it provides a disciplining device or consistency check. By their nature econometric models tend to pick up a number of theoretical inconsistencies or mistakes in their development, and the examination of a systems property like the natural rate can be useful in picking these errors up.

Is there a useful flow of information in the other direction? Have econometric models told us much about the natural rate? For the past the answer is essentially 'no': while theory does respond to empirical evidence, it has not responded positively to the evidence provided by macro-econometric models. My second proposition is that this situation could change in the future. I illustrate this with three examples of departures from the natural rate, where in each case econometric models may be in a position to inform theoretical analysis.

The natural rate as a systems check

Most academic macroeconomists prefer to distance themselves from the properties of established empirical macro models. However, whether they like it or not, macroeconometric models are the major way in which macroeconomic ideas get used in the wider world of business and government. One of the reasons for academic disdain is a well founded view that the theoretical foundations of these models are generally problematic. The natural rate in these models is a good example of this.

When econometric models contained a wage equation in the form of an

299

expectations-augmented Phillips curve (i.e. an equation determining wage inflation only as a function of expected price inflation and the level of unemployment) then the natural rate implied by the model could be derived from the wage equation directly. If the long-run coefficient on inflation expectations was unity, then the equation implied a unique level of unemployment consistent with steady inflation that was invariant to the rest of the model.

In this situation it was still interesting to ask what determined deviations away from the natural rate. In an important sense it was this question and its answer that provoked the new classical critique of traditional Keynesian and monetarist macro models. (This could be regarded as theory responding to the results of econometric models, but in a negative way!) Unfortunately some influential US macro modellers did not accept the validity of that critique, and in my view the development and reputation of US econometric macro models has suffered partly as a result. The position in the UK was very different, with the Lucas critique leading to the widespread adoption of consistent (rational) expectations solutions in UK macro models. These UK models still tend to show substantial and sustained short-term deviations from the natural rate, often for good 'new Keynesian' reasons, as we shall see below.

In UK econometric models the expectations-augmented Phillips curve was gradually replaced in the 1970s as modellers investigated the implications of imperfect competition in the labour market, although they remain more common in US models (see Visco, 1993). They were replaced by wage equations in which unemployment was accompanied by terms in the level of real wages. The wage equation now implied a real wage–unemployment combination in steady inflation equilibria, and it required another relationship between these variables determined elsewhere in the model (involving either the price equation or the labour demand and supply curves) to calculate the model's natural rate. In this situation it was no longer obvious what the model's equilibrium unemployment rate was, and what influenced it.

At first these natural rate calculations were not done, and as a result the medium-term properties of these models were not well founded. I will illustrate this with one example.

Empirical wage equations normally use some measure of consumer prices, both to construct expected inflation and to deflate nominal wages and to derive a real wage term. If the wage equation contains no additional terms in taxes or import prices, then combining this equation with a standard mark-up equation for the price of domestically produced output will imply that the natural rate is influenced by sales taxes (VAT, etc.) and the real exchange rate. Although this point is reasonably well known, some algebra will be helpful for subsequent discussion. To focus on the longer run, we ignore all dynamics in wage and price equations.

Suppose consumer prices (P_c) are a geometric weighted sum of the price of domestically produced goods (P) and overseas goods priced at P_w in foreign currency, and that all sales taxes are fully passed on. We then have

$$p_c = \alpha p + (1 - \alpha)(p_w - ex) + t$$

where ex is the foreign currency per unit of domestic currency exchange rate, t is a function of the sales tax rate and all lower case letters denote logs. This can be written more simply as

$$p_c = p - (1 - \alpha)e + t \qquad (1)$$

where e is the real exchange rate $(= p + ex - pw)$. $t - (1 - \alpha)e$ is often called the 'wedge' between consumer and producer prices.

Suppose total output (Y) is produced by a number of identical monopolistic competitors, each of which produces Y_i, and each firm maximises profits given by

$$\text{Profits of firm } i = P_i Y_i - w_i N(Y_i).$$

We ignore non-wage labour costs and other variable costs for simplicity. As firms are identical the technology embodied in $N(\ )$ is common. The demand curve facing firms is given by

$$Y_i = h(P_i/P, Z) \qquad (2)$$

where P represents competitors' prices (including overseas competitors) and Z is a measure of aggregate demand.

If firms take wages as fixed or predetermined when maximising profits, we obtain the familiar first-order condition

$$P_i/W_i = N'(Y_i)(1 - 1/\mathcal{E}_i)^{-1}$$

where $\mathcal{E}_i = h_p(.)P_i/h(.)$ is the elasticity of demand. Aggregating across firms when wages are common implies

$$P/W = N'(Y)(1 - 1/\mathcal{E})^{-1}.$$

A typical aggregate wage equation might take the form

$$w - p_c = y - n - fU$$

so that the real wage, defined relative to consumer prices, rises in line with labour productivity but is inversely related to the level of unemployment U.

These last two equations can be combined to give

$$fU = t - (1 - \alpha)e + \ln[N'Y/N] - \log(1 - 1/\mathcal{E}) \tag{3}$$

which relates the equilibrium level of unemployment (the natural rate) to the wedge, the output elasticity of labour demand and the price elasticity of product demand.

A fall in sales taxes, or an appreciation in the real exchange rate, will, *ceteris paribus*, reduce the natural rate of unemployment. There will be a reduction in wage pressure in the labour market, but there is no reason why firms should reduce their mark-up on costs to compensate, so the equilibrium level of unemployment must fall to apply countervailing upward pressure from the labour market.

In the 1970s and early 1980s this was a property of more than one of the major UK econometric models. The policy implications for the long-run effects of sales tax increases are very strong: a balanced budget increase in government spending financed by higher VAT, for example, would permanently raise the natural rate. The real world could conceivably work like this, but in the initial development of wage equations based on imperfect competition for UK econometric models this property was often assumed and untested, because the specification seemed natural from the point of view of the wage equation alone.

In the last 10 years this has been an issue which has been formally addressed, both at the theoretical level and empirically, largely as a result of a focus on the natural rate implied by these models. It turns out that specifying wage equations in terms of consumer prices rather than producer prices may not be the natural thing to do if the theoretical framework is based on bargaining between unions and firms (see Layard, Nickell and Jackman, ch. 2). The empirical case for long-run wedge effects remains unclear, both in the UK and elsewhere (see Darby and Wren-Lewis, 1993; Drèze and Bean, 1991). Whatever the outcome of this particular debate, UK macro modellers no longer specify wage equations in terms of consumer prices uncritically.

This is one example that I hope illustrates the usefulness of a system property like the natural rate for the analysis and development of econometric macro models. In an ideal world all equations would be based on consistent theoretical foundations, and cross-equation restrictions would always be applied, so system checks would not be required. This is not how econometric macro models have developed in practice. The reasons for this reflect in my view the focus of these models on short-term forecasting, with an associated disaggregation of the model (particularly on the demand side) and the involvement of large forecasting teams (see Wren-Lewis, 1993). The researcher who estimated the wage equation was often not the individual responsible for prices, and there may have been many price equations. Both researchers may have been concentrating on the short-term forecasting properties of their equations, with less attention being paid to equilibrium properties.

As these models began to be used over medium-term time horizons, and as the introduction of rational expectations brought the influence of the long-run equilibrium into the short run, this tendency to specify equations in isolation and ignore cross-equation restrictions became a serious deficiency. In these circumstances it became very useful to ask what determined the natural rate in these models, as I hope the example above illustrates.[2] I should stress that this does not presume that econometric models should contain an invariant natural rate, or that deviations away from the natural rate might not be prolonged. Instead it ensures that if departures from the natural rate occur, they are theoretically well founded.[3] In the UK in the last 10 years I believe it has been part of a progressive research strategy in macro modelling.

In the rest of this chapter I want to explore three particular reasons for departures from a natural rate. The common thread is that they are all departures that it might be particularly useful to explore with econometric macro models. They concern the short-, long- and medium-term respectively.

Price dynamics and Keynesian effects

My first example concerns short-run deviations from the natural rate. The most popular and familiar explanation for Keynesian-style fluctuations in activity is nominal inertia in either wage- or price-setting, or both. This was illustrated for a large UK econometric model by Joyce and Wren-Lewis (1991), who examined the National Institute's UK macro model, NIDEM. This model was particularly interesting because it embodied a substantial degree of rational expectations, including expectations in wage and price equations, but there was also a degree of nominal inertia in the dynamics of wage and price adjustment. As a result, the model could be described as new Keynesian in structure. The study showed that it took about 5 years for the model to approach its natural rate.

Figure 14.1 shows the response of unemployment and capacity utilisation in the model to one particular demand shock, a cut in the VAT rate, under the assumption that the authorities held nominal interest rates constant. (For full details of the model and the accompanying policy assumptions see Joyce and Wren-Lewis, 1991.) In this model a fall in sales taxes would produce a long-run fall in the natural rate of unemployment for reasons outlined earlier, but the model also produced a typical Keynesian response

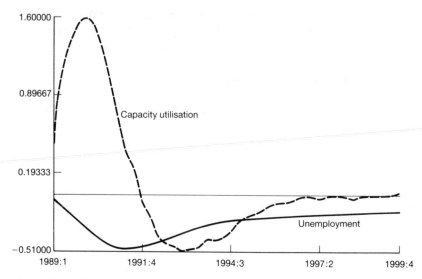

Figure 14.1   Unemployment and capacity utilisation following a tax cut

in capacity utilisation and unemployment in the short run. (GDP rises in the long run for the same reasons as unemployment falls, but capacity utilisation returns to base because of increases in the capital stock.)

At first I assumed that this short-run response was a consequence of nominal inertia alone. This turned out to be only half true. One great advantage of working with a structural rational expectations model is that deep parameters are identified and can be changed. In this model it was possible to isolate the few parameters in the wage and price equations which embodied nominal inertia. If they were set to zero, would the Keynesian property of the model disappear? Figure 14.2 provides the surprising answer. The initial increase in output is much smaller, but it remains substantial.

The reason for this comes from a combination of price dynamics, exchange rate movements and real exchange rate effects on supply. The exchange rate equation in the model was an open arbitrage condition with a weak risk premium term. The latter ensures that the exchange rate jumps to remove any disequilibrium in net overseas asset accumulation. The assumption of fixed nominal interest rates ensures that after the initial jump the exchange rate path is roughly parallel to its base trajectory, and this is shown in figure 14.3.

Figure 14.3 also plots the path of consumer prices. In the absence of nominal inertia these also jump following the shock, and their movement is governed by the need to equate demand and supply in each period. How

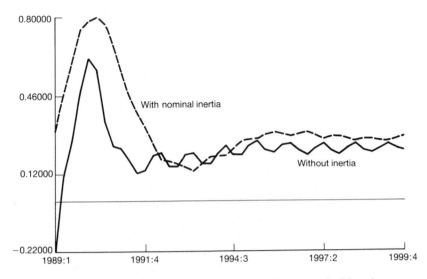

Figure 14.2   GDP following a tax cut with and without nominal inertia

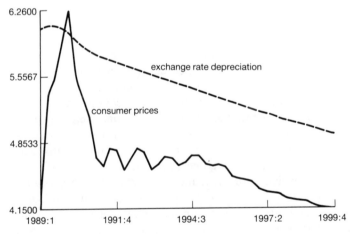

Figure 14.3   The real exchange rate after a tax cut with no nominal inertia

much they move will therefore depend on the way changes in prices influence demand, which involves a combination of wealth effects, real interest rate effects and the autoregressive behaviour of demand itself. This is likely to be quite complex, and explains why the path of prices in this simulation is relatively erratic.

The contrast in the behaviour of these two variables affects output because movements in the real exchange rate influence the supply side in this model. In our earlier example we saw how such effects might arise, but there are other channels. One is that the real exchange rate could influence the non-accelerating rate of unemployment (NAIRU) by changing the elasticity of product demand. In either case these influences could be limited to the short run, as it is only short-run adjustment which we are interested in here.

In the long run the real exchange rate depreciates, to compensate for the effect of higher GDP on import demand, and this provides some offset to the expansionary effect of the sales tax cut (see Joyce and Wren-Lewis, 1991). In the short run, however, the real exchange rate appreciates relative to this new equilibrium, which allows the natural rate of unemployment to fall by more in the short run compared to the long run. The Keynesian-type behaviour in unemployment which we observe in figure 14.2 is in fact a movement in the natural rate itself. The fact that output overshoots in the short run is entirely conditional on the dynamic path for prices, and a different path (reflecting different dynamic effects from prices on demand) could produce undershooting.

By eliminating all nominal inertia, we vividly illustrate the importance of these dynamic effects because they influence output directly. In the more general case where inertia is present they influence output through the speed of price adjustment. While we are familiar with the effects of the real exchange rate on demand in dynamic adjustment through the models of Dornbusch and others, the supply-side effects of the real exchange rate on dynamic adjustment paths have received less attention.

These results give one illustration of how an economy might exhibit Keynesian features even without wage and price inertia. There may perhaps be a more general point here about the relationship between theoretical development and econometric macro models. Dynamic paths will be influenced by many features of macroeconomic behaviour, and it is usually not possible to say which features are more important than others *a priori*. Econometric macro models represent an ordering which at least has some relationship to the data, and therefore may represent a useful guide to which areas of dynamic analysis would repay further theoretical and empirical research.

Demand elasticities and the natural rate

The second departure from an invariant natural rate that I want to consider concerns the longer run, and involves the aggregate elasticity of product demand. In the model outlined earlier, and in most models of imperfect competition, this is assumed to be constant across components of expenditure, and in particular is assumed to be unaffected by changes in government policy. As a result, the NAIRU determines the long-run level of aggregate demand (Z in the earlier notation), and not vice versa. Demand may adjust towards its equilibrium level either through direct effects from inflation and changes in the price level, or because governments change fiscal or monetary policy to stabilise inflation.

The form of the demand curve (2) is, however, rather special. Suppose firms sell their goods to two sets of agents, consumers and the government. Suppose each individual household h maximises a utility function of the form

$$U_h = (M_{+1,h})^\gamma (\Sigma_i a_i q_{ih}^{-\rho})^{-1/\rho}$$

where M_{+1} is next period's money balances, q_i is consumption of good i and a, γ, ρ are parameters. Their budge constraint is

$$\Sigma_i p_i q_{ih} + M_{+1,h} = p.y_h + M_h$$

where y_h is the share of aggregate wages and profits received by the household, and M_h is their initial money holding. Optimisation implies a demand for good i of the form

$$q_i = A(p_i/p)^\alpha (M/p + y)$$

where A and α are functions of a, γ and ρ.

It is not clear how we should derive the government's demand elasticity, but there is no *a priori* reason why this should be identical to the households'. As a result the firm's demand curve might look like

$$y_i = A(p_i/p)^\alpha (M/p + y) + B(p_i/p)^\beta g \tag{4}$$

where g denotes the total level of government spending (i.e. $B(1) = 1$). (4) cannot be written in the form of (2), i.e. as

$$y_i = h(p_i/p, Z(g, M/p, y))$$

as long as α and β differ. Instead we have the elasticity of aggregate demand

$$\mathcal{E}_i = \alpha + (\beta - \alpha) g_i / y_i$$

being a function of the share of government spending in output. An increase in government spending will shift both the price equation and the wage equation, leading to a permanent, long-run change in the natural rate, as (3) clearly shows.

Wren-Lewis (1987) explores the quantitative importance of this relationship in the case of a simple version of this model with imposed parameters. However the general issue of how important such effects might be can more usefully be explored in a standard macroeconometric model. This is because the hallmark of such models is disaggregation of aggregate demand. In the simple model above we focused on private consumption and government spending, but another interesting contrast might be between domestic demand and overseas demand. If the price elasticity of overseas demand is greater than domestic demand, then movements in the real exchange rate could influence the natural rate through the route examined here.

Vintages and the two mark-ups

The following appears to be a fairly general proposition. The mark-up of wages over prices in the goods market depends on the level of productivity on the marginal machine, i.e. prices depend on marginal costs. In the labour market, the mark-up of wages over prices will depend on average levels of productivity. Workers are typically not paid according to the productivity of the machine on which they work. If the natural rate is the resolution of a 'battle of the mark-ups' along the lines presented above, then changes in the relationship between marginal and average productivity can change the natural rate, as (3) shows.

In a putty, putty Cobb–Douglas world the relationship between the two is constant. In a vintage model, however, changes in output and investment are likely to alter the age of the oldest machine used, and so alter the relationship between average and marginal cost. Wren-Lewis (1992) and Darby, Ireland and Wren-Lewis (1993) analyse this effect at a theoretical level in the context of a change in real interest rates. However the limits to algebraic analysis are severe, and it is impossible to tell how important such effects could be in practice.

Figure 14.4 plots results from a new UK econometric model, COM-PACT, which embodies a vintage production technology. (The model's properties are described in Wren-Lewis et al., 1993.) It shows the response of unemployment to an increase in government spending in the complete model (labelled 'with vintage effects'), and in a version where prices always depend on average rather than marginal cost (labelled 'without vintage effects'). By comparing the paths of unemployment in the two models, we can isolate the importance of the vintage effects on the natural rate.

In the model with average cost pricing, an increase in government spending leads to a Keynesian-type expansion in the short run, but after about 10 years unemployment has returned to its natural rate. In the model with marginal cost pricing we note two major differences. The first is that the initial output expansion is smaller. This is because much of the extra output is produced on older, less efficient machines, which raises marginal

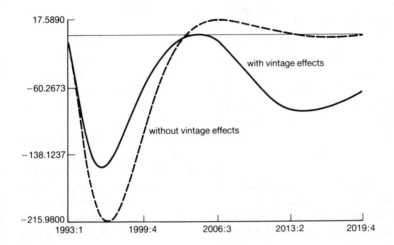

Figure 14.4   Unemployment and fiscal policy with and without vintage effects

costs and therefore leads to a more rapid wage–price spiral. The second difference is that the fall in unemployment is much more persistent. The initial increase in output increases investment, and investment also rises because higher inflation reduces real interest rates. (The monetary policy assumption involves a constant nominal interest rate.) As a result, when output falls back in the medium term firms find they are using relatively younger, more efficient machines at the margin. As as result, the natural rate falls.

The magnitude of these beneficial medium-term effects on unemployment is substantial. By construction, they come entirely from the influence of the vintage structure of production on marginal costs. At the very least, they suggest that such effects warrant further investigation.

All three of the examples above involve complexity at the systems level. In these situations theoretical analysis is often intractable, or it may be difficult to know which effects can be abstracted out of the analysis. At the very least, econometric macro models can provide some guide in this situation.

Conclusions

This chapter has been about a two-way relationship between the concept of a natural rate and econometric macroeconomic models. In the past I believe the natural rate has been useful for the development of empirical macro models. It has allowed modellers and others to focus on the reasons for departures (short- or long-run) from the natural rate in these models, a focus which is often not present in their original construction.

Until now it is probably fair to say that this examination has told us a good deal about the failings of econometric models, but rather little about the validity or limitations of the natural rate concept itself. In this chapter I have tried to be a little more optimistic about the future, and have given three illustrations of how econometric models may have a particular advantage in exploring some aspects of the natural rate.

Each example is I believe of some interest in its own right. The first examined how real exchange rate effects on supply (be they short- or long-run) can have a significant influence on short-term deviations from the natural rate. The second considered the possibility that changes in the composition of demand could shift the natural rate by changing the aggregate price elasticity of demand. The third looked at how a vintage production structure could lead to prolonged departures from the natural rate in the medium term.

Whatever the eventual verdict on any of these examples, they are also designed to illustrate a more general proposition. In complex systems (where the complexity comes from dynamics, disaggregation, non-linearity or another source) econometric macro models have a potential comparative advantage over other forms of analysis. This may be useful in increasing our understanding of the natural rate or any other system property. Time will tell whether econometric macro models are able in practice to fulfil that potential.

Notes

My thanks are to Rod Cross for helpful comments, but errors and opinions are my responsibility alone.
1 By the 'natural rate concept' I mean that the equilibrium level of unemployment and output is independent of shifts in the aggregate demand for goods.
2 Turner (1991) analyses the natural rate in a specific UK model, where deviations from a natural rate also reflect unintended outcomes of individual equation specification, but of a rather less interesting variety.
3 It could also be the basis for testing whether the implied natural rate was data coherent.

References

Darby, J. and Wren-Lewis, S., 1993. 'Is There a Cointegrating Vector for UK Wages' in Rod Cross (ed.), The NAIRU, Journal of Economic Studies, Special Issue, 20, 87–115
Darby, J., Ireland, J. and Wren-Lewis, S., 1992. 'Interest Rates, Vintages and the

Natural Rate', University of Strathclyde, mimeo

Drèze, J.H. and Bean, C.R., 1991. *Europe's Unemployment Problem*, Cambridge, MA: MIT Press

Joyce, M. and Wren-Lewis, S., 1991. 'The Role of the Real Exchange Rate and Capacity Utilisation in Convergence to the NAIRU', *Economic Journal*, 101, 497–507

Layard, R., Nickell, S.J. and Jackman, R., 1991. *Unemployment*, Oxford: Oxford University Press

Turner, D., 1991. 'Should Large Scale Models have Simple Long-run Properties?', *Oxford Bulletin of Economics and Statistics*, 153, 225–42

Visco, I., 1993. 'A New Round of U.S. Model Comparisons: A Limited Appraisal', in L.R. Klein (ed.), *Comparative Performance of U.S. Econometric Models*, New York: Oxford University Press

Wren-Lewis, S., 1987. 'Is There a Natural Rate Under Imperfect Competition?', *National Institute Discussion Paper*, 98

1992. 'Between the Medium and Long Run: Vintages and the NAIRU' in Colin Hargreaves (ed.), *Macroeconomic Modelling of the Long Run*, London: Edward Elgar

1993. 'Macroeconomic Theory and U.K. Macromodels: Another Failed Partnership?', International Centre for Macroeconomic Modelling, *Discussion Paper*, 9

Wren-Lewis, S., Ricchi, O., Ireland, J. and Darby, J., 1993. 'The Macroeconomic Properties of an Econometric Model with Consumption Smoothing, Vintage Production, Nominal Inertia and Rational Expectations', International Centre for Macroeconomic Modelling, *Discussion Paper*, 16

IV

Political economy

15 Is the natural rate of unemployment a useful concept for Europe?

Maria Demertzis and Andrew Hughes Hallett

With increasing integration between the European economies, and with full monetary union planned for the end of the century, it has become commonplace to examine performance indicators and policy concepts at the level of European averages. But such indicators can be highly misleading because no member economy need lie at or even near the average. Similarly, an improvement in the average need not imply an improvement for all, or even a majority of, participants. At the very least we need to know how our performance indicators would be affected by changes in the dispersion in national performance levels. More generally, interactions between the national markets means that the *distribution* of activity levels can have a profound effect on the level of performance in the aggregate even when monetary conditions remain constant. Given this, the usual performance measures and policy concepts are hardly likely to be either stable enough at the European level, or well enough focused, to be of much use for policy purposes.

This chapter therefore examines the extent to which using European averages for policy purposes, and the concept of a European natural rate of unemployment in particular, may be misleading. Our purpose is to show how the process of aggregating labour markets contributes towards worsening the natural rate of unemployment, and hence the EU's medium-term sacrifice ratio or inflation–unemployment trade-off. We show that if the variation in unemployment rates is taken into account, the aggregate sacrifice ratio will move up and to the right of the average of the national/regional curves. This implies a worsening of the inflation–unemployment position under monetary union: every unemployment rate will be accompanied by a higher inflation rate, or alternatively every inflation rate will imply higher rates of unemployment.

We argue that this deterioration in the sacrifice ratio is sustained by the segmentation of the EU's labour markets, which is due to a lack of labour mobility and various supply-side rigidities. In the chapter's empirical section, we are able to make estimates of this rightward movement in the period leading up to just before the Maastricht agreement (1991), noting the contribution and increasing instability of each component in that rightward displacement. That allows us to put a number on how much worse cyclically adjusted unemployment would have to be to maintain current inflation rates, as a result of integrating the European economies into a monetary union.

The micro foundations of a European Phillips curve

The natural rate of unemployment is defined as that level of unemployment which is consistent with unchanging inflation. Such a level of unemployment would depend on the structural characteristics of the economy and would, *in the long run*, remain unaffected by shifts in aggregate demand. However, even accepting the natural hypothesis in its own terms, aggregate demand may influence the natural rate of unemployment in the medium term if: (a) the *costs* of anticipated inflation vary with the rate of inflation (Friedman, 1977, for example); or (b) current demand and employment levels are *path dependent* (Cross, 1993, for example); or (c) if the *distribution* of unemployment changes. This chapter is concerned with the last factor in the context of European monetary union.

It is straightforward to demonstrate that an unequal distribution of unemployment between two sectors, regions or countries in a union will have a positive impact on wage inflation and hence on the natural rate of unemployment. That implies an upward shift in the aggregate sacrifice ratio faced by the EU as a whole. We show this

(1) For the case of convex downward sloping Phillips curves.
(2) Where the long-run Phillips curves are vertical.
(3) For the case of linear, region-specific Phillips curves.

The result holds in all three cases: any one of them is sufficient, but none of them is necessary.

The aggregation hypothesis with segmented labour markets

Suppose we have a union of two economies, involving either a single currency or integrated product markets, but labour markets which are segmented with different levels of unemployment. Certainly that has been the case within all the EU's member countries for a long time. And it will be no less the case across the EU as a whole since the variation in EU unemployment rates must be at least as great as that within any one member state. Delors (1989), in his evidence to the EU Commission, pointed out that the unemployment distribution in the EU was two to four times worse than that in comparable monetary unions such as the US or

Canada, and had been getting worse during the market integration of the 1980s.[1]

No doubt there are structural rigidities, supply-side distortions and market imperfections which (together with differences in infrastructure, amenities and institutional inertia) could account for this persistence in unemployment differentials. But in a single market for goods and services, these supply-side differentials would, in due course, tend to be reduced through migration and matching wage/labour cost differentials under a common inflation rate. So supply-side rigidities and distortions could sustain differences in unemployment only into the medium term.

Yet the best explanation of the persistence in unemployment differentials is perhaps the simplest: namely that the European labour markets are separated by a lack of labour mobility and are likely to remain so despite a single market. Migration remains low because it is expensive both for the migrant and for the host country, *and* because it is difficult to cross cultural and institutional barriers – to say nothing of language barriers. As a result, migration has not adjusted by enough either within or between countries to emove these regional differentials in unemployment. Recent research reflects the strength of this labour market separation. Migration in Europe, and within member countries such as the UK and Italy, remains lower than in existing monetary unions (such as the US) with comparable differences in activity and employment rates (Eichengreen, 1990). Moreover, those differences have become semi-permanent even in the US (Krugman, 1991; Blanchard and Katz, 1992).

Hence, labour market separation, if not supply-side rigidities as well, is likely to support unemployment differences for much longer than just into the medium term. In what follows, we therefore assume that different unemployment rates persist – despite common inflation and fixed exchange rates. They may go away eventually; but their endogenous resolution is likely to be extremely slow and their impact on the rate of wage inflation will remain meanwhile. We do not model these differentials here: we simply record them as a fact of life and examine the consequences.

Case I: downward sloping non-linear Phillips curves (Lipsey, 1960)

Suppose that the labour force is divided equally between two labour markets so that:[2]

$$U = \tfrac{1}{2}(u_A + u_B), \qquad \dot{W} = \tfrac{1}{2}(\dot{w}_A + \dot{w}_B). \tag{1}$$

From now on we use upper case letters to denote aggregate variables and

318   Maria Demertzis and Andrew Hughes Hallett

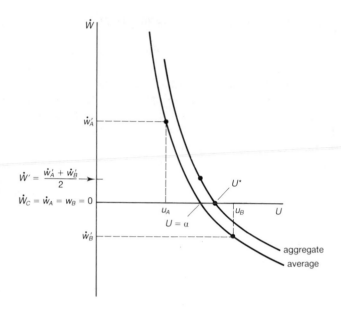

Figure 15.1   The average and aggregate inflation–unemployment trade-offs with identical convex Phillips curves

lower case letters for country/region-specific variables. For the moment we will assume that identical convex relationships hold between $\dot{w}_A$ and u_A, and between $\dot{w}_B$ and u_B, but relax that assumption on p. 322 below. If unemployment is the same in both markets, then $\dot{w}_A = \dot{w}_B$. The relation between the union-wide aggregates $\dot{W}$ and U would then be identical to that between their regional counterparts, $\dot{w}_i$ and u_i.

But if unemployment in the two regions is different (for example, $u_A < u_B$), and only *on average* corresponds to a natural rate of $U = \alpha$ and constant wage inflation $\dot{W}_c$, then the outcome is quite different.[3] The average unemployment rate $(u_A + u_B)/2$, i.e. $U = a$, will generate $\dot{w}_A = 0$ in A and $\dot{w}_B = 0$ in B. But that is as if the unemployment were redistributed between A and B because wage bargaining took place in a single market with *perfect* mobility. If the markets are segmented by a lack of labour mobility, then u_A would generate $\dot{w}'_A$ and u_B would generate $\dot{w}'_B$. For the union as a whole the outcome would be positive wage inflation at the average natural rate $U = \alpha$ since $\dot{W}' = (\dot{w}'_A + \dot{w}'_B)/2 > 0$. Similarly, the natural rate of unemployment will rise from $U = \alpha$ to $U = U^*$. That gives the aggregate curve in figure 15.1, when u_A and u_B are varied with a fixed disparity between them. The aggregate inflation–unemployment outcomes are Pareto inferior and lie along a curve to the northeast of the average of the national outcomes. In addition, the greater the disparity in the underlying unemployment rates, the greater the northeasterly displacement. In short the assumed convexity of wage responses leads demand pressures to increase wages faster in the market with excess demand (where $u < \alpha$) than they fall in the market with excess supply (where $u > \alpha$). Hence, across the union as a whole, wage inflation will be positive at the average natural rate $U = a$, i.e.:

$$\dot{W} = \tfrac{1}{2}(\dot{w}_A + \dot{w}_B) > 0.$$

Alternatively, for a constant rate of inflation, the natural rate of unemployment will have to rise from $U = \alpha$ to $U = U^*$.

Can we rely on downward sloping Phillips curves?

It is widely argued that in the long run, wage bargains will compensate for anticipated inflation (Friedman, 1968; Phelps, 1967). There may therefore be a trade-off between inflation and unemployment in the short to medium term. But in the long run the Phillips curves will be vertical, and inflation will match monetary growth while unemployment reverts to its natural rate. To what extent can we then legitimately refer to downward sloping Phillips curves and conclude that variations in the unemployment distribution can affect inflation and the natural rate of unemployment?

There are many reasons for arguing that figure 15.1 is indeed the appropriate analytic framework to use. First, and not least, we may simply be interested in the (policy) implications of the shorter term rather than the very long term because people are concerned about their employment and inflation prospects in this time horizon. And, as the lack of mobility/market segmentation argument makes clear, this shorter term may in fact be rather long. Second, if the long-term position cannot be influenced by expenditure patterns anyway, then the analysis which alters the distribution of unemployment favourably and moves the aggregate trade-off inwards in the shorter term is a Pareto improvement and worth having for its own sake. Third, vertical Phillips curves depend on further conditions being met: that the past history of unemployment does not affect the natural rate, that the costs of inflation do not vary with the inflation rate, and that wage bargains *fully* compensate for price inflation. If any of these conditions does not hold, we must use figure 15.1. Fourth, and significantly, many of the new results from the micro foundations literature support the existence of downward sloping (and non-linear) Phillips curves. For example Blinder (1991) finds clear evidence of asymmetric pricing strategies among firms.

Prices are raised more flexibly and by larger amounts in boom periods than they are cut in periods of excess supply. That implies a positive relation between price and output changes. And if wages respond to actual and /or expected price changes during the bargaining process, then some of this relationship must also feed through to wages. Hence figure 15.1. Similarly, Dornbusch's (1990) demonstration that the sacrifice ratio, which he defines as the marginal increase in the rate of unemployment necessary to secure a unit reduction in the inflation rate, has increased as inflation fell in the European economies during the 1980s, suggests that downward sloping relationships do hold in practice. Ball (1993) goes further and examines that ratio for its dependence on the underlying levels of activity, inflation, wage responses and contract length. Any of those factors would imply relationships as in figure 15.1. And they would be supported by theoretical micro foundations models. For example, in a study of the macroeconomic impacts of state dependent pricing rules, Caplin and Leahy (1991) have shown that aggregating across agents subject to nominal shocks automatically implies a conventionally signed (and non-linear) Phillips curve.

But perhaps the most interesting reason derives from Phillips's original work which, as Alogoskoufis and Smith (1991) are careful to point out, was actually conducted in terms of real wages although the effects of inflation expectations were incompletely specified and accommodated. However, Phillips did implicitly have an extra equation for prices (a price mark-up relation) which he used to substitute prices out and leave a quasi-reduced form for wage inflation as a function of unemployment, the change in unemployment, productivity growth and import prices. This shows the importance of distinguishing between the direct or *structural* Phillips curves (as usually studied in the theoretical literature), and its *reduced form* sacrifice ratio counterpart which also draws on all the indirect unemployment–inflation linkages which go through other equations in the model. In general there will be a number of such indirect linkages (in additiion to that provided by the price mark-up equation); and the process of substituting out the associated endogenous variables will introduce a number of extra partial derivatives which may offset those from the original structural Phillips curve, when determining the slope of the overall (reduced form) trade-off.[4]

Thus, only in the simplest models where the other variables (i.e. beyond inflation and unemployment) in the structural relationship are treated as exogenous, do we get the separation between the expenditure side and the supply side necessary to sustain a vertical Phillips curve. In the longer term, variables such as productivity, technical progress and human capital, and investment itself, will be endogenous and a function of activity levels and financial conditions.[5] Indeed Alogoskoufis and Smith develop just such a model and show that it has a downward sloping Phillips curve trade-off even when rational expectations of inflation are introduced. We adopt a similar approach here, arguing that the effects of different unemployment distributions will ultimately depend on the underlying inflation–unemployment trade-offs. That provides a general formulation, within which vertical (structural) Phillips curves are just one special case. Hence figure 15.1, as its diagrammatic representation, refers to the general reduced form trade-off or sacrifice ratio, rather than to any structural relationships.

Case II: vertical Phillips curves

How, if the long-run structural Phillips curves really are vertical as postulated in the natural rate hypothesis can sacrifice ratios be accommodated in our story? Price inflation would then be determined by monetary policy, and wage inflation by price inflation adjusted for productivity growth. In the long term, standard models of endogenous growth imply that productivity levels will be endogenous. That would be represented here by persistent (positive) productivity 'disturbances'. Therefore, in a world with wage bargaining we may expect that:

(a) The market with higher long-run productivity will enjoy larger (or at least not smaller) *real* wage increases than others with the same rate of price inflation.
(b) For a unit decrease in unemployment, the market operating under conditions of relative excess demand is in a position to increase wages by more (or at least not less) than a market with higher unemployment. On the other hand, since wages are ultimately constrained from below by social security benefits, the market with relative excess demand will suffer a larger fall in wages per unit increase in unemployment than a market with higher unemployment.

Together, those two propositions imply figure 15.2. Country A operates at a lower level of unemployment and relatively high excess demand. Hence, according to our model, $\dot{w}_A > \dot{w}_B$. Moreover, should any disturbance shift the curves to the left, wages in country A will increase by more than those in country B because its relative excess demand is greater. Similarly, if the curves shift to the right, wage inflation will fall, but by more in country A.

Thus, even when the underlying Phillips curves are vertical, we still get a negatively sloped aggregate sacrifice ratio which lies above and to the right of the average inflation–unemployment trade-off. The downward sloping nature of aggregate curve is due to condition (a) above, while the upward displacement to condition (b).

The displacement effect itself, however, depends on the initial variation in

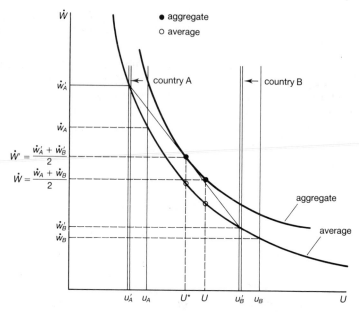

Figure 15.2   Average and aggregate trade-offs with vertical national Phillips curves

the natural rates of unemployment: the closer are u_A and u_B (*ceteris paribus*), the steeper the aggregate curve and hence the closer it comes to overlapping both the component curves and the average curve.

Case III: country-specific Phillips curves (Archibald, 1969)

Suppose now that countries A and B have the Phillips curves marked in figure 15.3.[6] Suppose also that country A has the lower unemployment ($u_B > u_A$). That implies expected inflation rates of $\dot{w}'_A > \dot{w}'_B$ respectively if the individual economies remain separated, and an average (union-wide) unemployment rate of

$$U = \tfrac{1}{2}(u_A + u_B)$$

consistent with a constant inflation rate of $\dot{W}_C$ under perfectly elastic migration.

However, if labour markets remain segmented after unification, the average rate of inflation consistent with union-wide unemployment rate U is

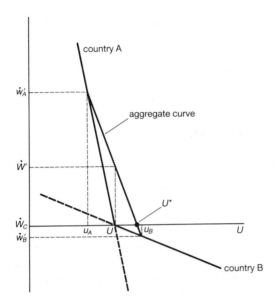

Figure 15.3   Average and aggregate trade-offs with country-specific Phillips curves

$$\tfrac{1}{2}(\dot{w}'_A + \dot{w}'_B) > \dot{W}_C$$

because the economy with relative excess demand for labour (country A) is generating greater upward pressure at that aggregate unemployment level than the economy with relative excess supply is generating downward pressure. That is not consistent with an unchanged inflation rate; either inflation must start to rise, or unemployment will have to increase to U^* to contain those inflationary pressures. There is therefore an outward shift in the aggregate Phillips curve and a worsening inflation–unemployment trade-off. Our result now depends on different countries having differently sloped Phillips curves; but the degree of displacement still depends on the disparity between the underlying unemployment rates.

Thus, in all three cases, variations in the rate of unemployment between countries (or regions) will displace the aggregate sacrifice ratio above and to the right of the average of the corresponding national trade-offs, *either* as a result of convexities in the wage bargaining process, *or* because different countries (regions, sectors) have different wage responses to demand pressures, *or* both. That implies a Pareto worsening of the infla-tion–unemployment possibility frontier. That means that there will be greater scope for, and a greater need for, policy interventions at the European than at the national level.

A formal model of the aggregation process

The next step is to express the upward displacement as an explicit function of the variations in unemployment across regions; to determine whether any other factors play a role and examine their relative importance. After all we have only shown that unequal unemployment rates cause a displacement, not whether different distributions within a given range will cause different displacements.

The displacement effect in detail

Consider the case of n distinct labour markets, with rates of unemployment and wage increases u_i and $\dot{w}_i, i = 1 \ldots n$. Let α_i be the weight of the ith economy, defined as total employment in region i as a proportion of total employment in the union as a whole. Thus $\Sigma \alpha_i = 1$ and $\Sigma \alpha_i u_i = U$ is the union unemployment rate. Suppose now that wage adjustments in each labour market follow an (inflation-compensated) Phillips curve of the Friedman–Phelps type:

$$\dot{w}_i = k\dot{P} + f(u_i) \tag{2}$$

where $\dot{P}$ is the anticipated rate of change of the European or union-wide price index. We further assume that excess demand exerts convex pressure on wage formation: $f'(u_i) < 0$ and $f''(u_i) \geq 0$, with linearity as a special case. These relationships are taken to be identical in each market (but recall Case III above). Moreover, if firms pay labour its marginal product, so that prices are a mark-up on labour costs corrected for changes in productivity, then (as a special case) the implied Phillips curve trade-off becomes vertical if $k = 1$. But if $\dot{P}$ enters with a lag and $k = 1$, we get full compensation and a natural rate or rational expectations equilibrium only in the long run.

The aggregate wage change over all regions is now:[7]

$$\dot{W} = \sum_{i=1}^{n} \alpha_i \dot{w}_i = k\dot{P} + \sum_{i=1}^{n} \alpha_i f(u_i). \tag{3}$$

Alternatively (3) can be derived directly from a fully specified multi-country model containing IS, LM, wage, price, employment and exchange rate equations for each country. This is demonstrated by Alogoskoufis and Smith (1991), who derive (3) from just such a model and show that the average (i.e. system-wide) rate of wage inflation will be independent of the exchange rate regime (which may include fixed or floating exchange rates, or monetary union). Expanding $f(u_i)$ around the aggregate unemployment rate U then yields:

$$f(u_i) = f(U) + (u_i - U)\frac{df(U)}{dU} + \frac{1}{2}(u_i - U)^2\frac{d^2f(U)}{dU^2} +$$

$$\frac{(u_i - U)^3}{3!}\frac{d^3f(U_i)}{dU^3} + \frac{(U_i - U)^4}{4!}\frac{d^4f(U)}{dU^4} + \cdots \tag{4}$$

Hence,

$$\sum\alpha_i f(u_i) = f(U) + \sum_{j=2}^{\infty}\sum_{i=1}^{n}\frac{\alpha_i(u_i - U)^j}{j!}\frac{d^jf(U_i)}{dU^j}$$

$$= f(U) + \frac{1}{2}s^2\frac{d^2f(U)}{dU^2} + \frac{1}{6}\mu_3\frac{d^3f(U)}{dU_3} \tag{5}$$

$$+ \frac{1}{24}\mu_4\frac{d^4f(U_i)}{dU^4} + \cdots$$

where $s^2 = \mu^2$, and where $\mu_j = \sum\alpha_i(u_i - U)^j$ for $j \geq 1$ define the sample moments from the regional distribution of unemployment rates.[8] Note that $s^2 \geq 0$, $\mu_4 \geq 0$ and $d^2f(u_i)/du^2 > 0$ necessarily follow, and we may also expect $d^4f(u_i)/du^4 \geq 0$.

Now substituting (5) into (3) yields:

$$W \simeq kP + f(U) + \frac{1}{2}s^2\frac{d^2f(U)}{dU^2} + \frac{1}{6}\mu_3\frac{d^3f(U)}{dU^3} + \frac{1}{24}\mu_4\frac{d^4f(U)}{dU^4} + \cdots$$

$$\tag{6}$$

(6) is similar to that used by Archibald (1969) in that it shows that the variance among unemployment rates will put upward pressure on inflation.[9] But it is also an extension since it recognises that the tendency of the unemployment rates to become bunched together in some places (and spread out in others) will increase that pressure if the asymmetries in the unemployment distribution, μ_3, *and* in the responsiveness of wages to increasing levels of excess demand, d^3f/dU^3, have the same sign.[10] Conversely, those asymmetries will reduce the wage pressure if they have opposing signs. Similarly, any tendency for unemployment rates to spread evenly over a wide range or to bunch together into two or more distinct groups (μ_4 large) will also increase the upward pressure on wages. Conversely, no extra pressure is implied if they bunch close together in one group ($\mu_4 \approx 0$).[11]

An interpretation of the displacement effect

These displacement factors are easy to interpret. The variance term (s^2) reflects the existing inequalities in unemployment and activity levels across the regions and countries of the EU. That signals an efficient use of resources. The asymmetry term (μ_3) may be positive or negative. If it is positive most regions will enjoy unemployment a little below average, but a few will suffer unemployment significantly above average. But if it is negative, most regions have above-average unemployment while a lucky few enjoy unemployment significantly below average. Thus $\mu_3 > 0$ signifies a *prosperous core* with a few struggling economies, and that the benefits of monetary union will be fairly well spread. But $\mu_3 < 0$ implies economic *leadership* from a few prosperous regions with a strong centripetal force, and a larger but less prosperous periphery. The benefits then go largely to the leaders.

Finally, the spreading term (μ_4) reflects clear differences between different economies, or groups of economies, within the EU: a prosperous core of low unemployment economies and a periphery of high unemployment economies – a 'two-speed' Europe in fact.

Whatever the interpretation, (6) shows that wage inflation will be affected significantly – and almost certainly adversely – by factors beyond the usual price and demand pressures in the regional or natural labour markets and, hence, beyond the control of national authorities who might try to restrain wage inflation by acting directly on expectations or demand pressures in their own markets. Since both migration and stronger regional policies are not costless, higher inflation and/or higher unemployment will be the likely outcomes.

Decomposing the displacement mechanism

If the impact of excess demand is correctly modelled as a weighted sum of convex functions, the successive derivatives in (6) will be linked to one another. Unrestricted estimation would inevitably yield poorly determined and highly collinear parameter values.[12] The alternative is to estimate the convex functions directly in (3). That avoids making any approximations.

For maximum flexibility of functional form, we adopt a Box–Cox transformation and allow the data to pick the best fitting specification:[13]

$$f(U) = \alpha + \beta U^{-\gamma} \text{ with } \beta > 0 \text{ if } \gamma > 0$$
$$\beta < 0 \text{ if } \gamma < 0 \tag{7}$$

but

$$f(U) = \alpha + \beta \log U \text{ but } \beta < 0 \text{ if } \gamma = 0. \tag{8}$$

This formulation covers all the specifications used in previous work with $\gamma = 1, 0, -1/2, -1$ being the most popular choices. The linear case implies no displacement effect. But if $\gamma = 1$ we get,

$$\dot{W} = \alpha + k\dot{P} + \frac{\beta}{U} + \beta\frac{s^2}{U^3} - \beta\frac{\mu_3}{U^4} + \beta\frac{\mu_4}{U^5} + \cdots, \qquad \beta > 0 \quad (9)$$

or if $\gamma = -\frac{1}{2}$,

$$\dot{W} = \alpha + k\dot{P} + \beta U^{\frac{1}{2}} - \frac{1}{8}\beta\frac{s^2}{U^{3/2}} + \frac{3}{48}\frac{\beta\mu_3}{U^{5/2}} - \frac{15}{384}\frac{\beta\mu_4}{U^{7/2}} + \cdots,$$
$$\beta < 0 \qquad (10)$$

or if $\gamma = 0$,

$$\dot{W} = \alpha + k\dot{P} + \beta\log U - \frac{\beta s^2}{2U^2} + \frac{\beta\mu_3}{3U^3} - \frac{\beta\mu_4}{4U^4} + \cdots, \qquad \beta < 0 \quad (11)$$

Hence the impact of the higher-order moments may diminish, but whether it does so rapidly depends both on the size of those moments *and* on the level of aggregate unemployment (the higher-order moments have increasing impact, at lower levels of unemployment).

Given estimates of β and γ, we can now calculate how much each characteristic of the unemployment distribution will increase inflation at each unemployment level. More interestingly, we can also determine the impact of each of these displacement factors on the natural rate of unemployment. If (7) and $\gamma = 1$ turns out to be the best model, then unchanging wage/price inflation in (9) implies:

$$\frac{\partial U^*}{\partial s^2} = \frac{U^3}{(U^4 + 3U^2s^2 - 4U\mu_3 + 5\mu_4)} = \frac{U^3}{A} > 0 \qquad (12)$$

if $\mu_3 \leq 0$ or $0 < \mu_3 < (U^3 + 3Us^2 + 5\mu_4/U)/4$. Similarly,

$$\frac{\partial U^*}{\partial \mu_3} = -\frac{U^2}{A} < 0, \quad \frac{\partial U^*}{\partial \mu_4} = \frac{U}{A} > 0 \qquad (13)$$

under the same restrictions. The negative sign in (13) implies that an increasingly positive skew, $\mu_3 > 0$, will offset the upward pressures on wage inflation. On the other hand, increasing degrees of variance (s^2), spreading (μ_4) or hegemonic leadership[14] ($\mu_3 < 0$) will raise the inflation pressure and unemployment levels, although the marginal impact of these distributional characteristics begins to fall off the worse they become. These developments are illustrated in figures 15.4, 15.5 and 15.6. And if we find the log-linear

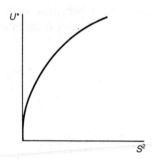

Figure 15.4   The natural rate of unemployment as a function of the dispersion in unemployment rates

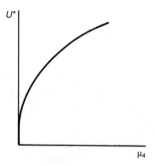

Figure 15.5   The natural rate of unemployment as a function of the skew in unemployment rates

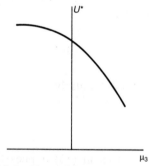

Figure 15.6   The natural rate of unemployment as a function of the kurtosis in unemployment rates

model to be the best, the conclusions are exactly the same: (11) with constant inflation implies:

$$\frac{\partial U^*}{\partial s^2} = \frac{U^3}{2B} > 0, \ \frac{\partial U^*}{\partial \mu_3} = -\frac{U^2}{3B} < 0, \ \frac{\partial U^*}{\partial \mu_4} = \frac{U}{4B} \tag{14}$$

where $B = U^4 + U^2 s^2 - U\mu_3 + \mu_4$ and $\mu_3 < U^3 + Us^2 + \mu_4/U$ is assumed. Figures 15.4, 15.5 and 15.6 still apply.

Econometric specification of the aggregate Phillips curve

We have run a series of regressions to get an idea of the size, numerical importance and composition of the worsening of Europe's sacrifice ratio in the 1980s. These regressions are designed to test the following specific propositions:

(a) that an unequal distribution of unemployment rates across the EU will have a significant impact on the inflation–output trade-off which policymakers face;
(b) that it is important not to truncate after the variance term, cutting out the higher moments which show how hegemonic leadership and a 'two-speed' Europe affect that trade-off;
(c) that the upward pressure on wage inflation or on the natural rate of unemployment, after economic and monetary union, has been underestimated;
(d) that the stability of that trade-off, and the degree to which it is displaced unfavourably, is sensitive to the kind of deterioration recently experienced in the EU's unemployment record;
(e) that, as a consequence, any measure of a natural rate of unemployment for the EU will be significantly higher than the average of the component economies.

The estimating equations

To test these propositions, we have to specify a suitable short-run model and introduce expectations explicitly. We take a model of the Friedman–Phelps type, as presented in Brechling (1974), to match (2):

$$\dot{W}_t = \beta_0 + \beta_1 f(U_t) + \beta_2 s_t^2 + \beta_3 \dot{P}_t + \beta_4 (\dot{W}_t^e - k_0 \dot{P}_t^e) + e_t \tag{15}$$

where actual and expected wage changes are now measured as deviations from actual and expected price changes. We may select a suitable functional form for $f(U)$, and add higher-order moments (μ_3, μ_4), and/or add parameter restrictions between β_1 and β_2, etc. It would be less ad hoc to set

$\beta_2 = 0, f(U_t) = \Sigma \alpha_i f(u_i)$, and recover the higher moments from (9), (10) or (11). In either case the remaining variables are aggregated (EU-level) variables. However, we have differentiated between the weights used for each of the aggregated variables: wages and unemployment are weighted by the proportion of each region's employment in the total, while expenditure shares have been used to weigh price changes. Having distinguished the effect of actual price changes from expected price changes, consistency with (2) requires $k_0 = \beta_3$ since otherwise the aggregate Phillips curve could never tend to any equilibrium or steady state relationship. But if, in addition to $k_0 = \beta_3$, we find that $\beta_4 = 1$, the long-run curve is vertical. That can be determined by the data; for the moment we maintain $k_0 = \beta_3$ only.

It might be attractive to impose a rational expectations mechanism in the short as well as the long term, but given the existence of wage contracting and other institutional reasons for price stickiness, that hardly seems realistic. Instead, we suppose adaptive expectations for the quarterly wage data we use:

$$\Delta \dot{W}_t^e = (1 - \lambda)(\dot{W}_{t-1} - \dot{W}_{t-1}^e) \text{ where } 0 < \lambda < 1. \tag{16}$$

Lagging (15) once, pre-multiplying by λ, subtracting the outcome from (15) and imposing expectations, yields:

$$\begin{aligned}
\dot{W}_t = {} & \beta_0(1 - \lambda) + \beta_1 \Delta f(U_t) + \beta_1(1 - \lambda)f(U_{t-1}) + \beta_2 \Delta s^{2t} \\
& + \beta_2(1 - \lambda)s_{t-1}^2 + \beta_3 \Delta \dot{P}_t + [\beta_3 - \beta_4 \beta_3](1 - \lambda)\dot{P}_{t-1}) \\
& + [\beta_4(1 - \lambda) + \lambda]\dot{W}_{t-1} + v_t
\end{aligned} \tag{17}$$

or,

$$\begin{aligned}
\dot{W}_t = {} & \gamma_0 + \gamma_1 \Delta f(U_t) + \gamma_2 f(U_{t-1}) + \gamma_3 \Delta s_t^2 + \gamma_4 s_{t-1}^2 \\
& + \gamma_5 \Delta \dot{p}_t + \gamma_6 \dot{P}_{t-1} + \gamma_7 \dot{W}_{t-1} + v_t
\end{aligned} \tag{18}$$

where:

$$\begin{aligned}
& \gamma_0 = \beta_0(1 - \lambda) \\
& \gamma_1 = \beta_1 \qquad \gamma_2 = \beta_1(1 - \lambda) \\
& \gamma_3 = \beta_2 \qquad \gamma_4 = \beta_2(1 - \lambda) \\
& \gamma_5 = \beta_3 \qquad \gamma_6 = \beta_3(1 - \beta_4)(1 - \lambda) \\
& \gamma_7 = \beta_4(1 - \lambda) + \lambda \\
& v_t = e_t - \lambda e_{t-1}
\end{aligned} \tag{19}$$

We have 8 estimated values but only 6 parameters to be fitted. Nevertheless we have two identifying restrictions:

$$\frac{\gamma_4}{\gamma_2} = \frac{\gamma_3}{\gamma_1} \tag{20}$$

$$\gamma_6 = \gamma_5(1 - \gamma_7).$$

Similarly, adding higher-order moments is straightforward; we attach

$$\gamma_8 \Delta\mu_{3,t} + \gamma_9\mu_{3,t-1} \text{ where } \gamma_9 = \beta_5, \gamma_8 = \beta_5(1-\lambda)$$

when $\mu_{3,t}$ appears in (15) with parameter β_5. A term in $\mu_{4,t}$ can be attached in the same way. However, (9), (10) and (11) make it clear that once a specific functional form is chosen for $f(U_t)$, the parameters of the s^2, μ_3 and μ_3 terms will bear a fixed relationship to one another. We can easily incorporate those parameter restrictions. Suppose we want to include only the s^2 term. We can match a short-run version of (9) to (15) as follows:

$$\dot{W}_t = \beta_0 + \beta_1\left[f(U_t) + \tfrac{1}{2}s^2\frac{d^2f(U)}{dU^2}\right]$$
$$+ \beta_2\dot{P}_t + \beta_3(\dot{W}_t^e - \beta_2\dot{P}_t^e) + e_t. \tag{21}$$

If we now write $\Pi_t = f(U_t) + \tfrac{1}{2}s^2 d^2f(U_t)/dU_t^2$, insert the expectations mechanism, and sort out terms, we get:

$$\dot{W}_t = \beta_0(1-\lambda) + \beta_1\Delta\Pi_t + \beta_1(1-\lambda)\Pi_{t-1} + \beta_2\Delta\dot{P}_t$$
$$+ [\beta_2 - \beta_3\beta_2](1-\lambda)\dot{P}_t + [\beta_3(1-\lambda) + \lambda]\dot{W}_{t-1} + v_t \tag{22}$$

where
$\Pi_t = U_t^{-1} + s^2U_t^{-3}$ if (7) is selected with $\gamma = 1$ or, $\Pi_t = \log U_t - \tfrac{1}{2}(s_t/U_t)^2$ if (8) is selected. Of course Π_t may contain more terms if μ_3, μ_4, etc. prove important.

Finally we estimate the most general model by setting $\beta_2 = 0$ in (15) and replacing $f(U_t)$ by $\Sigma\alpha_i f(u_{it})$.[15] For example, if the semi-log model (8) were chosen we would get:

$$\dot{W}_t = \beta_0(1-\lambda) + \beta_1\Delta\Sigma\alpha_i\log u_{i,t} + \beta_1(1-\lambda)\Sigma\alpha_i\log u_{i,t-1}$$
$$+ \beta_3\Delta\dot{P}_t + [\beta_3 - \beta_4\beta_3](1-\lambda)\dot{P}_{t-1}$$
$$+ [\beta_4(1-\lambda) + \lambda]\dot{W}_{t-1} + v_t \tag{23}$$

and parameter β_2 drops out since s_2 is incorportated in $\Sigma\alpha_i\log u_{it}$. This can be rewritten as:

$$\dot{W}_t = \gamma_0 + \gamma_1\Delta\Sigma\alpha_i\log u_{i,t} + \gamma_2\Sigma\alpha_i\log u_{i,t-1}$$
$$+ \gamma_3\Delta\dot{P}_t + \gamma_4\dot{P}_{t-1} + \gamma_5\dot{W}_{t-1} + v_t \tag{24}$$

where

$$\gamma_0 = \beta_0(1-\lambda) \qquad \gamma_1 = \beta_1 \qquad \gamma_2 = \beta_1(1-\lambda);$$
$$\gamma_3 = \beta_3 \qquad \gamma_4 = \beta_3(1-\beta_4)(1-\lambda)$$
$$\gamma_5 = \beta_4(1-\lambda) + \lambda \qquad v_t = e_t - \lambda e_{t-1}.$$

Only one parameter restriction now applies, but that ensures that all parameters are identified: $\gamma_4 = \gamma_3(1 - \gamma_5)$. And the only change, if the $f(u_{it}) = 1/u_{it}$ functional form were preferred instead, would be to replace $\Sigma \alpha_i \log u_{i,t}$ with $\Sigma \alpha_i/u_{i,t}$ throughout (23) and (24).

Comments on the econometrics

The data used is from the four largest European countries,[16] Germany, France, Italy and the UK. The data cover from the first quarter of 1975 to the last quarter of 1990 (64 observations).[17] Our estimation technique has five features:

(a) The mechanism used in deriving the final estimating equations left a lagged dependent variable on the right-hand side of each equation. That, in combination with the usual problem of simultaneity between wages and prices, implied that some regressors were correlated with the error term. Instrumental variables, in the form of a non-linear two-stage least squares estimator to cope with the cross-parameter restrictions were therefore used. The choice of instruments was conventional, if somewhat arbitrary, being the lags of the variables being instrumented (except for lags in multiples of 4 which would have been correlated with the errors) as well as some variables which are theoretically meant to be exogenous (e.g. GDP for Europe). Their suitability as instruments was then judged by the Sargan test. However, the latter is not entirely satisfactory because it assumes that the errors satisfy the classical assumptions, which in our case they clearly do not (feature (b) below). It is not known, however, to what degree this renders the test unreliable. It must therefore be treated with caution.

(b) When applying adaptive expectations to the theoretical model the error term becomes a fourth-order moving average (MA) process (the degree of the MA process is justified from the fact that the frequency of the data is quarterly). The software used does not allow us to use IV with a MA(4) error process incorporated; we can however correct for it and obtain consistent standard errors based on the Newey–West test with equal weights.

(c) A productivity[18] term was included initially, appropriately weighted, but it proved to be insignificant.

(d) Moving to quarterly data in a world of annual wage rounds, and where inflation (and inflation compensation) is judged on annual inflation rates, requires the one-year lags in $\dot{P}_{t-1}, \dot{W}_{t-1}$ be re-specified as 4 quarter lags.

(e) All variables are $I(1)$ (based on Dickey and Fuller's Φ_2 and Φ_3 statistics), and are cointegrated in groups. The equations specified are therefore balanced.

Table 15.1   *The determinants of aggregate wage inflation in Europe, 1975–90*

Model no.	β_0	β_1	β_2	β_3	β_4	λ
			Parameter estimates:			
I	0.0386	−0.0183	0.0060	1.073	0.1329	0.1886
	(2.61)	(4.44)	(3.15)	(13.62)	(1.31)	(0.943)
II	−0.0096	0.2801	0.2801*	0.3351	0.5299	0.0285
	(13.11)	(8.89)	U_t^3	(1.99)	(35.77)	(0.299)
III	0.1878	−0.700	—	0.3333	0.3610	0.4067
	(7.04)	(6.54)		(1.67)	(6.29)	(2.23)
IV	−0.0176	0.3864	—	0.3688	0.4487	0.2383
	(5.79)	(7.37)		(2.04)	(12.11)	(1.47)

Model no.	Sargan	SC	FF	Normality	Heterosced.
			Diagnostic tests:		
I	20.72	12.48	6.80	0.72	0.49
II	21.47	10.42	0.01	0.04	0.66
III	7.25	8.46	0.11	1.40	4.38
IV	11.22	5.97	0.01	0.22	3.07

Notes:
[a]Functional forms were as follows: $f(U_t) = \log\Sigma\alpha_i u_{it}$ in (1); $f(U_t) = 1/\Sigma\alpha_i u_{it}$ in (2); $f(U_t) = \Sigma\log\alpha_i u_{it}$ in (3); and $f(U_t) = \Sigma\alpha_i/u_{it}$ in (4).
[b]* denotes a restricted parameter.
[c]t-ratios in parentheses (Newey–West standard errors).
[d]SC denotes the Lagrange Multiplier test for serial correlation, FF that for the correct functional form.
[e]The Sargan test is distributed as a χ^2 variable with 12, 13, 11, and 11 degrees of freedom in the 4 equations respectively.
[f]The remaining four diagnostic tests are all Lagrange Multiplier versions distributed χ^2 with 4, 1, 2, and 1 degrees of freedom respectively in all four equations.

The empirical results

Table 15.1 contains the regression results for the two best fitting functional forms: the semi-log specification (8); and the hyperbolic function (7) with $\gamma = 1$. Linear and square root functions (i.e. (7) with $\gamma = -1$ or $-1/2$) were also tried but produced inferior results. Diagnostic test failures, and estimated coefficients with theoretically incorrect signs were the main problem. Those results are therefore not reported.

The alternative specifications

In table 15.1, Model I is based on (15) with the semi-log specification (11), but without the μ_3 and μ_4 terms or any parameter restrictions. That translates into (18) subject to (19), (20) and $f(U_t) = \log U_t$. Model II uses the hyperbolic form (9), including the parameter restrictions but without the μ_3 and μ_4 terms. That translates into (22) with $\Pi_t = U_t^{-1} + s^2 U_t^{-3}$. Models III and IV, however, do not approximate $\Sigma \alpha_{if}(u_{i,t})$ at all. Instead, they are based on (3). The corresponding short-run specification is (15) with $\beta_2 = 0$. That translates into (24) subject to (25) when the semi-log form $f(u_{i,t}) = \log u_{i,t}$ is used (Model III); or with $f(u_{i,t}) = 1/u_{i,t}$ (Model IV).

Thus a comparison of Models III and IV is a test of functional form, and indicates where (and whether) that selection has a significant impact on the results. Of course to evaluate the impact of the moments of the unemployment distribution individually, it is necessary to compute the approximations in (9) or (11) term by term. But individual significance tests are not possible.

A comparison of Models I and II tests the importance of that functional specification at the aggregate (rather than the regional) level, inclusive of parameter restrictions. That might appear to muddle the consequences of changing functional form with those of imposing parameter restrictions. But a regression's overall significance must deteriorate when restrictions are imposed. Hence, if Model II's performance improves over Model I, as it does here, then it must be that the parameter restriction is unimportant but the results remain sensitive to the correct choice of excess demand function.

Finally, a comparison between Models I and II and their counterparts among Models III and IV, will show the importance of including the third-and higher-order moments of the unemployment distribution.

Empirical results: general observations

Given the existence of simultaneity between $\dot{P}$ and $\dot{W}$, the use of instrumental variable estimating techniques implies that the F as well as the R^2 statistics are not reliable measures for the goodness of fit and this is why they are not reported in table 15.1. The *quality* of fit therefore, and hence the accuracy of the explanation provided, will be indicated by the significance of the parameters and the diagnostic tests.

With the exception of the parameter which governs the dynamics of the expectations process λ, the individual coefficient estimates are all highly significant at a 5% level and of a plausible size. More important, they all have the expected signs. The sign switch from $b_1 < 0$ in semi-log specification of excess demand pressures, to $b_1 > 0$ in the hyperbolic function, is consistent with the theoretical models in (7) and (8) respectively. Similarly the constant terms switch in sign from $b_0 > 0$ for the semi-log excess demand function to $b_o < 0$ for the hyperbolic function. That switch is necessary if the estimated curves are both to have a small negative asymptote for large U values. This implies that wage changes are indeed bounded below by the needs of subsistence and the payment of certain social security benefits when U increases, but rise increasingly fast if U falls to a very low level.

Elsewhere, all the coefficient estimates are positive as we should expect, implying that price inflation, the accelerations in price inflation, and past wage changes all have a positive influence on the current level of wage inflation. Of greater importance for this chapter, the term reflecting the variance of unemployment rates over the EU area also has a positive and highly significant impact on the rate of wage inflation–explicitly in Models I and II and implicitly in Models III and IV. That confirms the empirical significance of the displacement effect.

The diagnostic tests

The diagnostic tests are mostly acceptable at a 5% significance level for all four models. We can certainly accept the hypothesis of normally and homoscedastically distributed errors for Models I and II, and that we have the correct functional form in Model II. However, a semi-log specification for the excess demand term – at least in the truncated form used in Model I – is rejected even at a 1% level. Moreover both the first two equations show that the wage dynamics have poorly determined parameters and significant serial correlation in the errors.[19] There are various possible explanations for this: mis-specification of the dynamics of wage bargaining, principally in the expectations mechanism, or from omitted variables and/or the wrong functional form. To the extent that the serial correlation problem is corrected for in both the third and fourth equations, and the estimated parameters of the dynamics and expectations terms improve, then we can lay those results at the door of omitted variables – in this case the skew and spread factors (μ_3, μ_4) which, as we see from figures 15.8 and 15.9 (p. 339), are highly volatile. It is important to incorporate those effects in some way therefore.

This however is not a complete story since the serial correlation tests are clearly less significant, and the dynamic parameters better determined, in the hyperbolic rather than the semi-log excess demand specifications. So getting the right functional form is important as well. Indeed, direct tests of functional form uniformly favour the hyperbolic excess demand function over the semi-log form; the former is accepted easily in Models II and IV, while the latter is rejected decisively in Model I and is clearly less acceptable in Model III.

Nevertheless, although the choice of a hyperbolic function plus the inclusion of all moments of the unemployment distribution resolves the serial correlation in Model IV, it also moves the test of the no heteroscedasticity hypothesis close to its rejection region; the p-values of acceptance fall from 49% in Model I to just 8% in Model IV. As a result we have used Newey–West standard error formulae throughout table 15.1, in order to adjust for any remaining biases in the usual standard error calculations.

Finally the Sargan mis-specification test has been used to check that our regressions, and that the instruments used in the two-stage estimation procedure, were correctly specified. Formally speaking, both hypotheses can be accepted at the 5% level in all four equations, but that acceptance is very marginal (p-values of just 6%) in the first two. Both hypotheses are easily accepted in the other two equations. That suggests that truncating the displacement effect introduces a significant mis-specification.

Equation comparison: the preferred model

Comparing Models I and II shows the latter to be preferable in terms of fit. More important, the diagnostic tests show lower (but still significant) serial correlation in the errors; but no heteroscedasticity or non-normality. The functional form test accepts the hyperbolic function but rejects the semi-log form. In particular, the fact that Model II performs better despite its parameter restriction indicates that it is the change in functional form which is important. That contrasts with the corresponding comparison between Models III and IV where the change in functional form is much less important. That says that wages are much more sensitive to variations in the pressure of demand at the EU level than they are to variations in the national demand levels.

Moreover, the parameters themselves are better estimates in Model II. They have the correct signs and, the expectations adjustment parameter λ apart, they are all highly significant. More important, perhaps, they are also more plausible in terms of size. Model I's estimate of the impact of a unit decrease in unemployment on wage changes is probably too small at 0.75% on the annual rate of wage inflation for a 1% point fall in unemployment, versus 1.5% on wage inflation in Model II.[20] On the other hand its estimate of the impact of an increase in the variance of unemployment is almost certainly too large; i.e. that each 1% increase in the variance adds 2.5% points to the annual rate of wage inflation. It is worth noting here that a 1% increase in variance between two countries, like Germany and the UK, with unemployment rates of roughly 6% and 10% respectively in 1990, would be equivalent to the unemployment differential between them expanding by 0.02% points. Model II's estimates that the same movement would add only 0.5% to annual wage change therefore seems more plausible. At the same time, Model I also implies that wage bargains will overcompensate for any price changes (β_3) and adjust almost completely to shift in market fundamentals within one year (β_4). Both estimates seem highly implausible given the contractual arrangements and traditional inertia of European labour markets. Again Model II's estimates of a 34% compensation and a 47% adjustment each year look more reasonable.

There is less to choose between Models III and IV. As before the hyperbolic function is superior, both in terms of fit and in *all* its diagnostic tests. With Model IV we can accept the hypotheses of no serial correlation, or heteroscedasticity in the errors, plus a correct specification of the instrument's functional form and normality. Model III, however, still shows significant heteroscedasticity and only a marginal acceptance of no serial correlation – which, in a dynamic specification, leaves open the possibility of biased parameter estimates. Moreover, the parameters appear to be better determined in Model IV. They all have the correct sign; they are all highly significant (λ excepted) and are of a more reasonable size. Using (9) and (11) we find that a 1% point rise in unemployment reduces annualised wage changes by 1.5% in Model IV but by 2.5% in Model III. And a 1% increase in the variance of unemployment rates adds 0.75% to the annual wage inflation rate in Model IV but adds 1.5% in Model III. Both of Model III's figures seem rather high compared to recent experience. On the other hand both equations imply a 35% price compensation and a 55%–64% adjustment to fundamentals each year. Hence both sets of estimates seem broadly reasonable, but those in Model IV clearly have the edge in parameter values, significance and diagnostic tests.

Finally we can compare Models II and IV to evaluate the importance of the extra displacement effects which the latter implies. Based on the diagnostic test, Model IV seems to produce better results. Both models accept the null of correctly specified functional forms, and normal and homoscedastic errors. But Model IV accepts no serial correlation in the errors and a correctly specified instrument set, while (2) rejects (or nearly rejects) both. The individual coefficients all seem well determined with the only clear difference being a near-significant expectations adjustment term in Model IV. Similarly, the estimated parameters imply almost identical impulse effects. Wage changes are reduced (on an annual basis) 1.5% if unemployment rises 1% points, but rise 0.5%–0.75% if the variance of unemployment rises 1% point. Similarly, wage changes compensate for

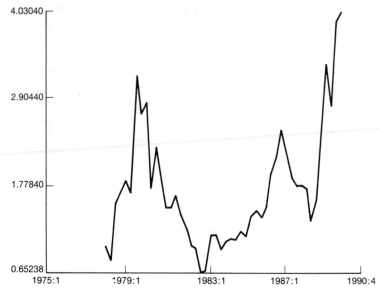

Figure 15.7   Variance $- \Sigma\alpha_i(u_i - U)^2$

35% of any price changes and adjust by 48%–55% for any change in fundamentals within a year. Expectations meanwhile adjust very quickly to actual outcomes, by 76% of the way each quarter.

We conclude that individually μ_3 and μ_4 may not be *quantitatively* important in explaining aggregate wage changes, but jointly they are important for obtaining *reliable* estimates of these changes. We therefore retain model IV as our preferred model.

The inflation and unemployment impacts of market integration

The final problem, and the ultimate focus of this chapter, is to calculate how much extra wage inflation will result from market integration and monetary union within the EU, and how far the natural rate of unemployment will rise as a consequence. To do that we evaluate the impact of the second- and higher-order terms in (9) on the wage inflation rate as determined in Model IV at the existing rate of unemployment and $\beta = \beta_1$. Similarly, we can evaluate and sum the partial derivatives in (12) and (13) at the same unemployment level, to get the corresponding rise in the natural rate of unemployment.

Figures 15.7, 15.8 and 15.9 show that the variance of unemployment across the four main EU economies has increased dramatically since 1985,

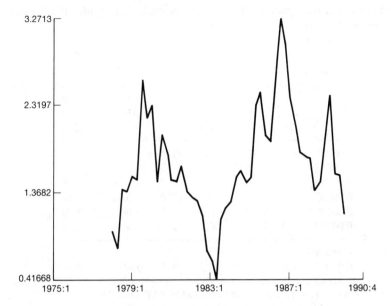

Figure 15.8   Skewness $-\Sigma\alpha_i(u_i - U)^3$

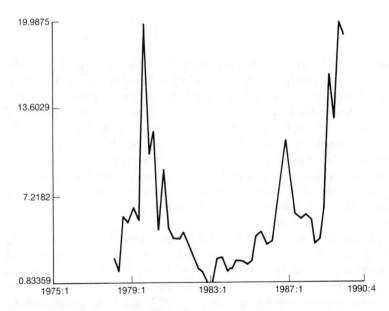

Figure 15.9   Kurtosis $-\Sigma\alpha_i(u_i - U)^4$

Table 15.2 *The worsening of the inflation–unemployment trade-off in Europe with unequal unemployment distributions*

Year	s^2 (1)	Contribution of: μ_3 (2)	μ_4 (3)	Extra wage inflation (ΔW) (4)	Rise in natural rate of unemployment in EU (ΔU^*) (5)
1985:1	0.00036	-0.6×10^{-4}	0.7×10^{-4}	0.15%	0.09
1986:1	0.00044	-0.2×10^{-4}	0	0.17%	0.12
1987:1	0.00061	-0.6×10^{-4}	0.2×10^{-4}	0.27%	0.18
1988:1	0.00053	-0.5×10^{-4}	0.1×10^{-4}	0.20%	0.14
1989:1	0.00130	-0.9×10^{-4}	0.7×10^{-4}	0.44%	0.30
1989:1	0.00200	-0.6×10^{-4}	0.1×10^{-3}	0.82%	0.39
Average	(1985–90)				
	0.00072	-0.6×10^{-4}	0.3×10^{-4}	0.34%	0.18

Notes: Columns (1)–(3) are estimated using Model IV, table 15.1, i.e. $\hat{\beta} = 0.38644$, in (9) to evaluate $\Delta \dot{W}$. Results in natural units are then converted into an annual rate of wage inflation in % of column (4). Column (5) is estimated using the formulae in (12) and (13) combined, whose units are percentage points.

most noticeably in 1986 and again in 1989. Hence inequality in the distribution of unemployment rates is highly volatile, but on an upward trend. The skew coefficient μ_3, meanwhile, is always positive – which indicates leadership by a small centripetal group of economies. In view of (9), this will act to reduce the upward pressure on wages because the employment benefits of monetary union are not widely shared. Again this factor is volatile, but it has been declining in importance since 1986. Lastly the spread coefficient, μ_4, shows the largest changes. It has risen by a factor of 8 since 1985, with sharp peaks in 1986 and in 1989. It too is pretty volatile, therefore, especially in periods of recession, with a trend to a *de facto* 'two-speed' Europe.

Inserting those figures into (9) term by term, with $\beta = 0.386$ from table 15.1, gives us the *increase* in wage inflation arising from a poor (and deteriorating) distribution of unemployment rates, all other factors remaining constant. The total increases and their composition by factor are given for the first quarter of each year in table 15.2.[21] It is clear, first of all, that the skew and spread factors do not contribute a great deal. They are smaller than the variance component by a factor of 10 or more and offset one another. The second point is that the extra upward pressure on wages has increased rapidly over the period 1985–90. It starts by adding 0.15% to the *annual* wage inflation rate in 1985, but rises to add an extra 0.82% to that annual rate (of about 5.5%) by the start of 1990. This, of course, was a period of increasing market integration. The third point is that the pressures for higher wage rises are evidently unstable. The extra wage inflation increases only slowly until early 1988; but it then jumps by a factor of 4 during 1988–9. That instability reflects the changing impact of the underlying demand pressures. The unemployment distribution, but not its average value, deteriorated sharply in 1988–9. That implies a significant increase in the pressure on wages. By contrast the mid-1986–7 period was a period when both the distribution and the average level of unemployment level worsened, so that there were no extra pressures on wage inflation.

But the critical observation from table 15.2 is to note how the natural rate of unemployment would increase as a result of monetary union between the big four EU economies. This has been obtained by solving our preferred model for the rate of unemployment consistent with an unchanged rate of wage inflation, and then computing the increase in that unemployment rate as a result of introducing the second, third and fourth moment of the unemployment distribution between the four economies: i.e., the sum of (12) and (13). The aggregate unemployment rate would in fact rise between 0.09% points in 1985 and 0.39% points in early 1990; that is about a 5% increase in the existing unemployment rate. Those are significant figures; they represent a steadily rising trend (up four-fold over the 1985–90 period), and involve something like 800,000 extra unemployed by 1989. However, most of the observations made of the increase in wage inflation also apply here. Not much is contributed by the μ_3 and μ_4 terms. It is likely that the big four EU economies will not contribute all that much to this increase in the natural rate. Introducing the other economies which have considerably higher rates of unemployment is likely to contribute much more since that will raise s^2 sharply and move us up the curve in figure 15.4. Given the curvature there, however, those increases may not be as dramatic as for the wage inflation case, just as the figures in column (5) of table 15.2 show less evidence of instability than those in column (4).

Conclusions

The policy implications are perhaps obvious: price stability and lower unemployment require policies which promote an equitable distribution of economic activities across the EU; greater attention to the incentive compatibility aspects of policy design; and stronger measures to counteract any centripetal or 'peripheralising' tendencies in market integration. By contrast a *laissez-faire* approach of relying on wage–price flexibility to resolve any differences in activity can be expected to prove both ineffective and damaging to the EU's overall performance.

The displacement of the inflation–output trade-off due to interactions between labour markets is not a small matter numerically. For the four larger EU economies it would have put an extra 1% point on the inflation rate, or a 0.5% point on the natural rate of unemployment in 1990, had their product markets been fully integrated. This kind of result will continue to hold so long as labour markets remain segmented by supply-side rigidities and a lack of labour mobility.

Notes

1 Currently the unemployment figures range from 40% to 2% on the EU's regional classifications or from 25% to 6% on national classifications.

2 The third section (p. 324) will extend this framework to any number of countries of different sizes.

3 For the sake of expositional simplicity we ignore productivity growth and assume that the constant rate of inflation (expected) at the natural rate of unemployment is zero. Relaxing these assumptions has the effect of shifting the horizontal axis in figure 15.1.

4 Hughes Hallett and Petit (1990) contains an explicit demonstration of this.

5 As postulated in the theory of endogenous growth, for example.

6 Following assumption (a) in the case of vertical Phillips curves, country A's trade-off is reflected in the steeper of the two curves.

7 For a country-specific parameter k, the proportion of price inflation reflected in wage inflation varies from country to country. In this case, anticipated price changes in each country cannot be represented by changes in the aggregate price level and $k_{\bar{p}}$ must be substituted by $\Sigma k_i \gamma_i \rho_i$ where γ_i is the ith country's weight in the European price index.

8 The linear term drops out of (5) only because we have assumed Phillips curves with identical slopes in every region. Generalising to country-specific Phillips curves would lead to additional terms of the form.

$$\Sigma \alpha_i [f(u_i) - f(U)] + \Sigma \alpha_i (u_i - U) \left[\frac{df(u_i)}{dU} - \frac{df(U)}{dU} \right] + \cdots$$

in (5) and so on for the higher-order derivatives. We can rewrite these terms as deviations from the average (union-wide) function and show that all these extra terms are small with a reasonable degree of convergence between the underlying markets. For example, suppose

$$\lambda + f(u_i) = a_i + \frac{b_i}{u_i}$$

Then we add

$$\Sigma\alpha_i\frac{[a_i - a + b_i - b]}{U} + \Sigma\alpha_i\frac{(u_i - U)(b_i - b)}{U^2} +$$

$$\Sigma\alpha_i\frac{(u_i - U)^2(b_i - b)}{U^3} + \cdots, \text{ etc.}$$

to (5) which all vanish as $a_i \to a$ and $b_i \to b$. Moreover these additions imply exactly the same terms as before, but with

$$\hat{\alpha}_i = \alpha_i(b_i - b)$$

replacing a_i throughout (where a and b are average curve's parameters). Thus unless the national/regional labour markets are *very* different in the way they operate, these terms add very little quantitatively and nothing at all analytically. So, almost without loss of generality, we can ignore the case of country-specific Phillips curves or a partially converged union.

9 However, Archibald's regression made use of a simple measure of statistical variation, whereas all the moments in (6) are deflated by the derivatives of the respective order. Archibald also used a measure of skewness but justified its inclusion in a different manner.

10 I.e. they reinforce one another because, while most regions have low employment $\mu_3 > 0$, the higher the excess demand, the *disproportionately* more pressure is put on wages if $f'''(U) > 0$ also holds.

11 These remarks assume $d^4f/dU^4 \geq 0$. It may be possible to find a convex function with negative fourth derivative, but it seems highly unlikely.

12 Omitting to deflate μ_3, μ_4, etc. by the powers of U indicated in (9)–(11) below, would be another important cause of collinearity. That deflation implies non-linear associations between the higher-order terms which would help avoid the collinearity that interfered with Archibald's original estimates. In a later paper, Archibald, Kemmis and Perkins (1974) attempted to overcome that problem by estimating with $f(U_i) = \Sigma\log u_i$, which obviously contains these higher-order moments. However, they never examined the aggregation of, and hence the impact of, those factors on wage inflation and the natural rate of unemployment.

13 The signs of β in (7) and (8) are required to ensure at least weak convexity.

14 See Thomas and Stoney (1971) for an alternative formulation of this leadership thesis.

15 The same model can be obtained by inserting $\Sigma\alpha_i f(u_{it})$ into (6) and using (3) and (5), without the need to invoke (15) at all.

16 All data are taken from Datastream, IMF series. Consistent quarterly data for the other EU countries is not yet available.

17 The P series had got some observations missing, a fact that reduces our data set significantly. To avoid losing degrees of freedom, the series is regressed on time and the fitted values replace the missing observations (Gilbert, 1977). We have tried estimating with both series, without much difference in the results.

18 Output *per capita*.
19 Theoretically (19) will have serially correlated errors if λ turns out to be significantly different from zero. Strictly speaking this does not happen in Models I, II, III or IV, although the value in the latter case is not far from significance at the 5% level. The Lagrange multiplier test did not find any evidence of serial correlation in Model IV, however.
20 All impulse values in this section are evaluated at current (1990) levels of the aggregate wage and unemployment values.
21 Due to differencing our sample size is reduced by one year, down to 1989:4; this last observation is taken to give the picture at the start of 1990.

References

Alogoskoufis, G.S. and Smith, R., 1991. 'The Phillips Curve, the Persistence of Inflation and the Lucas Critique: Evidence from Exchange Rate Regimes', *American Economic Review*, 81, 1254–75

Archibald, G.C., 1969. 'Wage–price Dynamics, Inflation, and Unemployment; the Phillips Curve and the Distribution of Unemployment', *American Economic Review*, 59, 124–34

Archibald, G.C., Kemmis, R. and Perkins, J.W., 1974. 'Excess Demand for Labour, Unemployment and the Phillips Curve: A Theoretical and Empirical Study', in D. Laidler and D.L. Purdy (eds), *Inflation and Labour Markets*, Manchester: Manchester University Press

Ball, L., 1993. 'What Determines the Sacrifice Ratio?', Department of Economics, Princeton University, mimeo

Blanchard, O. and Katz, L., 1992. 'Regional Evolutions', *Brookings Papers on Economic Activity*, 1, 1–76

Blinder, A.S., 1991. 'Why are Prices Sticky? 'Preliminary Results from an Interview Study', *American Economic Review*, 81(2) (May), 89–96

Brechling, F., 1974. 'Wage Inflation and the Structure of Regional Unemployment', in D. Laidler and D. Purdy (eds), *Inflation and Labour Markets*, Manchester: Manchester University Press

Caplin, A. and Leahy, J., 1991. 'State Dependent Pricing and the Dynamics of Money and Output', *Quarterly Journal of Economics*, 106, 683–708

Cross, R.B., 1982. 'Unemployment', in R.B. Cross (ed.), *Economic Theory and Policy in the U.K.*, Oxford: Basil Blackwell

1993. 'On the foundations of hysteresis in economic systems', *Economics and Philosophy*, 9(1) (Spring), 52–74

Delors, J., 1989. 'Regional Implications of Economic and Monetary Integration', in *Report on Economic and Monetary Union in the European Community*, Committee for the Study of Economic and Monetary Union, EC Office of Official Publications, Luxembourg

Dornbusch, R., 1990. 'Two-track EMU Now', in K.-O.-Pöhl *et al.* (eds.), *Britain and EMU*, London: Centre for Economic Performance, London School of Economics

Eichengreen, B., 1990. 'Is Europe an Optimal Currency Area?', *Discussion Paper*, 478, London: Centre for Economic Policy Research

European Economy, 1990. 'One Market, One Money', 44 (October), Commission of the European Communities, EC Office of Official Publications, Luxembourg

Friedman, M., 1968. 'The Role of Monetary Policy', *American Economic Review*, 58(1) (March), 1–17

1977. 'Nobel Lecture: Inflation and Unemployment', *Journal of Political Economy*, 85(3) (June), 451–72

Gilbert, C.L., 1977. 'Regression Using Mixed Annual and Quarterly Data', *Journal of Econometrics*, 5, 221–39

Hughes Hallett, A. and Petit, M., 1990. 'Cohabitation or Forced Marriage? A Study in the Costs of Noncooperative Fiscal and Monetary Policies', *Weltwirtschaftliches Archiv*, 126, 662–90

Krugman, P., 1991. *Geography and Trade*, Cambridge, MA: MIT Press

Lipsey, R.G., 1960. 'The Relation Between Unemployment and the Rate of Change of Money Wage Rates in the United Kingdom, 1862–1957: a further analysis', *Economica*, 27 (February), 1–31, reprinted in AEA Series (1966), *Readings in Business Cycles*, 456–87

Newey, W. and West, K., 1987. 'A Simple, Positive Semi-Definite, Heteroskedasticity and Autocorrelation Consistent Covariance Matrix', *Econometrica*, 55, 703–7

Phelps, E., 1967. 'Phillips Curves, Expectations of Inflation and Optimal Unemployment over time', *Economica*, 34(3) (August), 254–81

Thomas, R.L. and Stoney, R.J., 1971. 'Unemployment Dispersion as a Determinant of wage inflation in the UK, 1925–66', *The Manchester School*, 39, 83–117

16 The natural rate of unemployment: a fundamentalist Keynesian view

Meghnad Desai

Introduction

The theorising of the natural rate of unemployment (NRU) almost simultaneously by Phelps (1967) and Friedman (1968) was a significant step in the halt and ultimately reversal of the Keynes–neoclassical synthesis (neoKeynesian) in the field of macroeconomic theory as well as policy. Both Phelps and Friedman were of course reacting to the Phillips curve which in their view did not have sufficient grounding in neoclassical economics. The central issue was the seeming violation of the homogeneity postulate, since the Phillips curve purported to show a short-run, causal relationship between a nominal variable and a real variable. The neoKeynesians were uncomfortable with this because while they liked the macroeconomic simplicity of the Phillips curve, they also believed in the homogeneity postulate. The empirical/econometric connection between these ideas and the Phillips curve was made in two stages. In the first stage, Lucas and Rapping in two papers reversed the causal ordering between the rate of change of money wages (Δw) and the rate of unemployment (U) from that posited by Phillips, or rather more correctly by Lipsey (1960), (Lucas and Rapping, 1969, 1970; for the argument that Phillips did not have the same notion of causation that Lipsey and others have attributed to him, see Desai 1975, 1984). At this stage, price expectations were taken to be adaptive. In the second stage, Lucas engineered the creative union between rational expectations (RE) and the natural rate hypothesis (NRH), (Lucas, 1973). The effect of this reversal of the Phillips curve causal ordering and the undermining of any notion of a trade off between inflation and unemployment delivered the *coup de grâce* to official Keynesianism.

There has been a long debate since then about the rational expectations – natural rate hypothesis. New classical economics has been met by new Keynesian economics where the differences centre around the short-run versus the long-run nature of the natural rate of unemployment. A long list of inertial conditions – staggered wage contracts, unequal speeds of adjustment between labour markets and other markets, signal misperceptions, etc. can be evoked to make some room for a short-run trade off between inflation and unemployment. Recessions have certainly proved effective in bringing inflation rates down across OECD countries in the early 1990s, whatever the theoretical correctness of the natural rate hypothesis.

In this chapter I wish to distance myself from both the new classical and the new Keynesian schools. I shall argue that the rational expectations–natural rate of unemployment model is incomplete and that it is possible to close the Phillips curve model by adding an equation, not necessarily the quantity theory one, which endogenises unemployment and inflation and in which a pair of equilibrium values of inflation and unemployment can be derived. The issue I shall focus on is the non-homogeneity argument, providing some evidence in its support. In a second and radically different fashion, I wish to demonstrate that the way in which employment (or unemployment) is measured in all the schools in the natural rate of unemployment debate imposes the assumption of homogeneity of all types of labour regardless of skill, age, experience or gender differences. Keynes in the *General Theory* (1936) explicitly rejected this approach and proposed a different method of aggregating heterogeneous labour. Keynes' proposal on measurement of labour has been ignored by all subsequent macro-economic schools but in this particular context it is absolutely central to the Phillips curve – natural rate of unemployment debate. As it is not widely known, I shall exposit this measure by textual exegesis and then implement it with UK annual data. This will lead to a new way of posing the question of the natural rate of unemployment.

Phillips curve and the natural rate of unemployment

Much of what is said about the Phillips curve is more reflective of the work of Lipsey (1960) and Samuelson and Solow (1960) than of Phillips' own paper. Few people seem to have actually read Phillips' (1958) paper. (Friedman, 1968 contains no reference to Phillips, 1958, for example.) The glaring anomaly, which struck many people including Friedman, i.e. that a *nominal* price measure (Δw) was related to a *real* variable measuring excess labour demand, is carefully explained if one reads Phillips' paper. In what follows I offer a quick summary of Phillips' own model (Desai, 1984).

We start with an open economy. Assume that it is a growing economy in which Δq, the rate of growth of labour productivity, is constant.[1] The economy imports raw materials whose price level is growing at the rate Δp_m. Thus consumer price inflation Δp is given as

$$\Delta p = a\Delta w + (1 - a)\Delta p_m - \Delta q \tag{1}$$

where $(1 - a)$ is the share of imported raw materials in total costs.

Now if $\Delta w = \Delta p_m$, real wages will grow at the same rate as productivity. Thus this rate is an equilibrium growth rate of nominal wages $\Delta w = \Delta p_m = \Delta p + \Delta q$.

Now we can introduce Phillips' Phillips curve in two stages. One of them relates nominal wage growth *in the long run* to unemployment. Thus

$$\Delta w = \alpha_0 + \alpha_1 f(U). \tag{2}$$

When $\Delta w = \Delta p_m$, we could easily extract from (2) an equilibrium unemployment rate as

$$U^* = -f^{-1}(\alpha_0 - \Delta p_m)\alpha_1^{-1}. \tag{2a}$$

But Phillips makes a distinction between the long-run relationship as described in (1) and (2) and the actual economy. Since observed values are taken from a disequilibrium dynamic economy, he adds the cyclical influence of the rate of change of unemployment to equation (2). Thus, he puts

$$\Delta w_t = \Delta q_t + \alpha_0 + \alpha_1 f(U_t) + \alpha_2(\Delta U/U)_t. \tag{3}$$

I have deliberately added time subscripts to the variables in (3) because now these are time dated – annual in Phillips' case – observations.

Rather than estimate $\alpha_0, \alpha_1, \alpha_2$ by OLS or another suitable method from equation (3), Phillips collapsed his 52 annual observations in six data points by taking averages of U_t and Δw, falling within specified ranges of U, i.e. 0–2%, 2–3%, 3–4%, 4–5%, etc. He then estimated the parameters of (2) from the six data points. His averaging procedure was explicitly designed to be able to have values of U and Δw along which $\Delta U = 0$. Thus he was trying to extract unobservable long-run data from actual short-run observations (Desai, 1975; see, however, Gilbert, 1976).

Thus, the Phillips curve as estimated by Phillips is *a long-run relationship*. As far as approximating (3) was concerned, Phillips gauged the sign of α_2 from his loops which he drew around the fitted long-run curve.

Phillips' method of extracting a long-run relationship from short-run data is somewhat esoteric. We know now, following Denis Sargan's pioneering 1964 paper, that there is a better way of getting to the long-run relationship by first fitting a short-run relationship and letting the long-run relationship emerge from the estimated equations. (Sargan, 1964; for the error correction mechanism (ECM), see the introduction to Hendry and Wallis, 1984, which also reprints the Sargan paper).

If this above argument is correct then the Phillips curve is a long-run relationship, outside the time domain. As such, it is of no use for policy purposes and cannot by its nature display the short-run trade-off between inflation and unemployment. Lipsey in his 1960 paper did estimate (3), adding Δp_t as an additional variable. He thus estimated a short-run Phillips curve which started the mis-specification debate since the coefficient of Δp_t was significantly less than unity. Samuelson and Solow, who popularised the Phillips curve in their 1960 *AER* paper, do not even attempt an estimation. After displaying a scatter of US data which in their own words shows that 'there are points all over the place', they proceed to draw a smooth 'modified Phillips curve', between Δp and U. The debate surrounding the Phillips curve really turns on the Lipsey rather than the Phillips curve.

It is not necessary for the purpose of the present chapter to follow that debate. What is important is to note that (1) and (2) in defining long-run relationships constitute *an incomplete system*. We have two equations and three possible endogenous variables. (I take Δp_m to be exogenous.) These are Δp, Δw and U. We have a missing equation!

One way to complete the system is to argue that U is exogenous to the system. This argument is unclear as to whether it is the short-run value of U, i.e. U_t, which is exogenous, or the long-run value U^*. At the time of these debates, the Keynesians assumed that U_t was controllable by fiscal policy and hence the government could determine U_t to achieve the desired rate of inflation. But the neoclassicals (Phelps, Friedman) and the new classicals (Lucas, Sargent) showed that U_t was determined by Δp and its expected values.

The determination of U_t or its equilibrium value U^* is thus problematical. One defence is to say that U^* is determined by microeconomic behaviour, tastes and technology. This view is expressed in Friedman's reference to 'the dynamic Walrasian model' which grinds out the natural rate. Lucas and Rapping in their two papers reversed the causation and endogenised U, treating Δp as exogenous to the system (1) and (2) but determined by the quantity theory relationship.

It is inappropriate to leave the determination of U to some (non-existent) dynamic Walrasian model. For all practical purposes, we are speaking here of a macroeconomic measure in terms of percentage of labour force unemployment. The Lucas–Rapping effort and the subsequent rational expectations/natural rate hypothesis models of Sargent have the problem that the monetarist equation between Δp and money supply has proved to be fragile. (The debate here has been about the stability of the demand for money equation; for an examination of the econometrics of monetarism, see Desai, 1981; also Goldfeld and Sichel, 1990.)

A Keynesian theory for the natural rate: first attempt

It would be possible to close the model of equations (1) and (2) by fully endogenising U jointly with Δw, Δp. In Keynes' *General Theory*, there is an endogenisation of these three variables in chapters 19 and 20. This

Table 16.1 *The theoretical model*

(1)	$L = L(W,R,M_{-1})$
(2)	$R = R(M,W,L)$
(3)	$W = W(L^s,\underline{P}^e)$
(4)	$P = P(W,L;K)$

endogenisation also specifies a mechanism whereby the money stock affects unemployment. This is the Keynes effect. The Keynes effect works by variations in the ratio of money stock (M) to the prime cost of planned output (F) which for the present purposes can be equated to the import bill plus the wage bill (WL). Producers demand money to pay for labour and other inputs in the interval before output appears. Any increase in (M/F) is excess balance, *ceteris paribus*, and lowers the rate of interest (R). This in turn affects investment and, via the multiplier, income/employment.

To be able to incorporate the Keynes effect in a full econometric model it is necessary to endogenise w, p, U (or L) and R, in a full dynamic specification. Specifying a complete set of short-run, i.e. stochastic difference equations and estimating them by maximum likelihood methods, it is possible to extract long-run relationships to see how such a Keynesian model would fit the data. Such an attempt was made in Desai and Weber (1988). For the present chapter, it is sufficient to present the *estimated long-run* relationships. There were four endogenous variables U, R, w, p and three exogenous variables m (i.e. log M), p_m, q. The sample was UK quarterly data 1955–79 (stopping before the monetarist policy regime).

The four basic equations of the model are listed in table 16.1. (1) is for employment (L) derived from a Keynesian aggregate supply curve. (A word of caution is necessary here. This is not aggregate supply as in modern macro textbooks but as in the *General Theory*, chapter 3.) It is a function of wages, interest rate and money stock. (2) is for the rate of interest (R) as a function of the Keynes effect variable, the money stock as a proportion of the wage bill. (3) and (4) are for wages (w) and prices (p).

The results are summarised in table 16.2. These are the long-run equilibrium reduced form multipliers. In the course of estimation, employment (L) was translated into unemployment (U). Money stock, and import prices appear in logarithmic form as m and p_m. The two other exogenous variables are an incomes policy dummy (IPD) and the log of labour productivity (q). For each endogenous variable, the four multipliers for each of the four exogenous variables are shown. Besides the multiplier estimates, t values are displayed in parentheses.

The following remarks are appropriate:

Table 16.2 *Long-run multipliers*

	m		p_m		IPD		q	
U	-0.0718	(1.44)	0.0543	(2.10)	-0.0150	(1.30)	$+0.0639$	(1.40)
R	-3.4198	(1.40)	-0.9653	(2.85)	-0.0121	(1.18)	-0.0806	(1.31)
w	0.0016	(0.002)	0.4575	(1.20)	-0.2443	(1.57)	0.7184	(0.89)
Py	-0.0360	(0.12)	0.3981	(2.18)	-0.1541	(1.65)	-0.6584	(1.76)

(1) There is some, though weak, evidence of violation of the homogeneity postulate. Thus m influences U negatively but the t-value is only 1.44.
(2) There is a strong dichotomy in the estimated system which is Keynesian rather than monetarist. Thus m influences U and R but not w and p.
(3) Wages and prices are determined by costs – import prices and productivity.
(4) Import prices affect unemployment and interest rates as well. Indeed, given the t-values, one could impose a restriction that U is influenced by the $(m - p_m)$ money stock in terms of import prices.

Thus a Keynesian theory of unemployment would trace the effect of money on economic activity directly and leave prices to be determined by normal long-run costs. Clearly, much more work needs to be done in specifying and estimating larger and better models before this story can be fully persuasive. But to my knowledge this is the only attempt to specify and estimate a *General Theory* chapter 19 model of unemployment, wages and prices.

By tracing the influence of money on unemployment directly and by consciously violating the homogeneity postulate, the model described above makes room for a Keynesian (or what is called more often a post-Keynesian) version of the unemployment equation. It is not an easy task to relate this model to the natural rate of unemployment because the basic variables are levels of wages and prices as well as unemployment and interest rates. But we can make some remarks on the implication.

As can be seen from table 16.2, the real wage variable $(w - p_y)$ is independent of the money supply. To get a simple but meaningful expression we can write

$$(w - p_y) = q + \text{const.} \tag{4}$$

This is because the coefficients of m are insignificant and those of p_m cancel out. The coefficients of q come to 1.4 but the standard error attached will be large as is shown by the t-ratios. (4) of course implies a constancy of shares for which there is independent evidence in the original model (Desai and

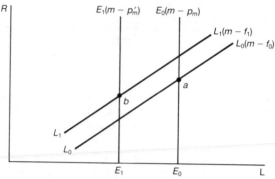

Figure 16.1   The impact of higher p_m on R and L

Weber, 1988, see (25b), p. 17; see also Goodwin, 1967 and Desai, 1973, 1984).

The other two equations determine U and R. A simple way to rewrite the long-run U equation is to use (4) above and get

$$U = -0.07m + 0.05p_m + 0.06(w - p_y) + \text{const.} \tag{5}$$

$$R = -3.4m - p_m - 0.08(w - p_y) + \text{const.} \tag{6}$$

The best way to illustrate the system of the other two equations implied by the model is to go back to (R,L) space. A stylised representation is given in figure 16.1, also reproduced from the original paper (Desai and Weber, 1988). Figure 16.1 illustrates the impact of higher input prices as in the oil shock. $E_0 E_0$ is the employment curve. The absence of any impact of R directly on U means that it is vertical which is similar to but conceptually different from a natural rate of unemployment. $L_0 L_0$ is the Keynes effect relationship, which is upward sloping. Its position is determined by the size of the money stock per prime cost of output, log (M/F).

To illustrate the stagflation of the 1970s, we start at position a. When there is an oil shock, real balances in terms $(m - p_m)$ go down (the coefficients of m and p_m are roughly similar in (5)). This is because p_m goes up to p'_m. $E_0 E_0$ moves to $E_1 E_1$. If the government increases the money supply to compensate for the higher costs, but not fully, we move from a to b with a higher money stock relative to both p_m and f but not high enough to prevent a rise in unemployment.

This Keynesian model thus tells the natural rate of unemployment story from a different angle and has an active role for monetary policy. This is because it endogenises U fully leaving the money supply to exert its full non-homogeneous effect.

Employment measured in wage units

I now move on to a totally different way of addressing the question of the natural rate of unemployment. No economist – Keynesian, post–Keynesian, neoclassical or new classical – has paid any attention to Keynes' discussion in chapter 4 of the *General Theory* as to how to measure employment. In chapter 4, entitled 'The Choice of Units' of the *General Theory*, Keynes addressed the question of measurement. He makes a distinction between *ex ante* and *ex post* measures, although he does not use these words. Keynes rejects concepts of real output and real capital. Not only is real output 'a non-homogeneous complex which cannot be measured, strictly speaking, except in certain special cases, as for example, when all the items of one output are included in the same proportion in another output' (*General Theory*, 1936, p. 38) but also the difficulties of defining real output or real capital 'never puzzles, or indeed enters in any way into business decisions and have relevance to the causal sequence of economic events, which are clear cut and determinate in spite of the quantitative indeterminacy of these concepts' (1936, p. 39). These concepts are thus no use for *ex ante* decision making but only useful for *ex post* historical comparisons. '[T]he proper place for such things as net real output and the general level of prices lies within the field of historical and statistical description'(1936, p. 40).

Instead of outputs, Keynes says 'that the amount of employment associated with a given capital equipment will be a satisfactory index of the amount of resultant output: – the two being presumed to increase or decrease together, though not in a definite numerical proportion' (1936, p. 41). The argument seems to be that employment is less heterogeneous than output and also the primary decision variable for a businessman is how many people to employ. So at the aggregate level, it is employment that is conceptually better defined and easier to measure.

But there is heterogeneity in employment. This is due to differences in skill and education experience. The problem of reducing heterogeneous labour to a homogeneous quantity has plagued Marxian economics for a long time. But in neoclassical and new classical *macro*economics, it is completely ignored. While at the micro level there is some attempt to account for the difference between the *stock* of workers and the flow of labour services and indeed an awareness of skill differences, etc. the new classical macroeconomics aggregates labour in a way just as crude as in the simpler versions of the Marxian model.

Keynes decisively breaks from this. As he puts it,

In dealing with the theory of employment, I propose, therefore, to make use of only two fundamental units of quantity, namely, quantities of money-value and quantities of employment. The first of these is strictly homogeneous, and the second can be made so. For, in so far as different grades and kinds of labour and salaried assistance enjoy a more or less fixed relative remuneration, the quantity of employment can be sufficiently defined for our purposes by taking an hour's employment of ordinary labour as our unit and weighting an hour's employment of special labour in proportion to its remuneration; i.e. an hour of special labour remunerated at double ordinary rates will count as two units. We shall call the unit in which the quantity of employment is measured the labour-unit; and the money-wage of a labour unit we shall call the wage-unit. Thus, if E is the wages (and salaries) bill, W the wage-unit and N the quantity of employment, $E = N.W$ (1936, p. 41).

This is one way to account for heterogeneity of labour, i.e. by regarding the relative wage levels as measuring productivity differences. It is obviously a strong equilibrium assumption about the workings of the labour market in the long run but also a rough and ready empirical measure. We can write Keynes' measure in slightly more formal detail. Let total earnings E be a sum of different types of labour L_i paid at wages W_i and let W_0 be the wage unit. Then

$$E = \sum_i W_i L_i \tag{6}$$

$$N = (\sum W_i L_i)/W_0 = L\sum\left(\frac{W_i}{W_0}\right)\left(\frac{L_i}{L}\right) \tag{7}$$

where

$$L = \sum_i L_i.$$

Now L is the usual measure of employment in terms of 'bodies'. (A further distinction in terms of hours would be desirable but for the purposes of this chapter, I wish to highlight skill heterogeneity rather than the stock-flow distinction.)

It is desirable to disaggregate L_i by industrial sector of employment as well as by skill differences. Empirical data on earnings are available more by industries than by skill differences. Thus we may rewrite (7) alternatively as

$$N = L\sum \frac{W_j}{W_0}\frac{L_j}{L} \tag{8}$$

where

$$L_j = \sum_i L_{ij}$$

$$W_j = (\sum W_i L_{ij})/L_j$$

where L_j is employment in the jth industry, etc.

Now it will be obvious from (7) and (8) that there is unlikely to be a one-to-one relationship in the variation between N and L. Thus excess supply of labour though defined in terms of L/L^s (L^s being labour supply) may bear no relation to N/L^s or, if we can construct it, N/N^s. Now natural rate of unemployment and the NAIRU are defined in terms of L/L^s rather than N/L^s or N/N^s. The concept of unemployment we have been using treats all labour as unskilled labour, abstract labour as Marx called it (see, however, Rissman, 1993 for a recent effort to allow for sectoral shifts when calculating the natural rate of unemployment).

How much difference does Keynes' measurement make to the actual employment data, i.e. how large is N relative to L? In order to derive estimates of N we have to choose a wage unit and then deflate the total earnings by that wage unit. As a first approximation to the measurement of N, I designated four sectors with the lowest nominal wages in the UK economy as candidates for defining the wage unit. These four sectors were

(1) Textiles;
(2) Gas, electricity and water supply;
(3) Food, drink and tobacco;
(4) Timber and furniture.

These four sectors were seen to be the lowest paid in the industrial sector in 'Trends in Earnings 1948–77' published in the *Department of Employment Gazette* (May 1978). The average weekly earnings in these four sectors weighted by their employment shares were taken as the wage unit. Thus

$$W_{ot} = \sum_{j=1}^{4} W_{jt}L_{jt} \Big/ \sum_{j=1}^{4} L_{jt} = \sum_{j=1}^{4} W_{jt}\zeta_{jt}.$$

Taking this estimate of W_{ot} for 1948–91, an estimate of N was derived by deflating total earnings by W_{ot}. In table 16.3, estimates of N are provided along with the data on L (employees in employment). As can be seen, 1948–68 is the Keynesian full employment period where N is consistently above L by about 2 to 3 million or 10–15%. The gap narrows dramatically between 1969 and 1973 and then reverses itself. For two years, 1974 and 1979, the gap is negative. From 1980 to 1991 the gap steadily widens and while L turns down sharply in the recession N moves down only fractionally. This indicates that unemployment is hitting the relatively lower paid (see figure 16.2).

The relation between the natural rate of unemployment and a 'Keynesian rate of unemployment' (KRU) can be developed as follows

$$N = L\Sigma\lambda_j\xi_j \tag{8a}$$

where $\lambda_j = W_j/W_0$ and $\xi_j = L_j/L$. Dividing both sides by labour supply L^s

Figure 16.2   Keynesian index of employees in employment, 1948–91

and taking logs we have

$$\log(N/L^s) - \log(L/L^s) \equiv \log(N/L) = \log\Sigma\lambda_j\xi_j.$$

Now $\log(L/L^s)$ is normally approximated by U, the rate of unemployment. Let us label $\log(N/L^s)$ as U_k. Then we get

$$U_k - U = \log\Sigma\lambda_j\xi_j. \tag{9}$$

It is clear that the difference between the two can be constant (zero) only if all the λ_j are equal to each other ($\lambda_j = \lambda$) or equal to one ($W_j = W_0$). Thus as long as there are interindustrial wage differentials, the Keynesian rate of unemployment will differ from the conventional measurement. If, for example, employment increases in the high wage sectors and diminishes in low wage sectors by an exactly matching amount, L does not change but N goes up.

From our empirical measurement of N we can infer something about the nature of unemployment. Through the period of high employment and relatively low inflation 1948–68, the relation between N and L seems to be fairly stable. It would seem then that $U_k - U$ is approximately constant. Wage differentials are stable during this period. Thus the average weekly earnings of the lowest quartile stays around 81–82% of the median through this period. Indeed, except for 1960 which is a high value (82.6), the numbers are nearer 81 than 82.

In the period 1969–80, there is a lot of movement of (N/L). This is the period of high inflation, changing differentials and rising unemployment.

Table 16.3 *Keynesian index of employees in employment, 1948–91*

N	Employees in employment L	Year
23.24482		48
23.32978		49
23.29509	20.758	50
23.5407	20.97	51
23.66247	20.916	52
23.6377	21.041	53
23.75285	21.404	54
24.20251	21.702	55
24.78666	21.965	56
24.70383	22.058	57
24.61363	21.884	58
24.59675	21.421	59
24.71081	21.899	60
25.37673	22.233	61
25.32209	22.452	62
24.85995	22.509	63
25.10003	22.816	64
25.02241	23.085	65
25.48417	23.257	66
25.0681	22.813	67
25.0531	22.655	68
24.68439	22.624	69
24.27383	22.479	70
23.31068	22.139	71
22.76262	22.137	72
23.00554	22.679	73
22.51909	22.804	74
23.17658	22.723	75
22.90031	22.557	76
23.46045	22.631	77
22.90989	22.789	78
22.94614	23.173	79
23.28527	22.991	80
22.5346	21.892	81
21.84023	21.414	82
21.4292	21.067	83
21.55597	21.238	84
21.96452	21.423	85
22.0753	21.387	86
22.44332	21.584	87
23.31966	22.258	88
24.13141	22.661	89
24.36287	22.9	90
24.20421	22.235	91

This is the period when the Phillips curve was said to have broken down or shifted. In the period 1981–7 the movements of N and L are again parallel. The boom in 1988–9 draws them apart and this divergence is heightened during the recession.

We can push the analysis a bit further by examining the effect of wage changes on the divergence between U_k and U (equivalently in $\log(N/L)$ from (9)). Although much of neoclassical and new classical economics analyses the impact of real wages on unemployment (U), Keynes emphasised the importance of nominal wages in a monetary economy. Differentiating ($U_k - U$) with respect to W_0 we get

$$\frac{\partial[U_k - U]}{\partial W_0} = \sum \xi_j \left\{ W_0 \frac{\partial W_j}{\partial W_0} - \frac{W_j}{W_0^2} \right\} + \sum \lambda_j (\partial \xi_j / \partial W_0) \tag{10}$$

$$= \sum \xi_j W_j (\eta_{jo} - 1/W_0^2) + \sum \lambda_j (\partial \xi_j / \partial W_0). \tag{10a}$$

Here η_{jo} is the elasticity of W_j with respect to W_0. If differentials are stable then $\eta_{jo} = 1$ for all j. Thus the first term on the right-hand side will sum to zero since we can take $W_0 = 1$, arbitrarily. The second term is the effect of the changing wage unit on the sectoral pattern of unemployment. It would be reasonable to assume that this term will be zero if differentials are stable since relative wage levels will stay the same as every wage moves up along with W_0. At best it will be mildly positive if low wage sectors shrink relative to high wage sectors. So with stable differentials, the right-hand side is zero or mildly positive. We can then say that the Keynesian rate of unemployment will move in parallel with the actual rate if wage differentials are stable in such a way as to leave sectoral proportions of employment unchanged.

But when differentials are unstable, it is difficult to predict the sign of the expression. Some η_{jo} may be greater than 1 and some smaller. The incomes policy of 1976 was deliberately designed to help the lower paid (£5 plus 5%). It is for this reason that we see N and L moving in non-synchronised fashion during the 1970s. In the 1980s the differentials were changing though not due to incomes policy as were the sectoral compositions. The joint effect is curiously similar to the earlier period of stability at least for 1981–7 when N and L move parallel again. It is the Lawson boom which again drives them apart and the recession heightens this effect.

A complete analysis of the interrelationship will require specifying the determinants of λ_j, ξ_j and W_0 in addition to the already explored nature of L. This is not done for the present but one further question needs to be asked. Regardless of the difference between U_k and U, how is the equilibrium level of U_k (or N) determined? Keynes tackled this problem in chapters 20 and 21 of the *General Theory*. His analysis is entirely in terms of N rather than L. It is worth noting it for this reason alone since the neoKeynesian models of the Hicks–Modigliani type drop N in favour of L.

In chapter 20, entitled 'The Employment Function', Keynes analyses the interaction of aggregate demand (D) on employment (N) with the aggregate supply curve. The AS curve can be inverted to show N as a function of aggregate supply price Z which in turn can be set equal to aggregate demand D. It is sufficient for our purposes here to take the summary expression Keynes derives

$$e_p = 1 - e_0(1 - e_w) \tag{11}$$

where

$$e_p = d\log P / d\log D$$
$$e_0 = d\log Y / d\log D$$
$$e_w = d\log W_0 / d\log D.$$

At this late stage in the *General Theory*, Keynes lets in the concept of real output (Y) albeit with a lot of qualifications and hedging. Now if you want a non-inflationary growth in aggregate demand, you wish to have $e_p = 0$ which in turn requires

$$e_0(1 - e_w) = 1.$$

Since $D = P.Y, e_0 + e_p = 1$ and then $e_w = 0$ is a sufficient condition for equilibrium. Thus equilibrium requires $e_p = e_w = 0$ and $e_0 = 1$. Of course a NAIRU-type equilibrium can be derived by setting e_p at some non-zero level. If we let the real wage be constant we get

$$e_w - e_p = (1 - e_0)(e_w - 1).$$

Setting the left-hand side equal to zero, we get the result that either $e_0 = 1$ or $e_w = 1$ will keep real wages constant. Of these $e_0 = 1$ is the non-inflationary condition and $e_w = 1$ is the 'perfect' wage inflation condition.

Keynes goes on in chapter 21 entitled 'The Theory of Prices' to extend this analysis to money supply influences. His summary equation is

$$e = e_d[1 - e_e e_0(1 - e_w)] \tag{12}$$

where

$$e = d\log P / d\log M$$
$$e_d = d\log D / d\log M$$
$$e_0 = d\log Y / d\log D$$
$$e_e = d\log N / d\log(D/w_0).$$

It can be seen from (12) that the money supply may have zero effect on the price level if $e_w = 0$, $e_0 = 1$, and $e_e = 1$. These are conditions for the non-inflationary expansion of output. A slightly weaker condition is

$e_e e_0(1 - e_w) = 1$ but this requires that the two elasticities $e_e e_0 > 1$ if $e_w > 0$. This is unlikely.

In terms of N, the equilibrium conditions for non-inflationary growth are similar to those in neoclassical or new classical economics though Keynes does not impose real wage rigidity ($e_p = e_w$). He also allows for violation of the homogeneity postulate by allowing e_p to take any value rather than just unity as the monetarists do.

Much more work remains to be done to determine the equilibrium value of $N(U_k)$ since the underlying model needs to be specified and estimated. It is hoped however that by recalling Keynes' different and hitherto neglected approach to measurement of employment, an avenue for alternatives to the natural rate of unemployment and the non-accelerating rate of unemployment (NAIRU) will have been opened.

Notes

I am very grateful to Taimur Baig who during his 'year aboard' helped me with the computations. Thanks are also due to Dilia Montes of LDE EDARC.
1 Hereafter I shall follow the convention that lower case denoted variables represent logarithms of upper case denoted variables i.e. $q = \log Q$.

References

Desai, M., 1973. 'Growth Cycles and Inflation in a Model of the Class Struggle', *Journal of Economic Theory*, 6 (December), 527–45
1975. 'The Phillips Curve: A Revisionist Interpretation', *Economica*, 42, 1–19
1981. *Testing Monetarism*, London: Frances Pinter
1984. 'Wages and Prices and Unemployment a Quarter Century After the Phillips Curve', in D.F. Hendry and K.F. Wallis, 253–74
Desai, M. and Weber, G., 1988. 'A Keynesian Macroeconometric Model of the UK Economy', *Journal of Applied Econometrics*, 3, 1–33
Friedman, B.M. and Hahn, F.H. (eds), 1990. *Handbook of Monetary Economics*, Amsterdam: North-Holland
Friedman, M., 1968. 'The Role of Monetary Policy', *American Economic Review*, 58(1) (March), 1–17
Gilbert, C.L., 1976. 'The Original Phillips Curve Estimates', *Economica*, 43, 51–7
Goldfeld, S.M. and Sichel, D.E., 1990. *The Demand for Money*, in B. Friedman and F. Hahn (eds.), *Handbook of Monetary Economics*, Amsterdam: North-Holland, 299–353
Goodman, R., 1967. 'A Growth Cycle' in S. Feinstein (ed.), *Capitalism, Socialism and Economic Growth*, Cambridge: Cambridge University Press
Hendry, D.F. and Wallis, K.F., 1984. *Econometrics and Quantitative Economics*, Oxford: Basil Blackwell
Keynes, J.M., 1936. *The General Theory of Employment, Interest and Money*, New

York: Harcourt Brace and London: Macmillan

Lipsey, R.G., 1960. 'The Relation Between Unemployment and the Rate of Change of Money Wage Rates in the United Kingdom, 1862–1957: A Further Analysis', *Economica*, 27 (February), 1–31, reprinted in AEA Series (1966), *Readings in Business Cycles*, 456–87

Lucas, R.E., 1973. 'Econometric Testing of the Natural Rate Hypothesis', in O. Eckstein (ed.), *The Econometrics of Price Determination*, Washington DC: Board of Governors of the Federal Reserve System

Lucas, R.E. and Rapping, L.A., 1969. 'Real Wages, Employment and Inflation', *Journal of Political Economy*, 77 (September/October), 721–54

1970. 'Price Expectations and the Phillips Curve', *American Economic Recview*, 59, 342–9

Phelps, E.S., 1967. 'Phillips Curves, Expectations of Inflation and Optimal Unemployment Over Time', *Economica*, 34(3) (August), 254–81

Phillips, A.W., 1958. 'The Relation Between Unemployment and the Rate of Change of Money Wage Rates in the United Kingdom, 1861–1957', *Economica*, 25 (November), 283–99

Rissman, E.R., 1993. 'Wage Growth and Sectoral Shifts', *Journal of Monetary Economics*, 31, 395–416

Samuelson, P.A. and Solow, R.M., 1960. 'Analytical Aspects of Anti-inflation Policy', *American Economic Review*, 80 (May), 177–94

Sargan, J.D., 1964. 'Wages and Prices in the UK: A Study in Econometric Methodology', in P.E. Hart, G. Mills and J.K. Whitaker (eds.), *Econometric Analysis for National Economic Planning*, London: Butterworths, reprinted in D.F. Hendry and K.F. Wallis, *Econometric Analysis for National Economic Planning*, Oxford: Blackwell (1984), pp. 275–314

17 Politics and the natural rate hypothesis: a historical perspective

Bernard Corry

Why does one economic idea or theory replace another? Why are some ideas discarded and others accepted or retained? Why are some apparently false notions brought back to centre stage some years later? These are difficult questions for economists to answer. The use of models of the development of science, such as those propounded by Popper or Kuhn or Lakatos[1] are increasingly found wanting as explanations of the actual development of economic ideas[2] and other approaches to the subject are increasingly advocated. It is not my purpose here to add to this literature, but rather to suggest that by looking at the politics of economic theory we can gain a useful insight into its development. By the 'politics of an economic theory' I shall mean both the political (policy) implications of a particular theory and the way in which political considerations may plausibly be said to have led to the statement of and the acceptance of that theory. Our specific concern is with the theory of the natural rate of unemployment (NRU).

Few would doubt that economics has made truly enormous strides since the end of the Second World War in the 'scientific' content of its endeavours. The typical economist is now far better equipped, both to undertake formal model construction and to subject these structures to sophisticated estimation procedures, than ever before. Of this there can be no doubt and the rate of growth of the scientific study of economic phenomena seems to be accelerating. Yet in the areas where the public expect most of them, economists have failed. I refer of course to their ability to forecast with tolerable accuracy and to suggest feasible policy measures that would ameliorate the lot of the ordinary person. Most people would argue that price stability and reasonably full employment are two major desiderata of economic policy, yet we seem as far away from a tolerable solution to these problems as 100 years ago. The optimism of the Keynesian years has gone. Now economists could and often do reasonably argue that an improvement in the scientific content of their subject does not *ipso facto* imply an improvement in forecasting accuracy or in better control. The 'future lies ahead' and it is not *a priori* obvious that the irreducible element of the unknown and unforeseeable will be so small as to improve the accuracy of forecasts. It is not clear to me that this accuracy has improved greatly over the last 50 years.

Today economists are seen as people with egg on their faces; this certainly is the public perception of this increasingly isolated breed. Whereas in the 1950s and 1960s, on both sides of the Atlantic, it was a proud boast, and indeed a social cachet at chattering classes soirées to announce in a stage whisper 'I am an economist', and the media for example gave liberal time to academic members of the profession, today economics is scorned and economists are in disarray and disgrace. They still make pronouncements about green shoots or other banal analogies, but certainly in the main, academic sorties in the media, especially TV and radio, have all but disappeared, and the right to feed the public with platitudes has been passed to 'real-world' financial and business experts. Insulting economists is now the sport of the moment and has taken the heat off that other pilloried group of forecasters – the weathercasters. To take but two examples – both from *The* (London) *Times.* Simon Jenkins writes of the 'Rout of the Economists' and has the sub-title 'the bluff of monetary models, theories and statistics has been called – a whole profession now stands arraigned'.[3] Or take a leader by Anatole Kaletsky dealing with a report by the Treasury panel of outside advisors and headed 'The Economics of Running a Whelk Stall' where he writes 'the best and brightest in British academic and business economics have argued themselves to a standstill after just four months. They could not even run a whelk stall, never mind the Treasury or even an advisory committee'.[4]

It would be unwise of me to suggest that there is anything new in the idea that basically economics is somewhat akin to the fashion business and that economists are not unlike fashion writers; fads and fashions come and go in economics just like trouser widths from skin tight to flares and back again. The next fashion may or may not be predictable but in the case of economic ideas it tells us nothing about the validity of those ideas. Economic ideas are fairly predictable; they will often be apparent from the logic of current debate in any particular area of economics. It is sometimes useful in trying to predict the next big idea to bear in mind Harry Johnson's homily on how to be a revolutionary in economics. Briefly, Johnson argued, for ideas to be successful they have to be sufficiently different (and difficult technically) for the old guard to find nearly impossible to absorb but easy enough for the young Turks to master. One useful weapon in the struggle is the invention of 'new' terminology.[5]

The cycle in economic ideas is also determined by political consider-ations, indeed I have long thought that this is *the* major determinant. Why does this seem to be the case in economics and why are economists currently in such public disarray? In fact it is nothing new, and in a way it is not basically the fault of economists other than their propensity when riding high to overstate the scientific nature of their discipline and its use as a predictive tool and as a control weapon. The reasons why we economists are so prone to forecast errors are many and have been stated time and time again for many years, but it behoves us to reiterate them every so often to prevent, or try to prevent, us being carried away by our own euphoria. Economic theories turn out to be extraordinarily difficult to test satisfactorily, by which I mean 'testable' in the sense that objective observers can say that because of this battery of tests we may now accept *this* theory and reject *that* theory. Consequently without these well-tested theories it is difficult to make forecasts that will have a reasonably high degree of accuracy. A random survey of the vast and growing literature on testing will show that the conclusion of most empirical work is: 'test inconclusive – further work (and funds!) required'. With hindsight the testing of economic theory – at least so far – via advances in econometrics has turned out to be another God that failed or at least has not lived up to expectations. The reasons for this are complex; I would give a good deal of weight to the continually changing parameter values of economic systems and, almost the same point, the continuous importance of 'news' in economic systems. 'Every day is a new day' or 'the future lies ahead' are slogans well worth carrying around in the economist's baggage.[6] It is perhaps for this reason that economists seem to have improved their performance mainly in their role as economic historians. We can now explain what happened in the past better, although some may even doubt this, witness the debate that still rages inconclusively about the causes of the 'great depression' of the 1930s, or the reasons for full employment growth after the Second World War.

Because of this, and for other more psychological reasons to do with the way in which the economics establishment has evolved its value set, the emphasis in economic research and especially in policy advocacy has been on new theoretical ideas at the almost total expense of empirical evidence for or against older or new ideas. Often, then, our 'revolutions' *appear* to be won or lost on theoretical grounds alone. But underlying these theoretical battles are the prior political positions of the adversaries. Let us take an example from the current UK scene; with the official demise of Keynesian economics and the victory of the capitalist market solution in so many areas of economic and social life, the left-wing economist has been hard put to find an outlet for her talents so we find 'lefties' reworking the theory of market failure under the guise of the economics of the environment. Whereas 'righties' faced with assaults on the static properties of the market solution ponder the theory of the dynamics of the market and have rediscovered Schumpeter (witness the surge of the New Austrians!). In a nutshell, economists find it difficult – nay, impossible – to settle disputes by an appeal to the evidence, so they engage in theoretical disputation. These theoretical disputes are often a mere facade for differing political agendas. The political agendas I have in mind are primarily the alternatives of free market provision and public sector interventionism. These swings between the two ideologies cannot always be associated with changes of government. For example in the UK it is arguable that for at least 20 years after the Second World War both Labour and Conservative governments were interventionist in that their prevailing ideologies favoured the intervention of government at both the micro and macro level and both parties accepted the view that the 'commanding heights' of the economy should be in public ownership. It is further reasonable to argue that since the 'rediscovery of the market' by the first Thatcher administration in 1979 economic policy statements by the Labour party have emphasised the benefits of market provision and the limits to government intervention. Recall that it was Mr (now Lord) Callaghan's Labour government that formally pronounced the end of Keynesian policies to fight unemployment!

The history of macroeconomics in the post-second World War era illustrates this theme very succinctly: from the end of Keynesianism[7] through monetarism (including the natural rate hypothesis, NRH) on to new classical and rational expectations (RE) and equilibrium business cycle theory, none of these ventures seem to have heralded not merely their theorectical arrival but their acceptance as a policy stance with a welter of substantiated empirical support. Clearly, for better or worse, economics just does not work that way and it is for that reason that older, 'outmoded' ways of thought cannot so easily be jettisoned as in the more empirically resolvable disciplines and hence can easily reappear as the current wisdom. (Witness the rise of the neo-Austrian and new classical schools; both are a direct revival of earlier modes of thinking.) What is current wisdom is not necessarily correct even though it may be the (only?) path to academic promotion.

In what follows I shall look briefly at the emergence of the concept of the natural rate of unemployment in the light of these thoughts about the actual development of economic ideas. Let us start our story by reminding ourselves just how the natural rate got into the act, which has to involve some thoughts about the Phillips relationship.

The Phillips curve and all that

We start with Keynes. It has often been noted that the *General Theory* was practically devoid of supporting empirical evidence for its theoretical structure and that the economics profession had been won over to the

Keynesian way of thinking well before the main building blocks had been estimated or tested empirically. The mood of the late 1930s, 1940s and 1950s was for interventionism on a grand scale and suggestions that the best solution was to improve the working of markets were barely entertained in respectable professional circles. Then mythical accounts grew up about the contents of the *General Theory*; the myths were sometimes used to discredit it; one version, and important for our story, was that Keynes assumed that the money wage rate and hence, in some versions of the story at least, the general price level, remained constant until 'full employment' was reached. This is often depicted in basic macroeconomic texts as a 'reverse *L*' aggregate supply curve. The truth is far less outlandish and much more sensible in terms of economic reasoning. Indeed it often strikes me that readers of what might justly be called 'bowdlerised' Keynes with all its ridiculous assumptions such as the fixed price world, must be amazed that the inventor of such puerility ever achieved star billing. Keynes assumed that as an economy emerged from depression, by which I do not wish to imply that he thought in terms of automatic recovery (more of this later), prices would continuously rise. This for two reasons: first, even in the absence of wage increases there would be an upward drift of prices because Keynes assumed that short-run diminishing marginal product of labour and hence short-run marginal costs were also typically assumed to be rising. It is true that later he modified this position in the light of the evidence presented about the cyclical pattern of real wages.[8] Secondly, Keynes argued that well before full employment there would be increases in the money wage rate and he implied, although not explicitly, that these increases would be at an increasing rate. His reasoning does of course create difficulties if we wish to define 'full employment' in an exact manner. We have thus two such definitions in the *General Theory*: the one defining it as the point where real output is no longer responsive to an increase in aggregate demand, and the other where prices begin to rise.[9] Keynes placed most weight on the former definition, as is obvious from his analysis of involuntary unemployment, but he did on occasions give credence to the latter.

In spite of Keynes' very clear and explicit remarks on the positive correlation between output increases and price increases, the early mathematical versions of Keynes' system, from which so many writers on macroeconomics learned their 'Keynes', included in their equations the fixed wage–price world.[10] It was thus concluded that the great weakness of the Keynesian system was its failure to explain prices – there was in the words of the then debate 'a missing equation' (see also chapter 16 in this volume). It may indeed be a reflection of the divorce between economic theory and reality that after the experience of wartime inflations and an upsurge in prices (at least in the UK) after the war as wartime controls were gradually dismantled, that many economists were still playing with fixed price models. There were of course plenty of discussions of inflation but they tended to go on separately from macro model construction. Indeed during and immediately after the Second World War the view was strongly expressed that any attempt to maintain full employment via aggregate demand control would lead to irresolvable wage inflation. These fears were voiced by pro- and anti-Keynesians, that is by right-wing, market economists and left-wing anti-market economists. One such approach to the understanding of inflationary pressures was to relate the rate of price increase to the relationship between actual output and 'full capacity' output. This approach was, of course, in the tradition of Keynes of the *General Theory*, encompassing both the diminishing returns and the pressure on wage costs aspects of the inflationary process.

A clear statement, among others, of this line of inquiry, but a key one for our story, was the initial work of Bill Phillips at the LSE. Phillips' Ph.D. thesis was entitled *Dynamic Models in Economics* and he presented it in 1953. Parts of it were published in 1950 – mainly relating to the actual construction of his hydraulic model and then in 1954 his famous article 'Stabilisation Policy in a Closed Economy'[11] appeared. Part 2 of this article was in fact chapter V of his thesis and dealt with the rate of change of prices in a 'model with flexible prices'. Frank Paish, also at the LSE, was working along similar lines. He had used the degree of capacity utilisation approach and had tried to estimate the 'optimum' degree of utilisation required to prevent spiralling inflation. It was in this milieu that Bill Phillips presented his famous estimate of 'the relationship between unemployment and the rate of change of the money wage rate'.[12] Phillips wanted a simple estimate of the full employment output–actual output gap (to become known as the Okun gap), and used unemployment as the easiest proxy although aware that in terms of labour market categories the 'correct' variable would have included vacancies as well. As Phillips presented his analysis he was clear that the direction of causality was from unemployment to wage changes, i.e. a demand driven system, and that the function related to non-equilibrium situations. He did not suggest any formal feedback mechanism such as would arise from a neoclassical labour market analysis, although he did hint at the impact of wage changes on prices and hence on further wage claims.

Several attempts were made to embody the Phillips curve – as it had become known – in a more explicit theoretical framework; the most famous of these attempts was that of Lipsey in his famous 1960 article.[13] At about the same time the idea of the Phillips curve as a trade-off curve was popularised; the key contribution here being Samuelson and Solow's 1960 paper 'Analytic Aspects of Anti-Inflation Policy',[14] where they referred to 'the fundamental Phillips schedule relating unemployment and wage changes'.

Lipsey's rationalisation of the Phillips relationship was based essentially on the neoclassical synthesis account of the 'Keynesian' labour market, and in this sense was fundamentally not Keynes' view of the operation of the system where employment and unemployment are determined in the output sector. This grafting of a neoclassical labour market onto Keynes' model was and still remains common practice; it leads almost inevitably to the conclusion that Keynes' proof of involuntary unemployment is – other than as a temporary disequilibrium phenomenon – due to downward wage inflexibility and we now have a whole series of competing stories to explain this phenomenon. Greater wage or more generally greater labour market flexibility would eliminate involuntary unemployment. Whatever the merits of this view – and recent UK experience would not suggest that it has much or any empirical validity – it emphatically was not Keynes' view.[15] In Keynes' story a reduction in involuntary unemployment can be achieved only by an increase in demand for output. In Keynes' economics the effects of downward wage/price flexibility are not clear as to sign, and indeed it is more than likely that output and employment would decline.

Politics and the Phillips curve

Now did people think that the Phillips relation embodied a political message? Yes! It was seized upon immediately for its political implications; the right wing seized upon the negative trade-off aspects of the debate and emphasised the 'you can't have your cake and eat it' message: full employment was a pipe dream and a level of employment compatible with price stability should be aimed for. The left wing saw it as a need for even more intervention and suggested that free collective bargaining had to be replaced by some sort of a prices/incomes policy either statutory or voluntary. In the UK the mood of the time was for an interventionist rather than a market solution and prices/incomes policies – or discussions of them – became the vogue. With careful government intervention it seemed possible to run an economy at close to full employment with only slow creeping inflation and real wages rising at the rate of increase of productivity. Welfare capitalism or socialism and water seemed to have arrived. In the UK this was not just academic babble, the economy seemed to be actually behaving this way. From 1950 to 1970 (with the exception of the Korean war) the unemployment rate never exceeded 3% and the inflation rate never exceeded 5%. On the whole the message from the combined Keynesian analysis of unemployment and the Phillips trade-off curve was an optimistic one, but a message that asked a good deal of government institutions and incidentally of organised labour via trades unions. Fiscal policy with a little help from its friend monetary policy was the instrument for the employment target and prices/incomes policy was to look after inflation. But lurking in the neoclassical synthesis approach to Keynes was the chink in the Keynesian armour that the market forces economists could lever into a chasm.

Enter the natural rate

Supporters of the market solution began to regroup after a decade or so of the academic ascendancy of the case for regulated capitalism plus strong doses of public ownership. The attack came initially at the microeconomics level – with agreement remaining on the 'Keynesian' (fiscal/monetary) control system for the macro economy. Academically the free market counter-revolution was spearheaded by several micro contributions. The most influential were firstly the Coase theorem, which cast doubt on the whole externality defence of interventionism. Secondly, and perhaps most important, the restatement of competition as a process rather than a state and hence a switch of the debate away from the static properties of capitalist markets to the dynamics and growth properties of such markets. The work of Hayek and his followers was crucial here. Thirdly, work on the theory of bureaux cast doubt on the public interest motivation of publicly owned organisations. What remained was fiscalism and what the right-wing economist desperately needed was a similar reworking of macroeconomics to underpin the rightward, market provision belief that was sweeping the western world in the 1960s and which was to gain momentum in the 1970s and 1980s. The stage was set for a new macro rightism.

It is at this stage in the political debate that the natural rate hypothesis appears on the scene in the two seminal papers by Friedman and Phelps.[16] It has been argued that the catalyst for both these writers was the empirical breakdown of the Phillips curve. But this certainly was not the case for the UK; yet as the anti-Keynes bandwaggon accelerated some commentators suggested that not merely had the relationship broken down but that on reflection it was not really there in the first place! Phelps' attack was of the theoretical type. He emphasised the logical difficulties in the structure of the Phillips model; Friedman made a much more open policy attack and emphasised the political implications of his arguments. Empirical testing of the natural rate has not really been a central research area, indeed its very definition makes such testing extremely problematic. Take, for example, the definition given by Haltiwanger which is very much in line with Friedman's original definition: 'the natural rate of unemployment is the rate towards which the dynamic system is converging for a given underlying general equilibrium stochastic structure. It takes into account the actual structural characteristics of the labour and commodity markets, including market imperfections, search and mobility costs'.[17] Efforts have been made to sort out the natural rate of unemployment from total unemployment by trying to identify non-cyclical and cyclical components of unemployment but the two aspects are too interrelated for this to be of much value. Friedman also brought in another key aspect of the debate which stands out clearly in Haltiwanger's definition. The system is assumed to adjust to equilibrium and this state to which the real world system is supposed to tend is full employment – defined as being where the demand for labour equals the supply rather than a specific percentage of the labour force without work. This again is a complete break with Keynes and modifies employment policy from one of cyclical and secular concern to one of just anti-cyclical policy. Furthermore, Friedman emphasised the importance of market imperfections in the natural rate and included in these imperfections were wage fixing policies and trade union activities. A reduction in both would lower the natural rate and hence the average actual rate of unemployment.

Now the 'expectations-augmented Phillips curve' – as Friedman's version of it came to be known – still had a crucial weakness as far as the free marketeers were concerned. The Friedman–Phelps model still allowed for an exploitable short-run trade-off between inflation and unemployment; this arose because fluctuations in aggregate demand could cause forecast errors and hence deflect the real wage from its equilibrium value. Thus it could still be argued that government-inspired increases in the demand for output would lower unemployment in the short run at the cost of increased inflation, and society might well decide that this cost was well worth paying. Thus quite a strong residual claim for the efficacy of macro intervention strategies on the demand side of the economy remained. As the free market philosophy swept the West the last step in the defusing of macro intervention was almost inevitable. This was the new classical policy proposals which were obtained by combining Friedman's model with rational expectations. From this revolution came the two important results, firstly that unemployment would, with fully anticipated inflation, be at its natural rate plus a random error term, and secondly that attempts to change the level of unemployment by systematic fiscal or monetary policy are doomed to failure. Now however ludicrous this may all sound to readers who have experienced the great depression of the 1990s and watch governments in all countries trying to dream up measures to stimulate aggregate demand, it must be recalled for UK readers that this policy neutrality doctrine invaded both political parties. But the policy worm has turned again. A combination of the reality of world depression, the massive problems with the 'market solution' in the ex-communist countries, and increasing environmental fears, are beginning to turn thoughts back to market failure at both the macro and micro levels. Apart from the work on supply-side features – skill upgrading and retraining programmes, replacement rates, length of payment of unemployment benefits, etc. – there now seems to be growing support among economists for macro intervention – or at least the anti-interventionist babble has quietened down. What is also of interest is the fact that the most common explanation currently given for the reduction in inflation in country after country is the rise in unemployment! Moreover even before the recovery has clearly got under way dire warnings are being voiced about the pressure on wages that the fall in unemployment will induce. Are we about to have another spate of incomes policy literature? Certainly 'free market economics' is not what it was, especially with the dubious outturns in ex-command economies and the growing underclass in the older capitalist economies. Is it time to dust down those old lectures on market failure and the case for macro intervention?

Conclusion

There is obviously a strong interplay between economic ideas and political beliefs, and however much we may wish to espouse the neutrality of economic theory the reality is far different. This interplay is a two-way process: our economics may lead us to policies that have clear political implications but – perhaps more importantly – we should be aware that our formulation of and our acceptance of economic ideas may be a consequence of our prior political/philosophical beliefs. A casual survey of economists' thoughts on the nature of unemployment would seem to confirm this thesis.

Notes

1 For an excellent introduction to the work of these writers see Blaug (1993).
2 For example, McCloskey (1986).
3 Jenkins (1993).
4 Kaletsky (1993).
5 See Johnson (1971).
6 There is also the much-discussed added complication that the very activity of forecasting may affect the structural parameters of the system and hence invalidate the forecast.
7 By 'Keynesian' I mean what has been termed bastard or neoclassical synthesis, Keynesian economics. It should not be confused with Keynes' economics, see Corry (1986). New Keynesian economics is but a variant of these interpretations.

8 Keynes (1939, 1973).
9 For the two definitions of full employment see Keynes (1936, 1973, p. 30, p. 292 *et seq.*).
10 Among the key articles in this dissemination process were Hicks (1937) and Modigliani (1944).
11 Phillips (1954).
12 Phillips (1958).
13 Lipsey (1960). See also his reflection on the meaning and interpretation of the Phillips curve in Lipsey (1978).
14 Samuelson and Solow (1960).
15 Keynes (1936, 1973, ch. 15).
16 Phelps (1967), Friedman (1968).
17 Haltiwanger (1987).

References

Blaug, M., 1993. *The Methodology of Economics, or How Economists Explain*, 2nd edn, Cambridge: Cambridge University Press

Corry, B.A., 1986. 'Keynes's Economics: a Revolution in Economic Theory or in Economic Policy?', in R.D.C. Black (ed.), *Ideas in Economics*, London: Macmillan

Friedman, M., 1968. 'The Role of Monetary Policy', *American Economic Review*, 58(1) (March), 1–17

Haltiwanger, J., 1986. 'The Natural Rate of Unemployment', in J. Eatwell, M. Milgate and P. Newman (eds), *The New Palgrave Dictionary of Economics*, vol. 3, London: Macmillan

Hicks, J.R., 1937. 'Mr Keynes and the "Classics". A Suggested Interpretation', *Econometrica*, vol. 5

Jenkins, S., 1993. 'Rout of the Economists', *The Times* (London) (3 February)

Johnson, H.G., 1971. 'The Keynesian Revolution and the Monetarist Counter-Revolution', *American Economic Review, Papers and Proceedings*, 61(2) (May), 1–14

Kaletsky, A., 1993. 'The Economics of Running a Whelk Stall', *The Times* (London) (7 July)

Keynes, J.M., 1936, 1973. *The General Theory of Employment, Interest and Money*, New York: Harcourt Brace and London: Macmillan (reprinted as vol. 7, *Collected Writings of John Maynard Keynes*, London: Macmillan)

1939, 1973. 'Relative Movements of Real Wages and Employment', *Economic Journal* (March) (reprinted as Appendix 3 to vol. 7, *Collected Writings*) London: Macmillan

Lipsey, R.G., 1960. 'The Relation between Unemployment and the Rate of Change of Money Wage Rates in the United Kingdom, 1862–1957: A Further Analysis', *Economica* (27 February), 1–31; reprinted in AEA Series (1966), *Readings in Business Cycles*, 456–87

1978. 'The Place of the Phillips Curve in Macroeconomic Models', in A.R.

Bergstom *et al.* (eds), *Stability and Inflation*, New York: John Wiley

McCloskey, D. 1986. *The Rhetoric of Economics*, Madison, WI: University of Wisconsin

Modigliani, F., 1944. 'Liquidity Preference and the Theory of Interest and Money', *Econometrica*, vol. 12

Phelps, E.S., 1967. 'Phillips Curves, Expectations of Inflation and Optimal Unemployment Over Time', *Economica*, 34(3) (August), 254–81

Phillips, A.W., 1953. *Dynamic Models in Economics*, University of London, Ph.D. thesis, unpublished

1954. 'Stabilisation Policy in a Closed Economy', *Economic Journal*, vol. 54

1958. 'The Relation Between Unemployment and the Rate of Change of Money Wage Rates in the United Kingdom, 1861–1957', *Economica*, 25 (November), 283–99

Samuelson, P.A. and Solow, R.M., 1960. 'Analytic Aspects of Anti-Inflation Policy', *American Economic Review*, 50 (May), 177–94

Index